Expectations

Expectations

Teaching Writing from the Reader's Perspective

George D. Gopen
Duke University

New York San Francisco Boston
London Toronto Sydney Tokyo Singapore Madrid
Mexico City Munich Paris Cape Town Hong Kong Montreal

Senior Vice President and Publisher: Joseph Opiela
Vice President/Publisher: Eben W. Ludlow
Executive Marketing Manager: Ann Stypuloski
Production Manager: Douglas Bell
Project Coordination, Text Design, and Electronic Page Makeup: Electronic
    Publishing Services Inc., NYC
Cover Designer/Manager: Wendy Ann Fredericks
Cover Photo: Copyright © Ryan McVay/Getty Images, Inc.
Manufacturing Buyer: Roy L. Pickering, Jr.
Printer and Binder: Courier Corporation—Stoughton
Cover Printer: Phoenix Color Corporation

Library of Congress Cataloging-in-Publication Data

Gopen, George D.
  Expectations : teaching writing from a reader's perspective / George
D. Gopen.
      p. cm.
Includes index.
  ISBN 0-205-29617-3
  1. English language—Rhetoric—Study and teaching. 2. Report
writing^Study and teaching (Higher) 3. Reading (Higher education).
4. Reading comprehension. 5. Books and reading. I. Title.
PE1404.G645 2003
808'.042—dc22

                                                          2003055626

Please visit us at http://www.ablongman.com

ISBN 0-205-29617-3

1 2 3 4 5 6 7 8 9 10-CRS-06 05 04 03

For
Sara Gopen
and
Sarah Gopen

Contents

Chapter **6**

Paragraphs: Issues, Points, and Purposes   194

P A R T   T w o

Pedagogy   261

Chapter **7**

Learning and Teaching the Reader Expectation Approach   263

Chapter **8**

"I Knew That"   324

P A R T   T H R E E

Appendixes 355

Preface

*Form is the creation of an appetite in the mind of the auditor,
and the adequate satisfying of that appetite.*

(KENNETH BURKE, *COUNTER-STATEMENT*)

*To guide the reader's expectations is already to have some
conquest over him.*

(KENNETH BURKE, *COUNTER-STATEMENT*)

I nterpretation and the Sibyl of Cumae

Ancient Greek mythology tells us that the Sibyl at Cumae was granted a wish
by the gods. She wished for immortality; but she neglected to wish for im-
mortal youth. As the years fled, she shrank with age, until she was but a few
inches high. But also as the years fled, she saw all that happened, until there
came a time when little happened that she had not already seen. She came to
understand the patterns. As a result, she gained a reputation for being a
prophet. Having seen it all, she could predict what would most likely be.

She lived in a cave. Those who wished her to predict their future and facilitate their decisions would approach the cave, send in their questions, and
retreat to wait for her response. She recorded her response on palm leaves,
each leaf inscribed with only a single word. She would lay out the leaves in
their proper order at the mouth of the cave and then retire. Only when she
had disappeared from view was it appropriate for the questioner to draw
near enough to read the message. But at that very moment, every time, a sudden gust of wind would scatter the leaves about. The would-be readers could
retrieve all the leaves; but they were left with the puzzle of how to order
these pieces of semantic substance to produce a structure that would unlock
their hidden meaning. All too often, they would make their interpretive decisions, rely on them, and find themselves ruined.

When they returned in anger to the Sybil, insisting she had misled
them, she produced the leaves and asked them what order they had made
of them. When they recreated the sentence, she would show them how
they had mistaken the structure and therefore arrived at a false conclusion.
She changed the location of a leaf or two and behold! -- the "new" sentence
offered a completely different solution. Had they followed *that* advice, they
would have achieved prosperity and happiness.

Substance without structure is interpretable but not effectively communicative. Substance with a misleading structure is highly likely to be misinterpreted. Substance with a helpfully instructive structure may not be interpreted in exactly the same way by all readers; but the likelihood of shared interpretation increases greatly.

P ragmatic Music

The approach to writing presented in this volume is pragmatic. It values the reader more the writer: In the world after graduation, communication is usually more valued than self-expression.

Though pragmatic, the substance of this volume finds the deepest of its many roots not in grammar, rhetoric, logic, law, linguistics, psycholinguistics, nor cognitive psychology. Its deepest roots are found in music. Since notes carry little or none of the semantic baggage of words, their meanings depend almost entirely on context. Their presence in some configuration or structure raises expectations about what might arrive next; the fulfillments or violations caused by that arrival are the ways in which notes "mean." Establishing tonalities, destroying tonalities, effecting modulations, resolving cadences -- all these are present throughout the following chapters, though rarely explicitly invoked.

D ichotomies

-- Students who function as readers, not as critics;

-- Teachers who are student-centered, not materials-centered;

-- Teaching that is inductive, not deductive;

-- Classes that are collaborative, not competitive;

-- Prose that is helpful, not merely correct;

-- Principles that are descriptions/predictions, not rules.

T he Common Sense of Writing

Two hundred years of writing instruction in this country can clearly be traced back to the Common Sense school of philosophy of mid-eighteenth-century Scotland. The main text of that school was Thomas Reid's *An Inquiry into the Human Mind on the Principles of Common Sense* (1764). Among his colleagues was George Campbell, author of *The Philosophy of Rhetoric* (1776). Hugh Blair (1783) and Richard Whately (1828) followed later, and the agenda of composition instruction was settled until the 1970s.

The Common Sense school of philosophy maintained that humans share a sense in common with which they perceive the material world and intuit the spiritual world. The eighteenth and nineteenth centuries used the concept to establish standards of taste and excellence; whenever those standards are considered by some to have rigidified into rules, the resultant intellectual battleground is visited with bloodshed. This happens on a recurring basis every few decades.

In this volume, the same sense-in-common concept finds another manifestation, this time in the form of psycholinguistic reader expectations concerning the relationship between structure and substance in prose. The single greatest challenge for the teacher of this approach is to avoid allowing its perceptions to be rigidified into rules. Thought and writing are inextricably intertwined. Each must remain as malleable as the other.

R *ules*

The surest way to make all the material in this book come to naught is for you to reduce it to rules. "No rules," I will urge now and again -- and perhaps more than now and again. Any rule where the process of writing is concerned can be violated to good effect. Context controls meaning. (That is not a rule but a fact.)

As is so often the case, Quintilian put it nicely, almost two millennia ago, in the first great treatise on teaching the expression of thought:

> But let no man require from me such a system of precepts as is laid down by most authors of *books of rules*, a system in which I should have to make certain laws, fixed by immutable necessity . . . For rhetoric would be a very easy and small matter, if it could be included in one short body of rules; but rules must generally be altered to suit the nature of each individual case, the time, the occasion, and necessity itself. Consequently, one great quality in an orator is discretion, because he must turn his thoughts in various directions, according to the different bearings of his subject. (*Institutes of Oratory*, Book II, Chapter XIII)

R *eader(s)*

When I speak of "reader expectation" -- and even of "Reader Expectation" -- I always mean "what most readers expect most of the time." Nowhere do I intend to suggest that there is one Great Reader in whose image we have all been cast. If we can take good care of most of our readers most of the time, we are doing a good and great thing.

U *sing This Book*

This book is addressed to two distinct audiences: (1) It is intended for those who wish to teach writing using this reader-based approach; and (2) it is intended for anyone who wishes to understand how the English language functions by knowing better how readers go about the act of reading. It will sound like teachers are the primary audience; but since the best way to learn anything is to learn to teach it, non-teachers should benefit as well.

We have traditionally taught writing by demonstrating how the language *is constructed*. I am suggesting here that we would do well to deemphasize the language as an object of interest by itself and switch our attention to how the language *functions*. The bottom line, where the quality of writing is concerned, has less to do with the language than with how the text is perceived by readers. We can reduce the judgment of the quality of a piece of writing to a single question: "Did the reader actually get delivery of what the writer was trying to send?" If the answer to that question is "yes," the writing was "good enough"; if the answer is "no," the writing -- no matter how impressive it might have sounded -- was inadequate. In order to explore this central question, we must investigate how the reader goes about doing the act of interpretation. Knowing how a reader makes sense of the English language will allow us to be consciously in charge of sending the reader the proper signals.

This book methodically and in great detail explains the relationship between the *structure* of prose and its influence on how readers go about perceiving its *substance*. It is based on the discovery that *where* a piece of information appears has a great deal to do with *how* that information is processed. The "where" refers to two separate but related concerns: (1) in what structural location information appears, and (2) in what kind of unit of discourse it appears. By "structural location" I mean whether it appears at the beginning, middle, or end of a sentence, or whether it appears between a subject and its verb, or whether in a paragraph it appears before or during or after the discussion of the paragraph's issue. By "unit of discourse" I mean whether it appears in a main clause or a qualifying clause or a phrase. These concerns might sound terribly technical at the moment; but I trust that their great significance will slowly unfold as this book progresses.

Learning what readers do allows a writer to control what readers do. It de-mystifies the reading/writing process. It empowers writers. It also furnishes writers with a new way back into the thinking process. This "reader expectation approach" begins as a method of revision; but it ends as an aid to invention.

You need not believe anything in this book on faith alone. As a reader, you will be able to judge whether or not what I say readers do makes sense or not. I am not presuming that all readers read the same way all of the time; but we have discovered that most readers go through the same kinds of processes most of the time. To understand what most readers do is all we can hope for -- and that will take us a long way. So do not be threatened or frustrated if some students insist they can interpret a given sentence differently from the way you have. They have not proved you or these theories wrong; they have just demonstrated that interpretation is always infinite in its possibilities. No sentence can be nailed down so securely that it can support only one interpretation. Interpretation is always dependent on context: Change the context of a sentence, and the possible meanings of that sentence increase. Context controls meaning.

It should come as no surprise that both readers and writers are creatures of habit. How could it be otherwise? If either one were to choose a whole new way of doing things for every sentence, neither readers nor writers would remain sane very long. As readers, we depend on certain things showing up at certain times and in certain places. As writers, we continually use and reuse the same kinds of strategies when faced with the same kinds of writing tasks. This book tries to help you uncover for your students (if you are a teacher) or for yourself (if you are not) what their writing habits or your writing habits currently are. Some of those habits will already be reader-friendly; a few will not. That narrows the field, helpfully. Concentrating on the one or two reader expectations you or your students habitually fail to fulfill will change your/their writing permanently, and for the better.

A cknowledgments

Not only is it impossible to acknowledge all the people in my life who have influenced the present work but it is hard even to recognize them. The probable first source of influence was Esther Hewes, my childhood piano teacher, who taught me musical phrasing. Perhaps my first inkling of the power of the Stress position came from listening to that kindest of ladies chant with great forward-leaning emphasis (in teaching me to play Beethoven's "Für Elise"), "and then to *there*, -- and then to *there*!"

Foremost in my acknowledgments must be Joseph Williams of the University of Chicago, who was the groundbreaker for this new way of thinking about controlling language. The great influence of his work on mine will be evident to anyone who takes even a quick glance at his oft-reprinted textbook, *Style*. We worked together in the Clearlines consulting group from 1981 through 1990.

I also learned a great deal from the other two original members of that group, Gregory Colomb and Frank Kinahan. Greg Colomb's intellectual contributions to our joint work have been, I believe, somewhat underestimated over the years. I thank him here for his sagacity, his wit, his insight, and his friendship. Frank Kinahan was a joy to work with and is much missed by everyone who knew him.

I wish to thank David A. Smith of the Duke Mathematics Department for his collaboration in importing writing and the analysis of writing into the teaching of calculus. If that sounds strange and you want to know more, see our article, "What's an Assignment Like You Doing in a Course Like This? Writing to Learn Mathematics," *College Math Journal* 21 (1990), 2–19. I also thank Judith A. Swan, with whom I have worked on scientific writing in a partnership we have called "The Science of Style." Together we published "The Science of Scientific Writing" in *American Scientist* (Nov.-Dec. 1990).

In my role as Director of Writing Programs at Duke University, I taught this approach and these materials to hundreds of graduate students as they began their teaching careers. From observing each of them teaching an hour's class, I have learned untold amounts about what works and what does not, and about the problems one can have in teaching this for the first time. I have also benefited more than I can account from the feedback, problem-sharing, support, and complaints of those hardworking and entirely earnest new teachers. Although I owe something to almost every one of them, I wish here to record just a few of the most memorable names: Mark Amos, Jill Beimdiek, Stan Blair, Chris Chism, Richard Dickson, Rick Fehrenbacher, Brandi Krantz Greenberg, Scott Harshbarger, Lee Lawrence, Scott McEathron, Fred Neumann, Lori Newcomb, Charlie Paine, Anne Scott, Martha Yeide, and Paul Yoder. I offer special thanks for the pleasure of collaborating with Kary Smout (now of Washington and Lee University) and for the research assistance of Wendy Gwathmey Brooks.

I also wish to thank former Duke University deans Richard A. White and Malcolm Gillis (now president of Rice University) for their long-standing support and encouragement.

Special thanks also to two people who were extraordinarily important to me at two specific moments in time -- and who may have little or no idea of what part they have played in it all: John Muller, former Director of Writing at the University of Utah, and Professor Charles Nesson of the Harvard Law School.

This Reader Expectation approach was developed not in the academic classroom but in the conference rooms of law firms, corporations, and government agencies. The thousands of professionals who have listened to two days' lecture and a 30-minute individual tutorial created for me and my partners a sense of accountability. Whenever this newborn approach had a weakness, one of those devoted, high-powered professionals was sure to let us know all about it. Over the years, as we grew wiser and more experienced, the complaints dwindled, and the sharp edges on the corners of their arguments were replaced by a coating of intellectual curiosity. It would be inappropriate to list all 115 professional clients I have served in the last 25 years; but a few of them -- recidivists all -- ought to be named to symbolize the contribution they have made to the progress of this work. Law firms: Epton, Mullin, Miller & Druth (Chicago); Jenner & Block (Chicago); Fulbright & Jaworski (Houston); Davis, Graham & Stubbs (Denver). Legal Publisher Matthew Bender & Company -- with thanks to David Epstein. Scientific research companies: Bristol-Meyers Squibb; FMC; Trimeris. Businesses: IBM; Bank of America. Government agencies: CDC; NIOSH; FDIC; GAO, NIH.

I have also benefited greatly from the opportunity to teach at four law schools -- Maryland, Loyola of Chicago, Harvard, and Duke. In addition, I have had the opportunity to offer workshops at the Duke University Medical Center that have been attended over the last 17 years by more than 2,700 faculty members. They have contributed far more than any of them realize.

I wish to mention Terry Bell and Joseph Dixon, two high school teachers from Dayton, Ohio, who have for several years now imported these materials into their classes with marked success. I continually find their enthusiasm uplifting. The same is true for the support and interest shown by Cynthia Buffington of the Philadelphia Rare Book & Manuscript Company, and another student of mine, Jinan Joudeh.

I wish to thank four reviewers of the manuscripts for their cogent and helpful suggestions: Valerie Balester, Texas A&M University; Robert Funk, Eastern Illinois University; Peter Richardson, Public Policy Institute of California; and -- most especially for his multiple readings and detailed responses -- William Vande Kopple, Calvin College.

It is a privilege to work with Eben Ludlow of Longman. He has maintained a confidence and interest in this work for a far longer time than should have been necessary.

Jim Hill of EPS did a masterful job of overseeing the process of transforming the manuscript into a book.

Part of the illumination that has allowed me to do my work happily for the past fourteen years has come from my son, Xander. He lights up my life.

I have saved the final two thank-yous for the volume's dedicatees. Sara Liberman Gopen Weintraub, my 94-year-old mother, has born me, and borne me up, and borne up with me through thickest and thinnest. She endured my laboring at my Ph.D. and my J.D. simultaneously for eight years. Sometime during the fifth year she began telling her friends, "Most mothers pray that their son gets into Harvard. Me -- I'm praying mine gets out."

But whatever good this approach to writing may have done or may do in the future for anyone else, it has brought me not just "benefits" or "profits," but the greatest gift of all. As a young lawyer in 1986, Sarah B. Duncan (now a justice on the Texas Fourth Court of Appeals in San Antonio) listened to me lecture for two full days. She came back to listen to me for another two days in 1987. A decade passed before we encountered one another again: After my lecture at the State Bar of Texas convention in 1996, she came up to ask if I would give a lecture at a University of Texas Continuing Legal Education conference she was helping run in 1998. It was only at that conference in 1998 that we had our first conversation of more than three sentences. We were married in April of 2000. I cannot promise, dear reader, that you will experience the same kind of wondrous results from this Reader Expectation Approach I have, because there are nowhere near enough Sarah Duncans to go around. That being said, I wish to thank my wife for her energetic support of this work -- long before I knew her -- and for the pervasive vibrancy she brings to my life.

A *n Invitation*

Despite the length of this volume and the extent of its detail, you may still have questions about this approach or experience difficulties in trying to put it to work. If you wish to write me about any of this, please feel free to do so. I will respond as promptly as I am able. You can reach me by e-mail at ggopen@duke.edu.

A Reader Expectation Approach to Writing

1

The Problems of Interpretation and the Efficacy of a Reader Expectation Approach

How do we describe our response to good writing?

-- It was clear as a bell.
-- I couldn't put it down.
-- It just flowed.

What are the characteristics of writing that produce such responses?

-- Nothing arrives that cannot be handled the moment it arrives.
-- Everything leans forward.
-- Then everything actually goes in one of the directions in which it was leaning.

Readers constantly need to know where they are coming from in order to recognize where they are and to have some idea of where they are going. We read from left to right and through time, seeking cohesion: In that sense, our experience is linear. But we also must strive to understand a number of parts of the text simultaneously, seeking coherence: In that sense, our experience in nonlinear. The trick (if you are a reader) is to be able to do these two things at the same time, constantly. The trick (if you are a writer) is to make it possible for your reader to do this and to receive what it is you intended to send. Nothing, we could reasonably argue, is more crucial to the exercise of government, the function of commerce, the sustenance of law, the progress of discovery, or the communication of knowledge. Because of this, all universities offer, and most universities require, instruction in writing.

For most of the twentieth century, no college course in the United States was more widely dreaded and disliked than the Freshman Composition course; yet by the end of the century it was the most frequently required course. In many schools it remains the only required course. As educators, we seem to agree on its crucial value to undergraduate education; yet in our many decades of effort, we have struggled mightily in an attempt to find approaches to the language that work well for both student and teacher.

Since the mid-twentieth century, it has become commonplace to lament a perceived decline in student writing ability "in recent years." The most oft-cited causes are too much TV and too little reading. While these have certainly taken their toll, they have been aided by equally powerful but far more subtle developments in language instruction: Before World War II, Greek disappeared almost entirely from the curriculum; after World War II, Latin slowly faded to a shadow of its former importance; in the 1960s and 1970s it was demonstrated to the satisfaction of many that knowledge of grammar and ability to write well were not necessarily digitally interconnected, which allowed English teachers to do away with grammar; and requirements for the study of modern foreign language were reduced in number and extent. As a cumulative effect of all these disappearances, students are now left to learn the English language primarily by ear or by imitation. Lacking instruction in Greek, Latin, grammar, and modern foreign languages, they have little opportunity to experience language as a system of functioning structures.

I am not suggesting that we return to the "good old days" of requiring Greek and Latin and the rest. Those old days were not so good that we need to reinstate their burdens and their narrowness. We will not easily return Latin and Greek to prominence in a country that is so pressured to keep up with new developments in technology; we are unlikely to witness a widespread and enthusiastic return to grammar, even though imaginative people like Martha Kolln are showing us why and how we should; and foreign language instruction will always remain a difficult task in a country where the great majority of its youngsters never have the opportunity to use another language on a daily basis. Without these traditional opportunities to experience linguistic structure, we need an approach for teaching writing that is capable of offering students what is missing from their intellectual diet -- a way to perceive the *shape* of modern English prose. We need a pedagogy that makes explicit how a reader experiences the relationships between structure and substance.

S *ynthetic Problems*

Many of our problems in teaching writing are forced upon us by the essentially synthetic nature of the composition course. The problems are numerous, intertwined, and therefore collectively substantial.

The first synthetic problem for our students: What is the nature of the writing tasks they are assigned? Over and over again in their Composition class they are asked to do something they may never be asked to do as a functioning adult -- to produce a piece of writing exclusively for the purpose of being evaluated on how well they can produce a piece of writing. In most adult or professional writing tasks, something other than that is at stake: A client or a colleague must be informed; a court or a foundation must be persuaded; a friend or a foe must be humored; a community or a government must be challenged.

Separating a technique from the normal purpose it serves will often lead to a self-conscious, awkward, and (ironically) inefficient performance. Consider, for example, the following way of ruining a fine dining experience. You have looked forward for weeks to trying a new restaurant that has been receiving rave reviews. When the evening finally arrives and you are exploring with great delight the endlessly attractive menu, a rather stuffy-looking gentleman, formally dressed, approaches your table, stands imposingly at attention, clears his throat, and addresses you: "I am from the State Board of Regents for Table Manners. I have come to observe you dine. Please proceed." And with that he sits down. Throughout the meal you find yourself consciously and cautiously deciding when to shift the fork from one hand to the other, or how far down the head can go to meet the rising soup spoon. In short, you "eat" differently because you were giving to the technical support process the attention you should have been paying to the substance of the meal. You behave in an awkward, self-conscious manner in a nervous attempt to please the imposing authority figure. The same holds true far too often when students produce writing for a writing teacher.

The second synthetic problem: For whom do our students think they are writing? -- for that most dreaded of all audiences, the Big Red Pen in the Sky. They often view their writing teacher as someone who is paid to act as an unreasonable reader. Unlike anyone else, this tyrant reads not for substance, but for error -- not for communication, but for form. Students are convinced that a "real" reader would have no problem in extracting from that prose its "real" substance and intent.[1] When they receive a paper back from an English teacher with a marginal comment by the fourth paragraph that says, "I don't see what you are getting at here," they might think, "Oh sure. My *history teacher* would have understood. My *roommate* would have understood. You're just pretending not to understand because you are holding me to higher standards of style."

The third synthetic problem: What kinds of comments do we tend to put on their essays? Almost all of our marginal responses tend to be of two types: (1) detections of error; and (2) observations on content. Despite our best intentions, these comments do not accomplish nearly as much as we hope and trust they will accomplish. That is frustrating news indeed -- especially since it is the producing of these comments that saps the energy and deadens the spirit of so many who try so hard to be the maximum help to their students.

The Detection of Error

What is wrong with noting every error on the page? After all, if something's wrong, it's wrong. And if students are not corrected now, they will embarrass themselves later, when they are no longer students. All that is true; but constant and comprehensive detection of error eventually does more harm than good:

1) Some students become more and more afraid of committing future offenses. That can result in a dislike, a fear, and an unnatural rigidification of writing.

2) Most students get the message that if they had only avoided making those errors, then this would have been a good piece of writing. In actuality, however, if the errors hadn't distracted us, then we could have begun to judge whether or not this was a good piece of writing.

There is much more to be said on this issue. If you are interested in the question, please see the extended discussion of it in Appendix B.

Observations on Content

Despite all our good intentions, and despite the actual good some of our commentary may do, our substantive comments that fill the margin and appear in summary at the paper's end all too often serve a purpose that seems hypothetical. "Needs an example"; "Expand this"; "But don't you think that...?": Together they proclaim, "The next time you write *this* paper, here's a better way to do it." Realistically, students rarely have the experience of writing the same paper twice. Even when assigned a revision, students tend not to "revise" and "rewrite" the essay but only to correct the indicated errors and to respond to specific pieces of revisionary advice. They seek out the red marks and do damage control. No matter how sincere and how supportive the intentions of the teachers, these individual comments usually indicate to students a momentary failure; a request for the student to revise the entire paper can imply a complete failure. Many students believe that (1) there exists in the teacher's mind the paradigm of a Perfect Paper, and (2) the closer the student gets to duplicating that model of perfection, the higher the final grade will be.[2]

Comments that attempt to deal with substance often indicate only *that* something is insufficient without demonstrating *how* to do something about it the next time. The most well-worn of this kind are "vague," "wordy," "unclear," and the ubiquitous "awk." These leave the diligent student reminding herself that next time she should be "more clear" and "less awkward"; they do not train her how to go about attaining that higher state of being. Even detailed, well-articulated responses to the intellectual content of the essay tend not to help the students write other essays in the future, which will necessarily deal with different material.

I am not suggesting that students derive no benefit whatever from the energetic and committed efforts made by most composition teachers. Caring and careful comments communicate to students that their prose is being read seriously and with attention. Supportive comments can open students' minds to the possibility that through a more concentrated effort they might have produced a more effective piece of writing. But if we could demonstrate to students how the *readers* of that prose will most likely go about *the act of reading* it, then our students could make use of those insights in all their *future* writing tasks. That is precisely the aim and the claim of the approach described in this volume.

In 1783 Hugh Blair published his influential *Lectures on Rhetoric and Belle Lettres,* from which the next two centuries formed many of the main traditions of teaching writing. In summing up his chapter on "Means of Improving in Eloquence," Blair offered a half-dozen pieces of advice:

1) cultivate habits of the several virtues, to refine and improve moral feelings;
2) get a great deal of knowledge;
3) acquaint yourself with the general circle of polite literature;
4) apply yourself industriously;
5) attend to the best models; and
6) when imitating, be sure to notice the difference between the oral and written styles.[3]

It is difficult to argue against the purity and intent of all these exhortations; it is all too easy, however, to demonstrate how little they will help one improve writing. Will the student not be able to write well until all of these noble deeds are accomplished? Which of us would have the temerity to claim to have completed these tasks ourselves? Is it therefore true that "writing can't be taught"?

We have come a long way since the days when Hugh Blair ruled our classrooms. Especially since the 1970s, we have turned fresh eyes to myriad problems that used to make the Freshman English course the most vilified in the curriculum. This volume is one more effort in that direction. I would argue that we *can* teach writing, with good hope of consistent success, if we concentrate on techniques that help us to do the following:

1) Too see through the surface of any student essay to the composing habits that inform the rhetorical choices made at every level;

2) To forbear commenting on the substance of an essay as if the essay were more important than the writer;

3) To help students understand better the complex relationship between thought and the expression of thought;

4) To help students understand -- and therefore control to some extent -- how readers read.

By doing all this, we can stimulate students to replace the blind adherence to rules of writing -- still taught in far too many high schools -- with an understanding of procedures of reading. The rest of this volume is dedicated to the task of explaining, developing, and complexifying these four aims.

Failure-proof Students

Students can fail math exams. They can fail physics exams. But it is not easy for students to fail a writing assignment -- as long as they fill the required number of pages with content that is considered appropriate to the assignment. And students absolutely cannot fail on a paper if they show improvement since their last effort.

Such is not the case in the professional world they will enter after their last graduation. There, people fail a lot. Working hard, following the rules, and even showing improvement will not keep them safe from failure.

Academics are fortunate if a manuscript is turned down only a few times before acceptance. Business people may have several deals fall through before one clicks. Baseball players are considered first-rate if they can hit safely in one out of three batting attempts -- which means that even the best is expected to fail two out of three times. Can you imagine a judge looking at a lawyer's brief and saying, "This is a real piece of junk; but since it is so much better than the last one you submitted, you win the case"?

In the professional world we enter after our final graduation, the success of a piece of prose no longer depends on how hard the writer worked or how much the writer has improved since last time. The important person is no longer the writer but rather the reader. The bottom-line question concerning the quality of a piece of writing is simply stated: Did the *reader* actually get delivery of what the writer was trying to send? If the answer is yes, the writing is good enough; if the answer is no, the writing fails, no matter how elegant or powerful it may look or sound.

P roblems That Arise When We Turn Our Attention to the Reader

When we turn our attention to the reader -- and especially to the reader's interpretive process -- the outlook for potential improvement at first seems dim. The reasons are many, and as we consider them, the situation may look increasingly unpromising but there is a comforting light of hope at the end of this dark tunnel into which we now shall peer.

First: Once a piece of writing has been handed to the reader, it "belongs" to the reader. The writer cannot stand over the reader's shoulder and correct misinterpretations as they happen. The whole idea of writing is to allow the writer's thought to be present when the writer is not.

Then it gets worse with the arrival of a rhetorical fact: All units of discourse are infinitely interpretable. By "unit of discourse" I mean any continuous stretch of prose that has a beginning and an end. The term thus refers to words, phrases, clauses, sentences, paragraphs, subsections, sections, chapters, documents, books, etc. All of these refuse to be pinned down to a single "correct" signification or even a single set of meanings; they are infinitely interpretable.

By "infinitely interpretable" I do not mean that for each unit of discourse an unthinkably large number of interpretations is simultaneously known or knowable. Instead, I am using the term in the following way: If the number of interpretations perceivable at a given moment for a unit of discourse is N, then $N + 1$ is always a possibility. Someone with a different frame of mind or semantic experience or cultural bias could come along and perceive in the unit of discourse something that no one yet had noticed -- and then the number of interpretations would increase yet again.

Apply this concept to a simple sentence: "I will break for lunch tomorrow at half past twelve." Ask 20 people gathered in a room what this sentence "means" to them. Though all might be on the same track, there will surface a larger number of slight variations than you might at first expect. Then issue to each person a clipboard and a sheaf of paper, with the target sentence inscribed on the top page, and have everyone disperse into the surrounding community to interview people at random, asking what this sentence "means." At the end of the day, the 20 interviewers return to the room and collate the responses: The list of interpretations will have grown. Repeat this process day after day until at the end of one day no new interpretations have surfaced. We will be exhausted, and our list will be, presumably, exhaustive. Make a final count: Call that number N. No matter how high the number that N might be, $N + 1$ will still be a possibility. We might meet a person who simply "thinks" differently than anyone yet encountered in the process. Perhaps there is somewhere a person on a crash diet for whom the term *lunch* pushes buttons we have not yet experienced.

If nothing else, time passes by, creating new contexts into which that sentence falls; and since context controls meaning, new "meanings" will appear. For example: Fifty years pass by and the Revolution comes, sweeping away all the failings of the old, corrupt way of life and installing a new, moral order of living. In this newly created world, none of the old practices that used to produce moral failings are allowed. In the professional world, one of these weaknesses was the three-martini business lunch. Therefore, under the new order, breaking for lunch in the business day is forbidden. Anyone apprehended "breaking for lunch" will be thrown into moral debtor's prison. Suddenly the statement "I will break for lunch tomorrow at half past twelve" has moral and political significations it could not have had before the Revolution.

For example, recall the well-loved family situation comedies of the 1950s and 1960s, like *Father Knows Best* and *Ozzie and Harriet*. In watching them at that time, we as a community were in agreement that the fictional mother portrayed was the ideal American mother, acting out her role in quiet perfection. Father and the kids made human errors nearly every week as they took turns starring in episodes; Mother was almost always quietly wise and correct, but rarely was she allowed the conscious, manipulative force necessary for her to be the dominant figure. Every few weeks she was allowed to be intuitive and solve the episode's central problem; but even then she was hardly the central or primary focus of our attention. Today, as we look at the same shows in light of our raised consciousness of women's roles in our society, some of us wonder how we ever missed noting her subjugation, her lack of equal partnership, her partially denied personhood. Even if only as a function of time, all discourse is infinitely interpretable.

If that is so (the counterargument might be raised), how does one escape the logical conclusion that nothing means anything, or that everything means everything? Stanley Fish offered an answer to this question in his influential book *Is There a Text in This Class?* We tend to form what he calls "interpretive communities," through which we tacitly agree that for the moment we all will understand certain combinations of signifying words to produce certain significations -- not because they articulate the "truth" of something, or because they "must" mean something particular, but because we must rely on a certain amount of communal certainty in our communications in order to function. Learning to write well, I would argue, depends on learning to recognize and manipulate the assumptions, agreements, and expectations of all the discourse communities to which we belong.

So far we have noted two major problems: Once a piece of writing reaches the hands of the reader, it is the reader's; and every unit of discourse is infinitely interpretable. That is already rather daunting.

But it gets worse. Readers summon what I call *reader energy* for the reading and interpreting of every discreet unit of discourse. For example, we summon what we might call *clause energy* for the reading and interpreting of a given clause; but simultaneously, we have summoned *sentence energy* for the reading and interpreting of the sentence of which that clause is a part; and again simultaneously, we have summoned *paragraph energy* for the reading and interpreting of the paragraph of which the sentence is a part of which the clause is a part -- and so forth, all the way up to the document as a whole. That means that whenever we read a single word, we are interpreting it not only as a word but also as part of a phrase, a clause, a sentence, a paragraph, a section, and a whole document.

And it gets worse still: Each of these discrete units of reader energy must be used to perform a single task that has two inseparable components: (1) to perceive the *structure* of the unit -- (e.g., "here's the subject -- where's the verb?") -- without which the unit cannot hold together; and (2) to perceive the *substance* of the unit -- (e.g., "what does all this mean?") -- without which the unit does not make sense. These two (perceiving structure, perceiving substance) may be discussed separately; but they happen simultaneously. You cannot separate one from the other. Therefore, they have a zero-sum relationship concerning the available pool of reader energy: Whatever energy is devoted to one depletes the store of energy that could be devoted to the other. As a result, we could almost define bad professional writing as that which continually forces the reader to devote a disproportionate amount of reader energy to the discerning of structure. If readers are overburdened by trying to figure out *how* these words can go together to make a sentence, they cannot be as free as they need to be to discover *what* that sentence might "mean."

The problem might seem without solution. We can understand better why so many say that writing cannot be taught. Combining all the above, it may seem overwhelming: (1) A text belongs to the reader, not the writer; (2) All units of discourse are infinitely interpretable; (3) Readers simultaneously summon a number of different mental breaths of reader energy to read and interpret a number of different units of discourse simultaneously; and (4) for each of those mental breaths, the reader energy must be divided to perform two tasks simultaneously -- the perception of structure and the perception of substance. What to do? The answering of this question is the task undertaken by the rest of this volume.

I call the perspective presented here the Reader Expectation Approach (REA). It might also be called Structural Stylistics. Though the term is new, almost no single detail of it is announced here for the first time. Lines of development can be traced all the way back to the beginning of the Western rhetorical tradition. The newness derives from the bringing together of reader-based perceptions of rhetoric into a single cohesive and coherent approach. Much of this material was developed over eight years of collaboration between professors Joseph Williams, Gregory Colomb, and myself, but most of the articulation of it here is my own. They share in the credit for anything you might find persuasive; I will take responsibility for the rest. I have also benefited from a collaboration with Dr. Judith Swan.

The central tenet that informs this approach can be stated in a single sentence -- not nearly as exciting to read as it turns out to be functional in practice. Here it is:

Readers of English have relatively fixed expectations of where in the structure of any unit of discourse to expect the arrival of certain kinds of substance.

By "English" I am referring to the present-day language used by people who grew up with it as their first language.

All of us are *intuitively* aware of these structural expectations in our role as readers; this work attempts to make these expectations *consciously* available to us in our role as writers. Once thus aware, we can then knowingly manipulate our prose to fulfill or violate those reader expectations, for whatever purposes we intend. By doing this, we will not have succeeded in making even so little as a single sentence "mean" exactly the same to all readers; every unit of discourse will still be infinitely interpretable. We will, however, be able to control the interpretation of 95% of our readers instead of 25% or 45% or 65%.

This Reader Expectation Approach allows writers to predict where in the discourse unit (sentence, paragraph, essay, etc.) a reader will be most likely to look for the arrival of certain kinds of information. By placing that information in that expected location most of the time, the writer accomplishes two major objectives: (1) The reader will label or identify each piece of information as performing a particular function -- the function that the occupant of that syntactical location is expected to perform; and (2) the reader will minimize the amount of reader energy necessary to discover the unit's structure, thereby increasing the energy available for understanding its substance. These are two substantial rhetorical victories. They give writers great influence over readers in their interpretive process. They also put writers more in touch with their own thought processes.

A generic example: I will be arguing in a later chapter that there is in the English sentence a place where readers tend to expend their greatest reading emphasis. Let us call this structural location the Stress position.[4] For the moment, let us oversimplify the matter by identifying that place as the end of the sentence. Most *readers* of English are *intuitively* aware of this structural invitation for emphasis. If a *writer* can become *consciously* aware of the location of the Stress position, she can then manipulate the material so the information intended for the reader's greatest emphasis will appear exactly at the moment the reader is naturally expecting that emphasis to arrive. As a result, the chances greatly increase that reader and writer will value the same piece of information the most. The structure of the sentence thus becomes a signifier of the relative values of the sentence's substance.

What tends to happen when writers violate readers' Stress position expectationson a regular basis? Let us imagine a writer who regularly positions the most important information in the middle of the sentence. One of two things is likely to happen -- and both of them are bad. (1) Readers approach the Stress position, ready to give emphasis, but find located there material that clearly is not worthy of emphasis. (It might be something readers already know is of lesser import; or it might be something they have encountered several times in recent sentences and that cannot be considered to be of fresh importance.) In such a case, readers realize that they have already missed it. There is no fallback structural clue -- no sense of "If the important material is not in the Stress position, then look for it over here instead." In order to get the meaning the writer intended, therefore, readers must turn backward to discover what material in that sentence -- *already read* without emphasis -- *had been* the most important. But in most cases, readers are already hurtling forward into the next sentence. Thus readers are caught trying to move backward *and* forward in the prose simultaneously. That produces, I would argue, that all-too-familiar cotton-headed sense of non-comprehension we so often have when we struggle to make sense of prose. This may not be much of a problem in the shortest, simplest sentences, which contain few other viable candidates for emphasis; but in denser or longer or more sophisticated sentences, the chances soar that readers will interpret the sentence differently from the writer's intention. When this happens sentence after sentence, a general sense of non-comprehension settles over readers, and the cognitive mists thicken.

Even worse, readers may find located in the Stress position something that appears eminently capable of receiving emphasis -- but unfortunately it is *not* what the writer intended readers to emphasize. In that case, readers are highly likely to stress this imposter material; and the writer will have lost an important opportunity to influence the reading process. As bad as it is for a reader to be confused as to what is important in a sentence, it is even worse for readers to choose the *wrong* material for emphasis -- and do it with a misleading sense of confidence.

Style is choice. An individual's personal writing style is the sum total of all the choices that person tends consistently to make when faced with the rhetorical problem of structuring a particular kind of discourse. Since we are so relatively consistent in these choices, we can use the information REA presents to judge which of our students' rhetorical habits prove consistently helpful to readers and which prove misleading. That in turn will allow us to analyze not merely the essay at hand but, far more importantly, the student's continuing and pervasive writing style. If we can tell a student that (for example) she *constantly* puts the emphatic material of a sentence elsewhere than in the Stress position, then she can come to recognize that bad habit and learn how to repair that structure for *every* sentence she creates in the future. This begins as a revision strategy but soon becomes part of the invention process. Eventually, it will become natural for her on a regular basis to choose the structure that will be of greatest help to the reader; and in doing so, she will be understanding better her own inventive thinking process.

Is there a serious problem created by teaching most readers make the same structural assumptions most of the time? If we advise students exactly where readers tend to expect things to arrive, will not that advice quickly rigidify into rules and tend to turn everyone into rhetorical clones of one projected ideal writer/reader? That may *seem* to be a concern; but it need not be. Two welcome complications prevent such rhetorical cloning: (1) There are too many rhetorical structural choices to make at any one time for any significant percentage of individual thinkers to be likely to make precisely the same set of choices. When I work with a group of 20 people on a single badly structured sentence (even a relatively short one), I rarely find more than two people producing exactly the same revision. The sentence's main problem was that it offered too few structural directions for reader interpretation, leaving each reader too much to her own interpretive devices. Since each of these readers possessed a different intellect, each quite reasonably could come up with a slightly different interpretation, which in turn resulted in a different revision. Each revision was clearer than the original; but each reviser made different sense of the sentence. We will work through many such examples in later chapters.

The second complication is actually an attractive and comforting one: Any reader expectation can be violated to good effect. In fact, our greatest stylists turn out to be our most skillful violators. But in order to violate effectively, one has to fulfill expectations most of the time. Only then will a violation be perceived as a special occasion rather than as part of a general chaos.

REA therefore does not propose a new set of rules that must be slavishly followed. It only sets before the writer the expectations that most current readers of English tend to have most of the time, thus giving the writer some insight into the most probable reader interpretations. I cannot overemphasize that when I speak of "the reader" or "a reader" I mean "most readers, most of the time." There is no single, all-encompassing "Reader"; there are only strong patterns that surface during the act of interpretation.

In addition, REA allows the writer a relatively objective way of reentering the thought process. (The writing process *is* part of the thought process, and vice versa; but more on that later.) Let us take once again the example of the Stress position: It is no mere *cosmetic* matter to ask yourself where your emphasis lies and then to transport that material to the Stress position if it was not located there already. In order to engage in that search, one has to ask the essentially *substantive* question, "What was it I wanted to emphasize here?" You might find it hiding somewhere else in the sentence. You might find that the sentence contains more than one viable candidate for the Stress position, which might mean you have been conflating two separate thoughts or juxtaposing two thoughts without making their relationship explicit. You might find that the thought to be emphasized is not explicitly articulated anywhere in the sentence but rather is hovering above it in the form of an implication. Or you might find that nothing in the sentence was worthy of emphasis -- in which case the sentence should not have been granted the important status of "sentence"; it should have been a clause or a phrase in some other sentence. Any of these discoveries leads to an intellectual act of revision, not merely to a cosmetic act based on convention and propriety.

We probably do our students a disservice when we comment that they "had good thoughts" but "expressed them badly." I say this only in part because this makes them think of us as unnecessarily nitpicking, more concerned with style than substance; more importantly, it is a statement we cannot make with any confidence. If the writing was bad, how can we judge what thought it was trying to express?

When we see that a particular writer (for example) never occupies the Stress position with emphatic material, we should not presume that our interpretation of any given sentence necessarily coincides with what the author meant to communicate. Our ability to make *an* interpretation of a sentence does not ensure that it was *the one* the writer had intended us to perceive. My experience in working with this approach has convinced me that most of my interpretations of poorly structured sentences have missed the mark intended by the writer. You can judge for yourself in later chapters. All we can tell a writer who constantly puts unimportant information in the Stress position is that *we know that we do not know* what she meant to tell us.

Once we notice such a habit, we can free ourselves from the burden of interpretation by shifting it back to the author: We hand the text back with instructions to fill Stress positions with the appropriate information. That gives the writer a surefire way of demonstrating to us what was intended to be considered important.

Most of these rewrites will surprise you at some point; many will surprise you continually. We know well enough how *we* might combine that information to form a thought; but we are no experts on how *they* would do so. By abandoning our own sense of synthesis, we can free ourselves to ask *them*, "What do *you* consider the most important thing here?" It is failure-proof on our part; it is empowering on theirs. Everybody wins. In the process, we will be teaching our students how to go about dethinking and rethinking their ideas.

Revising your own prose, I would argue, is one of the most difficult intellectual tasks there is. In attempting it, your mind plays a trick on you. When you revisit a sentence you have written in order to judge whether it needs revision, you *think* the following is happening:

You see these words.

You know the meanings of each of these words.

When you put these words with those meanings into this syntactical structure, the meaning of the whole is X.

Since X is what you intended to convey, you judge the sentence to be fine.

You move on.

What *actually* is happening is the following:

You see these words.

You *remember* those words.

Those are the words you summoned when you were trying to articulate X.

Mere association. Since those were the words you chose when you were trying to convey X, naturally they will remind you of X when you reencounter them. The question remains whether those words will communicate X to most of your readers.

Let me extend that to the ridiculous. You are at the breakfast table one day, looking over last night's writing. Suddenly you are struck by a scathingly brilliant idea. In your haste to record it, you overturn your coffee cup. The coffee spills and stains the corner of your page. For all of time, I would argue, that coffee stain might recall for you, through mere association, that scathingly brilliant idea; but it is highly unlikely to communicate that idea to a future reader of that page.

The coffee stain problem is a provoking one. If we can never disengage ourselves from the associations involved in our having created a text, how can we ever get enough distance from that text to judge the likelihood of its communicative power and accuracy? The answer lies in knowing *consciously* what readers *intuitively* expect to find in certain structural locations. If in checking our prose for the location of substance (a relatively objective task) we find that the material is often not where readers will be expecting to find it, then we know the odds are worse than we would like that our readers will perceive our intended meaning. Repairing the structural weaknesses will lead us inevitably back into the thought process, where we will discover what it was we really had been trying to say. And to boot, this process is eminently teachable.

E xpectation and Reader Energy

Some expectations are relatively fixed; others are fluid. Some can demand most or all of one's attention; others can function simultaneously with no sense of discord. Sometimes the fulfillment (or violation) of one expectation immediately gives birth to another. Just as meaning is controlled by context, expectation can be controlled by perspective. Here is an example of the fixed and the fluid, the focused and the simultaneously diverse, the immediately regenerative, and the multiperspective, all happening at once.

The scene is Fenway Park, home of the Boston Red Sox, a professional baseball team. They are playing their arch-rivals, the New York Yankees. The Red Sox are leading by two runs in the final inning. After two outs, the Yankees manage three singles to fill the bases. The next batter is crucial to the game's outcome: If he fails to hit safely, the game is over, and the Red Sox win; if he manages to hit safely, anywhere from one to four runs could score, thus altering the two-run deficit.

On the first pitch, the batter strokes a high fly ball to center field. The ball arches into the darkness of the night, reaches its apex, and begins its descent. The Red Sox center fielder positions himself for the catch that would end the game. A number of different expectations are engendered among various kinds of spectators.

In the stands are three people of interest to us: a rabid Red Sox fan, scarred by decades of late-season team collapses; an equally rabid Yankees fan, essentially hubristic and condescending, but with traces of mistrust and self-doubt; and an Unwilling Participant, trapped by social needs into attending the game, uncaring of the outcome, and thoroughly bored.

First consider the moment from the perspective of the avid Red Sox fan. While the crack of the bat may well have produced a moment of terror, the perception that the result should be a routine fly ball for an out raises an equally strong feeling of potential delight. The expectational tension increases dramatically with the parabolic progression of the ball. The height of the ball at its apex and the resulting shape of its curve are instantaneously calculated by the experienced eye so accurately that the very moment of the contact between descending ball and expectant glove can be predicted. Therefore, the force of the fan's expectations increases geometrically as the play draws ever closer to its conclusion.

Scenario #1: The center fielder catches the ball. The sight of the completed catch transforms the potentiality of delight into actuality, producing the explosive sounds and actions of emotional closure/release for which the price of admission had (in part) been paid. The fan's reaction is extreme because several expectations have been fulfilled simultaneously: (1) The ball was caught; (2) As a result, the inning has been ended; (3) As a further result, the game has been ended; (4) Therefore, the threat of the Yankees gaining ground in the standings has (for now) been ended; (5) Most importantly, morality, faith, patience, and loyalty have all been rewarded, producing a sense of complete self-satisfaction only occasionally encountered in the rest of life. All these expectations had been increasing as the ball descended toward the glove of the fielder.

Scenario #2: The center fielder drops the ball. All the expectations mentioned above are violated. The result is not only a destruction of all the desired closure experiences above but also a simultaneous creation of a confusing and anxiety-raising new set of expectations. How long will it take the center fielder to recover the ball and heave it toward home plate in a second attempt to put an end to the play? Though one run will surely score, will the second and score-tying run reach the plate before the throw arrives? The fan now is calculating a new geometric curve -- the throw to the plate -- and simultaneously gauging the concurrent linear progression of the Yankee runner to the same spot. The context has changed from potential triumph to potential disaster, bringing with it new, yet more dire expectations. Whatever the result of the play at the plate, the fan will reach a moment of explosive closure.

These new expectations may function as a protection against the tormenting results of the previously violated expectations. Through them the fan can "win" no matter what the outcome: Either the expectation of disaster is fulfilled ("I *knew* we'd blow it"), producing the satisfaction of accurate prophecy; or that expectation is violated by a superb throw to the plate resulting in the final out and a one-run Red Sox triumph, in which case the thrill of the delayed moment of victory immediately compensates for the anxiety of the previous violation. The emotional expectations may be complex and unconscious, but their force is clearly felt. It is also significant that they are fluid or flexible. One replaces another instantaneously, until closure -- or finality without closure -- is achieved.

If we shift our attention to the perceptions and expectations of the New York Yankees fan, we note that the same fly ball and the same two scenarios would produce almost exactly opposite emotional results. The difference in interpretation stems directly from the difference of context: One fan's victory is another fan's defeat. The expectation of arrival creates the moment; the context colors the interpretation.

The experience is yet different for the Unwilling Participant. Again, the same athletic act functions in a different context. If Unwilling's middle name is Ignorant, then the elegant parabola of the white ball against the blue-black sky might raise no expectations whatever; no context would be naturally constructed within which interpretive possibilities would be suggested. On the other hand, if Unwilling's middle name is Knowledgeable, then the fly ball would raise hope of relief and release, both of which will be activated by a successful catch. Then everyone can go home.

In all these cases, a single act produces widely varying interpretations because of the different contexts in which it is perceived. The interpretation of the ninth-inning fly ball is infinite in its possibilities because the potential number of different and differing perceivers is infinite. Without question, the play will be described in distinctly different terms by (a) the Red Sox radio broadcaster, (b) the Yankees radio broadcaster, and (c) the national network (presumably nonpartisan) television broadcaster.

Every act of discourse -- small or large -- is just such a fly ball. If we want our particular audience to interpret our particular discourse act in a specific way, we must control the context so that it will position the greatest possible percentage of readers to be transformed into knowledgeable fans on our side. We must know the bases for their expectations and their responses.

We lean into the structure of prose much in the same way the baseball fan leans into perceiving the parabolic descent of the fly ball. We read from left to right and through time. As we proceed, we expect certain kinds of substance to appear at certain structural moments. In general, we are most pleased and most at one with the reading experience when everything arrives about where it is expected to arrive. On occasion, a violation of our expectations (the ball being dropped by the outfielder), through its momentary disruption of our reader energy, can result eventually in much greater satisfaction in the postponed fulfillment of those expectations (throwing out the potential tying run at home plate). Knowing consciously the nature of these expectations allows the creator of the discourse to manipulate the probabilities of reader response.

Just as the baseball fan summons a certain amount of fanatic energy for the viewing of this particular play, increasing and decreasing exertion as the various moments of the play require, so readers summon what I have called *reader energy* for the perception of each unit of discourse, no matter what its size. At the beginning of that unit, the reader takes a kind of mental breath; with it is summoned the tension with which the reader will pay attention to the various parts of the discourse, breezing through less important matter and building toward moments of emphasis. If the reader is called upon to use a great deal more or less mental breath than that which was summoned, problems can ensue.

Have you ever suffered the following surprise at the hands of a paragraph? Imagine having begun that paragraph 10 or 12 lines from the bottom of a right-hand page. You read those lines. As you turn the page, your eye notes that there is no indentation in the left-hand margin. In other words, no new paragraph will begin on this new left-hand page. What happens? Your heart sinks. But why should you feel so oppressed? You knew you would have to read this page. You knew you would have to read this page and the next 12, if like me you always are aware of how much is left to read. What do readers tend to do at this moment? Some speed up; some turn back and start the paragraph over; and most, whether they know it or not, grab a glimpse of the new right-hand page to see where the next paragraph break will come. What is going on here?

I suggest that as readers we summon a "normal" amount of *paragraph energy* for the reading of all paragraphs that are suspected to be of normal length. Having read 10 or 12 lines on one page, we expect that the paragraph's issue has been stated, that the discussion is well underway, and that as we turn the page we should be coasting toward closure. Suddenly, we discover that we are much closer to the beginning of the task than its end, that the development of the paragraph's thought has hardly gotten underway, and, as a result, that an inadequate amount of *paragraph energy* is left to us for finishing this paragraph. That is why some of us speed up, in an attempt to complete the paragraph before our mental breath is exhausted and we start choking for mental air. That is why others of us return to the beginning of the paragraph, where we can summon a much larger *paragraph breath*, which we will dispense differently this time around. We are going to have to run the mile, not the 100-yard sprint. That is why most of us grab that glimpse of the new right-hand page: None of us like to be burned twice.

Apply the same concept of mental breath to the reading of a sentence. Sentences can come in all sorts of shapes and sizes; but we tend to expect (in English) that a sentence of any size will begin more or less immediately with the subject of the main clause, which will in turn be swiftly followed by the verb and then by the complement. We expect all that -- unless we are otherwise informed. We are "otherwise informed," for example, if the sentence begins with a word like *although*. Any initial *although* communicates in a split second all of the following to a reader: "Dear reader, I know you were expecting the main clause, but this is not the main clause. This is the "although" clause, which will qualify the material you will later encounter in the main clause. This qualifying clause will trundle along for a bit. You will know it is over when you see the appropriate comma; and after that you will find the subject, verb, and complement of the main clause. Thank you very much. Have a nice day." *Although* says all of that to us when we encounter it at the beginning of a sentence.

If the promise of the "although" clause is fulfilled, readers may well have no structural problem in reading the sentence. The experience would proceed something like this:

> Although xxxxx xxxxxx xxxxxx xxxxxx xxxxx xxxxx xxxx xxx xxxx, (pause) SUBJECT VERB COMPLEMENT.

But if those reader expectations are violated, the reader might find the summoned mental breath inadequate for the journey, making the reading process unduly burdensome:

> Although xxxxx xxxxxx xxxxxx xxxxxx xxxxx xxxxx xxxx xxx xxxx, (pause) and although xxxxxx xxxxx xxxxxxx xxxxx xxxx xxxxxxxxx xxxxxxx xxxxxx xxxx, (pause) despite which xxxxxxxx xxxxxxx xxxxxxx xxxxxxxx xxxxxxx xxxxxx and xxxxx xxxxx xxxxx xxxxxx, (pause) subject verb complement.

By the time the reader arrives at the *main* clause, he is unlikely to have sufficient reader energy remaining to endow the reading of that clause with the *main* emphasis it presumably deserves. Even worse is the case when the delayed arrival of the main clause brings material decidedly *not* central to the writer's point.

> Although xxxxx xxxxxx xxxxxx xxxxxx xxxxx xxxxx xxxx xxx xxxx, (pause) and although xxxxxx xxxxx xxxxxxx xxxxx xxxx xxxxxxxxx xxxxxxx xxxxxx xxxx, (pause) despite which xxxxxxxx xxxxxxx xxxxxxx xxxxxxxx xxxxxxx xxxxxx and xxxxx xxxxx xxxxx xxxxxx, (pause) blip.

At that point, the reader feels either incompetent or ill-used. A steady diet of such structures destroys the communication process. (Note: I am not suggesting that all multiple-clause sentences are dysfunctional; but the skillful handling of multiple clauses depends on a writer knowing what a reader can handle at any given moment.)

Indeed, how many times do we all, as readers, come to the end of a sentence and realize that in our cloudy mind *nothing* has registered? Feeling bad about ourselves, we give thanks that our friends and colleagues cannot see into our minds as this moment, for they all think we are relatively intelligent. Thank goodness they do not know how often this happens to us. Reprimanding ourselves, we try the sentence again -- this time with an increased energy and devotion to the task. Many a time, sad to tell, we once again fail "to understand" by the time the sentence has once again ended. Now we feel *really* bad about ourselves. Well, I would urge us all to stop feeling so bad. If we, with our education and reading experience and good conscientious will, have failed to make sense of that sentence, the chances are good that it is not *our* fault but rather the fault of the writer. All the "right" words might appear on the page; but the chances are high that those words were not in an *order* that would make their synthesis possible on a first reading.

All prose is persuasive. Readers assume we had a "meaning" to convey. Where we put information makes a difference: It "persuades" readers to believe they know what we meant to say. We all "know" this as readers. Example: Which of the following reports will get this employee a raise, and which will get her a reprimand?

-- Although she is often late for work, she is always thorough.

-- Although she is always thorough, she is often late for work.

-- She is often late for work, but she is always thorough.

-- She is always thorough, but she is often late for work.

This book concentrates on how a writer's structural location of information controls a reader's perception of meaning.

Reader expectations change over time and from place to place, but by relatively slow sociological, psychological, and linguistic processes; it is enough to be able to spot those we are dealing with here at the moment. Recognizing them can empower us and our students over the experience most of our readers will most likely have of our text. Given the infinite interpretability of text, corralling most of our readers into interpretive agreement would be quite an accomplishment.

Endnotes

1. For a dramatic exposition of this point, see Joseph M. Williams, "The Phenomenology of Error," *College Composition and Communication* 32 (1981): 152–168. In that essay, Professor Williams explores the subject at some length, during which most readers note that he commits four or five obvious grammatical errors. At the article's end, he confidently announces, "If by this point you have not seen the game, I rest my case." His essay contains "about 100 errors."
2. Other students believe that teachers are either capricious or dedicated to demonstrating their power through the medium of negative commenting. Both of these evils -- whether in the student's mind or the teacher's attitude -- can be moderated or eradicated by the Reader Expectation approach described in the rest of this volume. For a detailed example of the difference between the traditional types of comments found on student papers and the kind that can be generated from the Reader Expectation approach, see the end of Chapter 9.
3. Blair, Lecure XXIX, pp. 180–187.
4. The perception of the special importance of the end of a unit of discourse has a long history that stretches at least as far back as Aristotle and probably much further. It is noted in many of the English writing textbooks from the Renaissance to the present. I follow Joseph Williams in using the term *Stress position*.

2

Action and Agency

To explain these reader expectation concepts, I begin with the smaller units of discourse and proceed to the larger. Other orders would work; but the material is more easily taught from the bottom up because readers' structural expectations tend in general to vary in specificity with the size of the unit of discourse: The smaller the unit, the fewer structural choices exist. That makes the smallest units the neatest with which to begin.

Beginning with the sentence level in college composition courses sometimes frustrates students, who feel they should have progressed beyond such picayune considerations several years back. It might also seem too slow to teachers, who receive whole essays, not just sentences, from the beginning of the term. A word of pedagogical advice at the outset: Be patient in feeding this material to students. It is not important that their every paper be hypothetically revisable for publication; it is important that by the time the course is finished, they understand all the concepts and can shift from one level to another without stripping their intellectual gears. As Ezra Pound said in his *ABC of Reading*, it does not matter which leg of a table you make first, as long as by the time you are finished it stands firmly on the ground. I am reminded also of one of my law professors, who was fond of deflecting potentially distracting questions with the solemn pronouncement that "Sufficient unto the day is the evil thereof."

It would also be both kind and helpful to tell our students an important fact of life that is rarely mentioned in the entire educational process: The first time through anything can be rough. Old habits are not just reflex actions; they have seeped into the blood stream and are part of the brain's communication with the rest of the mind and body. It will be a challenge for students to open themselves up to this new way of seeing. We should help them see it that way -- and not as a "correction."

As a result, I tend not to grade student essays during the first half of the term. I see no need to punish or reward students for their previous preparation in writing. I much prefer to give them a chance to learn something from my efforts first, after which they can demonstrate how far they have come in this particular class.

I begin, therefore, with a consideration of what happens during the reading of a sentence.

S *ingle Actions*

Consider the following familiar-sounding sentence, which could have been written by an undergraduate trying to sound grown up or by a professional person already grown up trying to sound grown up:

1a. What would be the employee reception accorded the introduction of such a proposal?

Unmistakably, the sentence possesses a quality of professional sobriety and gravity. The words are individually respectable, and the grammar is unobjectionable. Compare it to the following revision:

1b. How would the employees receive such a proposal?

Putting aside the qualitative judgment of "better" and "worse," we can probably agree that, compared to the (a) version, the (b) version is *easier* to read. What makes that so? At first we might suggest that (1b) is shorter than (1a); it turns out, however, that although length by itself is sometimes a symptom of poorly constructed writing, it is not often its cause. In part, (1b) is shorter than (1a) because it omits the concept of "introduction" -- presumably a worthless word in this sentence, for the employees could hardly receive a proposal that had not yet been introduced. (We will revisit this below.)

This long-standing concern with sentence length has led us badly astray. We often teach students that where a sentence is concerned, to make it better, make it shorter. This is one of several widespread myths about writing that ought to be abandoned. In the 1930s and 1940s, a number of "readability formulas" were established -- the most notable being that of Rudolph Flesch, who created the "Flesch Test." Its results led him to the extraordinary conclusion that a sentence is too long when it exceeds 29 words. Why this conclusion was not laughed off the stage long before this is hard to understand. Instead, it has made a strong comeback in recent years, showing up in major software grammar checks. Now without asking you can be told when you venture over the 29-world line in the sand. One can almost hear the growing thunder of the wrath of the gods in the distance. I urge you to ignore it.

The average professional sentence has been calculated as varying between 24 and 26 words. (The average freshman sentence tends to vary between 13 and 15 words.) Think how many published sentences must have exceeded 29 words to balance off all those 8- , 10- , and 14-word sentences that have found their way into print. Flesch did good work, but came to the wrong conclusion. The professional sentence tends to be double the length of the freshman sentence because freshmen tend to produce sentences of one clause only, while professionals often produce sentences of two or more clauses. Exceeding 29 words often results when a sentence extends to *three* clauses or major units. Three are significantly harder to control than two. A sentence of more than 29 words then is not, as Flesch insisted, harder to *read*, but rather harder to *write*. You can find sentences of 30, 50, or 80 words that ring clear as a bell; you can also find sentences of 10 or 13 words that remain opaque to the closest scrutiny. Length *by itself* is no indication of the clarity of a sentence.

Back to the drawing board:

1a. What would be the employee reception accorded the introduction of such a proposal?

1b. How would the employees receive such a proposal?

We might also suspect that (1b) is easier to read than (1a) because of voice: Sentence (1b) forcefully uses the active voice, while (1a) may seem clouded by its use of the passive. This active/passive distinction, again *by itself*, is another myth of writing that must be abandoned. The passive is not only acceptable but a necessary tool if a writer is to have complete control over the structuring of sentences. We will be exploring a number of circumstances along the way in which the passive is not only acceptable but highly preferable to the active. At the moment we might begin with the simple tautology that the passive is superior to the active in all those sentences in which the passive does a better job than the active. Or perhaps we should turn theological: God would not have invented the passive if there were not a good use for it. Or we could make a Darwinian argument based on its survival over the centuries. Perhaps we should settle for the more modest statement that both active and passive have their uses. The difference between (1a) and (1b) cannot adequately be explained by the difference in voice.

Since many of our students were never taught the difference between active and passive, we might have to do that for them. Here is one way that works well:

1. Take an active sentence, which is one where the subject does the action to the object.

> Jack loves Jill.

2. To make it passive, you do the following:
   a) Make the object the subject. ("Jill" comes to the front of the sentence.)
   b) Replace the active verb by the verb "to be" plus a participle (=verbal adjective) made out of the previous verb. ("Loves" becomes "is" + "loved.")
   c) The former subject can then be included, if necessary, as the object of the preposition "by." (. . . "by Jack.")

3. The result:

> Jill is loved by Jack.

Returning to our consideration of example (1b), if the cause of the greater reading ease of (1b) is neither length nor voice, to what can it be attributed? I suggest the answer lies in a careful consideration of what will be our first Reader Expectation concerning the structural location of information.

When I use this example in workshops for professionals, I request that the participants underline the word or words in (1a) that denote actions taking place within that sentence. The task tends to take them much longer than anyone might have predicted. In a group of 20 or more people, virtually every time some underline zero words, some one, some two, some three, some four, and some five. Occasionally someone underlines six. But that produces more than just six different answers: The "three" people can choose different combinations of three; the "two" people can chose different pairs of two. As a result, there may be as many as 12 to 15 different responses in a group of 20 people. It might seem strange at first that in a group of well-educated, highly intelligent adults there could be so much disagreement as to what is happening in a 13-word sentence of no great intellectual depth whatever. The problem, it soon appears, lies not with the readers but with the writer. Sentence (1a) contains inadequate structural instructions for interpretation -- especially concerning what is "going on."

Although those workshop participants do not recognize it at the time, this is a phenomenal moment. No single person in the room considered the sentence beyond their intellectual abilities to understand. Each tended to assume that having perceived *an* interpretation, that must be *the* interpretation the writer intended to suggest. But were the results to be made public, most people would find only one or two others had chosen as they did; and some would find their choice had been unique. In other words, there was no communal agreement on "what is going on" in this sentence. That comes as a surprise.

I then ask the same workshop participants to perform the same task for (1b): Underline the word or words in (1b) that denote actions taking place within that sentence. This time the task requires less than 10 seconds. Every time, an overwhelming majority underlines only one word -- the verb "receive." In other words, for sentence (1b), there is widespread agreement as to "what is going on."

The difference in reader response between (1a) and (1b) can be explained by our first significant reader expectation:

Readers expect the action of a sentence to be articulated by the verb.

Why this is such a well-kept secret is hard to understand. Most of us were taught in high school that a verb is an "action word"; we should have been taught instead that the verb "ought to be the word that articulates the action." I have found it essential to emphasize this distinction for students, who tend to have difficulty grasping it at first. The distinction will be made clearer by the redefinition of "strong" and "weak" verbs below.[1]

Workshop participants designate a number of different words in (1a) as actions because they are interpreting the sentence in a number of different ways. Here it is again:

1a. What would be the employee reception accorded the introduction of such a proposal?

Some underline "would" or "be" or "would be." They expect "would be" to signify the action because they recognize that those words are *part of the verb*. That makes them "sound" like they ought to be at least part of the action. The concept of existence (the primary meaning here of "would be") is not the intended action of this sentence; I know this only because the author of (1a) told me explicitly what her intentions were.[2] Without that insider knowledge, my attempt at interpretation would be no more valid than that of any other reader. Only the writer knew for sure what the writer intended. She just neglected to inform us.

To make matters worse, she split the verb into two parts -- "would be" and "accorded." As we lean into the "would be," we expect to encounter the whole verb, which we hope will state the whole action. But we are made to stumble. We must hold on to the "would be" for a bit before it is at too much length resolved by the arrival of "accorded," four words later.

"Would be," or any other form of the verb *to be*, is quite capable of being the action of some *other* sentence. The meanings of the verb *to be* concern existence, equality, or labeling. Those are the things *to be* does well. When those are the things happening in a sentence, *to be* is a fine verb. (The verb *to be* has appeared four times in this very paragraph -- "is," "are," "are," and "is." Each time it tells us what is going on.)

A great many of the workshop participants underline "reception." The author agreed; she intended that the employees in this sentence perform the action of "receiving" something. "Reception," however, is not a verb but rather a noun constructed from a verb. Such a noun can be referred to as a *nominalization*.

Between two-thirds and three-quarters of workshop participants underline "accorded." The word sounds so formal, so involved, so important; its etymological dignity exceeds that of any other word in the sentence; but even more significantly, it is a major part of the verb. It turns out, however, that "accord" was not one of the author's intended actions. She told me straightforwardly that if the concept of "accorded" were removed from the sentence, none of her meaning would be lost. (Had the same sentence been authored by someone else, with different intentions, "accorded" might have indeed been an important action. In her case, it was not.) So many people underline "accorded" because they have been *waiting* for it to arrive to complete the verb -- "would be *accorded*." That expectation of completion, plus the long wait, makes the arrival of the important-sounding word "accorded" all the more convincing as the answer to the question "What is going on here?" Because she chose for her verb a word that has nothing to do with the action of the sentence, the author sent her readers a false interpretational clue.

About half underline "introduction"; it also sounds like an important word, referring to a recognizable concept of some potential complexity. Is it an action in this sentence? Again, it is a nominalization. Again, only the author would know for sure. Left to my own devices as the creator/reviser of (1b), I decided that "introduction" was excess baggage, for the reason offered above: How could the employees have received a proposal that had not yet been introduced? I threw it out.

A few underline "proposal" -- yet another nominalization -- perhaps with the sense that proposing is often a lively human action; but in this particular sentence, according to its author, "proposal" is no action at all. It *had been* an action in a previous sentence: Someone had proposed something, the result of which was this proposal. But no one was proposing anything in sentence (1a).

Readers lean forward to the verb in a clause or a sentence in expectation of discovering the action around which that clause or sentence is organized.[3] When a verb makes great sense as the potential action of the sentence, most readers are satisfied with that and seek no further. Once an interpretation makes sense to us, we tend to cease interpreting. If, however, the verb makes little or no sense as the action, then the reader must continue to look elsewhere to figure out what is going on. Unfortunately, once the verb is clearly perceived not to be the action, no other structural location offers itself as the next best place to look. Different readers will choose different words (or combinations of words) to supply their interpretive needs. That is why there is such widespread disagreement among workshop participants in discerning what is going on in sentence (1a).

Look again at sentence (1b):

1b. How would the employees receive such a proposal?

In processing this sentence, most readers lean forward to the verb and are gratified to find at that location the word "receive" -- something that makes sense as the action of this sentence. That is why sentence (1b) has what we might call *flow* or *shape*. The expectation evident in the leaning forward is fulfilled. You can "hear" the flow toward the verb: "How would the employees RECEIVE such a proposal?" Do not let people tell you it is impossible to teach flow or shape, or that one must simply have an ear for this sort of thing. If you know the reader expects the action to appear in the verb, then putting it there will create a natural flow toward that verb, thus helping produce a shape for the sentence.

Conversely, sentence (1a) lacks that kind of focused shape precisely because as a community of readers we are uncertain which word or words articulate the action. "Would be" is only half of the verb; if we have been leaning forward to it (which is the reason many underline it), we find ourselves unable to "arrive" at it with a sense of fulfillment -- because the remainder of the verb, "accorded," does not appear until later in our reading experience. "Accorded" fails to make enough sense as the main action, even though most people cloudily assume for it some significance, assured it is only their own intellectual limitation that prevents them from clearly understanding that significance. In what other word might the action be articulated? "Reception"? "Introduction"? "Proposal"? All that struggle to select and construe the *structure* of this sentence misuses the store of reader energy the reader summoned for the uncovering of its *substance*.

This uncertainty is reflected in the shapelessness of the sentence. It has too many potential "arrivals" where the question "What is going on here?" could be answered. That in turn creates a rhythmic jerkiness. Which of these capitalized words should be emphasized -- and how much?

What WOULD BE the employee RECEPTION ACCORDED the INTRODUCTION of such a PROPOSAL?

These five choices for emphasis (counting "would be" as a single choice) can generate 31 permutations and combinations of choice.[4]

Readers are so caught up in trying to decide *how* these words could be made to come together to form a coherent unit that they are unable to feel confident in deciding *what* these words might mean. In contrast, prose that continually places information where readers expect to find it allows readers to perceive the shape of local structures, to build and maintain momentum in the reading process, and thereby to feel more confidence, justifiably, in their interpretive decisions:

1b. How would the employees RECEIVE such a proposal?

Having said that, it must now be revealed that sentence (1b) -- my revision of (1a) -- for all its seeming improvement, turned out to be a totally inadequate representation of the author's intentions. The author looked at (1b), praised its flow, shape, and concision, and informed me that I had missed the interpretive boat completely. I had left out "introduction," which, together with "reception," had been the words she intended to be perceived as the sentence's action. So that was the answer to the question "What's going on here?" -- "reception" and "introduction." In a group of 20 people, only two or three -- sometimes fewer -- tend to choose these two and only these two words to underline. They are the only people who had a shot at understanding the sentence as she had intended. And, as you will see, it is only a shot.

When I was told that "reception" and "introduction" were the intended actions in the sentence, I told her "I now know that I do *not* know what you are trying to say. I *do* know, however, how to help you revise the sentence effectively. If 'reception' and 'introduction' are meant to be the actions, then they should both be transformed into verbs. Then make the doers (the *agents*) of those actions the subjects of those verbs, and the intended meaning will rise to the surface."

In no time she produced the following revision:

1c. How would the employees receive such a proposal if the Executive Board introduced it at this time?

Now we can discern two centers of action, each focusing on a verb. The action of the "how" concept balances the action of the "if" concept: "How ————→ receive, . . . if ————→ introduce." The seemingly precise and concise revision in sentence (1b) was not only inadequate -- it was worse than (1a). For all its difficulty, sentence (1a) was *capable* of being interpreted as the writer had intended; sentence (1b) was not. We cannot tell whether a sentence is good or bad without knowing what meaning it was intended to communicate. If the author is not around to tell us, we have to make our decisions based on the best clues we have -- not merely word choice but, more importantly, the structure and the context.

Note in (1c) the arrival of some strangers. Where did this "Executive Board" come from? Well, to be fair to the writer, we must remember that I have taken this single sentence out of the context of the whole document. The Executive Board had made its appearance earlier; this reappearance would come as no shock to someone who had read the entire text up to this point. In articulating the action in the verbs, the author was prodded by syntactic necessity into adding the "Executive Board"; she had to identify the agent of the action "introduce." As long as the concept of "introduction" was represented only by a noun, no one had to be around (in the sentence) to *do* it. As soon as it became a verb, the syntactic need for a subject became apparent. The author knew who did the introducing; after her revision, so do we.

But yet more important is the appearance of the concept of "at this time." By making this explicit, the author reveals to us the critical concept of immediacy; for her, that sense had been clearly enough implied by the word "introduction." The chances that most readers would perceive the concept of *immediacy* in "introduction" are not high. Once the author transformed "introduction" to the verb "introduce," it called attention to the need for a modifier. With "at this time" made explicit in the sentence -- especially in the sentence's Stress position -- our chances of perceiving the concept of immediacy increase dramatically. As it turns out, it was not the *mere existence* of "introduction" that mattered but rather its *timing*.

The author would have been able to make this clearer for us in sentence (1a) had she been able to read it *aloud* to us. No doubt she would have underemphasized "accorded" and given special emphasis to the word "introduction" by eliding it with the phrase that follows it:

What would be the employee reception (accorded the) INTRODUCTION of such an agreement?

But nothing on the page alerts a reader to assume these dynamics. On the contrary, the arrival of "accorded" as the long-awaited conclusion of a three-word verb structure would lead most of us to accent "accorded" and underemphasize "introduction":

> What would be the employee reception ACCORDED the introduction of such an agreement?

Both "reception" and "introduction" are nouns made from verbs -- which we are calling nominalizations. At present, these abstractions are extremely in vogue among writers in America's professional worlds. Nominalizations are neither good nor bad in and of themselves, but only when used in a particular context. They tend to be especially unhelpful to the reader when they usurp the action of the sentence from its verb. This is most problematically the case when a weak-verb sentence like (1a) above contains multiple nominalizations: Different readers will tend to select different combinations of nominalizations (and other nonverb words) to represent the sentence's action.

On the other hand, nominalizations have a number of good and helpful applications. They can be both powerful and subtle when functioning as a backward link to an action/verb that has appeared in some previous sentence. For example:

2. Senator Budd proposed a bill that would decrease Social Security payments for all citizens over 90 years of age. The proposal failed to garner enough votes for passage.

In the first sentence, "proposed" is the verb and "proposed" is the action. In the second sentence, the verb "proposed" has reified into a noun, "proposal," so it can become the agent of the new verb/action "failed to garner." The linkage is secure and powerful; and the action clearly flows from the verb of the first sentence through the nominalization to the verb of the second.

A warning: Our students seem to have great difficulty in understanding the subtlety of this usage. They have been trained to memorize prescriptive rules that are unambiguously inclusive or exclusive. The distinction between good and bad nominalizations is not nearly as easy to deal with as the rigid, overconstrictive, seriously unhelpful RULE that "all nominalizations are bad." Nominalizations, when effectively used, perform feats of reference in such an elegant and powerful way that readers rarely recognize the effect consciously. As Michael Halliday has pointed out, conceptualization itself might be impossible without nominalizations. Before Aristotle, many people had noted that things "moved." It took Aristotle to lead us to think about the concept of "motion."

On the other hand, when nominalizations are misused, they become all show and no action; indeed, they actually obscure the action. We must therefore be vigilant to prevent students from oversimplifying these perceptions into a false rule that "nominalizations are bad."

Here is an example to demonstrate another way in which to talk about "bad" versus "good" nominalizations:

3a. The North Carolina proposal involved the manufacture and interstate shipment of mobile homes.

This example contains three nominalizations -- "proposal," "manufacture," and "shipment." If none of them represent actions happening in this sentence, then they all perform their functions better as nominalizations than they would as verbs. In other words, if the sentence is well written, then no one is "proposing," "manufacturing," or "shipping" anything here. All those actions would have happened previously or will happen in the future. If the action of this sentence reflects the relationship between the proposal and the other two nominalizations (an action of "involving"), then "involve" is the best choice for the verb. We cannot judge the quality of sentence (3a), therefore, without knowing the *context* in which it exists. Here is a context that makes (3a) "well written":

3b. The Legislature was confused as to what the proposal from these three States actually involved. The answer in one case, however, was clear: The North Carolina proposal involved the manufacture and interstate shipment of mobile homes.

On the other hand, sentence (3a) would be "poorly written" if, in a different context, the author had been trying to highlight the action of "proposing" and the nature of the proposal. In that case, the following would do better:

3c. In response to new quality control problems in the housing industry, North Carolina proposed to regulate the manufacture and interstate shipment of mobile homes.

A sentence cannot be considered either good or bad apart from its context.

The same is true of verbs. Most of our students were trained to believe that there is a list of verbs in the English language that could be called "weak" and therefore are best avoided. (The list would include *to be* and *to have* and *to seem* and other existential formations.) The corresponding list of "strong verbs" comprises all those we learned as part of the 10 vocabulary-words-of-the-week -- ("use each in a sentence") -- the employment of which would help us develop an aura of respectability and sophistication.

These lists falsify the reality. No single verb should be considered strong or weak by itself. Since every verb in the language has meaning, every verb is potentially strong; since every verb can be used in a sentence that has little or nothing to do with it, every verb is potentially weak.

With reader expectations in mind, we can redefine for our purposes the terms *"weak verb"* and *"strong verb."*

-- A weak verb is one whose meaning has little or nothing to do directly with the action of the sentence as a whole.

-- A strong verb is one whose meaning is the focal point of the action of the sentence as a whole.

Although that may sound clear enough, students have difficulty putting it into practice. Here is a helpful little quiz. I give my students five seconds to decide whether the verb in this sentence -- "articulated" -- is weak or strong:

4. Jack articulated his love for Jill.

Those who vote for "weak" are wrong. Those who vote for "strong" are also wrong. We cannot effectively judge whether the verb is weak or strong because we are presented with no surrounding context: We do not know what the sentence as a whole is trying to say. For example, consider Context #1 -- an 800-page novel about Jack. Jack is a fine fellow -- a top student, a crack athlete, the president of the student government, and an altogether nice guy. His problem is that he has never experienced any really deep emotions. He meets Jill on page 46. After 700+ pages of tempestuous relationship, on page 752 Jack suddenly feels overwhelmed by a inner sensation he had not yet in life experienced -- a new and unexpected emotional sensation. The next sentence reads, "Jack articulated his love for Jill." "Articulated" is a weak verb, since we do not care at the moment about his expressive abilities. The appropriate verb/action might have something to do with feeling or loving or being capable of emotion.

Compare with that Context #2 -- a different 800-page novel about a different Jack. This fellow has felt things deeply since the cradle; his (typically male) problem is the inability to communicate those feelings to other people. He meets his Jill on page 39. More than 700 tempestuous pages later, on page 764, he finally splutters, "Jill, -- I -- LOVE -- you." "Jack articulated his love for Jill": "Articulated" is a strong verb, since the concept of expressing himself through articulation is intended to be the main action of the sentence.

We have now a Reader Expectation piece of advice that works well for the majority of sentences in contemporary English professional prose:

....
Usually express the action of a sentence as a verb.
....

Only the author knows what she intended as the action of any given sentence. Therefore, only the author can judge accurately whether the verb of any particular sentence is weak or strong. If an author uses what we are defining as a weak verb, then the chances are higher than she would like that many readers will misperceive what she intended as the sentence's action.

Generally, you should be able to get some sense of what is going on in a paragraph just by looking at a list of its verbs. Be careful, however, not to take this too far: A collection of uninteresting-looking verbs will not necessarily be weak; nor will an impressive list of dynamic-looking verbs necessarily be strong. Each verb must be judged in its own context.

If the author is revising the prose, he or she will probably know whether or not the verb expresses the intended action. If a teacher is reviewing the prose, he or she can either (1) chance a judgment based on the surrounding prose or (2) call the verb in question to the attention of the student and ask if it represents the intended action. The former is a gamble, and with bad odds; the latter is both safe and appropriately exploratory. You will often be surprised by your students' responses.

The action/verb piece of advice has a corollary:

....

Usually use verbs only for expressing actions.

....

Just as the reader expects to find the action in the verb, the reader expects any verb to express an action. A sentence can suffer from having too many verbs. Reconsider Example (3c) from above:

3b. North Carolina proposed to regulate the manufacture and interstate shipment of mobile homes.

If we turned all the available nominalizations into verbs, we might come up with the following:

3c. North Carolina proposed to regulate all who manufacture mobile homes and ship them interstate.

If the discourse that follows this sentence tries to focus on North Carolina and its proposal, then the verb/actions of the manufacturers and shippers simply clutter the cognitive horizon. The reader would actually benefit from the absence of those people -- as in (3c) -- and the understating of their having done actions. The point: By understanding what readers expect to do with a verb, a writer is empowered to some extent over the ways in which a majority of readers are likely to interpret the writer's prose. If the writer wishes to make it more likely that a reader will consider a particular piece of information as representing the action of the sentence, all the writer need do is to articulate that action as a verb.

These action/verb principles increase the power and control a writer has over the language. Here is an example that combines both the main principle and its corollary, resulting in a revision that simultaneously produces greater clarity and greater subtlety.

5a. The reorganization of the old Department into two new Departments should also include the institution of separate detailed bookkeeping procedures and the maintenance of separate bank accounts for each.

Context: An organization wishes to divide one of its Departments into two smaller Departments. It asks a lawyer to advise it as to what it must *do* to affect this change. Sentence (5a) is a part of the lawyer's response.

Again, I have asked many workshop groups to underline the words in this sentence they think denote actions. Again there is usually a great range of responses -- everything from one to six words. The most frequently underlined words are "reorganization," "institution," "maintenance," and "include."

Most people underline "include." Even without a consultation with the author, we can begin to see -- given the question he was asked -- why "include" does not belong on this list. The organization asked the lawyer, "What actions should we *do*?" If his answer comes back "*Include* stuff," the organization is unlikely to be happy to pay its legal bill. Why, then, do most people underline "include"? Because it is the verb. Since it inhabits that grammatical location, we expect it to be the action. It sounds like the action; but unfortunately, in this context, it is not the action.

The other three -- "reorganization," "institution," and "maintenance" -- are all nominalizations. Some students might be tempted to oversimplify the principle and make all action-seeming nominalizations verbs. In the present case, such a response might produce something like the following revision:

5b. When you reorganize the old Department into two new ones, institute separate detailed bookkeeping procedures and maintain separate bank accounts for each Department.

Better. Now we have a check list of things we should *do*: We should "institute" this and "maintain" that. But does the author really want to call as much attention to the concept of "reorganizing" here as the presence of the verb "reorganize" seems to command? Have not we been talking about this "reorganizing" throughout the whole document? Was not this concept part of the original question? "Institute" and "maintain" will shine even more brightly if the possibility of action being attached to "reorganize" is diminished.

Note that "reorganize" in (5b) already appears slightly less important than the other verbs because it appears in a subordinate "when" clause rather than in the main clause. The syntactic unit known as the *subordinate clause* tends to be interpreted by readers as containing material "subordinate" to that of the main clause. At the least, readers would dearly like to assign those relative values with some confidence. As long as we have demoted the concept of "reorganize" here to a subordinate position, why not continue in that vein and demote it even further, from the higher syntactic status of clause to the lower status of phrase? Note the effect:

5c. In reorganizing the old Department into two new ones, be sure to institute separate detailed bookkeeping procedures and to maintain separate bank accounts for each Department.

We have made the verb "reorganize" into the "-ing" form, "reorganizing." Now most readers will hear the opening phrase not as a repository of emphasis and a statement of action but rather as a structural marker, nodding backward and leaning forward, with little force of its own. The difference is subtle but significant. In (5c), there are two actions that dominate our attention; they are the two things the lawyer is telling the organization to *do*.

Our advice to students, then, can be relatively clear, even though the resulting procedure may involve complexity and subtlety. Ask whether the verb of a sentence articulates the sentence's action. If it does not, decide what you intend the action to be and express that as a verb. Summon to the side of that verb as its subject the agent (doer) of that action. Then reconstruct the rest of the sentence by moving backward and forward from there, being sure to include all the information and concepts that existed in the original sentence. Make all actions verbs; make all verbs actions. If there are pieces of the old sentence that simply will not fit into the new sentence, then they probably belong in some other sentence; their connection to the present material needs to be explicitly articulated.

When students hear this advice for the first time, they often mistake it for the other, less helpful advice -- "Use strong (that is, 'impressive') verbs" -- they have heard for many years concerning the efficacy of developing a strong vocabulary. They hear it as the English teacher's prejudice against simple, weak-sounding, flabby verbs, especially the verb *to be*. In trying to make the teacher feel better, they might search out some of the wimpy-*looking* verbs in their essay, consult a thesaurus, and replace them with *impressive*-looking words -- usually of Romance rather than of Teutonic lineage. If the verb they are replacing was indeed weak as newly defined here, then the verb they choose -- no matter how distinguished its pedigree -- must by definition also be weak. The original verb was weak because it did not articulate the action of the sentence as a whole; the action was lurking somewhere else in the sentence or was missing altogether. That action will remain hidden where it was no matter how impressive the new verb may sound; hence, that replacement verb must also be weak.

All too many of today's American 18-year-olds do not yet accept that (1) they have their own thoughts, and that (2) they should be allowed to have their own thoughts. ("Thoughts" must be distinguished from "opinions.") They have just completed a dozen years of education in which acceptance and regurgitation have usually functioned as highly desirable coping skills. Part of their composition course in college ought to be devoted to introducing them to this new sense of power, this new recognition of self. It can be a stunning experience (for student and teacher alike) when students are allowed/commanded to make their *own* decisions as to what is going on in a particular sentence. They have a hard time believing it actually is "their" sentence, as opposed to one you have prewritten for them. We can further empower them over their own thoughts by convincing them that the structural choices they make in creating discourse actually help them discover and develop those thoughts. At the same time, those choices will help persuade a majority of their audience to interpret the words on the page in accordance with their intentions. We need to emphasize for them the importance of their role in their own writing process: "Only *you* can tell me what's going on in your sentence. Whatever the action may be, express it as your verb." In doing so, they will begin to perceive the relationship between writing and thinking -- and especially the relationship between *their* writing and *their* thinking.

A String of Actions

While no single weak-verbed sentence might seem to present much of an interpretive challenge to an able reader, the cumulative effect of a string of such sentences can confound even the ablest. How well do you comprehend the following paragraph on first reading at a normal speed?

6a. The effects reported in this study have one of two explanations. Either the congeners themselves have direct and permanent effects upon the central nervous system, or there may be a retardation of the metabolism of ethanol by the congeners so that it has a stronger effect. The probability of the latter is less, because the observation of the effects occurred well after the blood alcohol concentrations were immeasurably small.

Most readers unacquainted with congeners assume they have difficulty with this paragraph because of their lack of technical knowledge. That lack turns out to be far less a problem than the lack of instructional help we get from sentence structure throughout. We can revise all of this paragraph without looking up the definition of "congener" or any of the other technical terms. We need instead to determine whether the action of each clause is articulated by the verb. If it is not, we might try to identify the action and turn it into a verb.

I know the intentions of the author of sentence (6a) because I have worked through this paragraph with him, asking the questions we will be exploring below. If in the development of this example you guess "incorrectly" the action of a given clause, do not blame yourself; blame the author. It is his duty to make clear to as many readers as possible what is going on in any given clause. That task is best done by giving structural clues as to the relative worth of different pieces of information. I will be bold enough to state here that almost *no* reader can perceive the author's intentions in one reading of this paragraph; very few will succeed even with a second, third, or fourth reading. Truth to tell, the author himself failed to recognize clearly enough the specific point toward which he was driving.

For this example, we will proceed clause by clause to determine the following:

1) Does the verb articulate the action of the clause/sentence?

2) If not, what is that action, and how may that be transformed into a verb?

3) Given our new verb, how does the rest of the information fit around it? (Who performed the action? On what was the action performed?)

The original first sentence:

The effects reported in this study have one of two explanations.

Ask any group of 50 people which word in this sentence represents the main action taking place and you will get almost equal votes for each of five choices: "effects," "reported," "study," "have," and "explanations." The author intended only one of these to convey the action. (I know this only because he told me. I could not have determined the correct one by myself.) "Have" was his verb; but "have" was not his action. We could rewrite this sentence four times, each time transforming one of the other candidates into the verb. Each of those four would be a clearer sentence than the original; but only one of them would represent the author's intention. By choosing "have" as his verb in a sentence that has nothing to do with "having," he missed his best opportunity to tell us what was going on.

He told me the action in this sentence was the nominalization "explanations." Let us then begin revising by making "explain" the verb. The question then arises, who did the explaining? The answer turns out to be "the people who did the study." Who would they be in the context of this paragraph? They would be represented by the first-person pronoun "we."[5] What did "we explain"? The "effects reported in this study," otherwise known as "our results." All that remains is the concept "one of two," which can fit in neatly at the end. (The neatness of that fit and the propriety or impropriety of first-person usage will be explored in later chapters.)

The first sentence revised:

6b. We can explain our results in one of two ways.

The first clause of the original second sentence:

Either the congeners themselves have direct and permanent effects upon the central nervous system,

The author informed me that to express the action of this clause he again used a nominalization, "effects." When we change the noun "effects" to the verb "affect," we do not have to change our subject; it remains the congeners. The adjectives "direct" and "permanent" transform into adverbs so they still modify "effects/affect." Note that the original verb again was "have" -- and again was of no help to us in discovering the sentence's action. He never intended "possession" to be an action in this paragraph.

The first clause of the second sentence, revised:

6c. Either the congeners themselves directly and permanently affect the central nervous system,

The second clause of the original second sentence:

or there may be a retardation of the metabolism of ethanol by the congeners

The author told me that, once again, he had expressed his intended action in a nominalization -- this time, "retardation." The agent of that action was again the congeners. (If it takes time and effort to unearth the structure at this pace, consider how burdensome the task must be when a reader is proceeding at a normal reading pace.) Note that the original verb was "may be" -- again of little help to us here, since the sentence was not talking about the action of "existence."

The second sentence, second clause, revised:

6d. or the congeners retard the metabolism of ethanol

The third clause of the original second sentence:

so that it has a stronger effect

Although it is not easy for us to perceive it, the author's intended action was again "effect." The agent of that action was "it." Most groups of people, in my experience, have difficulty agreeing on what "it" refers to; they offer a variety of five different referents -- "congeners," "retard," "metabolism," "ethanol," and "metabolism of ethanol." The author intended "it" to refer to "the metabolism of ethanol." The resulting object of that action was the absent but implied "central nervous system." Note that once again -- for the third time out of four -- the original verb was the verb "to have." Three "have's" and a "may be" have offered us no direction whatever in our search for action and our construction of meaning.

The third clause of the second sentence, revised:

6e. so that it affects the nervous system more strongly.

(Notice that the "it" is no longer as difficult to interpret, since it comes right on the heels of its referent, "the metabolism of ethanol.")

If we put together the revised sections of the second sentence, we get the following:

6c-e. Either the congeners themselves directly and permanently affect the central nervous system, or the congeners retard the metabolism of ethanol so that it affects the nervous system more strongly.

When compared to the original sentence, this seems clarity itself; but, as it turns out, it will require still more attention.

The first clause of the original third sentence:

The probability of the latter is less,

This is point in the paragraph when most first-time readers drop the ball and give up the struggle. "The latter"? What "latter"? In order to answer this annoying question, we would have to stop our forward progress, return to the jungle of the earlier part of the paragraph, find two of something, latch onto the second of those two, and transport it back to the word "latter" -- and nobody is paying us enough to undertake this burdensome effort. The best effort we can muster, probably, is to struggle forward in hopes of being brought up to date by the words that still lie in front of us.

If we do return to the previous sentences in the paragraph, we find there were indeed *two* explanations, the second of which was the "retardation" explanation. That was what was meant by "the latter."

The verb is "is." Is "is" a strong verb or a weak one? It looks like "is" is weak, because "is" always *looks* weak. But in this case, "is" is strong. All the author wanted to do in this clause was to *label* the second explanation "less probable." Since the verb *to be* is admirably suited to this task of labeling, it is, in this context, a strong verb.

For its agent -- and an elegant backward link -- we can employ the nominalization of the previous verb/action -- "retardation."[6] The first clause of the third sentence, revised:

6f. Retardation is less probable, though,

The remainder of the third sentence:

because the observation of the effects occurred well after the blood alcohol concentrations were immeasurably small.

The author had no problem in identifying the main action here as the nominalization "observation"; but he had some difficulty in explaining to this scientifically underinformed reader the importance of the concentrations already being "immeasurably small." He foreshortened his attempt by assuring me that the intended audience for this prose would understand the connection. We can therefore let that remain as it is for the moment.

The remainder of the third sentence, revised:

6g. because we observed the effects well after the blood alcohol concentrations were immeasurably small.

Here, then, is our entire revised paragraph:

6b.-g. We can explain our results in one of two ways. Either the congeners themselves directly and permanently affect the central nervous system, or the congeners retard the metabolism of ethanol so that it affects the nervous system more strongly. Retardation is less probable, though, because we observed the effects well after the blood alcohol concentrations were immeasurably small.

Again, this version is neither "correct" nor final nor the best; it simply attends to one important recurrent structural problem. We can profitably make further revisions. To suggest to students that *any* particular version of a sentence, paragraph, or essay is "the right answer" will keep them subservient to the language instead of empowering them over it. It will also belie language's infinite interpretability.

If we run a slow-motion replay of this revised paragraph, we can see that it has assumed a clearer shape. Though important problems remain, several kinds of reader expectations are more clearly raised and more clearly fulfilled. Here is the text of the revision, piece by piece, with interpolated comments from a reader's perspective.[7]

We can explain our results . . .

The paragraph will concern an explanation of what the authors found.

in one of two ways.

We expect two ways to appear -- the first immediately, the second sometime thereafter. Both may come in the next sentence; or one may come in the next sentence to be followed by the other in the following sentence; or one will arrive in the next sentence and be discussed for some time -- perhaps even the rest of the paragraph -- before we turn to the second. Whatever the progression, we hope to be notified in timely fashion of the advent of the second explanation. In other words, we want to know it when we see it.

Either . . .

Lovely. We now know that both of the "ways" referred to in the first sentence will appear in this sentence, the second way following hard upon the arrival of the sign-word "or."

the congeners themselves directly and permanently affect the central nervous system,

Whatever "congeners" are, they are doing something "directly and permanently" to the central nervous system. If we want to know more, we can look up "congeners"; but we do not have to reach for the dictionary in order to understand the interrelationship of these actors, their actions, and the central nervous system.

or . . .

Very nice. Here comes the second of the two ways we were promised.

the congeners . . .

Good. The congeners are the subject in both cases. So the two ways of explaining the results here are (1) the congeners do this, or (2) the congeners do that. The difference between the two explanations does not reside in a difference in agency.

retard the metabolism of ethanol so that it affects the nervous system more strongly.

OK. Before, the congeners did the action of "affecting"; now they are doing the action of "retarding." It is not quite clear -- although it *sounds* like it ought to be clear -- how these two clauses talk to each other. (We shall return to this.) But at least we know the two things that the congeners *do*.

Retardation is less probable, though,

The nominalization "retardation" elegantly connects backward to the verb "retard" in the previous sentence. Of the two explanations proposed, the second one (the "retardation" one) is now being discarded as less probable.

because we observed the effects well after the blood alcohol concentrations were immeasurably small.

Whatever this means, we know it is the reason offered for the discarding of the second explanation.

As we see, many concerns have been addressed, and the paragraph has improved; but something remains unclear: What was the main distinction between the two alternative "explanations" we finally unearthed in the second sentence? Consider them again:

1) Either the congeners themselves directly and permanently affect the central nervous system, or

2) the congeners retard the metabolism of ethanol so that it affects the nervous system more strongly.

Wherein lies the difference between the two?

-- It is not a question of agency: In both cases, the congeners were the doers of the action.

-- It is not a question of action: In both cases the main action was that of "affecting."

-- It is not a question of who got affected: In both cases, it was the central nervous system that wound up being the object of the action.

So in both cases, the congeners affected the central nervous system. The difference between the two lies in the immediacy of this "affecting": In the first explanation, the congeners did this task "*directly*" -- and it says so, right there on the page; but in the second they did it *indirectly*, by taking a billiard shot off the metabolism of ethanol -- and the word "indirectly," which is perhaps the single most important word for this paragraph, never made it onto the page. This is a failure not only of writing but of thinking: The two are inextricably intertwined. This author had never clearly realized that the direct/indirect distinction was the primary product of this paragraph's thinking.

To improve this sentence further, then, we can do two important things: (1) Articulate the concept of "indirectly" by explicitly using the word; and (2) create a structure that will focus appropriate attention on the direct/indirect contrast.

| CONGENERS | AFFECT | CNS | DIRECTLY |
| CONGENERS | AFFECT | CNS | INDIRECTLY |

Here is one possibility:

6h. Either the congeners themselves affect the central nervous system directly, or they affect it indirectly by first retarding the metabolism of ethanol.

Here is another:

6i. Either the congeners affect the central nervous system directly by themselves, or they affect it indirectly by first retarding the metabolism of ethanol.

Through this essentially *structural* investigation, we have uncovered a serious problem of *substantive* thought.

Yet another problem: Nowhere in our revision have we found a place for the author's original words "permanently" and "more strongly." In alternative explanation #1, what is the significance of that word "permanently"? Does it suggest that explanation #2 concerns, by comparison, an effect more "temporary"? And what does "more strongly" signify in explanation #2? Does it suggest that the "direct" effect of explanation #1 was somehow "less strong"? These are questions that remain unanswered -- because I did not think to raise them when I was talking with the author. He might well have been able to tell me *what was on his mind* when he selected those now missing words. Although they found no place in our revision, they must have had a place in his original thinking process. That part of his thought is now lost to us. Had *he* made these structural changes for himself, he would have discovered the mental noise caused by these problematic terms and might have been able to salvage them by making explicit their connection to his thought. This revision procedure would have engendered a new invention procedure.

In our revised paragraph, the next sentence began with "Retardation is less probable, though . . . . " We had been so pleased to have substituted "retardation" for "the latter," thereby making a smoother backward link; but now that we have made explicit what the real difference is between the two explanations being offered (direct versus indirect), we can substitute a far more descriptive -- and therefore a far easier to process -- backward link:

6j. The "indirect" explanation is less probable, though, because . . . .

Our newly revised paragraph now proceeds more sure-footedly, with more direction in its intellectual movement and energy:

6k. We can explain our results in one of two ways. Either the congeners themselves affect the central nervous system directly, or they affect it indirectly by first retarding the metabolism of ethanol, which in turn affects the central nervous system. The "indirect" explanation is less probable, though, because we observed the effects well after the blood alcohol concentrations were immeasurably small.

We are left at the end of this paragraph with a distinct expectation about the contents of the paragraph to follow: It will leap into an investigation of the first explanation -- the *direct* effect congeners have on the central nervous system. Our revised paragraph turns out to be more than a collection of better-shaped sentences: The thought progression of the paragraph as a whole has taken on a new shape -- a funnel shape -- that proceeds from the broad to the narrow. It tends toward elegance:

We can explain our results in one of two ways.
Here is #1, and here is #2.
Please discard #2.

Next paragraph:

So let's take a closer look at #1.

The author of this paragraph about congeners had consistently chosen weak verbs. It came as no surprise to me to find the same weakness reappearing in most of his paragraphs, in this and other documents. He had adopted (or fallen into) a weak-verbed structure as part of his rhetorical style. This kind of rhetorical recidivism can work to the advantage of composition teachers. Instead of attacking the sentences and shaking up the paragraphs of a *particular* document for the supposed purpose of improving *it*, we can tussle with the decisions that the writer *constantly* makes in constructing sentences, thereby improving *him*. Transforming him from a weak-verb writer to a strong-verb writer will affect every document he produces from that moment on.

Excessive nominalizations proved to be a major problem for this writer. Examples of nominalizations are easy to come by; but they are also easy to misuse in the classroom. It is tempting to insist that sentences like (7a), below, are always inferior to their denominalized version, (7b).

7a.   There was a <u>modification</u> of the program by the Director.

7b.   The Director <u>modified</u> the program.

With no context to influence us otherwise, we might well be tempted to prefer (7b) as being crisper, clearer, more forceful, and more direct. Our students, however, may balk at agreeing that *all* sentences like (7a) should be transformed into sentences like (7b). They argue that such restrictions deprive them of their individuality. I would agree with their instinct but not with their reasoning. I would argue that (7a) and (7b) are equally valid sentences; but their actual worth depends not on any sense of personal freedom or individuality but rather on the *context* in which they appear.

Sentence (7b) is likely to be the superior sentence in a context in which the Director is our primary agent and the action of "modifying" is the main action of the sentence. If the question lurking in the context of this sentence is "What did the Director do?" then (7b) would make a far better response than (7a).

Change the context, and sentence (7a) could become the better choice. What if the discourse immediately preceding sentence (7) concerns the existence and nature of modifications? What if the Director at this point is just a minor character, not the star of the show? If the questions lurking in the context of this sentence are "Was there any modification whatever made in this program?" and "If so, who did it?" then (7a) would be the stronger, more applicable response. Its verb, the lowly verb-*to-be*-plus-past-participle that we call the passive, would become the appropriate action of the sentence.

This example offers an opportunity to reconsider a piece of advice commonly given these days concerning prepositional phrases. For some decades now, there has been a "Plain English" movement in this country to get all laws and legal documents written in prose that non-lawyers can understand. While I agree, of course, with the general goals of this movement, its approach to the language often seems to me based on misguided concerns. It mainly urges the abandonment of jargon and the shortening of sentences. Jargon, I would argue, works just fine, if it is within the grasp of the intended audience. Then it saves time and effort. If the audience does not know the jargon, or French, or Chinese, then do not use that jargon, or French, or Chinese.

We have already seen that length -- or the lack of it -- has nothing to do directly with the quality of prose; but some states now have Plain English laws that limit sentence length. (See especially Connecticut, where one definition of Plain English says that legal sentences cannot exceed 34 words and must average, over the span of the document, no more than 22.) Some

Plain English advocates now have noted that long, cumbersome legal sentences often contain a large number of prepositional phrases. They are therefore advising us that to produce clearer prose, we should get rid of as many of prepositional phrases as possible. Get rid of the symptom (prepositional phrases), they say, and the disease (bad writing) will disappear by itself. But if that were true, we could obliterate the common cold by telling people never again to cough or sneeze. There is something to this prepositional phrase "problem"; but the advice currently being offered will not work.

Look again at the two versions of Example (7):

7a. There was a <u>modification</u> of the program by the Director.

7b. The Director <u>modified</u> the program.

True, the (b) version is shorter (5 words instead of 10) and lacks the two prepositional phrases of the (a) version -- "of the program" and "by the director." But how would anyone know *which* prepositional phrases should be cut? The real question is why those two prepositional phrases disappeared "by themselves" when we attended to the structural problem of articulating the action in the verb.

Why did the "by the" disappear? We made "the Director" the subject of the sentence. By definition, the subject is the "by the" person. Therefore, if the Director becomes the grammatical subject, there is no longer any need to articulate her role by articulating "by the."

Why did the "of the" disappear? In (7a), "modification" and "program" were both nouns. You cannot merely place two such nouns next to each other and expect readers to understand their relationship. You therefore have to articulate the relationship explicitly: "modification *of the* program." But once we have made "modification" into the verb "modified" and made "program" its direct object, the grammatical relationship makes the substantive relationship self-evident, and the need for the prepositional "of the" evaporates. The subject did the action to the object: "The Director modified the program."

Take care of the structural locations and the prepositional phrases will take care of themselves.

Just as we noted where nominalizations were concerned, structural advice concerning verbs should not be allowed to deteriorate into a *rigid rule* of *what writers must do*; instead, it should function as a description or *prediction* of *what readers generally expect*. The latter approach leaves all the controls of decision making to the individual writer. There are times when it is in the writer's best interest to undercut the forcefulness of an action; no "rule" should get in the way. In using REA, it is essential to keep Reader Expectations from deteriorating into Reader Demands. REA must not be used to substitute a new set of requirements to replace the high school requirements from which REA is to act as liberator.

For example, there are circumstances when the principle of expressing the verb as an action produces a rhetorical result that is less than desirable. Consider, for example, the following two sentences:

8a. The Dean made a <u>decision</u> to conduct a <u>review</u> of the matter.

8b. The Dean <u>decided to review</u> the matter.

I have underlined the words the author identified as actions in each case. Sentence (8a) expresses the actions as nominalizations; its main verb is "made" -- which is not, in this case, the action of the sentence. Sentence (8b) collects the two actions and combines them into one extended verb structure. But even if this decision concerning the likelihood of this sentence's action is correct, (8b) is still not a "better sentence" than (8a); it is better only when its author wishes to communicate the actions forcefully, straightforwardly, clearly, and unmistakably. Since those are *usually* admirable qualities, this version of the sentence tends to *sound* the more preferable of the two.

It is possible, however, to construct a context that does not favor those usually admirable qualities; in that case, (8a) becomes the better choice. Perhaps, for example, the hot political issue on campus this month is the fear that the Dean has become an administrative tyrant. Many believe she is deciding matters too swiftly and without adequate consultation. Let us also imagine that the Dean has decided she must call for a review of a particular matter and must announce this decision to the academic community. In such a climate, sentence (8a) would serve the Dean's needs far better than sentence (8b). The very power and forcefulness suggested by the concision of (8b) would exacerbate the problem of her perceived tyranny. In the nominalized (8a) version, the Dean presents herself not as "deciding" or "reviewing" anything; she is only "making" something -- a decision. As a result of that decision, a review will take place; but she will not "review" anything, but merely "conduct" a process. Her agency will have been significantly underplayed -- which, in this case, would be for her the preferred result. The marshmallow version -- (8a) -- would then be preferable to the far more forceful, tyrannical, in-your-face version, (8b). Both sentences are "right" or "good" or "acceptable"; they just elicit different interpretive responses from readers. Once again, context controls meaning.

A *gency*

The agent of a clause or sentence is quite simply the person or thing that performs the action. If the sentence is written in the active mode, the agent and the grammatical subject are one and the same; if it is written in the passive mode, the agent may be elsewhere or missing altogether.

Most often, but not always, writers need to let the reader know who is doing what. In other words, they have to name the agent explicitly.

7b.   The Director modified the program.

Once again I advise strongly against constructing any rigid, oversimplified rules for students. It will not do to tell them to articulate agency "at all times" or even "whenever possible." That advice belies not only what professional writers *do* but also (more importantly) what they *need* to do. Instead, I would advise that we explain to students *the nature* of agency, which in turn will suggest principles by which they can decide whether the articulation of agency is needed in a given situation.

In English, there are essentially only two ways to get rid of agency: (1) by articulating the action as a nominalization:

7c.   The program underwent a modification. [or]
       There was a modification of the program.

or (2) by changing the active to the passive -- after which the agent can be eliminated:

7d(i).   The program was modified by the Director.
7d(ii). The program was modified.

When agency needs to be eliminated, I strongly advise the use of the passive. It is preferable to the shift to a nominalization because it keeps the action in the verb. More readers will find it.[8]

This is not covered in middle school training because children do not need to be taught to avoid agency. We spend a good deal of our effort in exactly the other direction as we try to instill in them a sense of moral responsibility. We do not praise the young George Washington for saying to his father "The cherry tree got chopped down" but rather for admitting "I chopped down the cherry tree." But in the adult world, there are many circumstances where the elimination of agency is a necessary and moral action.

Sometimes agency is simply beside the point. Example: You have saved money for years to build the dream addition to your home -- the family room with the large picture window. You come home one day to discover that wonderful window smashed to bits, with shards of glass littering the floor. You pick up the phone and call your spouse. Which of the following is the "better" sentence for this tragic moment?

9a.   Somebody broke the window.
9b.   Our window was broken.

Answer: Neither, by itself, can be judged "better"; it all depends on what you want to convey. If the uppermost thought in your mind is vengeance, then the agency of "somebody" in (9a) is a necessary part of your communication. Somebody -- you don't know who, but you sure intend to find out, and are they ever in for it when you do -- broke your window. If, on the other hand, your thoughts at the moment are concentrated on the broken state of your favorite Pittsburgh Plate, then the articulation of agency will mislead your listener. In that case, sentence (9b), "Our window was broken," avoids raising the question of agency and directs your spouse's mind more sure-handedly to your intended focus of communication -- the broken window.

There are many other reasons why one might wish to suppress agency. Sometimes, for example, the articulation of agency can be impolitic or potentially disruptive. Perhaps, after you hang up the phone, you notice among the shards of glass a baseball. The mystery evaporates. That pesky kid next door is always tossing the ball and hitting it, tossing the ball and hitting it. You were long ago convinced that this unfettered activity posed a threat to your family room window. But you also know something about the psychology of that youngster's father. He is the sort who is forthcoming and generous when allowed to control a situation but stubborn and resistant when he feels the threat of an attack. "Your lousy rotten kid broke my window" will not produce the response you desire. So you pick up the ball, carry it next door (as a semiotic clue to agency), attract your neighbor's attention, and inform him "Our window was broken." Your words have not thrust the identity of the agent at him; the ball in your hand suggests that agency in a milder, more digestible manner. He might well say, "Oh, that's Cheryl's ball. I've warned her this could happen. So sorry. Please send me the bill."

Another case: Sometimes the presence or lack of an agent becomes all-important when the morality of agency is in question. On any December 7, if you tune in to your favorite radio station for long enough, you may well hear a somber voice intone,

10a. On this date, in 1941, the Japanese bombed Pearl Harbor.

The Japanese were the agents; the bombing was decidedly their action; and Pearl Harbor was unquestionably their target.

On August 6, tune in again. You may well hear the same somber voice saying,

10b. On this date, in 1945, the atomic bomb was dropped on Hiroshima.

Nobody dropped this bomb. There is no agent in sight.

One of the most controversial books ever written about the question of agency was Charles Darwin's *On the Origin of Species*. In the last sentence of the first edition of that book he hints at the presence of a divine Agent

of creation; but he undercuts that agency by the use of passive constructions. The acknowledgment can hardly be called forceful or direct.

9a. There is grandeur in this view of life, with its several powers, *having
     been originally breathed* into a few forms or into one; and that, whilst
     this planet has gone cycling on according to the fixed law of gravity,
     from so simple a beginning endless forms most beautiful and most
     wonderful *have been, and are being, evolved.*
     (emphasis supplied)

How interesting it is that by the third edition he was convinced to go
one step further. He revised the sentence to make the agency explicit:

9b. There is grandeur in this view of life, with its several powers, having
     been originally breathed *by the Creator* into a few forms or into one; . . .
     (emphasis supplied)

By making explicit an agent that was formerly only implicit, Darwin
changed the effect of his sentence. Because that sentence is the last in the
volume, he also changed the nature of the work's closure. No one can specify in what way these rhetorical differences are perceived, because those
perceptions depend to a great extent on the nature of the person doing the
reading. Some angry people might be somewhat appeased by the change;
other angry people might be made more angry. Some supporters of Darwin's theories might have been relieved by the change; others might have
felt disappointed or even betrayed. Had Darwin chosen the active voice instead of the passive, each reader response may have been increased in fervor in whatever direction it was already headed. The sentence might have
looked something like this:

10c. There is grandeur in this view of life, with its several powers,
      the Creator having originally breathed it into a few forms or into
      one; and that, whilst this planet has gone cycling on according to
      the fixed law of gravity, but has evolved and continues to evolve
      endless forms most beautiful and most wonderful from so simple a
      beginning.

This puts a different spin on the concept of evolution altogether. The
verb "evolve" becomes transitive instead of intransitive. But no matter who
the reader is or how the reader is originally disposed to feel, a change from
active to passive (or vice versa) is likely to produce a change in the reader's reaction. The active and passive voices are not the better and worse
voices; they are just remarkably different voices. It will not do to prefer one
to the other by magisterial edict; it will do quite nicely to understand what

each voice is capable of producing and then to choose the one most likely to produce the desired effect.

We can use our knowledge of actives and passives offensively, defensively, and even deconstructively. The hidden can be made manifest; the otherwise manifest can be hidden. Sometimes we will be dealing only with a case of embarrassment, as in the case of this freshman writing about his writing:

11. I've always felt that writing was an academic weak spot for me. In high school English courses, my grade was constantly lowered by my writing assignments.

Notice, in the second sentence, what agent is to be blamed for the lower grades.

At other times, the ability to perceive the absence of agency may allow us to uncover a cover-up. Here is a report of a news conference called by a former Secretary of the Interior, Cecil Andrus. He was being questioned about the possible long-term dangers of "surface coal mining operations" -- otherwise known as *strip mining*. Strip mining is an activity in which a mining company cuts down all the trees in an area in order to unearth minerals beneath the surface.

12a. Andrus also concedes that surface coal mining operations will destroy wildlife. He contends that "while reduced populations will result from increased human activity in the areas and from the loss of habitat, no adverse long-term impact is anticipated."

The first sentence is written straightforwardly. "Andrus" is indeed the agent; his action is clearly to "concede" the material in the "that" clause. Within that clause, "surface coal mining operations" is the agent; its action is to "destroy" the wildlife.

The quotation from Andrus in the second sentence functions in a different manner altogether -- and it is by no means straightforward. Most people, on first reading, understand him to say that while strip mining has some negative short-term affects, it really poses no major threat in the long run. However, if we unearth the agents of his sentence by translating the nominalizations that are actions into verb phrases, a different message surfaces. What is meant by "reduced populations"? Is anyone losing weight here? If we translate the nominalized phrase into a verb phrase, thereby focusing attention on agency and action, we get something along the lines of "kill the bunnies." We can replace "increased human activity" with the more direct noun phrase "strip mining." And to what does "loss of habitat" refer? Has someone "misplaced" something? Since the agent is still the strip mining, the appropriate action/verb translation would produce something like "destroy their homes." Put that much together:

12b. "Although by strip mining we kill the bunnies and destroy their homes, no adverse long-term impact is anticipated."

Then we can question this agency-hiding passive construction, "is anticipated." By *whom* is this adverse long-term impact *not* anticipated? *Not* by the bunnies. The missing agent here is "those who profit from the strip mining." With all the agents now made explicit, we arrive at a new translation:

12c. "Although by strip mining we kill the bunnies and destroy their homes, it doesn't bother us."

This translation would probably raise a protest from the Secretary. If, during the ensuing discussion, all agents are made explicit and all actions are articulated as verbs, the essence of the environmental debate would eventually surface: We would be weighing and balancing how we as people benefit from the strip mining and, as a result, how much the local animal populations must suffer. The agent/action conflicts would become clearer:

We profit by strip mining ⎯⎯⎯⎯⎯→ Bunnies die

People benefit ⎯⎯⎯⎯⎯→ Bunnies suffer

The question then becomes how much of one is worth how much of the other or whether alternative results could be achieved.

Of course, this "translation" is not the only or the "true" interpretation of the sentence. Like any other sentence, this one cannot be limited to one interpretation. Perhaps Andrus meant the following: "Although by strip mining we may destroy the lives and habitats of a few animals who currently inhabit the area, we will be able to reestablish wildlife patterns after the mining is concluded, thus avoiding any long-term negative effects." REA cannot be used by readers to eradicate interpretive problems; it can, however, help discover the roots of interpretive problems that otherwise would remain hidden. Only Secretary Andrus -- or his speechwriter -- could tell us which version most accurately conveyed his intentions.

Questions of agency, then, go far beyond grammatical conventions and syntactical good manners. They cut right to the heart of questions concerning control and responsibility. Instead of giving students examples of nominalized or passive sentences to "correct," we would do better to encourage them to create a number of rewrites, articulating as they go the different effects produced by each. With this kind of experience, they will grow to recognize the kind of control they can have over the probable reception of their prose by a large percentages of their readers. They will also be led to realize underlying issues of greater moral ambiguity and complexity than they yet have come to expect from "proper" adult prose.

They may also come to realize how their own avoidance of agency, whether intentional or not, can often leave their readers completely in the dark. This is a common result of the heavy overuse of nominalization:

13a. If there could be the presentation of data that would indicate the representation of the status of the problem was accurate, then a decision could be made.

The sentence sounds like it means something specific. Perhaps it tires or annoys us a bit; but most of us feel that if we but concentrated a bit harder than we did on first reading, we would be able to perceive a specific, intended meaning. It is difficult to perceive how very *little* we can understand from reading this sentence when we leave the nominalizations to articulate actions, thereby stifling all agency. If we turn the three nominalized actions ("presentation," "representation," and "decision") into verbs, we discover we have no idea who the agents are and therefore no idea what the sentence is trying to tell us.

13b. If [?] presents data that would indicate that [?] accurately represented the status of the problem, then [?] could decide to do something.

Not only do we not know who should be filling the three brackets but we cannot even discern whether it involves one, two, or three people. All three questions marks could be replaced by the same person; or all three could represent different people; or the three could represent a variety of two-and-one combinations. The writer knew the answer -- but never sent us the necessary information.

Even more troubling than this kind of noninterpretative result is the potential misinterpretative result. In the following example, try to discover (1) who is the main agent and (2) what action that agent managed to do.

14. A study was performed on the causes behind the decrease in the identification of child abuse among emergency room service by the Social Services staff.

(This is one of those sentences that gets worse the longer you look at it.) With only a bit of effort, most readers can perceive that the Social Service staff is the main agent in this sentence. But what did those Social Service people actually do? In my long experience with this sentence, a large majority of readers quickly decide that the Social Services staff "performed a study" (an interesting visual image, is it not?) or, more directly, "studied." They *studied* why the appropriate people in the hospital were not identifying as many cases of child abuse in emergency room service as in the past.

But that may not be the correct reading. Perhaps someone from outside was called in to study why the *Social Services staff was identifying* fewer child abuse cases in emergency room service. That reading is equally possible from the syntax and equally probable as a solution.

But that also may not be the intended reading. Equally possible, but we hope far less probable, perhaps someone from the outside was called in to study why people on the inside were failing to identify cases in the emergency room in which the *Social Services staff was abusing* children.

(With the horrors we read in the newspapers about sexual assaults in day care centers, anything is possible.)

There is no *syntactical* clue in this sentence to help us determine which of these three actions the Social Services staff had done. All three are equally possible. Why, then, do such a large majority of readers identify "study" as the main action? I suggest the answer lies in an important general principle of interpretation: *Readers tend to cease the act of interpretation as soon as they are allowed to do so.* As soon as an interpretation makes *some* sense, we presume that must be *the* sense it was intended to convey. Since we read from left to right and through time, we come upon "study" in this example sentence *before* we discover the other possible actions. Our question ("What did the Social services staff do?") is answered right off the bat; and we cease our search.

It is rather like always finding your missing car keys in the last place you look. That makes great sense: After you find them, there is no need to continue looking. Rare is the person who, with keys in hand, asks, "Now if they hadn't been *there*, where *else* might they have been?" -- and then proceeds to look there. Of course, if that key turns out not to fit the lock, we then realize we have found the wrong key and resume our search. In the same way, we may reopen an interpretive search for meaning in prose at some later moment if our first interpretation fails to make good enough sense in some later context. How important it becomes, then, to recognize which interpretive clues readers will tend to fasten on -- and when.

Most of us were taught in school to favor the active voice and to avoid the passive. We were young then, and unsophisticated. We had little legitimate need for the passive. Most of the ethical lessons we were being taught urged us *never* to avoid the responsibility of articulated agency.

But later in life, we come upon many circumstances when it is better, wiser, more effective, more accurate, or more politic *not* to articulate agency. Here are some, but by no means all, of those circumstances:

1. We do not know who the agent was;
2. We do not care who the agent was;
3. Everyone already knows who the agent was;
4. The resulting action is more to be focused on than the agent who performed it;
5. It would be bad manners to confront the reader with agency;
6. It would be bad psychology to confront the reader with agency.

Recalling that there are only two main ways in English to obliterate agency -- (1) by nominalization and (2) by the use of the passive -- we should urge our students to tend to prefer the passive, thus leaving the action in the verb. This is the first of several strong, subtle, and sophisticated uses of the passive.

A *Few Pedagogical Hints Reviewed*

Undergraduate students often hear the material in this chapter with a somewhat jaded ear, protesting that they have heard it all before. They are probably mistaken. I suggest here a few of the most common misapprehensions.

(1) Many students somehow interpret the structural advice "articulate the action in the verb" as equivalent to the semantic advice "use important-sounding words." They persist in believing that there exists a list of "strong" verbs and a list of "weak" verbs, the latter of which they have been taught to avoid. They are quick to take out the thesaurus and replace what looks to them like a weak verb with what looks to them like a strong verb. They must be reminded many times that "weak" and "strong," in terms of reader expectations, have to do not with impressiveness of diction but rather with whether or not the verb articulates the action happening in that sentence.

Any verb chosen just to replace a weak verb, with no further changes, must also be, by definition, weak: The word that describes the action will still be lurking elsewhere. To change from a weak verb to a strong, you usually have to change the whole sentence's structure, making the action that was not a verb into a verb.

(2) Students also demonstrate a great need to reduce everything to rules. We must remind them that these methodological principles are not rules but rather descriptions and predictions of general reader expectations. We must also remind them, constantly, that any reader expectation can be violated to good effect. So the rule "Don't use nominalizations" will not do. Some nominalizations are bad, and some are good. Even the rule "Don't use bad nominalizations" will not do. (A "bad nominalization" might be one that usurps the action from the verb position.) There are some occasions when you might *not* want to be clear and forceful and straightforward in stating what action is happening. The rule "Don't use bad nominalizations unless you have a good reason to do so" starts to sound less like a rule and more like an invitation to make a judgment call. That is the activity in which we should like students to be engaged. It works for nominalizations, passives, and any other of the rhetorical tools available.

(3) Students and teachers alike can forget all too easily that *any* piece of discourse under examination lacks context. No matter how much context you supply, there is always more beyond that. A sentence by itself lacks context; but if the sentences on both sides of it are produced, then those three together still lack context. Evan a whole document has a greater context in which it was produced. Thus there are no *right* answers in a revision exercise; there are only different *versions*, each of which will "mean" in a different way, and none of which will "mean"

in only one way. Therefore, any student can demonstrate that what *you* say a sentence "means" might not be its only possible meaning. In a classroom situation, it will always be possible to create new contexts; and with new contexts come new meanings. Do not be frustrated by it; embrace it. Comparing the effects of different revisions is the best we can do -- and that best is good enough. It may well be all there is.

With this material behind them, students should start to digest the message that the mere *articulation* of information conveys far fewer clues for interpretation than does the *placement* of that information. The structure of prose sends signals to readers concerning how they should interpret the substance of that prose. Instead of trying to teach our students what is right and wrong to do, or what will appear good manners amid enlightened and educated company, we should be helping empower them over prose by showing them how to manipulate -- as best as we can -- the audience response to what necessarily must remain infinitely interpretable discourse. If agency is articulated at the front of the sentence, then *the chances go up* that a majority of readers will note the agency and consider it an important component of the sentence's communication. If the action is articulated by the verb, then *the chances go up* that a majority of readers will identify that particular word as the action of the sentence. We do our students a service when we put them in charge of improving their chances.

Endnotes

1. Many people have been taught that in addition to being an "action word," a verb can also express a "state of being." I make no distinction between these two. Either can be "what is going on here." The reader expectation is that the verb will tell us what is going on here.
2. The author may have forgotten, or may have been lying; I have taken her words at face value.
3. Note what happens to a reader when the writer splits the verb into two different locations -- "would be . . . accorded." The reader's sense of leaning forward in expectation of the verb's arrival is uncomfortably extended *beyond* the beginning of the verb ("would be") and *through* other information (". . . the employee reception . . .") and not finally resolved until the arrival of the long-awaited participle (". . . accorded . . ."). That expectation invites all sorts of structural emphasis to be expended on "accorded," which the writer considered a non-important word. This is a major cause of the sentence's interpretive difficulties.
3. Since every clause has a verb, the "what's going on" question is first and foremost a clause-level concern. If a sentence has only one clause, its verb is the expected repository of the action for the sentence as a whole. If a sentence has more than one clause, each clause is expected to be "about" its own verb; but the "what's going on" question for the sentence as a whole becomes more complicated. For a discussion of

the relevant importances of clauses in a multiclaused sentence, see the "Fred and His Dog" example in Chapter 4 (page 119ff).

4. For the five elements A, B, C, D, and E, the following are the 31 possible permutations and combinations from which the reader would have to choose:

   A, B, C, D, E
   AB, AC, AD, AE
   BC, BD, BE
   CD, CE
   DE
   ABC, ABD, ABE, ACD, ACE, ADE
   BCD, BCE, BDE
   CDE
   ABCD, ABCE, ABDE, ACDE
   BCDE
   ABCDE.

   That choice must be made almost instantaneously.

5. Scientists are often loathe to insert the first person into their written discourse. The issue is one of great interest and complexity, requires.... Let it be sufficient for the moment to state that the first person, singular or plural, should always be used when the first person has a legitimate and important role to play in the statement; otherwise, it should be repressed.

6. For a discussion of this tactic, see Example (2) above (page 30).

7. It bears repeating that "*a* reader's perspective" does not mean to suggest "*the* reader's perspective." There is no single reader. These reader comments, therefore, are suggestive ones, not inevitable ones.

8. As William Vande Kopple has reminded me, a third possibility is to transform the verb into its "ergative" sense:

   1. Active: Joe opened the door.
   2. Ergative: The door opened.

This is not always an option. We do not say, "The program modified."

3

Subject-Verb-
Complement
Separations

In this chapter, I deal with examples that are sometimes far more sophisticated and complex than most freshmen are capable of producing. Despite
that, I have two reasons for doing this: (1) These examples of professional
prose can demonstrate to our students the reasons some professional prose
has become so unnecessarily difficult to read; that, in turn, may prevent them
from adopting bad habits by imitation. (Law professors often complain that
third-year students write a great deal worse than first-year students.) (2) If
we can solve this structural problem for the most clogged and difficult prose,
we should be able to apply it with far greater ease to the somewhat simpler
prose with which we are faced in our classrooms.

Here is a reading experience all too familiar to lawyers and all other
professionals:

1a. The trial court's conclusion that the defendants made full disclosure
    of all relevant information bearing on the value of Knaebel's stock is
    clearly erroneous.

It is familiar not because Knaebel is a household word nor because the
nation in general has been obsessed by issues of "full disclosure." It rings
a rhetorical bell because its burdensome structure raises problems of interpretation we all have faced many times, whether or not we were consciously aware of their sources.

The sentence is hard to read. Why? It feels long; but it cannot be considered long just on the basis of word count. It extends only to 24 words, quite a
common length for a publishable sentence and well within the (not-to-be-trust-
ed) 29-word limit of most readability formulas.[1] Nor is it hard to read because
of its intellectual content -- although the content is made to seem more complex than it actually is by our inability to focus on the important information.

The sentence is hard to read, I would argue, because of the structural
location of the verb. There are two problems here -- a lesser and a
greater. (1) The lesser problem: The sentence's verb, "is," appears as the

third-to-last word out of 24. Since the verb in English is expected to announce "what's going on," it is often problematic for the reader if that piece of information arrives too late in the sentence to be of optimal help. This problem is to be considered a lesser one because there are so many exceptions to this general statement.

(2) The greater problem brings us to the next reader expectation to be considered. The verb in this sentence is separated from "conclusion," its grammatical subject, by 17 words -- which in this case is 71% of the sentence. This is a burdensome wait -- one we neither wanted nor expected.

> **Readers expect every grammatical subject will be followed almost immediately by its verb.**

As a result of the subject-verb-complement order of English sentences (hereafter "S-V-C"), readers have come to expect they will discover what is happening (articulated by the verb) the moment after they discover who or what is the agent of that action.[2] Until the verb arrives, we do not know how to conceive of the subject. Conversely, if by the time the verb arrives the subject has been forgotten, then the verb will also fail to make complete sense. The two parts of speech, subject and verb, rely on each other's presence. We need to "hear" them reverberating at the same silent decibel level in our reading process. whether they appear together --

SUBJECT -- VERB

or at a distance from each other --

SUBJECT -- (interrupt, interrupt, interrupt) -- VERB

For the reader, therefore, waiting for the verb to appear is like waiting for the second shoe to drop; if that arrival is delayed long enough, eventually it commands all available attention.

We invest a special kind of reader energy in the reading of a verb. Given a subject, we lean forward toward the verb in expectation of its arrival, ready to invest it with that special energy we reserve for the reading and processing of verbs. Therefore, anything that intervenes between subject and verb is read as interruptive. If the interruption is brief and easily distinguishable, it causes no problem:

SUBJECT, however, VERB. . . .

If it is slightly longer, but still digestible in one gulp, it still is unlikely to overburden us:

SUBJECT, except on Tuesdays, VERB. . . .

If, however, that interruption grows to great length, we begin to weary under the burden of expecting the verb:

SUBJECT, except on Tuesdays, but not if it is raining, unless it had also rained on the previous Monday, VERB. . . .

But worst of all is the case when the interruptive material is the information the writer wanted us to emphasize most. Its structural location tells us one thing -- "Don't pay much attention to me because you're still waiting for the verb to arrive"; but at the same time, the writer would like its substance to be shouting "Look at me! I'm the most important thing here!" *That* is the most serious problem with sentence (1a) -- and in all the thousands of sentences just like it that come a professional reader's way on a regular basis.

Think of the energy we summon for reading verbs as if it existed in liquid form, available in a keg, to be accessed by the operation of a tap. The moment a grammatical subject appears, we reach our hand toward the tap, ready and expectant to open it as the verb arrives; by opening that tap, we produce the liquid "verb energy" we need to supply the proper emphasis to the verb as it arrives. If the verb fails to arrive just then, we find ourselves awkwardly extending that arm in readiness at the tap while other prose passes by. If the verb takes a great deal of time to arrive, our arm begins to tire. We also find ourselves not paying sufficient attention to the words that intervene: We have been "instructed" by the structure to undervalue the information that is interrupting us as we wait for the verb. We cannot invest energy in the interrupting material if we must be saving energy for the arrival of the verb.

Back to our sentence:

1a. The trial court's conclusion that the defendants made full disclosure of all relevant information bearing on the value of Knaebel's stock is clearly erroneous.

The moment we read the grammatical subject "conclusion," we are put on guard for the arrival of the verb. But instead of the verb, we get a "that" clause. As we read the "that" clause, much of our reading energy must be preserved in anticipation of the arrival of the main verb.

But within the interruptive "that" clause, we encounter a second subject-verb combination. When that subordinate subject appears, we formulate a second verb-arrival expectation -- this time for the verb of the "that" clause. We are now dealing with *two* expectations aimed at the arrival of *two* separate verbs, the second of which must arrive first. That is a complicated reading task. When the verb "made" arrives, we have to open the tap on our verb energy keg -- but close it quickly in order to retain enough verb energy for the arrival of the other verb, for which we have long been waiting. That is complicated.

When that verb finally arrives, we open the tap with all the strength we have left, only to find a disappointing "is." The verb, so long awaited, tells us nothing we did not already know about the subject. Then we encounter the negative label, "clearly erroneous," and the door slams shut. We realize that whatever the sentence was meant to communicate, we have missed it.

We blame ourselves for our lack of comprehension. We rejoice that our friends and colleagues do not know the real truth about us -- that we are not the keenly perceptive and elegantly effortless readers we have long appeared to be. We beat ourselves up for a moment, take a deep breath, and return to the beginning of the sentence, determined this time to make something of our reading effort.

If that describes you, then, please, stop feeling bad. The fault here is not yours but the writer's. By placing the important material of the sentence between the subject and the verb, the writer has sent us an interpretive instruction that directly opposes the one intended to be sent.

So don't feel bad; feel mad. If you have been paying even a modicum of attention to a sentence whose words are recognizable but whose sense is imperceptible, it is most likely the fault of the writer. Perhaps all the necessary *words* are on the page; but they do not appear in the proper structural *locations* to send you the necessary *instructions* for the interpretive process. There are enough things in life to engender legitimate feelings of guilt. This is not one of them. Let it go.

We can repair damaging subject-verb separations straightforwardly enough: Just move the verb up next to its subject and reconstruct further as seems logical or necessary. Let us do this to our example sentence.

First, we move the main verb, "is," forward until it is united with its subject, "conclusion."

The original:

1a. The trial court's conclusion that the defendants made full disclosure of all relevant information bearing on the value of Knaebel's stock is clearly erroneous.

The revision:

1b. The trial court's conclusion is clearly erroneous . . .

We now have a unified clause. As in the previous chapter, we check to see if the verb represents the action of the clause as a whole. According to the author, with whom I have spoken, it does not. (Recall that only the author knows what the sentence was intended to communicate.) At first it might appear that "conclusion" is the prime suspect for the main action, since it is a nominalization that represents an action taking place in this sentence. But according to the author, the main action was intended to be "erroneous." "Conclusion" is an action, but a subordinate one: The court did indeed "conclude" something; but more importantly, it "erred" in doing so. Can we indicate structurally that two actions are happening simultaneously, with one being more important than the other? Certainly. We make "erroneous" into the main verb and "conclusion" into a lesser verb form, like one with an "-ing" construction:

1c. The trial court clearly erred in concluding that . . .

Notice how we are now free to pay full attention to whatever comes after the "that." We are no longer holding something in reserve for a main verb that has yet to arrive. We also are now informed to color everything in the "that" clause stupid. We know in time that the court *erred*. In the original, we learned this important fact only *after* we have processed the "that" clause material. Whether we knew it or not, that had caused us two problems: (1) We had expended a good deal of extra effort to go back and color all the previous material "erroneous"; and (2) we may not have succeeded psychologically in retroactively making completely negative that which we had initially processed as positive.

We must understand, however, that version (1c) is not necessarily the "right" version, or even a "better" one. It certainly is *stronger* in the force of its accusation of the court's error; but there are times when strength is a drawback. Under some conditions, "The trial court clearly erred in concluding that . . ." would be too strong. Perhaps the writer will have to appear in front of this Court at some future time to argue another case. The Court might well remember having been chastised in the past by this person as having "clearly erred." If that were the case, what could we do?

The court had done two actions: (1) They had "erred" -- which they were *not* supposed to do; and (2) they had "concluded," which they *were* supposed to do. To soften the accusation, we can shift the main action from the former to the latter. Let the court do the acceptable action, with a disappointing modifier:

1d. The trial court erroneously concluded that . . .

This is softer than (1c).

Is (1d) still too harsh? If so, add marshmallow to soften. Make the verb a non-action of the court altogether. Bring back the verb *to be* and have the conclusion, not the court, be in the wrong:

1b. The trial court's conclusion is clearly erroneous . . .

Students of all ages delight in learning how much control they can have over probable reader responses. It is similar to the power of a recording engineer running a sound-mixing studio: Move this lever for more volume; flip that switch to lower the treble; press that button to increase the intensity of the vibration. All sounds are potentially appropriate; but only one combination fits the present situation best. The trick is to know how each structural choice is likely to be read by most readers; the power of control is in choosing the right one to fit the right situation.

Let us turn now to the long-awaited "that" clause:

. . . that the defendants made full disclosure . . .

Once again (according to the author) the main action had not appeared in the verb. The defendants did not "make" anything; they "disclosed" something -- or failed to disclose it. We can transfer the action here from the nominalization "disclosure" to its verb form:

1e. . . . that the defendants fully disclosed all relevant information bearing on the value of Knaebel's stock

Should we also transform the nominalization "information" into a verb by changing "all the relevant information" into "everything they knew"? That depends entirely on whether we want the reader to concentrate on the defendants having done one action or two. Back we go into the sound-mixing studio. If we will be dealing later in this document with two actions -- what the defendants *disclosed* and what they *knew* -- then the clause would benefit from having two verbs. If, on the other hand, the document will concentrate only on whether or not they disclosed something, then the single verb "disclose" will direct our attention to that sole target here and now.

Note that both of these options *sound* equally fine out of context.

-- . . . defendants had fully disclosed all the relevant information . . .

-- . . . defendants had fully disclosed everything they knew . . .

We must begin to guide our students -- and ourselves -- away from judging prose primarily (or even initially) *by the ear*. The ear will mislead at least as often as it guides us well. We do better to use *the eye and the mind*: *Look* in the important structural locations and *judge* from their occupants what readers are likely to make of the prose. The eye and the mind; not the ear.

We would presume that the final revision of this sentence (1a) should now read with considerable ease, compared to the original. Looking back, however, we discover we have not produced a "final revision" but rather a number of *choices* for revision, all of which depend for their quality on the contextual situations. Each clause has multiple possibilities, three of which have been noted above for the first clause and two for the second:

1st clause

a. The trial court clearly erred . . .

b. The trial court erroneously concluded . . .

c. The trial court's conclusion was clearly erroneous . . .

2nd clause

x. defendants had fully disclosed all the relevant information . . .

y. defendants had fully disclosed everything they knew . . .

We can mix and match from these six combinations:

a + x; a + y; b + x; b + y; c + x; c + y

Each of these is easier to process than the original; but each of these has a different focus and a different purpose. Here is the one the author might choose if (1) he is quite sure he will never have to argue before that trial court again, and (2) he will proceed to discuss both what the defendants *disclosed* and what the defendants *knew*:

1f. The trial court clearly erred in concluding that the defendants fully disclosed everything they knew that was relevant to the value of Knaebel's stock.

The concepts communicated by sentence (1f) are not as difficult as they appeared to be in sentence (1a). The sentence no longer seems "long," even though it contains essentially the same number of words (23) as the 24-word original. The big difference: Sentence (1f) does not misuse reader energy by placing information in unexpected locations. To experience how powerful that mislocation can be, read once again the original sentence (1a), noting how difficult the sentence remains, even though we have just spent a good deal of conscious energy investigating it:

1a. The trial court's conclusion that the defendants made full disclosure of all relevant information bearing on the value of Knaebel's stock is clearly erroneous.

As long as we have to wait for the arrival of the verb, we cannot be paying enough appropriate attention to the intervening material.

There are at least three more reasons (1f) reads with so much more ease than (1a):

-- In (1f), no piece of information arrives for which we are not already somewhat prepared;

-- In addition, every new arrival seems to "lean forward" with possibilities as to where we might go from here; and

-- We continually find ourselves actually going to one of those advertised places.

These are the three benchmarks of good, clear writing, established at the beginning of this book. To demonstrate how these function in sentence (1f), here is a slow-motion replay of how many readers experience the journey through this sentence.

The trial court . . .

("Well, what did they do?")

clearly erred . . .

("Made a mess of things, did they? How did they do that?")

in concluding . . .

("In concluding what?")

that the defendants . . .

("And what did *they* do?")

fully disclosed . . .

("What did they disclose?")

everything they knew . . .

("Knew? About what?")

that was relevant . . .

("Relevant to what?")

to the value of Knaebel's stock.

("Ah, yes.")

Compare example (1a) to example (2):

2. Any assertion that chemical "retesting" is a valid technique but because of a time lag has not been recognized by the scientific community is untenable.

These two sentences are essentially the same sentence -- only with different words. Both begin with a nominalized subject; both suffer a lengthy subject-verb separation; both arrive at the main *to be* verb at the next-to-last moment; both *to be* verbs are then followed by a negative label; and then door slams shut. Example (2) might be a tad harder to read than (1a) because the interruptive material contains two verb phrases instead of one; but it does us little good to compare the severity of one headache with that of another -- especially when we are in the throes of either. Students who can see that (1a) and (2) are essentially the *same* sentence, *structurally*, are beginning to be able to perceive sentences as units of structure.

Here is a metaphor to describe this that has worked well with students. Someone asks you to help him carry something to his car. You agree. He hands you a large package. You now want to know precisely what you should *do* with it. Instead of telling you, he hands you a second package. You can handle this one; but you are slightly annoyed not to have known it was coming. If he then hands you a third package, chances are you no longer can manage everything and you drop them all. Had you been informed beforehand how many packages would be coming and what you were to do with them then, you might have been able to function helpfully and without undue strain.

The same applies to syntactic packages of thought: If readers are asked to carry too many of them through a sentence before being told beforehand (by the verb) what *to do* with them all, they feel grossly overburdened. This is especially true if they have no idea how many more packages are coming before the verb will mercifully appear. So we can be assured that if the grammatical subject is severely separated from its verb, most readers are going to have trouble handling all the intervening packages and making sense of the sentence as a whole.

This S-V separation has become a hallmark of contemporary professional prose, often resulting from an overdeveloped defensive posture. A subject-verb unit in English is capable of conveying a sense of completeness; premature completeness can be open to attack as oversimplification. To defend against this kind of vulnerability, it seems prudent to insert the necessary qualifications before the arrival of the verb. Take, for example, a seemingly straightforward legal statement:

3a. Whether Congress intended X has long been a matter of debate.

Now spell out the "X."

3b. Whether Congress intended to include interspousal wiretapping within the scope of prohibited acts under Title III has long been a matter of debate.

Then qualify it, being careful to have the qualification in place before the verb gets a chance to bring the sentence to closure:

3c. Whether Congress intended to include interspousal wiretapping within the scope of prohibited acts under Title III, when no deleterious use was made of the surreptitious products, has long been a matter of debate.

The problem gets serious when this *method* for qualification-by-insertion is allowed to repeat itself -- under the reasoning of "it worked once, so why not again?"

3d. Whether Congress intended to include interspousal wiretapping within the scope of prohibited acts under Title III, when no deleterious use was made or was threatened to be made of the surreptitious products, has long been a matter of debate.

and again . . .

3e. Whether Congress intended to include interspousal wiretapping within the scope of prohibited acts under Title III, when no deleterious use was made or was threatened to be made of the surreptitious products, and the results were no more serious than would have been the case had the third party been listening in on an extension, has long been a matter of debate.

and yet again,

3f. Whether Congress intended to include interspousal wiretapping within the scope of prohibited acts under Title III, when no deleterious use was made or was threatened to be made of the surreptitious products, and the results were no more serious than would have been the case had the third party been listening in on an extension, and insert here any of the other arguments that you might plan to bring up somewhere else in the memo, brief, or letter, and want to be sure not to leave out at this point because who knows what might be considered of primary importance at some later date and you do not want to appear to have missed any of the salient points, has long been a matter of debate.

The sad truth, however, is that the ridiculous at times can become the reality. Here is one of New Jersey's Public Questions of 1996. This is not to be read only by lawyers or lawmakers but rather by every citizen in the state in the privacy of a voting booth. Then those citizens are supposed to take action, by voting.

4. Public Question No. 1

Shall the "Port of New Jersey Revitalization, Dredging, Environmental Cleanup, Lake Restoration, and Delaware Bay Economic Development Bond Act of 1996," which authorizes the State to issue bonds in the amount of $300,000,000 for the purposes of financing, in whole or in part, the costs of constructing subaqueous pits and a containment facility or facilities for the disposal of materials dredged from the Kill Van Kull, Arthur Kill, and other navigation channels located in the New Jersey/New York port region; projects related to the decontamination of dredged material; dredging the Kill Van Kull, Arthur Kill, and other navigation channels located in the New Jersey/New York port region; dredging navigation channels not located in the New Jersey/New York port region; remediating hazardous discharge sites; and constructing Water supply facilities to replace contaminated water supplies; the restoration of lakes; and economic development sites in the Delaware River and Bay Region; and which provides the ways and means to pay the interest on the debt and also to pay and discharge the principal thereof, be approved?

That was real; and that was ridiculous. The problem is felt most keenly when the intellectual content is complex enough to obscure the fact that the result is ridiculous. Try this memorable moment from our extraordinarily unwieldy Uniform Commercial Code, a book-length document in use in 49 of the 50 United States:

5. §1-201(9)

"Buyer in ordinary course of business" means a person who in good faith and without knowledge that the sale to him is in violation of the ownership rights or security interest of a third party in the goods buys in ordinary course from a person in the business of selling goods of that kind but does not include a pawnbroker.

When we untangle this mess by bringing together the subject and its verb, we find that a "buyer in ordinary course of business" is being defined as "a person . . . who buys [goods] in the ordinary course of business." Not very helpful.

Much the same reasoning that controls S-V separations applies to verb-complement (V-C) separations. (By "complement" I simply mean everything that comes after the verb to complete the thought.) Many writers who constantly construct S-V separations also separate the verb from the complement, even in the same sentence.

6. The younger generation, which never seems to want to listen to its elders or follow set patterns of acceptable behavior, will often choose, to its own detriment and without much conscious thought, novelty for the sheer sake of novelty, it seems.

Not all separations are harmful. Some are short enough or straightforward enough not to bother most readers. That is especially so when the interruptive material presents nothing new or complicated. For example, you may not have had much trouble following this recent sentence of mine:

7. Many writers who constantly construct S-V separations also separate the verb from the complement, even in the same sentence.

The interrupting clause -- "who constantly construct S-V separations" -- was familiar enough at the time not to cause much trouble in the interpreting of the sentence.

Nor are all separations anti-productive. Some can run to extreme lengths and yet produce powerful results. These are examples of an important corollary mentioned earlier: Any reader expectation can be violated to good effect. Here is an oral example of a V-C separation so familiar to us that we actually have developed an expectation for it. It has tended to recur every four years, during the Democratic and Republican national conventions, at the end of presidential nominating speeches:

8. And so my friends, I give you a man who . . . , a man who . . . , a man who . . . , a man who . . . -- I give you, my friends, -- the next president of these United States of America, -- Tennessee's favorite son, --- Richard ---- P. ----- BAX - TER.

And the balloons rise as the cheers fall. This V-C separation works for several reasons: (1) We do not need the information being withheld from us, since we already know what it is: The television commentator has already informed us that Congressman Rodriguez will be nominating Senator Baxter. Throughout the speaker's final crescendo, there is no mystery; there is instead an increasingly heightened expectation of the closure to be achieved with the arrival of the candidate's name. (2) The purpose of the speech is not only the creation of the candidacy by naming the candidate; it is also to demonstrate to the television public how enthusiastic the Party is about this new candidate. The delay of the expected name, in this case, serves well to increase the sense of expectation, releasing a maximum response of energy when the syntactic closure is finally achieved.

Such effective S-V-C separations used to appear with much greater frequency before the twentieth century, which suggests that the nature of the expectation itself has changed.[3] Consider the following paragraph from *Rambler* #121 of Samuel Johnson, written in the year 1751. (I have begun every sentence at the left margin and numbered each.)

9.

1 When Ulysses visited the infernal regions, he found, among the heroes that perished at Troy, his competitor Ajax, who, when the arms of Achilles were adjudged to Ulysses, died by his own hand in the madness of disappointment.

2 He still appeared to resent, as on earth, his loss and disgrace.

3 Ulysses endeavored to pacify him with praises and submissions; but Ajax walked away without reply.

4 This passage has always been considered as eminently beautiful; because Ajax, the haughty chief, the unlettered soldier, of unshaken courage, of immoveable constancy, but without the power of recommending his own virtues by eloquence, or enforcing his assertions by any other argument than the sword, had no way of making his anger known, but by gloomy sullenness and dumb ferocity.

5 His hatred of a man whom he conceived to have defeated him only by volubility of tongue, was therefore naturally shown by silence more contemptuous and piercing than any words that so crude an orator could have found, and by which he gave his enemy no opportunity of exerting the only power in which he was superior.

Every sentence but #3 contains at least one S-V-C separation. (Note how swift in action sentence #3 seems compared to those that surround it.) In sentence #4, the subject, "Ajax," is separated from its verb by 34 words, which are distributed in six separate phrases; yet the rhetoric works with some power. Why?

-- Perhaps eighteenth-century readers had the time and inclination to proceed at a pace deliberate enough for them to glory in the complexity of intricately wrought syntax. Today we tend to hurtle through prose in search of information.[4]

-- Perhaps the sense of grandeur in the subject matter justified and supported a grandness of structure. The eighteenth century cared for the sublime and the beautiful; we tend more to value accuracy, clarity, and efficiency.

-- Probably eighteenth-century readers had a great deal more practice reading artistically imbedded sentences, not only because such sentences were particularly fashionable but also because Latin and Greek, the languages of their education, so regularly left the verb till the end of the sentence.[5]

Note that despite the many interruptions, the S-V separation of sentence #4 does not burden the reader the way those separations tend to do in the scientific, bureaucratic, and legal prose of today. Compare Johnson's sentence with our Example (2) from above, a far shorter example from modern science:

9a. [Johnson, 18th century:] This passage has always been considered as eminently beautiful; because Ajax, the haughty chief, the unlettered soldier, of unshaken courage, of immoveable constancy, but without the power of recommending his own virtues by eloquence, or enforcing his assertions by any other argument than the sword, had no way of making his anger known, but by gloomy sullenness and dumb ferocity. [61 words; 34-word subject-verb interruption]

2. [21st century:] Any assertion that chemical "retesting" is a valid technique but because of a time lag has not been recognized by the scientific community is untenable. [25 words; 21-word subject-verb interruption]

For any reader familiar with the characters of the Trojan War stories, the mere mention of the name Ajax brings to mind a number of characteristics and associations: He was a warrior of great size and awesome physical strength, but of slow intellect and limited in his powers of articulation. Taken together as a set, these characteristics provide a context sufficiently vivid and well-enough-defined for the reader to handle the six interruptive phrases that follow. Each of the six brings to the fore a single characteristic summoned by the mere name Ajax but otherwise not featured, not focused upon: Each of the six, therefore, acts not as an interruption of the thought process but as an appositive phrase that emphasizes and reemphasizes the identity and character of the subject. In a sense, Johnson has not suspended but rather extended the subject, restating it seven times before allowing the reader to arrive at the verb; that arrival is thereby all the more dramatic and climactic.

With that in mind, we can perceive the difference between our two examples more clearly. Again:

2. Any assertion that chemical "retesting" is a valid technique but because of a time lag has not been recognized by the scientific community is untenable.

The subject, "assertion," gives us no clearly identified concept or image. Its very vagueness required the interruptive definition that follows. Our understanding of the {subject + qualification} unit is not complete until the unit itself is completed, at the word "community." Given such disregard for the plight of the reader, the qualification could easily have continued for three or four more lines: " . . . by the scientific community most immediately concerned with the subject matter about which . . . . " In this sentence, we await the verb in order to make sense of what is already happening in the sentence; only with its arrival will we be able to assemble into a single unit all the semantic and syntactic packages with which we have been burdened. Even worse, when the verb -- "is" -- finally does arrive, *all* it achieves is the fulfillment of the grammatical requirement; by itself it adds nothing to our understanding of what is going on in the sentence. In the Johnson sentence, however, we know enough about Ajax at the start to make the arrival of the verb the arrival of the action, not merely the fulfillment of a requirement.

In sum, then, the Johnson sentence builds tension and heightens the expectation of the arrival of the verb by the very structural feature that makes of the scientific example sentence a garbled mess. The agent was revealed by the initial appellation, "Ajax," and then re-revealed and further revealed by each of the six interruptions. To increase this combined sense of redefining and tension building, Johnson fashions his six interruptions symmetrically and incrementally, pairing them as he goes:

1) the haughty chief

three words; single noun phrase; straight appositive; *two*-syllable adjective followed by a *one*-syllable noun

2) the unlettered soldier

three words; single noun phrase; straight appositive; *three*-syllable adjective followed by a *two*-syllable noun (producing an augmentation over its predecessor)

3) of unshaken courage

three words (thereby linking it to #1 and #2); prepositional phrase that qualifies (thereby differentiating it from #1 and #2); *three*-syllable adjective followed by a *two*-syllable noun (like #2)

4) of immoveable constancy

three word prepositional phrase that qualifies (thereby linking it to #3); *four*-syllable adjective followed by a *three*-syllable noun (producing the same kind of augmentation over #3 that #2 had provided over #1)

BUT

5) without the power of recommending his own virtues by eloquence

ten words (a great augmentation over #4); three-word prepositional phrase (thereby linking it to #3 and #4); qualified by a seven-word participial construction; *one* word follows the "by"

OR

6) enforcing his assertions by any other argument than the sword

ten words (thereby linking it to #5); ten-word participial instead of the seven-word unit of #5 (a great augmentation over #5); *six* words follow the "by" (another great augmentation over #5)

In augmented and augmenting parallel segments, the sentence has repeated the *concept* of Ajax seven times, carefully balancing but also increasing its increments to build a crescendo of expectation for the arrival of the verb. One could regraph the sentence as follows:

Ajax; Ajax, Ajax, A j a x, A J A X, A - J - A - X, **A -- J -- A -- X**, had no way of making his anger known, but by gloomy sullenness and dumb ferocity.

With such control of structure, a writer can violate reader expectation to stunningly good effect. Lacking that control, the writer can well be led by an aspiration for style into Frankensteinian syntactic deeds. The following paragraph was written by a Rhodes scholar matriculating at the Harvard Law School. That its architecture was fastidiously and consciously conceived, I have two proofs: (1) The sentence that preceded it was structurally its identical twin; and (2) He told me so.

10a. Similarly, in *Weaver*, the D.C. Court of Appeals held that the qualifying word "estimate" used in conjunction with the stipulations and conditions that the quantities were "to be used to canvass bids" and "not to be the basis for any payment by the ultimate consumer of the products" and that payments would be made "only for actual quantities of work completed," transformed the contract into a requirements contract.

I maintain that this sentence is impossible to process on first reading -- unless you are already so familiar with requirements contracts and the *Weaver* case that you need not have read it in the first place. Again, the difficulty does not stem from its length, its intellectual complexity, or its specialized topic; it stems instead from its lack of reader-friendly structure.

To make the point, let us reread the sentence in ultra-slow motion, focusing our attention on the reader expectation that a verb will appear directly after its subject.

Warning: Because sentence (10a) is so hard to read, this slow-motion replay will also be hard to endure; but that is precisely the point. Follow it as it unfolds, and you will see just what makes this sentence such a nightmare. It should be worth the effort. Here is the sentence again, with some helpful numberings.

$$S_1 \qquad\qquad V_1 \quad T_1$$

10a. Similarly, in *Weaver*, the D.C. Court of Appeals held that

$$S_2$$

the qualifying word "estimate" used in conjunction with

$$T_2 \qquad\qquad S_3 \quad V_3$$

the stipulations and conditions that the quantities were

"to be used to canvass bids" and "not to be the basis for

any payment by the ultimate consumer of the products" and

$$T_3 \quad S_4 \qquad\qquad V_4$$

that payments would be made "only for actual quantities

$$V_2$$

of work completed," transformed the contract into a

requirements contract.

(For this slow-motion replay, let us summon again the metaphor of verb energy being stored in kegs. The appearance of a grammatical subject initiates the reflex action of our reaching out for the tap of that keg, to let the verb juices flow.)

At the appearance of the first subject, "the D.C. Court of Appeals" (S1), we expect its companion verb (V1); we get it -- "held." The first "that" (T1) leads us to expect another subject (S2), which we also get -- "the qualifying word 'estimate.'" We then expect V2; but we are disappointed. Instead we get "used in conjunction with" -- a phrase that informs us we are being interrupted with a qualification of S2. Our sense now must be that V2 will not appear until this qualification has been completed. Our hand is now outstretched to the tap on the keg of verb energy -- and we must hold it there, suspended in the air, awaiting the arrival of V2.

We are slightly annoyed to find that this interruptive qualification is itself bifurcated, even if only slightly, by "the stipulations *and* conditions." This "and" does not annoy us in a serious way, however, because we can clearly sense that the two units being connected by the "and" are single words only -- "stipulations" and "conditions."

We are far more troubled to find at this point a second "that" (T2), which tells us the bifurcated qualification that has interrupted us will now itself be interrupted by a qualification of its own. Worse yet, T2 (like any other "that") leads us to expect yet another subject (S3), which we get. S3 in turn leads us to expect yet another verb (V3), which we also get. Here now is something especially burdensome: Our hand has been outstretched toward the tap on the keg of verb energy for some time now in expectation of the arrival of V2; by the arrival of S3, we are alerted to the need to open the tap to produce verb energy for V3 -- but when that verb arrives we must shut it almost as soon as we have opened it to allow enough verb energy to remain for the arrival of V2. This is a complex act -- and as painful to the mind as the physical act would begin to be painful to the shoulder muscles.

In this S3-V3 unit we encounter another, far more annoying bifurcation: "The quantities were 'to be used to canvass bids' *and* . . ." This "and" burdens us greatly: We now must deal with the reality that this second "that" clause (beginning with T2), which is already qualifying a bifurcated qualifier, is itself to be bifurcated. When we see the quotation marks that precede and follow the "and," we expect (or at least hope) that the second quoted phrase will neatly balance its predecessor, "to be used to canvass bids." What we get, however, is something a good deal longer and heavier: "not to be the basis for any payment by the ultimate consumer of the products." This imbalance (which begins at "by the ultimate consumer") causes even the most energetic reader to feel the strain of diminishing reader energy. We are still waiting for V2 to appear so we may at long last discover what S2 is supposed (all this time) *to have been doing*.

At this troubled moment, we encounter a small word that strikes great fear in our hearts -- "and." Already supporting a number of packages and subpackages, together with their bifurcated bifurcations, we must now endure yet a further bifurcation and receive a new subpackage. The next word is structurally obscene -- the worst four-letter word in the language we could possibly encounter at this moment -- "that" (T3). Now we are thrown into conceptual disarray: Is "that" #3 that-ing "that" #2, which in turn is that-ing "that" #1? Or is "that" #3 parallel to "that" #2, and together they are that-ing "that" #1? Or is . . . ? At this moment we are using ALL of our available reader energy to try to figure out the *structure* of what is unfolding; we can have precious little left for figuring out the *substance*. All we want to do at this point is to survive until the end of the sentence -- by which time we might have gained enough information to be able to put the whole thing together the second time around. If we give up now, we will have to start again at the beginning, with no hope of being better informed by the time we return to this point.

Unfortunately, after T3, like after any other "that," we expect another subject (S4), which we get. We then expect another verb (V4), which we also get. Our hand again turns the tap, and whatever liquid verb energy was remaining in the keg comes splashing out on V4 -- "payments would be made" -- leaving us with absolutely no verb energy available for the arrival of V2. When we finally encounter that long-awaited verb ("transformed"), how many of us could claim to have any lasting memory of S2 ("the qualifying word 'estimate'"), which had appeared several lines earlier? I repeat:

For most people, this sentence is virtually impossible to process on first reading.

One could almost define bad professional writing as writing that constantly forces the reader to devote a disproportionate amount of reader energy to the perceiving of *structure*. When that is the case, the reader cannot be maximizing reader energy for the perceiving of *substance*.

Am I suggesting that major improvements could be made to this sentence just by reuniting S2 and V2? Yes; at least that is the first and most important step toward that happy end. Watch now what happens when we revise by uniting S2 and V2.

$$S_1 \qquad\qquad\qquad V_1 \quad T_1$$
10a. Similarly, in *Weaver*, the D.C. Court of Appeals held that

$$S_2 \qquad\qquad\qquad V_2$$
the qualifying word "estimate" transformed the contract into

a requirements contract . . .

Simple enough so far. What follows logically? -- some word like "when" or "because." What is that cause? -- "it was used in conjunction with" certain stipulations and conditions. The rest of the material in the sentence turns out to be a list of those conditions. The list is three items long. All we need do now is announce there will be such a list and then produce it:

10c. Similarly, in *Weaver*, the D.C. Court of Appeals held that the qualifying word "estimate" transformed the contract into a requirements contract because it was used in conjunction with the following stipulations and conditions:

1) The quantities were "to be used to canvass bids";

2) They were "not to be the basis for any payment by the ultimate consumer of the products"; and

3) Payments would be made "only for actual quantities of work completed."

Note that we have been able to rewrite this sentence successfully without having been informed of what a "requirements contract" is or what the three stipulations and conditions actually signify. Why are we better off as readers now than we were with the original? We now know what questions to ask. Define for us the jargon, and we are on our way to understanding. Note also that the significantly more readable revision is actually four words *longer* than its unreadable predecessor (72 words instead of 68). So much for the readability formulae: Here is a sentence two and half times as long as the supposed 29-word limit that still reads clearly and cogently. Why? Because as each new word arrives, we are already adequately prepared to put it to work.

Once again, we cannot construct a simplistic *rule* to make our students feel both safe and familiarly oppressed. "Never interrupt between a subject and verb" simply will not accord with the realities of modern rhetoric. Example (10) was an S-V-C separation disaster; but other grammatical S-V structures, like the one I am currently interrupting, can benefit from the extra emphasis the separation will visit upon the arrival of the verb. Every S-V-C interruption should be a judgment call. Here, then, are the concerns we might consider when judging the probable reader response to any given S-V-C separation:

1) How long is the separation? (If it is only a word or two, most readers will not feel burdened. If it is two or three lines long, most readers will be taxed to or beyond their limit of sustained concentration.)

2) How difficult is it to comprehend the substance of the interruptive material? (Difficult material can make even the shortest of interruptions problematic. Crystal-clear material or extremely familiar material can make even the longer interruptions seem smooth sailing.)

3) How difficult is it during the interruption to make sense of the part of the sentence that preceded it? (The more certain we are of the identity of the delayed information, the easier it is to attend to the material causing the delay and to remain aware of the material at the beginning.)

4) Is anything to be gained from interrupting the syntax at this point? (Sometimes the writer has good reasons for delaying the arrival of the expected syntactic resolution: Interrupting the syntax might neatly yet subtly indicate to the reader the subservient quality of the interrupting information.)

The worst S-V-C interruption is that which contains the material the writer wished the reader to emphasize most. By locating words between a subject and verb (or between a verb and its object), the writer is signaling the reader to proceed quickly through that material, as if it were parenthetical. The very *location* of that material pronounces its relative *in*significance. If the material is actually worthy of great emphasis, then its location belies its significance.

S-V-C interruptions can be spotted with relative ease -- once the eye is trained to do so -- and can be revised with relatively little effort. They are a good example of how noting a structural problem in our prose can lead us to predicting the substantive and interpretive problems that will most likely burden and confuse our readers.

Endnotes

1. For information on these readability formulae, see Chapter 2, page 23.
2. This is the case when the verb is active; the subject is then, by definition, the agent of the verb's action. In all other cases, the verb is a form of *to be* and needs to reside as close to its subject as possible. There are, of course, any number of good reasons to violate this expectation.
3. Once again, when I speak of reader expectations in this book I am referring to that set of expectations shared by those reading expository and persuasive American prose at the turn of the twenty-first century. These expectations change over time and from place to place; but they are usually supplanted by yet other expectations. This passage from Johnson's *Rambler* demonstrates just such a change in expectations.
4. Richard M. Weaver (*The Ethics of Rhetoric*, Chicago: Henry Regnery, 1953) offered the following pastiche description of why we now tend to prefer the short sentence to the long:

   > It is a fair generalization to say that our age prefers the short sentence. The reasons for this are interesting in themselves, although they cannot be discussed at length here. The hurried pace at which one is forced to catch buses and subways, the necessity of meeting business schedules, the times precision of many forms of entertainment, the limitations which newspaper make-up imposes on style, the general tendency to estimate things by the degree of thrill they provide -- all of these factors discourage the kind of leisurely and sustained attention that our forbears gave to the written word on the printed page. Such conditions of living virtually compel people to favor the sentence whose meaning can be picked up quickly. In consequence, our age, as compared to an age like the eighteenth or nineteenth century, employs the relatively short sentence unit.

5. Most people think Latin became a "dead" language in the fifth century at the fall of the Roman Empire. That is not the case, by far. It was used as the exclusive language of higher education well into the nineteenth century. Until then, at English universities, all lectures, discussions, examinations, and papers were in Latin. The first lecture ever given in English at Oxford University was delivered by Matthew Arnold in 1859.

4

Beginnings
and Endings:
The Topic and
Stress Positions

S *tructure, Substance, Context, and Some Helpful Boxes*

In *Style: Ten Lessons in Clarity and Grace,* Joseph Williams presented the English sentence in a box paradigm that can be an elegant and powerful teaching device. In combination with other, similar boxes that pertain to units of discourse larger than the sentence, it is both simple and complex, helpful and challenging. Even its limitations can be used effectively to give students an overview of linguistic structure and the difficulties involved in communication. Here is the box unit that helps us investigate the unit of the sentence considered in isolation:

STRCT	SUBJECT	VERB	COMPLEMENT	FIXED
SUBS	AGENT	ACTION	GOAL	MVBL

The upper level, labeled "STRCT," represents the normal *structure* of the English clause -- and therefore of the one-clause sentence. It is true, of course, that a great many clauses do not conform to this order: Some lack one of the three normal components; some end in a question mark; some call attention to themselves by the abnormality of their structure to produce an effect either poetic or notably formal. For example: Consider the difference between "I will not do that," which fulfills the expected Subject - Verb - Complement (S-V-C) order, and "That I will not do," which violates that expectation by putting the complement before the subject. The difference in meaning or effect between the two -- whatever that difference may be for you -- is caused by the difference in structure. Such a large majority of English clauses conform to the S-V-C order that readers consider it a kind of default structural value: That is how they *expect* a clause to unfold. This structure is a societal product, and there is little an individual writer can do to alter the resulting expectations.[1] This relatively FIXED structure therefore brings with it certain relatively FIXED expectations on the part of readers. Those expectations concern the placement or arrival of certain kinds of substantive materials.

Many sentences consist of one clause only. Their relatively simple structure makes them ideal for articulating relatively straightforward facts or concepts. The more that is added to the self-enclosed single clause -- even if only by interruptive phrases -- the more potentially complex the structure can become. When thought becomes complex enough to warrant the articulation of a *connection* between two component subthoughts, then two clauses become almost a necessity. When sentence that extends beyond two clauses, it requires a good deal of sophistication on the part of the writer to control the structure, even when the contents themselves are not especially sophisticated. In order to explore the concept of the Topic and Stress positions (see below), we begin by considering one-clause sentences. When the concepts are in place and functioning, we can investigate the problems presented by more complex, multi-unit sentence structures.

The lower level of the boxes, labeled SUBS, represents the SUBSTANCE of the thought, which is, for the most part, in the control of the writer. In contrast with the structure, which is relatively fixed by society, the substance is relatively MOVEABLE (MVBL) by the writer. The relationship between these two, substance and structure, is the focal point of this Reader Expectation Approach. We can begin with a single piece of general advice for the writer, the significance of which will become increasingly clear as we proceed:

....

Whenever possible, try to locate the various types of substance in the structural locations where readers expect those types of substance to arrive.

....

As we have seen in Chapters 1, 2, and 3, this general statement translates into the following more specific pieces of advice for the sentence level:

1) Usually locate the action of the sentence in the verb.

2) Usually let the agent appear as the subject of that verb if the reader needs to know up front who is doing the action.

3) Do not separate a subject from its verb or a verb from its complement unless (a) the separation is particularly easy to process, (b) the interrupting material is intended to be considered of relatively little im-

portance by the reader, or (c) there is some good purpose in delaying the reader's syntactic resolution.

Again, these pieces of advice are based not on convention or on the rules of grammar but rather on the expectations shared by most readers of current professional American English.

I repeat the following for emphasis: None of this advice should be allowed to rigidify into rules. Any such rules will eventually self-destruct, for three major reasons:

1) They do not accurately describe the way people actually write. Good writers violate these supposed rules frequently. As soon as the student discovers this, the teacher will appear to be either unrealistic or a hypocrite; the rules will be discarded the moment the student is freed from the controlling force of the semester's grade.

2) The presence of rules will reinstate the teacher-student power structure all too familiar to them from high school days. Students learn more from teachers who present themselves not as adversarial representatives of an artificially cultured world but as co-conspirators against a common enemy -- the difficulties inherent in the production of effective discourse.

3) Rules tend to focus attention inward from the boundaries they create; but when readers read, they use much of their energy to focus outward, necessarily connecting the present moment of the reading experience to those that precede and follow it. Sentences seem to have boundaries -- the capital letter at the beginning and the period at the end; but sentences usually do not exist in a vacuum. In reading a sentence as part of a continuing piece of discourse, readers must be aware of what has gone before and be apprehensive of what is likely to follow. The present moment cannot be divorced from its past or its future. One could even argue that "the present" exists not in and of itself but just as the meeting-place of past and future. Readers must look inward at the sentence from its boundaries to perceive what it might be capable of communicating "by itself"; but simultaneously they must obliterate those boundaries and look outward (both backward and forward), to perceive how the sentence functions "in its context." In actual practice, the "by itself" and the "in its context" cannot be separated. Context controls meaning. By their very nature, rules oversimplify this complex set of relationships.

Interpretation is always dependent on context. If a writer wishes to control a reader's perception of meaning in a given sentence, that writer must try to construct a context for the sentence that will limit the possibilities of misinterpretation. Those contexts are highly complicated. They stretch from the very local to the very distant. Locally, every sentence talks directly to the sentences on either side of it; less locally, they relate to all other sentences in its paragraph; and yet less locally still, they relate to other paragraphs and other pages in the document. Yet further in the distance are all the social, psychological, political, economic, historic, and other forces that have produced the situation in which the writer is writing. In between and all about, there looms large the nature and character of the writer, the nature and character of the intended audience in general, and the complex individuality of each particular reader. All of these combine at all times to form the context for any given sentence. In the face of such complexity, any rule must be unhelpful because of its rigidity. Any rule must shatter.

W *hose Story?*

Context reveals itself in many ways -- some quite obvious, some wonderfully subtle. We deal in this chapter with making consciously available to writers a number of important clues to contextualization that are suggested by a sentence's structure and are intuitively available to most readers.

We begin with the following five prose accounts of a single incident:

1a. Mary smashed John in the face with the pie.

1b. Mary smashed the pie into John's face.

1c. John's face was smashed by the pie.

1d. John's face was smashed by Mary.

1e. The pie smashed John in the face.[2]

Though all five sentences of Example (1) deal with the same basic materials -- John, Mary, a pie, and a potentially dangerous, probably humiliating action, -- they all tend to "mean" differently to a given reader. Each sentence can still have meaning in an infinite number of ways; but for any given reader, each of these sentences tends to differ slightly from all of its variations. From what source does this differentiation arise?

Since we have recently looked at verbs in some detail, let us begin with them. Checking the five sentences for verbs, we find the following: "smashed," "smashed," "was smashed," "was smashed," and "smashed." In tracking down the interpretive differences, these verbs will be of little help.

Instead, let us try to determine for each sentence *whose story* is being told.

1a. Mary smashed John in the face with the pie.

Whose day does this describe? A majority of readers -- but by no means all -- will say this is Mary's story. Since the question itself is new and strange to most students, we can expect them to hesitate and offer varied responses; but in my experience, the more they consider the question, the more they tend to agree the story is Mary's. It is important to distinguish for them between the concept of "whose story" this is and the concept of "who did the action?" "Who did the action?" is a question of agency; "whose story?" is a question of perspective.

When I ask them the same "whose story" question for the other four sentences, the majority tend to agree on the following responses:

Sentence	Whose story?
1b. Mary smashed the pie into John's face.	Mary
1c. John's face was smashed by the pie.	John's face
1d. John's face was smashed by Mary.	John's face
1e. The pie smashed John in the face.	The pie

The responses to these questions suggest that something even stronger than reader expectation is functioning here:

Readers tend to read a clause -- or a one-clause sentence -- as being the story of whoever or whatever shows up first.

This goes beyond what readers expect or hope or wish; it describes what they tend to *do*.

As important a structural principle as this is, it will be worthless to students if they themselves are not convinced of its accuracy. First, they should be cautioned that this statement (and all others like it) applies to most readers, most of the time -- and not to everyone, all the time. If they are still incredulous, we can treat them to an ultra-slow-motion replay of the sentence. This is a technique that succeeds in part because so many students are familiar with examples of it on television -- from sporting event replays to highly dramatized moments of violence in prime-time drama. More significantly, though, it succeeds because we as readers experience a sentence from left to right and through time. The slow-motion replay reproduces, in microdetail, the first-time experience of reading the sentence.

Here is a dramatized play-by-play for the slow-motion journey through (1a):

Mary smashed John in the face with the pie.

M - - A - - R - - Y

    ("Yes, yes. What did she do?")

S - - M - - A - - SH - - ED

    ("She did? *What* did she smash?")

J - - OH - - N

    ("She smashed *John*? Really! Tell me more.")

IN - - THE - -

    ("yes, yes . . . ")

F - - A - - CE

("Aaahh . . . ")

W - - I - - TH THE

("with what -- the frying pan? the rolling pin?")

PIE

(expression of mischievous glee.)

As each word in a sentence appears, it is already contextualized by those that have preceded it. Each new arrival changes the discourse and combines with its predecessor to turn the reader's attention to a new set of future possibilities. With this principle in mind, we can begin to see why (1a) might differ from (1b):

1b. Mary smashed the pie into John's face.

M -- A -- R -- Y

("Yes, yes. What did she do?")

S - - M - - A - - SH - - ED

("She did? *What* did she smash?")

THE -- PIE

(At this moment, we see Mary smashing a pie.)

INTO

(Into what? Smithereens?)

JOHN'S

(Where did he come from?)

FACE

(Ha!)

Note how (1a) and (1b) differ from (1c) and (1d):

1c. John's face was smashed by the pie.
1d. John's face was smashed by Mary.

Sentences (1a) and (1b) tell the story of what Mary did; (1c) and (1d) tell what kind of a day John's face had. In the fifth sentence,

1e. The pie smashed John in the face.

the story line belongs to the pie. We cannot separate the way discourse affects us from the structure or order in which it is presented. Certain structures invite such significantly consistent reader responses that the structure itself can be viewed as a clue or as a force of persuasion for the reader engaged in a process of interpretation. Knowing about those clues gives us as writers much more control than we had before over the reader's *probable* interpretation. We will never have complete control.

Once again: We are dealing with clues, not rules. Readers who are predisposed to respond to certain semantic clues in certain ways may find these clues overriding those sent by structural expectations. A John-disposed reader may read all of these sentences as being John's story. A Mary-disposed reader will have Mary foremost in mind no matter where she turns up. But for those readers who do not bring with them such controlling contexts, the clues sent by the structure will exert powerful influence over their interpretation of each of these sentences: The sentences will tend to be read as the story of whoever shows up first.

It may be easier to teach this structural point using nonverbal examples. For instance, as part of an experiment, a scientist wishes to measures the change in the temperature of a heated liquid over a period of time. She sets up the apparatus, takes a number of measurements, and records the perceived temperatures. She then wishes to present her data in print. Here is one possible arrangement:

2a. t (time) = 15′ T (temperature) = 32º; t = 0′ T = 25º; t = 6′ T = 29º; t = 3′
     T= 27º; t = 12′ T = 32º; t = 9′ T = 31º.

For most readers, this linear arrangement makes it more than difficult to perceive how the writer would have us interpret the data. The prose equivalent of this linear presentation is of no greater help to us:

2aa. After 15 minutes, the temperature was 32º; at the beginning, it had been 25º; at the 6-minute mark it was 29º; after 3 minutes, the temperature was 27º; at the 12-minute mark it was 32º; and after 9 minutes it was 31º.

The numbers are all there, and the numbers are fastidiously accurate; but the structure sends us no instructions about how we are intended to put them alltogether. We have *received* the information; but to *perceive* what might be meant by it, we have to formulate our own sense of order. The writer has not done that job for us.

Here is a second possible arrangement of the same data:

2b. | **time (min)** | **Temperature (ºC)** |
|---|---|
| 0 | 25 |
| 3 | 27 |
| 6 | 29 |
| 9 | 31 |
| 12 | 32 |
| 15 | 32 |

This arrangement makes it far easier for us to interpret the data. It also will lead a greater percentage of us to interpret the data in the same way. If we are familiar with the conventions of reading such tables, we know we are to connect pieces of information both horizontally -- (at minute 6 the temperature was 29 degrees) -- and vertically (as time goes by regularly, something interesting and irregular happens to the temperature).

The structure of table (2b) provides the reader with an easily perceived *context* (the moment in time) in which the significant piece of information (the degree of temperature) can be interpreted. The contextual material appears on the left and is patterned by the experimenter to produce an expectation of regularity. How many of us could tell from the linear arrangement in (2a) that the temperature readings were taken at regular 3-minute intervals? The interesting results appear on the right -- and the discovery of its less predictable pattern is the very purpose of this bit of scientific discourse. The temperature rises regularly for a while at 2-degree intervals, then rises only by a 1-degree difference, and finally ceases to rise altogether. It is the relationship between the *regular* progression of time (3-minute intervals) and the *irregular* progression of the rise in temperature (2 - 2 - 2 - 1 - 0 degrees) that constitutes the thought being represented.

But yet more interesting than the difference between (2a) and (2b) is the difference between (2b) and the following variation, (2c). A curious thing happens if the two vertical parts of the table are reversed in location. The new table that results is much harder to use:

2c.

Temperature (°C)	time (min)
25	0
27	3
29	6
31	9
32	12
32	15

Since we read from left to right -- that is, since we *encounter* the material on the left before we *encounter* the material on the right -- we experience the former as context for the latter. In (2a), the left-versus-right arrangement of the information was of no help to us; it left us on our own to figure out a way to make it all coherent. In (2b), we experienced the material on the right -- the rate of the rising temperature -- as a *function* of the passage of time, which had continually and regularly contextualized us on the left. (2c) is such a bewildering experience because we are invited by the left-right organization to consider *the passage of time as a function of the rising of a temperature*. "If you want to make time pass," it tells us, "heat up a liquid."

This "whose story" principle lends yet more support to the argument that the passive voice is not always inferior to the active. "Bees disperse pollen" and "Pollen is dispersed by bees" are two equally respectable but different sentences about the same facts. The first tells us something about bees; the second tells us something about pollen. The passivity of the second does not invalidate its potential effectiveness; "Pollen is dispersed by bees" is probably the better choice of the two *if* it appears in a paragraph presenting a continuing story about "pollen." Instead of asking if this should this be active or passive, we would do better to ask whose story it is. If using the passive is the only way to get a particular "whose story" up front, then thank goodness for the passive. In such a case, the story turns out to be a passive one. It should come as no great surprise that the passive is much better than the active in communicating passivity.

In my experience, students *think* they understand this point before they actually do. To help them assess their real comprehension, offer them the following little quiz:

Which of the following is the best sentence?

3a. Miss Grundy taught me grammar.

3b. I learned grammar from Miss Grundy.

3c. Grammar I learned from Miss Grundy.

A certain number of hands may go up for each of the alternatives. I disagree with all who raised their hands. Each of these three sentences is "a good sentence"; but each is superior to the other two, depending on the context. If I were writing a biographical note for my high school reunion, the best choice among these three would depend on which kind of paragraph would be its home. If I were writing a paragraph about *the people* who taught me things in high school, then (3a) would be my preference:

3d. Mr. Jorgenson taught me algebra. Mrs. Simpson taught me history. Miss Grundy taught me grammar.

Whose story is each sentence? -- the story of the teachers.

Alternatively, if I were writing a paragraph that continually presented *my* story, then I would prefer (3b):

3e. I learned algebra from Mr. Jorgenson. I suffered through history with Mrs. Simpson. I learned grammar from Miss Grundy.

Now it is my story throughout.

However, if I were writing a paragraph that told the story about all the *subjects* I studied, then I would prefer (3c):

3f. Algebra I learned from Mr. Jorgenson. History I suffered through with Mrs. Simpson. Grammar I learned from Miss Grundy.

Now it is the continuing story of those subjects.

The problem of context is continually self-renewing. It is not solved simply by transporting the person or thing whose story it is to the beginning of the sentence. Every moment in the sentence responds to everything that has preceded it; each moment is taken together with those that preceded it to form a unit that immediately becomes the context for whatever appears next.

The slow-motion technique is again most effective for making the point. Stanley Fish used it in an early article, "Literature in the Reader: Affective Stylistics" (reprinted as Chapter 1 of *Is There a Text in This Class?*). He investigated the following sentence at length:

> That Judas perished by hanging himself, there is no certainty in Scripture.

He demonstrates that by the time we arrive at the comma, a number of distinct possibilities still lie reasonably before us:

> That Judas perished by hanging himself, <u>is</u> (an example for us all).

> That Judas perished by hanging himself, <u>shows</u> (how conscious he was of the enormity of his sin).

> That Judas perished by hanging himself, <u>should</u> (give us pause).

Although a great many more (indeed, an infinite number) are possible, the range of possibilities narrows,[3] he points out, with the arrival of "there is no."

> At this point, the reader is expecting, and even predicting, a single word, "doubt," but instead he finds "certainty"; and at that moment the status of the fact that had served as his point of reference becomes <u>un</u>certain. . . .
>
> The basis of the method is a consideration of the *temporal* flow of the reading experience, and it is assumed that the reader responds in terms of that flow and not to the whole utterance. That is, in an utterance of any length, there is a point at which the reader has taken in only the first word, and then the second, and then the third, and so on, and the report of what happens to the reader is always a report of what has happened <u>to</u> <u>that</u> <u>point</u>. (The report includes the reader's set toward future experiences, but not those experiences.)[4]

What he calls "the reader's set toward future experiences" I am calling "reader expectations." The new news is that for English prose, the most important reader expectations are tied to structural location.

Many of us might recall a piece of advice many of our English teachers gave us in the sixth grade: "Vary the way you begin your sentences to keep your reader interested." That was fine advice in the sixth grade, but works poorly for adult life. That teacher was dealing with student sentences of 6, 8, 10, 12, 14 words. If several words at the beginning of one sentence reappeared at the beginning of a number of others, the repetitions consumed far too great a percentage of the reader's time and attention. Here is an actual student essay that suffers from this malady.

4.   <u>**Spring**</u>

I like the Spring for many reasons.

I like the Spring because of the pretty birds. I like the Spring because of the robins. I like the Spring because of the blue jays. I like the Spring because of the cardinals. I like the Spring because of the pretty birds.

I like the Spring because of the pretty flowers. I like the Spring because of the tulips. I like the Spring because of the roses. I like the Spring because of the daffodils. I like the Spring because of the pretty flowers.

I like the Spring because of the fun things you can do. I like the Spring because you can go camping. I like the Spring because you can go swimming. I like the Spring because you can play baseball. I like the Spring because of the fun things you can do.

Therefore, in conclusion, I like the Spring for many reasons.[5]

We can easily see why this teacher could get frustrated enough to insist, "*Daffodils* are another reason I like the Spring. Vary the way you begin your sentences to keep your reader interested." Of course, "your reader" here is really "your teacher"; and "interested" really means "from going bonkers -- especially if this is the 36th such essay encountered that afternoon.

After we grow up and become professionals, we have far less need to "keep our reader interested." Most of our readers will have to read what we write whether they are "interested" or not. More to the point, our readers will be dealing with sentences of 25, 40, 55 words or more. In that case, our readers will be *delighted* to discover that our next sentence is *still* on the same topic we had been dealing with in the previous sentence. As we will see in chapters 5 and 6, carefully controlling the "whose story" perspective throughout a sophisticated paragraph allows us to control, to a great extent, how readers connect and interrelate even the most complex materials.

A far more effective piece of advice for sophisticated writers would be to "vary your sentence *structure* to accord with the *shape* of the thought it is presenting."

We have so far been considering this clause-level "whose story?" concept in sentences of only one clause. But what if a sentence has more than one clause? Compare the following two-clause sentences:

5a. Although Smith constantly complains, Jones plays the radio at a high volume.

5b. Jones plays the radio at a high volume, although Smith constantly complains.

In (5a), the first clause is the story of Smith, and the second is the story of Jones. Whose story is the sentence as a whole? Most readers would vote for Jones. In (5b), the first clause is the story of Jones, and the second is the story of Smith. Whose story is the sentence as a whole? Most readers would vote again for Jones. Why? Because in both cases, Jones is the subject of *the main clause.*[6] That leads us to another reader expectation:

In a multiclause sentence, readers tend to read the entire sentence as the story of whoever or whatever shows up first in the main clause.

That explains, at least in part, why readers can get so exhausted by sentences that pile up too many qualifying clauses before getting to the main clause. Here again is a "sentence" we considered in Chapter 1:

Although xxxxx xxxxxx xxxxxx xxxxxx xxxxx xxxxx xxxx xxx xxxx, and although xxxxxx xxxxx xxxxxxx xxxxx xxxx xxxxxxxxx xxxxxxx xxxxxx xxxx, despite which xxxxxxxx xxxxxxx xxxxxxx xxxxxxxx xxxxxxx xxxxxx and xxxxx xxxxx xxxxx xxxxxx, subject verb complement.

This "sentence" strikes most readers as burdensome not simply because it is "too long" but because we have to deal with far too much material before reaching the subject of the main clause; only then does it finally articulate for us *whose story* the sentence was supposed to have been all along. We needed to know that information a good deal earlier.

What of sentences that contain two main clauses -- [S-V-C and S-V-C]? Whose story is such a sentence?

5c. Jones plays the radio at a high volume, and Smith constantly complains.

Is it Jones's story? It is Smith's? Is it both? That ambiguity is one of the reasons the ", and" between two independent clauses tends to create an unhelpful structure. We will revisit this problem later.

T *he Topic Position*

Connections Between Sentences

Since the interpretive sense of context always reaches leftward/backward in prose, we cannot profitably dwell for too long on teaching the isolated sentence. Each sentence considered by itself is likely to persuade a reader to a different interpretation than it would if considered along with its neighbors. We would do well to devote a substantial portion of time and effort to teaching how sentences connect with those that immediately surround them. In many ways, those connections can be considered the single most important thing to concentrate on in teaching writing. Teaching them will demonstrate how the control of style affects and is affected by the generation of substance.

Writing is not the reduction of preexisting thought to visible words; it is rather the constant interaction between thought and expression of thought, neither of which can exist effectively without the other. Since they are essentially inseparable, improving either one results in improving the other. This assumption has gained widespread support in recent years, as "learn to write" has become intertwined with "write to learn."

This stylistic Reader Expectation approach may look like it applies only to the Revision process: "Was my action articulated by the verb?" "Is this sentence really supposed to be the story of the subject of this main clause?" But once this approach is internalized, it becomes a crucial part of the Invention process: "What is going on here next? I'd better choose a verb to express it." "Have I anything more to say about the subject of the last sentence? If so, I had better keep the same subject up front." Every three or four weeks, someone comes up to me in a grocery store or post office or airport to tell me they took a workshop from me years ago and still think of these principles on a daily basis. Once they are yours, they are yours.

In order to investigate these inter-sentence connections, I will be referring to two crucial structural locations in the sentence -- the Topic position and the Stress position. I will oversimplify their definitions, for the moment: The Topic position comprises everything from the beginning of a sentence up to and including the grammatical subject; the Stress position is the sentence's end. Both these definitions will require substantial modification later.

Both of these terms refer not to things but to structural locations. They thus are "fixed," even more strongly than the subject-verb-complement syntactical order of the sentence. Like S-V-C, the Topic and Stress positions engender certain fixed expectations on the part of readers; as a result of that parallel, they become a second layer of boxes in the Williams paradigm, which I alter only somewhat here.

STRCT	TOPIC		STRESS	FIXED
SUBS				MVBL
STRCT	SUBJECT	VERB	COMPLEMENT	FIXED
SUBS	AGENT	ACTION	GOAL	MVBL

Once again we have dual-layered boxes, now superimposed on the Subject-Verb-Complement set of boxes. This upper level of boxes represents structural components that are relatively fixed and therefore raise relatively fixed expectations in the minds of readers; the lower level of boxes represents the cognitive substance, which remains in the control of the writer and is therefore movable. Once again, the major piece of advice for writers is to arrange the substance so it appears in the structural locations where readers expect it to appear.

The lower set of boxes, filled with Subject-Verb-Complement and Agent-Action-Goal, represents the sentence considered as an isolated unit. The upper set, filled on the structural level with Topic and Stress and not yet filled on the substantive level, suggests the way sentences connect backward and forward to the sentences that surround them. The reader-based concerns of the upper set of boxes are yet more important than those of the lower.

A warning: As we work through examples in this chapter, the revised sentences, considered in isolation, may well *sound* no better than the originals; but in terms of their linkage to the sentences surrounding them, the revisions will usually represent a great improvement. Students must be warned, and warned often, that they will not be able to judge the revisions by ear. It matters little which sentence *sounds* better; it matters a great deal more which sentence *connects* better to its neighbors and sends the reader persuasive instructions on how to value its various components.

If there ever arises a conflict between choices to be made on Agent-Action principles (the lower boxes) and choices to be made on Topic-Stress principles (the upper boxes), it is usually more effective to decide in favor of the latter. It is far more important for readers to be able to step securely from one sentence to the next than that they be able to luxuriate in the glow of a magnificent but artificially isolated sentence.

Old Information

Readers have two important needs as they read the beginning of a new sentence, both of which must be satisfied by the information that occupies the Topic position. The first of these we have covered already: They need to know "whose story" this is. But they also need to know, as soon as possible, how this new sentence connects backward to the sentence they have just finished reading. This anxiety is so pressing that readers tend to use the first opportunity afforded them to accomplish this mental task. If something up front in the new sentence *can* be used to forge that backward link, then the chances are high that it *will* be so used. As a result, it becomes essential for the writer to control with great care what kind of information appears at the beginning of every sentence.

We can use this understanding to formulate another reader expectation:

Readers expect the material at the beginning of a sentence to provide a connection backward to the sentence that precedes it.

All writers of English would be well advised, then, to put at the beginning of every sentence the piece of "old information" that forges the logical backward link to the previous sentence. The term "old information" does *not* refer to things that happened before the year 1800. Rather, it refers to any material that has already appeared in this particular piece of discourse. Often it will have appeared in the sentence immediately preceding. Sometimes it will hearken further back within the paragraph, or even to a previous paragraph. The further the leap in space, the more tenuous the connection is likely to be.

When a piece of old information appears at the beginning of a sentence, it offers the reader the following comforting instructions: "Dear Reader," it says. "Of all the information that has come your way most recently in this document, this is the one strand you should use to connect the discourse logically from where you were to where you are going." Having done that, it also helps provide the context in which to consider the "new information" yet to come.

This concept is trickier to work with than it may appear at first glance -- which should become more apparent as we look at several examples.

6a. The assignment of supplemental readings -- even if those readings were referred to in texts already approved by the official curriculum, were clearly germane to the subject in general, and could be demonstrated to be related to the core assignments -- would also require the School Board's permission.

Why is this sentence so burdensome to read? Many readers would suggest it was "too long." Creators of readability formulas, like Rudolph Flesch, would probably agree.[7] Sentence (6a) contains 46 words. Flesch demonstrated to his satisfaction (see Chapter 2, page 23) that English sentences should not exceed 29 words because at that point they become too hard to read. I contend that after 29 words sentences do not become harder to read; they only become harder to write. The larger the expanse of a sentence, the more skillfully the syntax must be structured to keep the reader continually contextualized.

Instead of relying on magic numbers, let us look closely at the structure of (6a). With the material of the last chapter in mind, we can immediately spot one glaring problem: There is a 37-word interruption between the subject and the verb. That interruption amounts to more than three-quarters of the sentence's bulk. We could lessen the reader's burden significantly by attending to this one problem.

However, there is another structural problem that also requires attention: The arrival of the old information in (6a) is delayed until the end of the sentence. We can recognize the old information here even without having before us the sentence that preceded it: The backward link is "would also require the School Board's permission." The word "also" flags us that the discourse has recently been discussing something else that required the School Board's permission and informs us that the material in this sentence "also" requires such permission. As readers, we would have been delighted to know *up front* that this sentence would discuss yet another such requirement.

Which should we work on first -- the S-V-C separation or the old information problem? It does not matter. Any sentence that displays one structural flaw may well contain several. Since revision of any one affects the structure of the whole, altering one structural feature might well in turn alter others, and possibly provide a remedy for them, too. It does not matter with which problem we begin.

If we get the requirement of School Board permission up front in the Topic position, where it will do the reader the most good as the appropriate backward link, the rest of the sentence will be likely to create far less of a burden for the reader. Here is one possible revision:

6b. The School Board's permission would also be required before teachers would be allowed to assign supplemental readings -- even if those readings were referred to in works already approved by the official curriculum, were clearly germane to the subject in general, and could be demonstrated to be related to the core assignments.

This revision actually turns out to be yet longer than the original it replaces -- 51 words to the previous 47; yet most readers find it easier to follow and interpret.[8] The original sentence made us hold in mind a great deal of complicated material about "readings" while we were still waiting for two crucial things to arrive: (1) the verb (without which the arduously retained subject would make no sense); and (2) some indication of how in the world all this material relates to material in the previous sentence. Another way of saying the same thing: The reader was too burdened by considerations of *structure* to be able to pay a sufficient amount of attention to the unveiling *substance*. Those structural considerations concerned both the present sentence (the S-V-C separation problem) and the relationship of this sentence to its predecessor (the misplaced backward-linking old information problem).

Please note that the revision (6b) brings with it a passive that did not exist in the original: "The School Board's permission would also be required. . . ." This, I would argue, exemplifies one of the strongest and most advantageous uses of the passive. The passive is to be preferred to the active in each of the following cases:

1) When it is the only way to move the backward-linking old information to the Topic position,

2) When it is the only way to move the person or thing whose story it is to the Topic position; or

3) When the story is a passive one and therefore benefits from the verb/action demonstrating that passivity.[9]

An active construction here would sacrifice those structural gains in favor of obeying a rule that has its origins more in convention than in logic or practicality.

When sentences remain simple, including only a few pieces of information, the lack of a clear backward link may not seem to be a severe problem. Few choices exist; and any choice will be close enough to the previous material to be "heard":

7a. Neither Chris nor Pat could be sure which city to choose. Chris thought that. . . .

7b. Neither Chris nor Pat could be sure which city to choose. Pat thought that. . . .

7c. Neither Chris nor Pat could be sure which city to choose. New York seemed. . . .

However, when information gets plenteous and choices multiply, the presence of a clear backward link allows a reader to maintain a steady and confidant stride forward. This is especially the case in professional prose, where these connections control not only the flow of thought but also the cohesion of thought. Here is a typical, factual, unprepossessing legal sentence:

8a. Petitioner Jane Doe filed this state-law tort action against respondent Acme Corporation in Massachusetts Superior Court in September of 1990.

Note in how many ways the prose can continue from here:

8b. Petitioner Jane Doe filed this state-law tort action against respondent Acme Corporation in Massachusetts Superior Court in September of 1990. Acme removed the case to the United States District Court for the District of Massachusetts on the basis of diversity of citizenship. The district court granted. . . .

8c. Petitioner Jane Doe filed this state-law tort action against respondent Acme Corporation in Massachusetts Superior Court in September of 1990. The question before this Court is whether by September of 1990 the statute of limitations had already run. In March of 1984, Acme had. . . .

8d. Petitioner Jane Doe filed this state-law tort action against respondent Acme Corporation in Massachusetts Superior Court in September of 1990. Robert Roe filed a similar suit against Acme in Missouri Superior Court one month later. In both cases, Acme responded by refusing to. . . .

8e. Petitioner Jane Doe filed this state-law tort action against respondent Acme Corporation in Massachusetts Superior Court in September of 1990. In that same month, Jane Doe also. . . .

Let me repeat an important caveat that applies to every example used in this entire volume: None of the revised versions offered for any of these examples represents the "right" way to write the sentence or paragraph. Rather, they represent one particular possibility of revision aimed at one particular structural problem. Other revisions are possible -- because other interpretations are possible. All of my revisions remain as infinitely interpretable as the sentences they replace. However, if they are good revisions, they will outdistance the originals in terms of the percentage of readers who interpret them in the way their author intended.

We have now seen that two major questions represent a reader's major concerns at the start of a new sentence:

1. Whose story is this?
2. How does this sentence link backward to its predecessor?

The answers to those two questions, taken together, form the CONTEXT for the rest of the sentence. "Context" is the last of the four key words of this Reader Expectation approach:

> Expectation
>
> Structure
>
> Substance
>
> Context

The reader's need for this contextualizing information is so pressing that the reader tends to use *whatever* is available up front to answer these questions. With the "whose story" question, the reader will always be able to find some answer, right or wrong, since something or someone has to occupy that up-front subject position. It therefore behooves the writer to get the *right* answer where it will be most likely to be discovered.

Which of these two sentences would most high school English teachers choose as the better construction?

A.   Jack loves Jill.
B.   Jill is loved by Jack.

Most would opt for (A), since it is shorter and -- more importantly -- active. But should anyone ask you, "Tell me all about Jill," and you started your response with, "Jack . . . ," they might well complain that they had asked about Jill. If you start with "Jill . . . ," then the passive follows naturally, since her story at the moment is a passive one.

With the question of backward-linking old information, however, it is possible to supply nothing up front that could be of help. Let us say your previous sentence contained seven bits of information, represented here by these seven letters:

> A B C D E F G.

If you start your next sentence with the new information

Q

your reader cannot adequately formulate an answer to the "how does this link backward" question. As a result, the reader has to hold on to "Q" while still searching for that answer. Should your sentence continue with

$$Q \ R \ S,$$

by the time the "S" arrives, the reader has to stop searching for a backward link in order to pay proper attention to the unfolding structure of this new sentence. The reader hopes that once this new sentence is comprehended in and of itself, the linkage between the two sentences will somehow become apparent.

But offering *no* old information, bad as it is for your reader, is not nearly as bad as offering the *wrong* piece of old information. Let us say that the sentence following your ABCDEFG sentence is meant to be connected to the previous sentence by the "F" piece of information. Should you start that new sentence with "D," you have not only blown an opportunity but also have seriously misled your reader. Your reader will continue with great confidence and for some time to presume this "D" connection is the proper way to form a context for the new sentence.

It will be extremely difficult and confusing to repair the damage. Think of a train approaching a station where there are multiple exit tracks labeled A through F. Your train is supposed to exit on Track F; but the stationmaster mistakenly makes Track D available before you get to Track F. Once your train of thought has switched to Track D, it will require a burdensome effort to back it up and send it on its proper course.

When you take good care of the Topic position by supplying the correct backward link and identifying whose story the new sentence will be, then you will have created the correct context to control the reader's interpretive journey.

....

"Whose story?" + backwards link = context

....

Here is an example of the chaos that can ensue when neither of those important pieces of information appears in the topic position.

9a. Churches exhorting members to sever family and marital ties, rodent infestation, and employee discharge, and a refusal to make a retraction in a newspaper, were all considered outside the net of "extreme and outrageous."

Once again, the slow-motion reading technique dramatically demonstrates the difficulties the reader encounters in trying to make sense of this sentence the first time around.

CHURCHES . . .

It's going to be the story of "churches." They will do something, which will be identified by the main verb.

... EXHORTING ...

That's a verb form, but not the main verb. So although I know these are "exhorting" kinds of churches, I still do not know what action they are doing in this sentence.

... CHURCHES EXHORTING MEMBERS TO SEVER FAMILY AND MARITAL TIES, ...

They sound like cult churches. I want to know what these churches *do*; but the comma tells me I will have to wait to find out -- probably at least until the appearance of another comma.

... RODENT INFESTATION, ...

!!?? The best I can do with this newly arrived information, given the context in which it appears, is to understand that churches, for some weird reason, are exhorting their members to rodent infestation. These must be some strange churches.

... AND EMPLOYEE DISCHARGE, ...

In the context of "rodent infestation," "employee discharge" sounds like a medical problem. What is going on here?

... AND A REFUSAL TO MAKE A RETRACTION IN A NEWSPAPER, ...

In the context of "employee discharge," "retraction" sounds vaguely like it has something to do with pet hygiene. That doesn't make much sense; but nothing at the moment is making much sense. All I am convinced of is that these four strangely assorted items have nothing whatsoever to do with each other.

... WERE ALL ...

All? I'm wrong. They *do* have something to do with each other. They form some kind of cohesive unit; and the presence of the word "all" suggests I must be awfully stupid not to understand *how*.

... CONSIDERED ...

Finally, the rest of the main verb has arrived. Now maybe we can make some sense of all this.

... OUTSIDE ...

"Outside?" Are these all outside activities? I thought that an "infestation" of rodents would have to have been inside.

... THE NET ...

"Net"? What "net"? Is that the net they are using to catch the rats?

... OF "EXTREME AND OUTRAGEOUS."

I am now totally confused. The sentence, even at its end, makes no sense whatever to me as a first-time reader.

Am I suggesting that if only the answers to the two important questions "Whose story is it?" and "What is the backward link?" were to be
found up front, this onslaught of seemingly disparate information might
actually make some sense on a first reading? Yes.

What is the backward link here? Even without having the previous
sentence before us, we can sense that it might well have been focusing on
the quoted term, "extreme and outrageous." Since the term is not defined
within this sentence, it is probable we already have experienced it before.
That turns out to be the case. (Of course, the author would know the answer to this right away.)

Whose story is this sentence? It turns out to be the story of four
examples of things that courts have decided fall short (bad as they are) of
the level "extreme and outrageous."

Get those two up front, and the pieces of the puzzle fall together neatly:

9b. Examples of actions considered outside the net of "extreme and out-
     rageous" have included churches exhorting members to sever fami-
     ly and marital ties, rodent infestation, employee discharge, and a
     refusal to make a retraction in a newspaper.

It now can make immediate sense. We could make yet further refine-
ments; but these changes would just be polishing an already comprehensible sentence. (The previous changes were structural repairs that took care
of the problem of incomprehensibility.) Putting the four examples in a
short-to-long order makes them easier for the reader to handle; and making their grammatical structure as parallel to each other as possible increases the ease of readability; and just in case "net" is not clear enough,
maybe "definitional net" would do a better job.

9c. Examples of actions considered outside the definitional net of "ex-
     treme and outrageous" have included rodent infestation, employee
     discharge, newspaper editors refusing to make retractions, and
     churches exhorting members to sever family and marital ties.

All three revisions of example (9) contain virtually the same information; but each delivers it in a different structural order, thereby producing
different effects.

Try one more example in the slow-motion technique -- this time less
bizarre but more recognizable in the professional world. Instead of seeing
the whole sentence first, we will encounter it bit by bit.

10a.
     MAXIMUM LEFT VENTRICULAR WALL VELOCITY, . . .

     The five-word phrase is burdensome enough by itself; but the arrival
     of a comma instead of the expected verb strikes fear into the heart of a
     reader in search of a verb.

. . . MEAN LEFT VENTRICULAR WALL VELOCITY, AND . . .

Is "mean" the verb after all? No, it would have had to have been "means." By the end of this five-word phrase, we might note that the only difference between the two phrases is the opposition of "maximum" to "mean." The comma plus the "and" suggest that we are in the midst of a three-part series. If we have had the "max" and the "mean," surely we are about to encounter "minimal left ventricular wall velocity."

. . . AMPLITUDE OF POSTERIOR LEFT VENTRICULAR WALL . . .

"Amplitude"? We were expecting "minimum." At the very least we were expecting another (parallel) adjective. Well, at least the presence of "left ventricular wall" makes us confident that the next word will be "velocity."

. . . EXCURSION . . .

A scientist who knows something about this field might still be standing; but most of the rest of us sink to our knees at this point, weighed down by the burden of unresolved questions: "What is going on here" (no verb yet); "Whose story is it?" (Unclear whether it is the story of one of these or all three -- or perhaps of something that has yet to appear); "How does this link backward?" (No old backward-linking information up front); and, as a result, "What does all this mean?"

. . . WERE CALCULATED DIRECTLY . . .

Finally, the verb has arrived. Perhaps the sentence may still turn out to be worth the wait and the struggle.

. . . BY PREVIOUSLY DESCRIBED TECHNIQUES.

Crash. After all that waiting, we are rewarded only by the appearance of the decidedly anticlimactic old information. Whatever this sentence was all about, we missed it.

Here it is without interruption:

10a. Maximum left ventricular wall velocity, mean left ventricular wall velocity, and amplitude of posterior left ventricular wall excursion were calculated directly by previously described techniques.

How were we to guess that this onslaught of scientific terms had something to do with "techniques" that had been described previously? If we had been contextualized in the Topic position by the old information ("previously described") and the identification of whose story it was ("techniques"), we would have had to use far less reader energy to unravel the sentence's structure; that would have left us with a great deal more energy for contemplating the sentence's substance. The simple revision tactic produces something like the following:

10b. We used previously described techniques to calculate directly the maximum left ventricular wall velocity, the mean left ventricular wall velocity, and the amplitude of posterior left ventricular wall excursion.

If the use of the first person seems inappropriate for the intended audience, we can easily obliterate agency by recourse to an agency-deleting passive:

10c. Previously described techniques were used to calculate directly the maximum left ventricular wall velocity, the mean left ventricular wall velocity, and the amplitude of posterior left ventricular wall excursion.

A Few Pedagogical Hints

The concept of the Topic position raises a number of problems for students. It sounds like it ought to be simple; it turns out to be rather complex. In general, I would advise that the complexity be stressed -- or at least never underrated. Here are some of the most common difficulties.

(1) Students will want to know how far into the sentence the Topic position extends. The length cannot be defined as a specific number of words. The Topic position continues as long as it is clear to the reader that the sentence is still beginning. (Therefore, different readers may perceive different length Topic positions in a given sentence.) In most sentences, the Topic position extends to include the grammatical subject of the sentence, but not its verb. Here are some examples, with the Topic position underlined:

   a) <u>The Topic position</u> extends to include the grammatical subject, but not its verb.

   b) <u>In most sentences, the Topic position</u> extends to include the grammatical subject, but not its verb.

   c) <u>Despite what anyone might try to say to the contrary, in most sentences the Topic position</u> extends to include the grammatical subject, but not its verb.

   It can extend past the subject if the backward link appears after the subject -- usually as an interruptive phrase.

   d) <u>The verb, being thus excluded from the Topic position</u>, begins to build on the context already established.

(2) In multiclause sentences, each clause has a Topic position of its own. The sentence as a whole will be the story of whoever or whatever shows up first in the main clause. No matter where the sentence's

"whose story" appears, the backward link must be established at the very beginning of the sentence. That is where the reader will be trying to make that connection.

(3) When a sentence must contain many pieces of old information, students sometimes get frustrated by trying to cram all of it into the Topic position. In trying to do this, they tend to be fearing the retribution that presumably is connected to the disobeying of a new "rule": Thou shalt put all old information into the Topic position. First, it should not be presented as a rule. Second, the advice being given is NOT "Put the old information into the Topic position." There may well be several pieces of old information in a sentence. The Topic position should not be the home for all of it, but rather for *that piece of old information that makes the appropriate backward link.*

(4) Students may mistakenly equate the two pieces of advice they have been given concerning the Topic position: (1) Fill the Topic position with "whose story" the sentence tells; and (2) fill the Topic position with the appropriate backward-linking old information. Sometimes these two refer to one piece of information; but sometimes they refer to two distinct pieces of information. The two coincide when the old information from the last sentence is also the "whose story" person in the new sentence: "The School Board's permission would also be required before. . . . " [See Example (6), above.]

    The two are not the same when old information is used to link two separate stories about two separate people/things/ideas. For example: A political proposal has been discussed for the last four paragraphs and therefore qualifies as old information; but the story of the new sentence belongs to someone not yet mentioned, Nevada's Senator Kirkenbaum. Both can be accommodated by the same Topic position: "Under this proposal, Nevada's Senator Kirkenbaum would. . . ." Taken together, the "whose story" material and the backward-looking old information form the context in which the rest of the sentence will function.

(5) Students may mistakenly assume that every sentence must contain old information. Such information may well be lacking in any sentence that begins a new piece of discourse. When the Topic position has nothing to look back upon, then its contextualizing, forward-looking function becomes all the more important.

We can sum up most of these observations in reader expectation predictions that concern the Topic position:

....

Readers tend to read a clause or a one-clause sentence as the story of whoever or whatever shows up first.

....

Readers tend to read a multiclause sentence as the story of whoever or whatever shows up first in the main clause.

Readers expect and desire sentences to begin with material that links backward logically to materials that have already appeared in the previous discourse.

Readers expect that material to the left contextualizes anything that comes to its right. Readers expect that the occupants of the topic postion contextualize the reader for the rest of the sentence.

T he Stress Position

I also have a hard time thinking of conclusions, so I will end this paper with that thought.

(A Freshman)

Saving the Best for Last

You may have often heard the advice, "Write the way you speak." It is almost always bad advice.[10] When I talk to someone, I have a great many ways of indicating which of my words I want emphasized in certain ways: I can wave my hand, each flourish directing my listener's attention to one word at the expense of others; I can summon all sorts of body English -- eyebrows that question, facial lines that frown, a nose that can smirk, a head that can incline to call things into question, or shoulders that can indicate anything from increasing concern to total helplessness; and, most directly, I can use my voice, either by accentuation, to emphasize particular syllables, or by modulation -- louder or softer, faster or slower, higher or lower -- to differentiate by variation. When I speak, I can use all of these, and more, in varying combinations and permutations, in an attempt to engage the attention and direct the comprehension of my listener. But when I write, all of these visual and auditory sources of input disappear: Aside from a few flag words and an occasional typographical accent (italics, underlining, capitalization), the main way I can indicate intended emphasis is through structural location.

If I had to choose one of the reader expectations about structural location as the single most important to keep in mind when writing, it would be this one:

> **Today's readers of American English expect to find the most important informaton of a sentence located in a stress position.**

To begin overly simply, let us think of the Stress position as "the end of the sentence." We will complexify the definition as we go.

That the end of something could be its place of greatest emphasis is by no means a new idea. Aristotle, Cicero, and Quintilian all claim the same for the oratorical Latin sentence. The principle was reiterated in the seventeenth century by Puttenham, Wilson, and other compilers of English handbooks, and then again by Campbell, Blair, and Whately, the eighteenth-century Scotsmen whose influence controlled the way composition was taught until the last quarter of the twentieth century. It has been reconfirmed by research in psycholinguistics, cognitive psychology, and composition theory. It is not new; but it also is not well known or well understood. It still calls for explanation.

It might well seem outrageous to state that most English sentences are read with the expectation that the most important material will arrive at their end. I cannot prove this is the case; but I can hope to persuade you it is so. Perhaps it can best be understood by investigating a number of sentences that have been rewritten to get different pieces of information into the Stress position. If several versions of the same sentence's information, differing only in arrangement, seem to differ in meaning, then we could safely ascribe the differing meanings to the differing arrangements. That we will do; but first I offer three abstract ways to look at the issue.

Here is the first. A commonsense proverb tells us to "Save the best for last." That does indeed make sense. The only people who begin a meal with the strawberry shortcake and work their way up to the broccoli are the people who consider broccoli the best part of the meal. If the most important material were to appear at the beginning of the sentence, what would the reader have to look forward to before the next capital letter appears?

Moreover, we seem to enjoy delayed gratification. We like to reward ourselves for having taken part, for having struggled, for having endured. A writer who consistently ends sentences with the new, important material repeatedly reproduces for the reader that gratification experience in miniature, making the reading experience a constantly fulfilling one. According to Kenneth Burke,

> We "think" in a crescendo because it parallels certain psychic and physical processes which are at the roots of our experience. The accelerated motion of a falling body, the cycle of a storm, the procedure of the sexual act, the ripening of crops -- - growth here is not merely a linear procession, but a fruition.[11]

Here is the second. As readers, we take what we might call a mental breath at the beginning of every sentence to summon the energy, the tension, with which we pay attention to the unfolding of the syntax. Unless we maintain our concentration on the unfolding of the sentence's structural and grammatical unity, we will be unable to perceive clearly the writer's intended thought. As the last portion of the syntax announces itself, we have no more need to retain that mental breath; we begin to "exhale" it. The breath must be completely exhaled by the sentence's end so we can summon a fresh, new breath for the next sentence. That act of exhalation produces a sense of arrival, which in turn produces a sense of emphasis: A destination, a cadence, a closure has been reached. The Stress position is the moment of greatest emphasis in a sentence because it is a moment of syntactic closure.

Here is the third -- and perhaps the most important of the three. In the culture of the United States, I would argue, closure is more than merely a basic human need and expectation: It is a compulsion. It has been deeply implanted in us by moral education and repeated experience. It has become such a part of us that we rarely recognize how dependent we are on it for our sense of happiness, fulfillment, and well-being. That statement may sound excessive; but examples of it are easier to find than you might think. Here are just a few. You may judge for yourself if any of them apply to you and your experience.

1. You are watching your favorite murder mystery movie -- a two-hour saga you have already seen four times. Two minutes before its end, when the detective has summoned all the suspects to the salon and is just about to expose the guilty party, you hear an urgent voice calling you to the dinner table and clearly indicating that EVERYone in the house is waiting for you to appear. What do you do? Do you abandon the movie lightheartedly and go to dinner? Or do you stall for two minutes, filling time with argument or explanation, as you back out of the room slowly, remote control in hand? The movie ends. Discarding the remote control, you enter the dining room to find a number of hostile faces glowering at you. You knew the outcome of the movie. You could even summon to mind the cinematographic blocking of the final scene. With that in mind, why then were you so insistent on watching it again to the end, knowing there would be a great price to be paid in terms of domestic infelicity? You are compelled by your need for closure. You have been watching for two hours, expectant of this moment of resolution. It is just too hard to walk away from such an investment of your time and your mental forward-leaning energy.

2. If that example does not describe you, then perhaps this one might. You are halfway through your hamburger at the fast food restaurant. You silently calculate how many french fries remain and how many bites of hamburger are likely to be needed. You balance the timing of your future actions accordingly, carefully arranging life so the last bite

of hamburger will coincide with the availability of the last fry. When you are about to reach for the last fry, your dining companion says, "Oh here, I'm not going to finish mine. . . ." and dumps 11 more fries onto your plate. You are extremely annoyed at what otherwise should seem an act of generosity. Or worse still: Just as you are about to reach for that final fry, it is whisked away by your eight-year-old son. Your annoyance stems not from your need for food but from your need for long-expected closure.

3. I sing to you: "My country, 'tis of thee, sweet land of liberty, of thee I . . ." and I stop. You wait. I smile. You wait. If I do not complete the cadence with ". . . sing," the rest of your day may be unsettled. You may even feel compelled to supply the final note yourself. The need for closure can be completely compelling.

The sense of urgency toward completion in these incidents comes more from psychological than intellectual sources. Knowing or foreknowing the end as we do, we are not lacking any "information" at those moments. It is not a sense of mystery that spurs us on but rather a sense of psychological completion that we seek. We experience that same sense of closure (to some extent) in every sentence we read. As the sentence draws toward its end and as the mysteries of its syntactical puzzle are about to be resolved, we experience the closure of the task we have been seeking ever since we encountered the sentence's initial capital letter.

An understanding of this need can be of great help to writers. In the reading of any sentence (which, we recall, is infinitely interpretable), how does a reader go about deciding which particular piece of information to emphasize? If the choice depended entirely on logic or intuition or personal experience, different readers would be highly likely to make different decisions. That choice, however, actually depends to a great extent on the "instructions" for interpretation that accompany the sentence. The writer could send these instructions by printing the most important words in red -- but custom prohibits; or the writer could revive the nineteenth-century habit of printing a hand with a pointing finger in the margin of the text -- but dignity forbids. Instead, a major source of those instructions, I would argue, is our set of expectations for how the sentence must unfold -- for how the grammatical structure of the sentence will invite us further and further on, toward the grammatical act of completion. If the writer is aware that the Stress position -- the moment of grammatical closure at the end -- is a natural attractor of emphasis, the writer can know to fill that position consistently with the material intended for emphasis. That turns out to work surprisingly well.

There is nothing simple or mechanical about this advice. Nor is it merely cosmetic. In order for a writer to decide what to put in the Stress position, the writer must know or be ready to discover what it is she or he wants to emphasize. Examples will makes this more evident. Example (11) is a lengthy, detailed one -- but an important one. I urge you to read it with patience.

11a. A gross violation of academic responsibility is required to dismiss a tenured faculty member for cause, and an elaborate hearing procedure with a prior statement of specific charges is provided for before a tenured faculty member may be dismissed for cause.

(11a) is an unpleasant sentence at best. What makes it that way? Some would say it was "long," noting that its 41 words greatly exceed the 29-word limit suggested by Dr. Flesch's readability formula; but as we will shortly see, improved versions can come in all sizes, even extra-large. Others might complain of the repetition of information, or that there are too many concerns attended to for one sentence. None of these complaints, however, gets to the heart of what causes most readers to be annoyed when reading this sentence.

Let us investigate the problem more closely by noting what information is presented where. There are essentially five chunks of information in the sentence, which appear in the following order:

1) "a gross violation of academic responsibility"
    This is the substantive action of the tenured faculty member that must be discovered and proved if the university wishes to consider dismissal.

2) "to dismiss a tenured faculty member for cause"
    This is a severe action the university may wish to take.

3) "an elaborate hearing procedure"
    This is a procedure the university must offer the faculty member in order to end a tenured contract.

4) "a prior statement of specific charges"
    This is a prior part of that same procedure. Note that the reader's confusion is increased at this point, because this "second" procedural act must be accomplished "prior" to the first one. That is complicated to understand on first reading.

5) "to dismiss a tenured faculty member for cause"
    This is a repetition of information chunk #2.

Of these five, which is the backward-linking old information? From looking just at this sentence, it is hard to tell; but a reader of the whole document from which this is taken would know that for over a page now we have been hearing about "dismissing a tenured faculty member." Where should that information have shown up in this sentence in order to be of greatest help to the reader? -- right at the beginning, as chunk #1. It was not there, where we needed it, which causes a problem in itself. But then, after encountering it in the #2 slot, and after struggling through a great deal of other information, we find it located a second time at the sentence's end, where we had expected to find the new and important information. So not only did it fail to arrive in the Topic position, where we needed it, but it arrived for a second time, in the Stress position, where we are burdened by it. No wonder the sentence is annoying to read.

The repeated information causes an even more bothersome problem: Because it usurped the Stress position, we cannot know which of the other three chunks of information (the substantive #1 or the procedural #3 and #4) the writer intended us to emphasize. It could be #1; it could be #3; it could be #4; it could be ##3+4; it could be ##1+3+4. None of these were printed in red or bold type or italics or with underlining or with any other artificial indication of emphasis. The major indication of emphasis in the English sentence is supplied by the structural location of the information in a Stress position; but that position was filled with a second coming of the old, backward-linking information. In short, the sentence is a structural mess.

This kind of mess, however, can be cleaned up fairly readily. Old backward-linking information? Put it up front.

11b. In order for a university to dismiss a tenured faculty member for cause, . . .

Important information, most to be emphasized? Put it at the end. But which piece of information is that? As readers, we cannot tell. Only the writer knew for sure. Let us produce two rewrites -- one that emphasizes the substantive chunk #1, and another that favors the procedural chunks #3 and #4, combined. Both of these will be clearer and easier to process than the original; but they will produce markedly different statements.

Where then do we put the two procedural matters? We could put them in the middle, in an interruptive (and therefore less important) location:

11c. In order to dismiss a tenured faculty member for cause, a university, after presenting the charges and through conducting an elaborate hearing, must demonstrate a gross violation of academic responsibility.

However, if the rest of this paragraph does not concern those procedural steps, they could easily be omitted and introduced later, in plenty of time to make them the primary focus:

11d. In order to dismiss a tenured faculty member for cause, a university must demonstrate a gross violation of academic responsibility.

Let us say we have chosen this alternative and then discussed for a page or two the nature of that "gross violation," and that the time has come to switch topics and introduce the procedural requirements. Now all of revision (11d) becomes backward-linking old information and can exist helpfully at the beginning of a sentence, leaning forward to the arrival of the procedural matters in the Stress position.

11e. Even when a gross violation of academic responsibility has been demonstrated, a university may still not dismiss a tenured faculty member until it. . . .

But we have *two* procedural items to discuss. Can two items occupy one Stress position? That leads us back to the task of defining "Stress position" with more care. I offer two definitions -- one awkward, one neat.

The awkward definition: A reader has just entered the Stress position when it is clear that nothing is left in this sentence other than that which the reader is now reading. The Stress position might consist of a single word, or of a few words, or even of several lines; but in all cases the reader can sense that when this next bit is over, the sentence will also be over.

Two or more items can therefore be united into one Stress position as long as it is immediately clear that (1) these items can be made into a unit, and (2) this unit is the last thing in the sentence. One way of signaling the approach of such a unit is to create a list -- especially a numbered list. For example,

11e. Even when a gross violation of academic responsibility has been demonstrated, a university may still not dismiss a tenured faculty member until it (1) formally makes the faculty member aware of the specific charges, and (2) provides an elaborate hearing.

Note how the reader is more or less assured upon reaching the "(1)" that this numbered list is the only material remaining in the sentence. That first number signals that the Stress position has begun.

One of the worst things a writer can do to a reader is to promise a Stress position and then not deliver. For example, take a relatively readable sentence, replace the period with a comma, and keep on going:

11f. Even when a gross violation of academic responsibility has been demonstrated, a university may still not dismiss a tenured faculty member until it (1) formally makes the faculty member aware of the specific charges, and (2) provides an elaborate hearing, except in those cases which involve criminal activity, in which case. . . .

In many professional disciplines, this sort of expansion has become epidemic. Legal statutes, for example, are often made hopelessly complex and unreadable when the committees that write them feel compelled to attend to everyone's substantive needs but have no concept of the structural function of the Stress position. The resulting mess tends to sound something like this:

11g. Even when a gross violation of academic responsibility has been demonstrated, a university may still not dismiss a tenured faculty member until it (1) formally makes the faculty member aware of the specific charges, and (2) provides an elaborate hearing, in addition to which a calendar must be issued and an opportunity for all those who wish to be heard in the matter must be made available, except on alternate Thursdays if the university official in charge and the faculty member in question are both left-handed, but not when either is between the ages of 36 and 43, unless one or the other was born west of the Mississippi River, in which case. . . .

That is the "awkward" definition of the Stress position.

A reader's primary job at the sentence level is to understand the unfolding of its syntactical structure. If the reader cannot figure out a sentence's structure, the reader will not be able to understand its substance. As the sentence draws near to an end, there is a moment when the reader has the sense that it is all downhill from here. The mysteries of the structure have been sufficiently revealed. The time for closure is approaching -- the time when the reader feels, ". . . and now the job is *done*."

Now we can understand the "neat" definition: A Stress position is any moment of full syntactic closure.

> **Contemporary readers of American English sentences expect to find the most important information in a stress position. A stress position is any moment of full syntactic closure.**

Such moments occur not only at the end, with the advent of a period, but also within a sentence at the appearance of those marks of punctuation that are stronger than a comma -- the colon and the semi-colon. The more sophisticated and complex a thought becomes, the greater need there will be for the creation of multiple Stress positions in a single sentence.

Multiple Stress Positions

The simplest way to multiply Stress positions is to multiply sentences; But often that very separation destroys the sense of connection between stressed items the writer wished to emphasize.[12] Despite the claims of Plain English movements across the country, making one long sentence into two or three shorter ones is often an inappropriate remedy. We need to find ways to keep related information in a single sentence without crushing the reader under the resulting interpretive burden.

Since the Stress position is not simply "the end of the sentence" but rather any point of full syntactic closure, we can introduce a second (and third and fourth . . .) Stress position into a sentence if we can manage to construct in mid-sentence additional moments of full syntactic closure. To signal such closure to a reader, we need marks of punctuation stronger than dashes and commas; we need colons and semi-colons. Since our students are probably unsure of the nature of the colon and possibly altogether uninstructed in the art of the semi-colon, we may need to offer them a momentary grammar lesson. The following explanations have worked well for those in need of explanation.

The colon has two main uses. In both cases, that which precedes it must be able to stand by itself as a complete sentence. (Students may or may not need to know this is called an independent clause. It is the function, not the terminology that counts.) What follows the colon redefines what preceded it. In one case, the second unit is an independent clause that finds a different way of saying the same thing: The colon functions as a kind of "equals" sign. (This last sentence is an example of that which it defined.) For this use of the colon, the second dependent clause requires an initial capital letter. That capital allows the reader to know at a glance which kind of colon it is and what kind of syntactical unit has now begun.

As an example of this type of colon use, consider what would happen to the familiar disclosure statement we have grown used to seeing on a movie played at home on a VHS or DVD should a colon replace a period. We usually see this:

12a. This film has been modified from its original version. It has been formatted to fit your TV.

We know from the first sentence that they have somehow altered the film for home use; but we are not at all sure what they might have done. Have they edited out offensive language, or nudity, sexuality, or violence? We know from the second sentence that, whatever else they might have done, they have changed the formatted shape of the film so it will fit our television sets.

What difference would it make if the first period were to be replaced by a colon?

12b. This film has been modified from its original version: It has been formatted to fit your TV.

Now the second clause restates and further explains the first clause. Now we know the *only* change they have made is to alter the shape of the format.

The other, more commonly encountered use of the colon is to introduce a list of examples.

13. To give your reader the best chance of understanding what you have to say, pay careful attention to the major reader expectations: action-centered verbs; helpfully filled Topic positions; and importantly filled Stress positions.

Most grammar books tell us the members of such a list of examples should be separated by commas, unless one of the members itself contains a comma. I disagree. If the members of that list are so slight as not to deserve semi-colons (e.g., if they are only one word long), the sentence is better served not by a colon but by a double dash.

14. This model comes in three colors -- red, white, and blue.

Such a list does not deserve or need multiple Stress positions. If the examples are deserving of individual emphasis, the semi-colons will do a better job of indicating that need.

I warn students to avoid a misuse of the colon that has become accepted in contemporary publishing practice: I urge them not to use a colon after a verb when the clause has not yet been completed. Here is an example of this unfortunate trend.

15a. The four most important things to consider are:

    1. Wwwwwwwwwwwwwwww,

    2. Xxxxxxxxxxxxxxxx,

    3. Yyyyyyyyyyyyyyyy, and

    4. Zzzzzzzzzzzzzzzz. [Stress]

This sentence allows the reader only one Stress position, at the end. Because the introductory segment has no syntactic closure of its own, we as readers must "hang on" to it throughout the reading of the whole sentence. The reading experience is something like this:

15b. The four most important things to consider are

    1. Wwwwwwwwwwwwwwww, and they are

    2. Xxxxxxxxxxxxxxxx, and they are

    3. Yyyyyyyyyyyyyyyy, and they are

    4. Zzzzzzzzzzzzzzzz. [Stress]

If the opening segment is completed to be a full independent clause, then a Stress position is created at the colon; as a result, each of the examples stands by itself as a full syntactic unit (even though they are not independent clauses), thereby generating four more Stress positions. Each unit of the sentence has a mental breath unto itself. As such, the examples deserve semi-colons rather than commas.

15c.The four most important things to consider are the following: [Stress]

    1. Wwwwwwwwwwwwwwww; [Stress]

    2. Xxxxxxxxxxxxxxxx; [Stress]

    3. Yyyyyyyyyyyyyyyy; [Stress] and

    4. Zzzzzzzzzzzzzzzz. [Stress]

The semi-colon is by far the more interesting, sophisticated, and useful mark of punctuation. It requires some explanation. For me, when I was a teenager, the semi-colon was shrouded in mystery by my instructors in much the same way my parents had disguised anything that had to do with sex: "You're too young to need to know about this. You'll find out later." Unfortunately, when the time arrived that I needed to be able to use a semi-colon, there was no one around to offer the instruction.

Like the colon, the semi-colon, properly used, requires that the material preceding it be able to stand by itself as a whole sentence. As such, that first half-sentence establishes its own moment of syntactic closure; that moment is therefore validated as a medial Stress position. The material that follows the semi-colon must also be able to stand as a complete sentence (although certain introductory words like "but" are commonly allowed); thus, the end of the sentence brings with it a second moment of complete syntactic closure. The choice of this structure by the writer will affect the interpretive act of the reader. It makes a difference whether the information is conveyed in two separate sentences or in a single sentence that includes a semi-colon. The difference is essentially this: The presence of the semi-colon suggests there is such an intimate relationship between the two halves that they need to be locked together into the same grammatical unit. The first independent clause pauses to achieve its own emphasis; but it also promises that the even-more-interesting clause about to begin will combine with it to form a whole perhaps greater than the sum of its parts. That turns out to be the subtle rhetorical element for which most teenagers have not yet developed the need. The same information isolated in two sentences lacks this necessary sense of intimate relationship.

One of my favorite poets, Edwin Muir, dreamed the night before his death of nothing but a semi-colon. That dream works well as a metaphor through which to teach this function of the semi-colon: death as a semi-colon; the semi-colon as the moment of death. It seems plausible. At that moment of existence, the whole life unit that has long been underway now comes to full syntactic closure. It is over, finished, complete. However, says the semi-colon, there is a new unit about to begin -- equally a whole unto itself. It will combine with the former unit to produce a greater whole, one that is larger than the sum of its parts. The semi-colon says, "Make no mistake about it: You are undergoing full syntactic closure this very minute. But understand that this now-concluding unit is only a part of the story, a half of the story. Lean forward to experience the rest of the whole."

The colon tells the reader to expect a repetition-clarification of the first clause; but the semi-colon tells the reader to expect a continuation-complexification of the first clause. Both are significant tools, tools that signify.

By the skillful use of colons and semi-colons, a writer can extend a sentence to dozens of words without unduly burdening the reader. Here is a rewrite of the original 41-word sentence of example (11a) that extends to 55 words. Along the way, it succeeds in constructing four Stress positions, each marked by a major mark of punctuation (colon, semi-colon, or period).

11h. In order for a university to dismiss a tenured faculty member for cause, it must meet three requirements:

> 1) It must make the specific charges known to the faculty member in question;
>
> 2) It must then provide an elaborate hearing; and
>
> 3) In that hearing, it must prove that the faculty member is guilty of a gross violation of academic responsibility.

This revision stresses that all three requirements are necessary. It also suggests that they are the only three.

A comma can never produce an internal Stress position because its nature is antithetical to closure. All other English marks of punctuation announce their function at the time of their arrival. An exclamation point says "Wow!"; a question mark says "Huh?"; and a period says "Stop here." But the comma performs so many different functions and fills so many needs that in order to discover its function at a given point, we have to go beyond it to see just which kind of comma this one is. Is it part of a series? or signaling a brief interruption? or announcing the advent of a new independent clause? Since we always have to travel past the comma to recognize what kind of a comma it is, the comma can never provide the closure required to create a Stress position.

(11h) is not a "better" revision than (11d) or (11e); it is only more persuasive toward a particular interpretation. All three revisions have better chances than (11a) of being interpreted in a single way by a majority of readers. It is important that we stop giving students revision exercises that ask for a "best" answer. They only learn more deeply the false lesson that a particular sentence can be absolutely restricted in its meaning to one particular interpretation. Better by far to give them an assignment to create a number of revisions for each murky sentence, each revision intended to emphasize a different choice of interpretation. Our students will grow intellectually as they realize the subtlety of the medial Stress position and the power of the final Stress position.

We can now dispense with Dr. Flesch's concept that a sentence is "too long" when it exceeds 29 words. In its place we can offer a more reader-based definition: *A sentence is too long when it contains more viable candidates for Stress positions than it has Stress positions.* When that is the case, revision should be based on the principle of creating a Stress position for everything that needs to be stressed. Sometimes that requires separating one sentence into two; sometimes it requires combining individual pieces of information into cohesive lists; sometimes it requires creating appropriate conditions for colons and semi-colons. Beyond 29 words, a sentence does not become harder to read; it becomes harder to write.

Conversely, *a sentence is too short when it contains no viable candidate for the Stress position.* Many of our students have been taught that brevity and concision are virtues in and of themselves: The shorter and more compact a sentence is, the more clean, clear, and therefore powerful it will appear. We should abandon such advice, supplanting it with attention to the relationship between stressworthy information and the nature of Stress positions. If from among all the pieces of advice generated by this reader expectation approach I had to choose one as the most powerful and empowering, it would be this twofold combination:

Fill every stress position with something stressworthy;
and
ensure that everything stressworthy occupies
a stress position.

If our students do this on a regular basis, it will be hard for them to go wrong. They will always be telling us as pointedly as possible what is on their minds. We cannot make them more brilliant than they naturally are; but we can help them to express as fully as possible all the intelligence they already possess.

Think how much clearer written communication would have been all these centuries had color printing been invented by Gutenberg. Readers would have been so much more likely to understand what writers were trying to say if (for example) every "whose story" had been printed in green, every backward link in orange, every action in brown, and every piece of information requiring emphasis in red. Even in this age of inexpensive color printing, we are not likely to switch to such a system; but were we to do so, I would lobby, in addition, for all Stress positions to be printed in blue. That way, the best prose would always have the red words (worthy of stress) printed in blue Stress positions. No red words would appear elsewhere; and no Stress position would be left an unadulterated blue. The best prose, therefore, would be purple prose.

Perhaps most importantly, what begins as a revision tactic evolves into an invention procedure. After students "correct" sentence after sentence in which they have not put the important bit in the important place, they will become aware of the structural layout of their sentences as they create them. It will help them discover the important things they have to say. If in every sentence they write, they (1) link backward to the previous sentence, (2) announce whose story the sentence is meant to be, (3) articulate the action of the sentence in the verb, and (4) drive forward toward the moment of syntactic closure, where they will inform us of the most important thing on their mind, how far wrong can they go? For better and for worse, they will be regularly communicating, as precisely as possible, what is on their mind.

Remember, however, that different readers will interpret the same sentence differently. As a result, your students may quite reasonably disagree with each other and with you as to what "ought" to be stressed in any given sentence. You should not waste any time or energy "correcting" them. They are "right." They are expressing, accurately, how the sentence reads *to them*.

A related matter[13]: Many people have been taught over the years that it is improper in formal prose to use numbers or letters to mark the members of lists. I suspect this prohibition has something to do with our being trained to construct an outline form before writing anything formal. Most of us tended to build the entire outline first -- terribly annoyed that there always had to be a (B)(2) if you wanted to use a (B)(1) -- and then "write" the paper by making all those sentence fragments into full sentences, eradicating the numbers and letters, and pushing everything all the way to the left margin except for sometimes when we indented to show the beginning of a new paragraph and then we were through. (That's why those essays sounded as pedestrian as they often did.) I think we were taught to do away with numbers and letters because they were vestigial traces of the original outline, not intended for public view. I would have us reverse that teaching. We should use any such indications -- numbers, letters, dashes, bullets -- if they will help a reader perceive the structure of a unit of discourse more quickly and more surely. We will have overused them if their presence insults a reader who could competently have perceived the organization of the piece without the additional signposts.

In my work with adult professionals, I have discovered that many are still troubled concerning the concept of outlining. During a great many of my visits to law firms and corporations, I have been quietly and privately asked by some worried soul whether or not it is really necessary to make a carefully constructed numbered-and-lettered outline of everything you write "before you write it." Two answers to this question can potentially cause this worried questioner some pain: The first is "yes," because he may be suffering guilt from not having written a single outline since grade 12; the second is "no," since he may have spent about 11% of his professionally billable hours making surreptitious outlines which he then carefully destroyed. My answer to both such people is the same: It is absolutely essential to make a carefully constructed, numbered and lettered preliminary outline of everything you write if you cannot write without one; otherwise, don't bother. Use whatever method of initial organization makes you comfortable. You need not be a slave to a rigid form if that goes against your nature. Over-outlining can inhibit the later flow of the composition process. And no one in the working world is going to give you partial credit for a neat outline if the final document fails to do its job.

We return to the consideration of the Stress position: It would seem that the shorter and the more uncomplicated a sentence is, the less likely a reader would be to misconceive the writer's intended emphasis. In some ways, that is true; but as we have seen several times in previous chapters, even short sentences can be wide open to misinterpretation. It does seem to be the case, however, that the longer a sentence becomes, the more likely it is that emphasis will be misassigned by the reader in the absence of accurate structural clues. Here is an example that has proved a most interesting one over years of experimentation in classes and workshops.

16a. As used in the foundry industry, turn-key means responsibility for the satisfactory performance of a piece of equipment in addition to the design, manufacture, and installation of that equipment. P et al agree that this definition of turn-key is commonly understood in the foundry industry.

    I ask the participants (everyone from freshmen to long-established professionals) to rewrite this example based on one controlling principle -- that everything worthy of a Stress position have a Stress position created for it. (I urge you to make your choice of your Stress position candidates for this example before continuing.)

    Usually about 50% find themselves combining the two sentences into one. That is neither "right" nor "wrong"; but those who do it tend to argue that nothing in the second sentence is worthy of a Stress position.

    A sentence is a unit of discourse that is presumed to present at least a single point. If there is no information in a sentence worthy of the Stress position, then that unit of discourse is not worthy of standing by itself as a sentence. It ought to be demoted to a clause or phrase and inserted in some other sentence.

    In the second sentence of (16a), all the information is old information to us (repeated from the first sentence) except for the agreement of "P et al."[14] Those who try to combine the two sentences into one have made the judgment that P et al's agreement is not important enough a piece of information to warrant its own Stress position. (It is perfectly possible, of course, that P et al's agreement is the single most important piece of information in the entire document.)

    When asked what information might justify a Stress position spotlight, students and workshop participants vary a great deal in their responses. Here is a list of the usual candidates:

1) the foundry industry;
2) turn-key;
3) responsibility;
4) satisfactory performance;
5) satisfactory performance of a piece of equipment;
6) design, manufacture, and installation;
7) P et al;
8) agreement;
9) satisfactory performance, design, manufacture, and installation.

    Each of these is supportable. Each of these, highlighted with its own Stress position, would transform that sentence into something clearer than the original but significantly different from each of the other revisions.

    For each, the assumption is made that almost everything else in the sentence is either old information or is clearly subordinate in importance.

For example, "foundry industry" could conceivably be the only new piece of information and therefore worthy of the Stress position. That would require all the rest of the material to have been recently discussed in some detail -- a somewhat unlikely state of affairs, but not an impossible one.

16b. The significance of the term turn-key to indicate responsibility for the design, manufacture, installation, and satisfactory performance of a piece of equipment has long been recognized by the foundry industry. That industry has refined the definition even further by. . . .

Almost no one ever chooses the bland phrase "a piece of equipment." They laugh when I ask if it might be deserving of a Stress position. But then I point out to them that this most unstressworthy "piece of equipment" turned out to be the actual occupant of the original sentence's only position of Stress.

In this particular case, I know what the author intended. I know that in the only way I am capable of knowing it: He told me. Other than that, my guess would be no better, no worse than anyone else's. He intended us to stress "satisfactory performance." He had made an unsuccessful attempt to indicate to us the importance of that term by using the phrase "in addition to." Through those words, he intended us to note his segregation of "satisfactory performance" from the other three parallel terms, "design, manufacture, and installation." His clue failed because we encounter the clue words "in addition to" only *after* we have finished reading the words "satisfactory performance." Because of that misplacement, we could not have known that the words "satisfactory performance" were to be emphasized while we were in the act of reading them. Once lodged in our understanding as nonstressed, "satisfactory performance" had only modest chances of resurfacing as the star of the sentence. It is rarely the choice for stress for more than 25% of my students and clients.

It is possible to reconstruct the two sentences of (16a) into one sentence, building inexorably toward a Stress position occupied by "satisfactory performance." We must take care, dealing with so much information, that no word arrives without being preceded by a context in which the new arrival can make sense. Here is one possibility:

16c. As P et al agree, the foundry industry uses the word turn-key to signify responsibility not only for the design, manufacture, and installation of a piece of equipment, but also for its satisfactory performance.

This 34-word sentence poses no pressing problems of comprehension, even for a first-time reader. It accords with the three characteristics of good prose mentioned in Chapter 1:

-- Nothing arrives that cannot be handled the moment it arrives.

-- Everything leans forward.

-- Then everything actually goes in one of the directions in which it was leaning.

Once again, a slow-motion read might be helpful:

AS P ET AL AGREE, . . .

> They agree, do they? Well, on *what* do they agree?

. . . THE FOUNDRY INDUSTRY . . .

> What do they do?

. . . USES THE WORD TURN-KEY . . .

> What do they use it for?

. . . TO SIGNIFY RESPONSIBILITY . . .

> Responsibility for what?

. . . NOT ONLY FOR THE DESIGN, MANUFACTURE, AND INSTAL-
LATION OF A PIECE OF EQUIPMENT, . . .

> Ah, for *those* three things. But also for something else even more important, right?

. . . BUT ALSO FOR . . .

> And now we are going to get the big pay-off piece of information . . .

. . . ITS SATISFACTORY PERFORMANCE.

> Thank you. I get the picture. Now tell me more about "satisfactory performance."

It is possible to indicate to readers that stressworthy material is appearing in a sentence in a location other than the Stress position. Sometimes a phrase like "most importantly" can highlight information even in the depths of the sentence's middle. At other times, capitalization, italics, underscoring, or change of type font can readily attract attention where it otherwise would not be generated. Overuse of these non-structural possibilities can lead to problems.

Some writers find themselves constantly tempted to underline words they wish to appear emphatic. They are probably recognizing, half-consciously, that the words in question are not likely to receive sufficient emphasis from readers unless some artificial emphasis indicator is provided. I can offer two correlative suggestions: (1) If the underlined word or passage can easily be moved to the Stress position, the writer should usually prefer the structural emphasis (Stress position) to the synthetic emphasis (underlining). The Stress position is the more powerful indicator of the two; moreover, it does not condescend to the reader with a brassy "Look *here*, stupid." It also keeps the writer's mind more finely tuned into the writer's thought process. Here is a delicious example from that hope-raising but often disappointing nineteenth-century source of rhetorical wisdom, Alexander Bain:

> Both usage and reason agree in regarding the END of the sentence as the place of greatest strength or emphasis.[15]

This particular sentence, given its message, seems ill chosen as a moment for him to have expressed emphasis through capitalization rather than structural location.

(2) The second suggestion: Writers should feel no qualms about underlining words that, because of their syntactic functions, cannot smoothly be transferred to the Stress position and will not otherwise be likely to attract the reader's special attention. This is the case especially for pronouns and adjectives, words that are difficult to get to the sentence's end position. Here is one example:

> It matters not *how* you deliver this message, but only *that* you deliver it.

Here is another, lifted from Chapter 2:

> They are so caught up in trying to decide *how* these words could be made to come together to form a coherent unit that they are unable to feel confident in deciding *what* these words might mean.

It is also possible that new, important information appearing in the Stress position will be accorded too much stress.

> Dear Sir: You are fired.

Nothing is simple. The bad news was bad enough without the Stress position location making its finality yet more dramatic. There are occasions when tact calls for a writer to undercut a certain amount of a force's natural emphasis by locating a counterforce in the Stress position. Rules do not work.

In fact, every Reader Expectation can be violated to good effect. Our best writers are often our most skillful violators; but to violate successfully, you have to fulfill expectations most of the time, so the violation will appear as an intended, unusual effect.

Here is an example from a legal brief of just such a skillful violation. The question before the Court in this hearing was a simple one: Should the case be heard in Massachusetts or in New Hampshire?

> 17. In this case, the private interests of the litigants, the Bentham children, is best protected by a resolution of the issues in the New Hampshire Courts. The children's mother, Hannah Bentham, dealt with an insurance company, Christian Mutual, incorporated in New Hampshire, with a principle place of business in Concord, New Hampshire, and purchased a policy which was issued in the State of New Hampshire, administered in the State of New Hampshire, and the proceeds of which would be paid from the State of New Hampshire.

The first sentence highlights "New Hampshire" by placing it in the Stress position. There is no question which outcome this advocate is seeking. But the second sentence *also* has "New Hampshire" in the Stress position. Even "worse," "New Hampshire" shows up in this second sentence no fewer than five times. By the end of that sentence, has not this old information grown moldy? No: The multiple repetitions of "New Hampshire" say to the Judge, "Your Honor, *wherever* you look in this case, you keep bumping into New Hampshire. No matter where you start, you always wind up in New Hampshire. In this case, New Hampshire is inescapable. And therefore, the case should be tried in New Hampshire." Every reader expectation can be violated to good effect.

Fred and His Dog: Competition for Emphasis

As powerful as the Stress position may be in persuading a reader to perceive emphasis, it is not the only such persuader. The Stress position tends most to dominate attention when a sentence contains only a single clause. When more than one clause appears, each clause calls attention to itself, although with varying amounts of force. The effect of the whole depends on a number of factors. Consider the following set of sentences that contain essentially identical information:

18a. Although Fred's a nice guy, he beats his dog.

18b. Although Fred beats his dog, he's a nice guy.

18c. Fred's a nice guy, but he beats his dog.

18d. Fred beats his dog, but he's a nice guy.

For the purposes of investigating this example, I beg your indulgence. Just for the moment, please assume the following:

(1) It is a very bad thing to beat your dog; and (2) it is possible to be an otherwise nice person in spite of having the one bad attribute of being a dog-beater. I do not subscribe to the latter assumption; I just wish to establish an extreme good side and an extreme bad side to Fred, to demonstrate how the two combine with or play off each other in different rhetorical presentations.

I have worked through this example with more than 300 groups of people. The results have been the same in every case but one. Taking each sentence by itself, I ask the participants to determine whether the writer wants us to approve or disapprove of Fred and to indicate their decision by a show of thumbs up or thumbs down. Here are the stunningly consistent results.

18a. Although Fred's a nice guy, he beats his dog:

> Unanimous or nearly unanimous thumbs down on Fred.

18b. Although Fred beats his dog, he's a nice guy:

> Nearly unanimous thumbs up on Fred. Some people cannot abide the thought of even a fictional dog being beaten and therefore vote negatively or abstain. (There will be more on this difficult part of this example below.)

18c. Fred's a nice guy, but he beats his dog:

> Some up, some down, many hesitating to vote, and some demon-strating a vacillating hand motion of ambivalence; overall, somewhat more negative than positive.

18d. Fred beats his dog, but he's a nice guy:

> Same response as (18c), except the overall result is noticeably more positive.

The facts, the "data," remain the same throughout the four sentences; yet the votes indicate four different majority interpretations. Since the facts do not differ, the "instructions" for these consistently varying interpretations must be being sent by the structure in which the facts are differently deployed. In other words, the same facts in different structural locations produce different interpretations.

If your own thumb did not vote with the majorities indicated above, do not feel either that the example is flawed or that you are abnormal. There is always a minority vote. You are therefore part of a normal minority. The structural interpretive clues I am about to discuss do not generate reliable probabilities for predicting the decisions of any individual reader; but they seem to be remarkably reliable in predicting the response of a whole community of readers.

The Topic and Stress positions are *places* in the sentence. Locating information there generates certain kinds of effects. Fred and his dog bring us a new consideration: It is important not only *in what location* a piece of information may be but also *in what kind of unit of discourse*. It can even matter in what *size* unit of discourse.

When two clauses compete with each other for attention and emphasis, there are several structural/syntactical factors that influence the reader. Of these, three are dominant:

(1) End placement

   Readers tend to give greater emphasis to the final clause because it contains the Stress position.

(2) The "main" clause (as opposed to the "qualifying" clause)

   Readers emphasize the "main" clause because they expect it to contain the main thought. (I put quotation marks around "main" because in technical grammatical terms, a sentence may have two main clauses. By the term "main" I refer to the clause whose substance is not limited by a qualifier such as "but" or "although." The "main" clause is therefore distinguished from the "qualifying" clause.)

(3) Length

   A disparity in length between two clauses invites a reader to emphasize one at the expense of the other. More often than not, readers tend to give more emphasis to the longer of the two, perhaps because more reading time is expended on it. It is possible, however, for a shorter clause to dominate the reader's attention because it is so comparatively brisk and forceful.

The consistency of the communal judgments on Fred and his dog can now be explained. Since the clauses in each of the four sentences of example (18) are of approximately equal length, we need only consider the effects of emphasis derived from end placement and from inclusion in the main clause. The dominance of these two structural indicators explain why there is such widespread communal consistency in how Fred is viewed.

18a. Although Fred's a nice guy, he beats his dog:

    End placement: dog-beating

    Main clause: dog-beating

    Both indicators of emphasis are negative, thus explaining why almost all thumbs are down on Fred.

18b. Although Fred beats his dog, he's a nice guy:

    End placement: nice guy

    Main clause: nice guy

    Both indicators of emphasis are positive, producing mostly thumbs up for Fred. The vote is never quite as strong as the previous one because Fred's negative trait is so repellent. This is so even though the vote is based on whether or not the *author*, not Fred, is seeking approval of Fred.

18c. Fred's a nice guy, but he beats his dog:

    End placement: dog-beating

    Main clause: nice guy.

    The two indicators point in different directions. This explains the hesitation and uncertainty within certain individuals and the ambivalence of the group as a whole. Some follow one sign; some follow another; and others cannot decide which to follow. In general, however, the vote is decidedly more negative than positive. At first glance, it might seem that when the structural indications conflict like this, they might cancel each other. That, in turn, would allow the moral inequality of the two substantive matters to prevail: Dog-beating is a worse negative than being a nice guy is a good positive. That turns out not to be the case, as the vote on (18d) will demonstrate.

18d. Fred beats his dog, but he's a nice guy:

    End placement: nice guy

    Main clause: dog-beating

    The fact that the structural emphasis indicators once again diverge in their instructions accounts for another ambivalent response. But the response to this variation (18d) is consistently more positive than is the response to (18c). That suggests that the moral balancing of the substance, mentioned above, is not the controlling factor. Instead, the difference can be explained structurally: Whenever end placement and main clause compete with each other for attention, the slight edge goes to end placement. The attraction power of the main clause is not quite as strong as the attraction power of the Stress position. It is clear that this does not hold for individuals, for that would once again produce a unanimous vote. But it is just as clear (from the consistency of the outcomes) that it does hold for a community of readers taken as a whole. The end placement of a qualifying clause will not eliminate the influence of an earlier main clause; it only results in a higher percentage of influence than its competitor.[16]

Now let us complicate the matter by introducing the factor of length:

18e. Fred is a good husband, a caring father, a fine colleague, and an altogether nice guy, even though he beats his dog.

18f. Even though he beats his dog, Fred is a good husband, a caring father, a fine colleague, and an altogether nice guy.

Audience responses to these are just as consistent as those in the previous four examples: (18e) engenders great consternation and a good deal of inability to vote at all.

18e:	End placement:	dog-beating
	Main clause:	nice guy
	Length:	nice guy

We saw before, with sentences (18c) and (18d), that when end placement and main clause compete for attention, end placement wins a narrow victory, probably due to the power of the Stress position. What happens, then, when the influence of main clause is increased by combining it with the influence of length? Does that combination outweigh the end-placed clause, negating somewhat the power of the Stress position? Or will the Stress position maintain a certain dominance no matter what is placed in opposition to it? In practice, neither of these is the result. Instead, reading communities respond most keenly to the turmoil raised by the conflicts. They find themselves less able to come to conclusions of any kind. If after all that information about being a nice guy, Fred ends up beating his dog, then something is drastically wrong with Fred. He's conflicted. He needs help. It is the turmoil, the conflict, the friction that dominates the reader' attention.

Sentence (18f), on the other hand, usually generates unanimous thumbs up:

18f: End placement: nice guy

   Main clause: nice guy

   Length: nice guy

   All three indicators are positive. "Although Fred beats his dog, he is wonderful, wonderful, wonderful, wonderful." Fred for president! By the time the sentence ends, the dog has disappeared from view.

From these experiments we can provide the following examples of advice (not rules) for our students when they have created two clauses that compete for reader attention. The advice is based on the likelihood of what most readers will do most of the time. It cannot predict interpretive results for any individual reader.

(1) Let us say you are a member of Congress and must vote on the expensive and highly controversial MRX plan. You poll your constituents and find they are split 50-50 on the matter. With an election coming up, you feel you must take into account both of those strong feelings by demonstrating an energetic ambivalence. State your decision clearly in the main clause; but do not place that clause at the end. Let the risks attract the attention provided by the Stress position. The conflict between the two indicators will convey your ambivalence to a majority of your readers.

   19a. We should invest in the MRX plan, even though the risks are high.

(2) Perhaps instead of indicating ambivalence, you wish to indicate the firmness of your positive conviction; but you feel it would be irresponsible not to identify the risks. After articulating those risks clearly in a qualifying clause at the beginning, put your opinion into the main clause and place it at the end. The combined strengths of the two indicators will make your opinion seem firm to a majority of your readers.

   19b. Even though the risks are high, we should invest in the MRX plan.

(3) Instead of merely indicating your opinion, you may wish to agitate for it. Although you still feel the need to identify the risks, you do not want your audience to consider them as a counterbalance to the positives of the MRX plan. To accomplish this, put your opinion into the main clause, place it at the end, and beef it up with additional length. The combination of all three indicators will give your opinion a sense of urgency for a majority of your readers.

   19c. Even though the risks are high, we should draw upon whatever funds are available and invest in the MRX plan.

Shorter is not always better. Length can sometimes act as ballast.

Those are the three main structural indicators, but not the only ones. There are three others to consider.

i) As we noticed in Chapter 3, anything that intervenes between a subject and its verb tends to be read with less emphasis. Therefore, another way to undercut the power of a piece of information is to place it between the subject and the verb. Compare the following responses to a grant proposal:

20a. Although the all-encompassing scope is a great conceptual strength of the proposal, it might prove to be overly ambitious.

20b. The all-encompassing scope, though it might prove to be overly ambitious, is a great conceptual strength of the proposal.

There is good news and there is bad news. The bad news is the "overly ambitious" quality. In (20a), the bad news is left to burble and fester in the spotlight of the Stress position. In (120b), the same bad news is undercut significantly by being tucked away not only in midsentence but between a subject and a verb. Most people read (20b) as a much more positive statement than (20a).

ii) Nouns weigh more than pronouns. Names weigh more than references. If "Fred" is in one clause and "he" is in the other, the "Fred" clause carries a bit more weight. Most readers feel that (18g) is a yet more negative statement than (18a):

18a. Although Fred's a nice guy, he beats his dog.

18g. Although he's a nice guy, Fred beats his dog.

iii) I have argued that structure accounts for 85% of the interpretive instructions sent to the reader, while word choice only accounts for 15%. The ratio of 85 to 15 is not 100 to zero: Word choice still counts for something. If a word is strong enough, extreme enough, perhaps even outrageous enough, it can dominate a reader's attention. Let us make one change in Fred's personal history:

18h. Although Fred's a nice guy, he commits genocide.

No matter how I might rearrange the information into varying structural permutations, I would expect a unanimous thumbs-down vote at all times.

This does not mean, however, that structural variations, even with such inflammatory information, will not create differences in interpretation. Compare (18h) with (18i):

18h. Although Fred is a nice guy, he commits genocide.

18i. Although Fred commits genocide, he is a nice guy.

The slow-motion reading technique is again helpful in demonstrating the differences.

18h. although FRED IS . . .

> It is Fred's story. The verb *to be* suggests we are soon to hear something about him; but the "although" qualification suggests we will be hearing something markedly different about him in the next clause.

> . . . A NICE GUY,

> So there is Fred -- a smiling, attractive sort, at the moment. But expect to hear something less flattering coming up after the comma.

> . . . HE COMMITS

> Uh-oh, here it is. Commits what? Adultery? Tax fraud?

> . . . GENOCIDE.

> Boom! Fred is an unsalvageable moral reprobate.

Now change the structural order.

18i. ALTHOUGH FRED COMMITS GENOCIDE, . . .

> What do you mean "although" he commits genocide? How can there be any "although" about such a thing?

> . . . HE'S A NICE GUY.

> "Nice guy" cannot possibly mean here what it meant (momentarily) in (13h). No smiling, lovely Fred can emerge. The term "nice guy" is not simply descriptive but clearly sardonic or parodic.

Such examples are particularly helpful in persuading students not to digest these principles as rules but rather as descriptions of reader behavior. As thought becomes more complex, one expectation will collide more frequently with another. The writer's task is to choose not only "the right words" but also the most efficacious structure, one that will *tend* toward persuading the largest percentage of readers possible to interpret the discourse as the writer intended.

Once again, the distinction between rules and descriptions of reader behavior is a crucial one. All the founding fathers of the accepted methods of teaching composition -- Hugh Blair in the eighteenth century, Richard Whately and Alexander Bain in the nineteenth -- perceived the relationships between clauses I have suggested above; but they all were quick to rigidify these perceptions into dogma. Here is one example from Bain:

> The distinction between principal and subordinate in a sentence, paragraph, etc., is marked by comparative length in the statement. . . . As in a state procession, the greatest space is accorded to the highest dignitaries, so the principal matter of a sentence is distinguished by the length of the expression. Hence the necessity of the condensing arts in the wording of subordinate clauses.[17]

Since length indicates emphasis, he tells us, and since principal clauses indicate emphasis, then, he rules, you should always make your principal clauses longer than your subordinate ones. Elsewhere he insists that "It is a law of economical thinking, that qualifying circumstances should precede what they are meant to qualify."[18] When we combine these two pieces of advice, we find that we must "always" construct a two-clause sentence by placing the briefest form of the qualifying clause first and the artificially elongated principal clause last. Bain apparently did not trust his minions to be able to work with varying structures and produce varying effects.

As another of his examples, Bain quotes a famous line from Bacon:

A crowd is not company, and faces are but a gallery of pictures, and talk but a tinkling cymbal, where there is no love.

Whether this sentence is a "good" one or a "bad" one, it is a memorable one for the effects it succeeds in creating. Here are Bain's comments on it:

Most readers will take the three statements in their broad generality, without suspecting the serious limitation, till it comes in at the end; and so the meaning of the sentence has to be reconstructed in the mind. This awkward effect would be entirely prevented by simply placing the condition at the beginning.[19]

His first sentence strikes me as perceptive; but its usefulness is undone by the conclusion that follows it. Bain assumes there exists a "best" way of arranging Bacon's words. He predicates that on the assumption that he knows the truth behind what Bacon was trying to say. The very "reconstruction" of which he speaks -- due to the surprise appearance of "where there is no love" -- might well have been precisely the dramatic effect Bacon was seeking to produce. Bacon's sentence emphasizes "no love" by reserving for it the climactic Stress position. Bain's suggested revision undoes that and transforms "no love" into the contextualizing material for the rest of the sentence.

Where there is no love, a crowd is not company, and faces are but a gallery of pictures, and talk but a tinkling cymbal.

This version is more calm, more settled, and less dramatic. Neither by itself is better than the other; they just perform different kinds of persuasive acts.

Difficult though it may be, we would do well to resist the temptation to make value judgments of all these examples and revisions. Instead of preferring one Fred/dog sentence to another, we would do better to limit ourselves to demonstrating the ways in which they differ. Students will probably be persistent in trying to ascertain which is the "right" version. We should get them instead to ask "right for whom?" and "right for what purpose?"

On page 86, we encountered Stanley Fish analyzing in slow motion the following sentence:

That Judas perished by hanging himself, there is no certainty in Scripture.

Later in his article he reverses the sentence's two clauses and performs a slow-motion Fred/dog examination of his own.

"There is no certainty that Judas perished by hanging himself."

> Here the status of the assertion is never in doubt because the reader knows from the beginning that it is doubtful; he is given a perspective from which to view the statement and that perspective is confirmed rather than challenged by what follows; even the confusion of pronouns in the second part of the sentence will not be disturbing to him, because it can easily be placed in the context of his initial response. There is no difference in these two sentences in the information conveyed (or not conveyed), or in the lexical and syntactical components, only in the way these are received. But that one difference makes <u>all</u> the difference -- between an uncomfortable, unsettling experience in which the gradual dimming of a fact is attended by a failure in perception, and a wholly self-satisfying one in which an uncertainty is comfortably certain, and the reader's confidence in his own powers remains unshaken, because he is always in control. It is, I insist, a difference in meaning.

Notice that he does not *value* the "comfortable" one more; he just points out the difference between the two. Were I to adapt his final sentence for the purpose of teaching composition, it would read, "It is, I insist, a difference in the structural forces that are at work persuading readers who are in the process of making interpretive decisions."

It does not take much practice or application for my students/clients to get the hang of manipulating Fred and his dog, whenever they encounter them. (And it is remarkable how often Fred and his dog show up in the prose of professionals, whose job so often is to make delicate balancing decisions.) The exercises that work the best are not the "right/wrong" examples but the "vary for different effect" examples. Here is one from a federal funding agency's letter of decision, telling a scientist of the results of his grant application. Judith Swan and I took a balancing sentence (some good news, some bad news) and created three permutations on it. Then we asked our audience of professionals at the funding agency to give a score for the proposal, assuming the value judgment indicated in this sentence was equivalent to the value judgment of the proposal as a whole. We asked them to rank the proposals by percentages, with 1% being the top, 99% being the bottom, and 15% being the funding cutoff level.

21a. This is an exciting, but somewhat flawed application from a creative investigator.

Their judgment: Not bad, not good. About the 50th percentile.

The bad news ("somewhat flawed") is hidden in the middle. It is only part of a phrase and does not have a whole clause to itself. However, "flawed" gets to live right next door to "application," making the application sound more flawed than exciting. The good news is similarly mixed in effect. The Stress position is filled with a compliment, but it is to the investigator, not to his application; and it is the application that will receive or fail to receive funding.

21b.   This creative investigator has produced an exciting but somewhat flawed application.

Their judgment: The score, compared to (21a), goes way down -- sometimes as far as the 70th percentile.

The Stress position is filled with the bad news. It is the "story" of a good guy ("creative investigator"), who for a brief moment in the middle of the sentence has done a good thing ("exciting"); but before the noun modified by "exciting" can arrive, the bad news intervenes and takes most of the excitement out of it.

21c.   This creative investigator has produced a somewhat flawed but exciting application.

Their judgment: The score goes up, not only above (21b) but also above (21a) -- often all the way to the 25th percentile.

The good news ("exciting") gets to live right next door to "application." Together, that most uplifting combination of words luxuriates in the Stress position. The bad news ("somewhat flawed") is not at the end and is immediately undercut by the "but." The sentence begins with good news and ends with better news. The flaw in the application will still keep it from reaching the funding cutoff level of the 15th percentile.

21d.   This creative investigator has produced a somewhat flawed but truly exciting application.

Their judgment: Bingo. This one rises above the 15% level and gets funded.

The addition of the semantic marker "truly" adds positive weight in two ways: (1) It intensifies the adjective "exciting," suggesting an over-the-top reaction; and (2) it structurally balances the adjective "somewhat," thereby making the word sound mild or even petty. The application may be "somewhat" flawed; but it is, in the Stress position here, "truly" exciting. A touch of semantics and a dash of structure suggests the check is in the mail.

A pedagogical note -- dog-beating revisited: I am aware that the beating of Fred's dog -- fictitious though it may be -- causes a certain amount of discomfort for many people. I retain the example, with some hesitation, for good reason. I have often had the opportunity to watch novitiate graduate students try to teach these balancing principles to a freshman composition class. Sometimes the graduate student, put off by the very mention of a dog being beaten, changes the example by substituting some other character flaw for Fred. The results usually get confused and confusing. "Fred's a nice guy," one graduate student tried, "but he cheats on his golf score." Most of the Duke undergraduates voted positively for Fred at all times. Another tried ". . . but he cheats on his taxes." Still there were constantly solid majorities for Fred throughout the process. The example requires a definitive positive and a definitive negative. Few such distinctions exist in our pluralistic academic society. The lack of contamination of "nice guy" and the outrageousness of "beats his dog" together do the trick. The silliness of the fiction (why would one bother to defend such a negative by positing that kind of positive?) allows the rhetorical principles to dominate our attention.

Grammar and Spelling, Too

Descending from the abstract to the mundane: Structural considerations often allow us to remediate students' grammar without having to take recourse to brute force. I had a colleague who threatened that she would fail any paper that contained even a single comma splice. Quite regularly, no comma splice ever appeared in her students' work -- but more from fastidious proofreading by roommates than from suddenly developed grammatical skills of the authors. If students simply cannot *hear* a comma splice, telling them they are inferior for not hearing it will probably not help. Why not substitute for the negativity of prohibition the positive possibility of better controlling reader interpretation? Here is a delightful comma splice from a recent freshman:

22a. If I am not sure, I will revise the sentence using a conjunction, then I know where to put the comma.

Pride goeth before a fall: In the very sentence in which he boasts of his control of the common comma, he commits a comma flaw. Could he hear the problem? Probably not. Telling him to listen harder would most likely have been futile. Instead, I asked him structural questions: Which pieces of information in this sentence did you want your reader to emphasize? Which therefore deserve a Stress position? He chose both "using a conjunction" and "put the comma." I advised him to create the necessary second Stress position. He did not like the option of creating two sentences:

22b. If I am not sure, I will revise the sentence using a conjunction. Then I know where to put the comma.

"Baby prose," he said. The two halves of his original sentence seemed to him in need of an intimate relationship. The effective solution: a semicolon.

22c. If I am not sure, I will revise the sentence using a conjunction; then I know where to put the comma.

By discovering the use of the semi-colon to create internal Stress positions, he had learned not how to obey a new rule but how to use a new power. Most comma splices disappear if everything stress-worthy resides in a Stress position.

The same kind of advice works to facilitate student comprehension of any number of grammatical problems: the need for capital letters; the proper use of commas before the "and" that joins two independent clauses; the proper omission of a comma before the "and" that joins an independent clause to a dependent clause; the function of the apostrophe; paragraph indentation; and many more.[20] This in turn helps isolate those details of our grammatical system that are strictly conventional from those that make logical sense. The merely conventional grammatical rules are then easier to memorize as isolated illogical instances in an otherwise logical and mostly coherent system. For example, it helps to know that both American and British rules are equally nonsensical concerning the placement of quotation marks relative to commas and periods. In America, those two punctuation marks always come within the quotes; in Great Britain, they always come without. Strangely, both countries use a logical rule for placement of quotation marks relative to semi-colons, colons, question marks, and exclamation points: If the punctuation is part of the quote, it is placed within the quotes; if it is not part of what is being quoted, it must follow the quotation marks. It is helpful to students to winnow out these examples of strict conventionality from the much larger number of grammatical usages that function as inciters of reader expectation.

An example of the latter is the grammatical comma rule for sentences that contain two long clauses conjoined by an "and." The rule is simple enough: If both clauses are independent clauses, a comma before the "and" is required; if one of the two is a dependent clause, then no comma is permitted. Teaching that as a bit of rote memorization will not work as well as teaching it in terms of reader expectations.

23a. Ted grew zucchini and thought it a good thing.

23b. Ted grew zucchini, and Alice detested him for it.

Instead of ruling whether or not *the writer* should put a comma before the "and," we can talk about what happens to *readers* when they find or do not find a comma there. In (23a), the lack of comma before the "and" warns a reader *not* to close down at that point. After the "and," the reader must expect material that will depend syntactically on a connection to something before the "and." In this case, the verb "thought" will make no sense unless the reader retains in active memory its subject, "Ted." The lack of comma keeps our memory of Ted alive and functioning.

In (23b), the comma tells the reader that "Ted grew zucchini" is a story complete unto itself. In addition, it promises that whatever comes after the "and" will also be able to stand by itself as a complete syntactical unit.

It comes as no surprise, therefore, that both the story and the agency shift after the "and" from Ted to Alice. Had the comma been omitted, "Alice" might have appeared at first as a possible (although illogical) second object for the verb "grew": "Ted grew zucchini and Alice . . . ." Reader energy would be unnecessarily expended in recognizing that "Alice" is an inappropriate object of Ted's verb "grew."

This structural approach also gives us a better way of explaining to students why spelling is so important and why "neatness counts." We usually tell them that if they clutter their papers with typographical errors and spelling mistakes, they will appear to readers to be uncaring or intellectually inferior. That may well *be* the case; but that explanation fails to *explain* the case. Readers summon only that amount of reader energy they consider necessary for making it through the particular unit of discourse they are presently engaged in reading.[21] (How many of us ascertain the number of pages of an article before we plunge into reading it? It makes sense to be prepared.) A reader should be called upon to expend no more reading energy than that required to perceive the intended message. If a reader constantly encounters typographical errors adn speling mistakes, reader energy is wasted in making the mental "corrections." It may be clear that "adn" is really the word "and" mistyped; but the energy necessary to make that adjustment comes out of the energy that could have been used for perceiving the sentence's structure and substance. *Anything* that distracts the reader, no matter how trivial, has the bad effect of raising the odds that the reader will misinterpret the writer's intended communication.

Summary

Here again are the boxes.

STRCT — TOPIC		STRESS	FIXED
SUBS — OLD, FAMILIAR INFORMATION ←		NEW, IMPORTANT INFORMATION !!!!!!	MVBL
STRCT — W.S.? SUBJECT	VERB	COMPLEMENT	FIXED
SUBS — AGENT	ACTION	GOAL	MVBL

The two lower boxes deal with the sentence as an isolated unit. The upper two boxes deal with the sentence itself but, more importantly, with the connections sentences make with each other. (The next chapter investigates the intersentence connections in great detail.)

The Topic and Stress positions are not things; they are places, fixed by definition. As locations, they engender relatively fixed expectations on the part of readers:

1) Readers tend to read a clause or a one-clause sentence as being the story of whoever or whatever shows up first.

2) Readers tend to read a multi-clause sentence as being the story of whoever or whatever shows up first in the main clause.

3) Readers expect and desire sentences to begin with that piece of "old information" that makes the appropriate link backward to the sentence they have just finished reading.

4) Readers expect that material to the left contextualizes anything that comes to its right. Readers expect that the occupants of the Topic position -- especially the backward link and the "whose story" person, thing, or idea -- contextualizes the reader for the rest of the sentence.

5) Readers expect that the most important piece(s) of new information in a sentence will appear in a Stress position.

6) Readers expect that every Stress position will contain material worthy of the emphasis they naturally tend to expend there.

Although the boxes are a powerful teaching tool, they raise the danger of being oversimplified by students. A few warnings are necessary. First, although the dividing lines within the boxes seem to be fixed at particular points, no suggestion is intended that those space proportions are fixed quantities. Only rarely will the subject, verb, and complement of a sentence occupy precisely one third of its "space." Either the Topic or Stress position may be as short as a single word or as long as several lines; they seldom occupy exactly the proportion of the sentence as their boxes indicate.

Second, the boxes, appearing as they do in print, must necessarily remain two-dimensional. To reflect the realities of prose, they really should be three-dimensional -- or even four-dimensional.

Third, the Topic/Stress boxes do not easily allow for the visualization of sentences that contain more than one clause. Placed above the S-V-C level as they are, they suggest that there can be only one Stress position in a sentence. This is not a serious enough drawback to invalidate the use of the boxes; it is something, however, that must be pointed out to students.

Fourth, the placement of old and new information on the substance level of the upper boxes suggests that all old information belongs at the front and all new information at the end. That would be an impossibility. The blank spaces must by definition always be filled with information that is either old or new: There is no other kind of information.[22] The piece of old information that functions best in the Topic position is that which best links the reader backward to previous discourse. (Hence I have added a backward-facing arrow to the SUBS box under the Topic position.) Often one has to choose between many pieces of old information in deciding which should come first -- and what the order of the rest will be. Conversely, the new information that deserves the Stress position is the *most important* piece of new information -- the one worthy of stress. (Hence I have added exclamation points to the SUBS box under the Stress position.) There may be a great deal other new information in the sentence that is worthy of a Stress position.

Therefore, we should not tell students to put old information in the Topic position and new information in the Stress position, as the boxes might suggest. Instead we should tell them to put in the Topic position *that piece* of old information that *makes the appropriate link backward*; and we should tell them to put in the Stress position *that piece* of new information that *deserves emphasis*. The most important printed marks in these boxes, therefore, are the backward-linking arrow and the series of exclamation points.

"Save the best for last" sounds proverbially convincing; but so does the equally proverbial "First things first." Does my advice about the use of the Stress position conflict with the journalist's advice that in a newspaper article, the most important things should come first, followed by the second most important thing, and so forth, until nothing important is left to be said? Not at all. I agree with the journalist; but the journalist is dealing with a unit of discourse known as the newspaper article; I am dealing here with the unit of discourse known as the sentence.

We have a firm expectation that a newspaper article will begin with its most important matters. Any other arrangement would cause us unending inconvenience and annoyance, because few of us reach the end of every article we begin. Either we lose interest, or the phone rings, or our bus stop comes, or we cannot find page 17. Were newswriters to leave the important information for the end, we would all tend to read newspaper articles backward. The journalists are therefore serving their readers well by putting first things first.

A sentence is a different affair altogether. Anyone who begins one of our sentences is likely to be around at its conclusion. They may depart shortly thereafter, but usually not in midstream. As a result, we can afford to delay the gratification until the last moment, where it will resound with an accumulated resonance. There is no place quite like the end.

Endnotes

1. A writer can alter a reader's S-V-C expectation in any given sentence by sending semantic or structural signals that give warning of that alteration. For example, a grammatical object followed by the grammatical subject can be "heard" quite readily: "Money most people never think they have in excess." (The lack of a verb directly after "Money" or after "most" suggests that "Money" cannot function as the sentence's subject.) There are no rules involved here -- only expectations based on what generally occurs.

2. These five sentences, to the best of my knowledge, were the creation of Frank Kinahan, one of the original founders of the Clearlines group that included Joseph Williams, Gregory Colomb, and myself.
3. The *range* of possibilities may narrow in the sense that the further we proceed in the sentence, the easier it becomes to discard certain interpretive possibilities. But the narrower range still contains an infinite number of possible interpretations, since there is still an infinite number of interpreters available to read it and an infinite number of directions in which to go from there. We are dealing, then, with the probabilities of interpretation, not with an approach to some objectively "right" single interpretation.
4. Stanley Fish. "Literature in the Reader: Affective Stylistics." Chapter 1 of *Is There a Text in This Class?* (Cambridge: Harvard University Press, 1980), p. 27.
5. This rigid five-paragraph theme format, together with its self-similar five-sentence paragraph components, is actually the focus of North Carolina state law. Middle school English teachers are forced to feed these formulae to their students. The students are tested by the state at the year's end; if a class demonstrates an unfamiliarity or incompetency with these formats, the teacher may not be rehired.
6. Please note the subtle but important distinction between "whose story" a sentence is and what is to be considered "most important" about the story as a whole. A great majority of readers would read both (5a) and (5b) as Jones's story; but an equally great majority would hear (5a) as emphasizing the high-volume radio and (5b) as emphasizing the constant complaining. This will be explained in detail later in the chapter; you will be referred back to this point by endnote #16 to this chapter.
7. To judge the work of Rudolph Flesch for yourself, see any of the following: *The Art of Clear Thinking* (New York: Harper's, 1951); *The Art of Plain Talk* (New York: Macmillan, 1962); *The Art of Readable Writing* (New York: Harper & Row, 1974); *How to Write Plain English: A Book for Lawyers and Consumers* (New York: Harper & Row, 1979); *How to Write, Speak, and Think More Effectively* (New York: New American Library, 1964).
8. The difference is even more noticeable when this sentence is returned to its context. Now two consecutive sentences will begin with the story of "the School Board's permission." We will deal with such multi-sentence examples later in this chapter and throughout Chapter 5.
9. A "passive story" is simply the story of anyone or anything that is not in control of the named action. It is always a question of perspective. "Senator X won the election" is an active story about Senator X; "the election was won by Senator X" is a passive story about the election. The two sentences may call upon the same facts -- but they tell two different stories.
10. I can think of one particular case in which "write the way you peak" may be good advice: It can help the writer who is so overly conscious

of the formal requirements of written discourse that he or she litters the page with convoluted syntax and rented vocabulary, making it impossible for a reader to discover what is being communicated. "Write the way you speak" can help unstuff this particular shirt; but once that is accomplished, the advice ceases to be of help. To be clear and effective, writing must be more than unstuffy.

11. Kenneth Burke, *Counter-Statement*, page 45.

12. Here is the first sentence of this paragraph once again:

> The simplest way to multiply Stress positions is to multiply sentences; but often that very separation destroys the sense of connection between stressed items the writer wished to emphasize.

Note how the sense of cohesion -- of "oneness of thought" -- can be diminished by separation into two sentences:

> The simplest way to multiply Stress positions is to multiply sentences. But often that very separation destroys the sense of connection between stressed items that the writer wished to emphasize.

13. Note the colon is used here after a unit that is not an independent clause. To this point, I have discussed only the formal use of the colon in which the first unit must be able to stand by itself as a complete sentence. There are other, less formal (but still acceptable) uses of the colon. Primary among them is the non-clause introducer of an example. This can be used safely when there is no significant chance of ambiguity.

> "An important note: One should never make categorical statements about. . . ."

It would be unnecessary or even burdensome to have said, "Here is an important note:" or "An important note is this:". No rules, only effects.

14. "P et al" may well be old information as well, though they did not appear in the previous sentence. They might have played a prominent part in the cast of characters throughout the entire piece of discourse.

15. Alexander Bain. *English Composition and Rhetoric*, enlarged edition (New York: American Book Company, 1887), page 4.

16. This explains further the distinction attended to in endnote #6 above (to page 88). The Topic position controls "whose story" it is; the Stress position controls the focus of emphasis.

17. Bain, page 49.

18. Bain, page 2.

19. Bain, page 2.

20. For a detailed exploration of English punctuation perceived from the reader's perspective, see Chapter 6 of my textbook, *The Sense of Structure: Writing from the Reader's Perspective*.

21. This pronouncement sounds at first simpler than it proves to be in practice. A reader of a clause is simultaneously a reader of a sentence, paragraph, subsection, section, and complete document. That

complexity intensifies the need for the reader's energy not to be wasted in the effort to correct grammatical and typographical errors.

22. No information is either old or new by definition or nature; it is only old or new by reader perception and interpretation. Even the repetition of a particular word cannot be defined as old information for the reader who perceives it to mean something quite distinct from the meaning it had in its previous appearance.

C H A P T E R

5

Using Topic/Stress to Control Development Within the Paragraph

O *vercoming Splat Prose*

To this point, we have been investigating the Topic and Stress positions primarily for the way they influence reader attention within a given sentence. While they are more than useful for such purposes, their real power emerges when we discover how they control the flow of thought from sentence to sentence. As the sentences roll by, the effect becomes cumulative. When Topic and Stress positions are consistently well filled, they make the shape of a paragraph's development more easily perceivable. When they are consistently structured in ways that violate readers' expectations, they often produce a shapeless product I call *splat prose*.

Splat prose results from writers not understanding the structural needs of readers. The reader presents an empty plate to the writer, interested to see how the writer will fill it up. The writer drops a sentence onto the plate -- splat -- and then another, fully formed but not clearly connected -- splat -- and then another of the same -- splat. With this delivery comes the implicit instruction, "*You* figure out what to do with these." Each sentence by itself may be grammatically and even substantively respectable; but together they fail to suggest specific ways in which the reader should connect them to form a whole, developing train of thought.

An example:

1a. A disease that progresses with few or no symptoms to indicate its gravity is an "insidious" disease, under this definition. Asbestosis, neoplasia, mesothelioma, and bronchogenic carcinoma are all examples of insidious diseases. Asbestos insulation installers who have inhaled asbestos fibers over a period of many years regularly contract these diseases.

If we were to limit ourselves to the kinds of responses writing teachers traditionally relied upon throughout most of the twentieth century, we could find little to say that would help the writer revise this paragraph and do a better job in creating future paragraphs. We can point to no grammatical errors, no diction problems, no lack of research, and no lack of effort. We can hardly offer an "unclear" or an "awk."

Despite that, serious problems pervade this paragraph. The individual sentences may sound relatively unobjectionable; but the writer has failed to provide the reader with sufficient instructions for connecting the second sentence to the first, or the third to the second. As a result, the intended shape of the whole paragraph has not been made evident to the reader. In the past 25 years, we have made good progress in teaching paragraph unity and coherence. Here is yet another way to approach these crucial concerns.

Let us start with a set of related questions: Do the frightening-sounding diseases of the second sentence exemplify the general definition of "insidious disease" offered in the first sentence? Do they refer to the specific diseases contracted by the unfortunate workers in the third sentence? Or do they do both? That second sentence simply *exists* between the first and the third; we cannot be sure how it was intended to connect backward and forward; yet those connections turn out to be an essential part of what this paragraph was trying to communicate.

If we revise these three sentences based solely on the Topic/Stress principles derived in the last chapter, we can begin to perceive some of the writer's intentions and realize how far we are from perceiving others. Sentence by sentence, we will ask which piece of new information deserves the most emphasis; then we will find a way to move it to the Stress position. We will ask whose story each sentence is, and which pieces of old information connect the sentence backward to previous discourse; as we have done before, we will find a way to move those pieces of information where they will be of most help, to the Topic position. After we do that for each of three sentences, we will take a look at the new paragraph that has resulted.

The first sentence:

1b. A disease that progresses with few or no symptoms to indicate its gravity is an "insidious" disease, under this definition.

The old information announces itself: "under *this* definition." The "this" indicates that a definition had been the subject of discussion prior to this sentence. At the moment, this backward-linking old information occupies the Stress position, which for the reader is *doubly* unhelpful: (1) The information is not up front in the sentence, where it can make the appropriate connection backwards; and (2) it is usurping the Stress position from the information the writer wanted emphasized. It can be moved to the Topic position with ease:

1c. Under this definition, a disease that progresses with few or no symptoms to indicate its gravity is an "insidious" disease.

Note that this new sentence, (1c), does not *sound better* than sentence (1b). We have to get our students to stop relying on the *ear* as their primary judging device. We have to get them to use the eye and the mind instead.

Now we turn to sentence (1c)'s newly created Stress position. Is "insidious diseases" the proper occupant? Or should we rather favor its definition, "a disease that progresses ... to indicate its gravity"? Most people again rely upon the ear to make that decision; but again the ear again will be insufficient as a guide. Instead, we have to ask which of these two, the term "insidious diseases" or its definition, was intended by the writer for us to emphasize. With the question put that way, we realize we are not able to answer it -- at least not within the confines of this single sentence. If the paragraph continues to focus on the *story* of "insidious diseases," then "insidious diseases" deserves the spotlight of this Stress position. Having called attention to the term in this way, we could switch it to the "whose story" location in the next sentence's Topic position, and we would be on our way. If, on the other hand, the paragraph proceeds to refine the *definition* of insidious diseases, showing in more detail how it "progresses" with "few symptoms" that "show its gravity," then that material deserves the Stress position so it may take over the "whose story" position in the next sentence. Since we have not enough information in the first sentence to make this decision, let us, for the moment, leave revision (1c) as it is. We shall return when we have revised the other two sentences.

The second sentence:

1d. Asbestosis, neoplasia, mesothelioma, and bronchogenic carcinoma are all examples of insidious diseases.

Once again, the old information is distinctly recognizable (although too late, on first reading): We have heard about "insidious diseases" before. Once again, the old information is doubly unhelpfully located in the Stress position. Once again, we can easily move it to the Topic position:

1e. Examples of insidious diseases are asbestosis, neoplasia, mesothelioma, and bronchogenic carcinoma.

Since the four intimidating diseases are all that is left in the sentence, they stake a reasonable claim to the Stress position. They deserve a Stress position, however, *only* if they are so important that we must keep them in mind for future usage. If that is not the case -- if they are only a "by the way, here are four examples whose names you need not remember" kind of lot -- then *nothing* in this sentence was worthy of the Stress position.[1] In that case, this information should be transplanted to some other sentence (e.g., "Insidious diseases, which include a, b, c, and d, . . .") In that case, leaving them in the Stress position would unduly burden the reader with a pointless task of memory.

Sentence (1e) is in no way superior to sentence (1d) as an isolated sentence, but only in the context where "insidious diseases" acts as the backward-linking old information. We shall soon be able to judge whether (1e) is an improvement over (1d) in the context of the resulting new paragraph.

The third sentence:

1f. Asbestos insulation installers who have inhaled asbestos fibers over a period of many years regularly contract these diseases.

Yet once again the old information arrives too late: We have heard about "insidious diseases" before. Once again, it usurps the Stress position and can be moved to the Topic position:

1g. These diseases are regularly contracted by asbestos insulation installers who have inhaled asbestos fibers over a period of many years.

Once we are attuned to this structural concern, we might ask, with some annoyance, "Can't the author *hear* that she's ending every sentence with the backward-linking old information?" The answer, of course, is "no." Until one understands the importance of these structural locations, one is unaware of one's own structural patterns.

If we try to select the right piece of new information for this Stress position, we can identify the following candidates:

a) "installers";
b) "asbestos fibers";
c) "asbestos insulation"; and
d) "over a period of many years."

Not being the author, we have no way of determining which of these four was intended to prevail; the structure of the original sentence gives us no clue which to prefer, since none of them were printed in red or boldface or capitals or italics or -- which is by far the most common mode of indicating emphasis -- in the Stress position.

At this moment of our revision, the Stress position is occupied by "over a period of many years." Question: If "over a period of many years" is indeed the best choice for the Stress position here, what would we as readers expect the next paragraph to discuss? Answer: We would expect to hear about something having to do with "a period of many years" -- perhaps a consideration of prolonged exposure to asbestos. How long does one have to sniff that stuff before it becomes hazardous to one's health? If that turns out to be the case, then sentence (1g) above is an effective revision of the original.

If, on the other hand, the next paragraph goes on to explore the nasty qualities of asbestos fibers, then those fibers deserve the Stress position. Because the substance is *movable* (recall the box paradigm), we can re-engineer the sentence to affect that structural change:

1h. These diseases are regularly contracted by asbestos insulation installers who, over a period of many years, have [constantly] inhaled asbestos fibers.

If, in yet a third possibility, the next paragraph proceeds to discuss the plight of the people who are exposed to these fibers, then we should rearrange things to have the Stress position occupied by those people:

1i. These diseases are regularly contracted when asbestos fibers are inhaled over a period of many years by asbestos insulation installers.

It is also possible that the next paragraph might concentrate on asbestos insulation. If so, we know what to do:

1j. These diseases are regularly contracted when asbestos fibers are inhaled over a period of many years by installers of asbestos insulation.

In order to answer the question of which piece of information most deserves to occupy the Stress position, we must have sure knowledge of the writer's intentions. As teachers, we often lack that knowledge and therefore mistake those intentions. As long as the sentence appears to be a reasonable sentence, we all too easily assume that our interpretation must be the one intended by the writer. We underestimate how often that assumption is ill-founded. I could make the argument that this mis-assumption is the single most prevalent and most unacknowledged handicap under which writing teachers function. We can avoid it by substituting a different assumption -- that when the Stress position is *not* filled by the obviously important material, we do *not* know for sure what the writer intended -- no matter how clear the sentence seems to us.

Instead of telling the writer what information *ought* to occupy a Stress position, we would do far better to ask the writer to make the decision for us. That question will force the writer to reenter the thought process in order to articulate exactly what it was she or he intended to say. The writer's answer will often surprise us. The more we are surprised, the more the writer needs the structural advice we can offer: "If you want us to know what you consider the most important information, put it in a Stress position. The chances will increase dramatically that we will discover it without having to ask." When this question is asked often enough of a student, she will eventually perceive that it is not enough to make a sentence sound respectable; she must also send with it instructions -- structural instructions -- so we may arrive at the intended interpretation by ourselves.

Since the original text actually did continue in the next paragraph to discuss the effects of prolonged exposure, we will leave "over a period of many years" in the Stress position. Here, then, is the new paragraph that results from our Topic/Stress revisions to this point:

1k. Under this definition, a disease that progresses with few or no symptoms to indicate its gravity is an "insidious" disease. Examples of insidious diseases are asbestosis, neoplasia, mesothelioma, and bronchogenic carcinoma. These diseases are regularly contracted by asbestos insulation installers who have inhaled asbestos fibers over a period of many years.

Although this may not yet be the smoothest and most powerful of paragraphs, it already does a great deal that its original failed to do. We can now return to our initial set of related questions: Do the diseases named in the second sentence exemplify the general definition of "insidious disease" offered in the first sentence? Or do they refer to the specific diseases contracted by the unfortunate workers in the third sentence? Or do they do both? With the Topic and Stress positions now occupied by helpfully placed information, we perceive that diseases of the second sentence lean both backward and forward: First they exemplify the general definition of the first sentence; then they specify the diseases involved in the third sentence. That also turns out to be the medical reality.

What if that had not turned out to be the medical reality? What if, of these four diseases, only asbestosis was contracted by the people in the third sentence? We could adjust to that fact by a simple structural change: We could place "asbestosis" last in the second sentence's list of four so it could be referred to with greater ease at the beginning of the third sentence by a simple semantic flag.

1l. Examples of insidious diseases are neoplasia, mesothelioma, bronchogenic carcinoma, and asbestosis. Of these, asbestosis is regularly contracted by asbestos insulation installers who have inhaled asbestos fibers over a period of many years.

Returning to the first sentence, we can now settle the question we raised earlier: Which piece of information deserves the Stress position -- the term "insidious disease" or its definition, "a disease that progresses with few or no symptoms to indicate its gravity"? In the revised paragraph (1k), the "whose story?" place in the Topic position of both the second and third sentences is occupied by "insidious diseases." The paragraph as a whole has therefore become those diseases' story. Given that, the term "insidious diseases" well deserves the spotlight of the first sentence's Stress position, where it announces its own importance and makes possible its future "whose story" appearances in Topic positions.

Another detail should be noted concerning the revised paragraph (1k). The third sentence, as a result of our revision, now contains a passive construction:

1m. These diseases <u>are regularly contracted by</u> asbestos insulation installers who have inhaled asbestos fibers over a period of many years.

I have argued before that the passive should be preferred to the active when (1) it is the only way to transport the backward-linking old information to the Topic position, (2) it is the only way to transport the person or thing whose story it is to the Topic position, and (3) it demonstrates that the story is a passive one. Those who argue for active over passive at all costs might protest that sentence (1m) could retain "these diseases" in the Topic position and still manage to support an active verb:

1n. These diseases regularly <u>afflict</u> asbestos insulation installers who have inhaled asbestos fibers over a period of many years.

I would argue that neither construction is superior to the other in and of itself; once again, it depends on the context in which the sentence appears and what the sentence was intended to do. The distinction between the two is subtle but potentially powerful:

1) If the original three sentences of (1a) were part of a six-sentence paragraph that continued to tell the story of "these diseases," the active voice of (1n) will do the better job. It keeps the focus on the continuing activity of the diseases:
   ". . . a disease . . . is an "insidious disease""
   "Examples of these diseases are. . . ."
   These diseases regularly afflict. . . .
   These diseases also afflict. . . .
   They make it impossible to. . . .
   They pose a serious threat to. . . . "
   The story remains that of what insidious diseases actively do.

2) If, on the other hand, example (1a) is a complete three-sentence paragraph that will be followed by a new paragraph that shifts to the story of "prolonged exposure," then the passive construction of (1m) does the better job. It subtly and intentionally dilutes the focus on "these diseases" (which are no longer actively or aggressively the agent) and thus transports our energy further on into the sentence to the new

agent ("installers") and the new information about that agent ("over a period of many years"). The passive may sometimes be "weaker"; but sometimes weaker is better.

One final concern: Did the naming of the four diseases in the original second sentence deserve the Stress position accorded them? If, upon reconsideration, the author tells us they did not, then we can helpfully combine the three sentences into two:

1o. Under this definition, a disease that progresses with few or no symptoms to indicate its gravity is an "insidious" disease. Four of these -- asbestosis, neoplasia, mesothelioma, and bronchogenic carcinoma -- are regularly contracted by asbestos insulation installers who have inhaled asbestos fibers over a period of many years.

This tells the reader the names of four such diseases without insisting that those specific names be kept currently available in the reader's mind for use in the near future.

Notice how the revised paragraph no longer suffers from the equally insidious disease of splat prose. The paragraph now has a helpful and discernible "shape" -- specifically, a funnel shape. It begins with the broad sweep of a definition producing a term of art, "insidious diseases"; it then narrows to producing examples of that first sentence's Stress position; and those examples further narrow the focus on some people who do a particular act "over a period of many years." We now have sentences that form a continuum, funneling us into the next paragraph, which will explore why "a period of many years" was the paragraph's final destination. This funnel shape has been an objective of many methods of teaching composition in recent years; this Reader Expectations approach is yet another way of achieving it.

Note also how this paragraph now accords with the three characteristics of good prose mentioned in Chapter 1:

-- Nothing arrives that cannot be handled the moment it arrives.

-- Everything leans forward.

-- Then everything actually goes in one of the directions in which it was leaning.

To see how this is indeed the case, try applying the slow-motion reading technique used so often in previous chapters.

I repeat here a warning I have repeated before: The revised paragraph does not necessarily "mean" what I have interpreted it to mean here. Rather, my interpretation will be assented to by many more readers than would have discovered it for themselves from reading the original paragraph. The original came equipped with too few helpful structural clues to persuade a high percentage of any reading community to any one particular interpretation. The revised paragraph provides structural clues that continually pay off, that make sense, and that direct our interpretive efforts. The interpretation suggested in one sentence finds confirmation in the next one. When that happens sentence after sentence in prose, readers learn to trust both the writer and the writer's structures. Such consistency we recognize as a writer's style.

S *tyle and the Consistency of Choice*

Style is choice. One's personal writing style is the sum total of all the habitual choices one makes when faced with the same rhetorical task. By investigating the patterned habits of our students where these reader expectations are concerned, we can identify what they naturally do well on a constant basis; by making that conscious, instead of intuitive, we can put them in better control of those already established strengths. We can also help them discover what they habitually do that is unhelpful for readers; by making them aware of those habits, we can help them change, permanently.

That which we call style, fairly or unfairly, represents the character and intelligence of the writer. By many it is considered unteachable, perhaps because it is assumed to be produced by those inner personal qualities that will seem to proclaim themselves no matter what the writer does. But the stylistic characteristics described by words like *flow* and *pace* and *power* and *forcefulness* are actually dependent, to a great degree, on controlling the reader's attention; that, in turn, has a great deal to do with what the reader is expecting to happen at any given moment. Therefore, even a single bad structural habit on the part of a writer, if it surfaces consistently enough, can be perceived as a flaw of mind or personality. Correcting that bad habit can change a writer's self-presentation of character dramatically.

As an example, here is a passage from a campaign speech of Walter Mondale, the unsuccessful Democratic presidential candidate who opposed President Reagan's re-election attempt in 1984.[2] Mondale was widely regarded as an honest, intelligent, well-intentioned person, sensible, well-balanced, and caring; and yet he lost by the greatest landslide in presidential election history. Exit interviews at polling places indicated that even the Democratic electorate feared he did not have the force, the spirit, the moral fire necessary for presidential leadership. Now where did they get that impression? Most voters had encountered him only through his public and televised appearances. What they "knew" of him was not based on biographical detail or previous experience but rather on his manner of self-presentation. They knew him from his style.

Let us take a brief look at that style. Throughout this passage from one of Mondale's speeches, note the occupants of the various Stress positions.

2a. I have refrained directly from criticizing the President for three years. Because I believe that Americans must stand united in the face of the

Soviet Union, our foremost adversary, and before the world, I have been reticent. A fair time to pursue his goals and test his policies is also the President's right, I believe. The water's edge is the limit to politics, in this sense. But this cannot mean that, if the President is wrong and the world situation has become critical, all criticism should be muted indefinitely.

A fair chance has been extended the President, and policies that make our relationship with the Soviet Union more dangerous than at any time in the past generation no longer deserve American support and support cannot be expected.

Reagan administrative diplomacy has had this grim result: We could face not the risk of nuclear war but its reality if we allow present developments in nuclear arms and United States-Soviet relations to continue.

None of the individual sentences can be considered ungrammatical or intellectually vacuous; but the weakness of every single Stress position suggests a political impotence that accords with his overwhelming defeat.

The Stress position occupant of the first sentence emphasizes that our candidate has done the action of refraining "for three years."

I have refrained directly from criticizing the President for three years.

Since that is exactly how long Mr. Reagan had been President, "three years" translates into "forever." He might as well have said,

I have refrained directly from criticizing the President forever. Vote for me.

It is a strange claim to make. He continued:

Because I believe that Americans must stand united in the face of the Soviet Union, our foremost adversary, and before the world, I have been reticent.

The long "because" clause increases our expectation of a powerful resolution in the main clause to follow. When that main clause arrives, not only is it disappointingly anticlimactic but also it features a Stress position that once again highlights the candidate's reticence. Putting the two sentences together, valuing the Stress position occupants as the most important information, we get a strange message: "I have said and done nothing, forever." Why should we vote for a man with this record? More tellingly, why should we vote for *such a man*? (The style proclaims the man.)

The final sentence of the paragraph, given this context, descends almost to the comical:

But this cannot mean that, if the President is wrong and the world situation has become critical, all criticism should be muted indefinitely.

The negative verb ("cannot mean") is so far separated from its resolving clause ("all criticism should . . . ") that its negative quality is undermined. As a result, we get a Stress position strangely filled with "all criticism should be muted indefinitely." It almost produces this comical argument: "Since all criticism should be muted indefinitely, you should vote for me, because I have made a good start on that, having said absolutely nothing, forever." Of course, that was not his intended argument; nor is it a *logical* interpretation. But it *is* a compilation of everything he has put into his Stress positions and therefore has offered to us as the important matter for emphasis. It therefore becomes at least part of his message.

In the second paragraph, he demonstrates his inability to make a point without backing away from it. "A fair time to pursue his goals and test his policies is also the President's right," he says, in what sounds like a definitive tone; but before he finishes, be backs away with a Stress position filled with "I believe." ("I think, maybe, well, perhaps. . . .")

If that were a sole instance of such a rhetorical retreat, it would not define his character; but he does the exact same thing in the next sentence. "The water's edge is the limit to politics," he declares with some force; but he then undercuts it by ending the sentence with "in this sense." ("Well, maybe in some other sense, no, but . . . .")

The weak Stress position poisons every single sentence. He ends with a Stress position that counteracts the concept of ending:

> Reagan administrative diplomacy has had this grim result: We could face not the risk of nuclear war but its reality if we allow present developments in nuclear arms and United States-Soviet relations to continue.

Potentially important arguments for his side appear, but never in the Stress position, where they would have been most noted and most valued. His prose (or, actually, his speechwriter's prose) presents the image of a man who cannot see things to their conclusion, who cannot stand up for his own insights -- who is, in short, lacking in power and force.

Am I suggesting that if his speechwriter had only filled all the Stress positions with the important material of the sentence, his style -- that is to say, his *character* -- would have been so transformed that he would have appeared a man of strength and force and insight? Yes. Here is a revision of this passage in which something of import has been moved into every Stress position.

2b. For three years, I have refrained from directly criticizing the President of the United States. I have been reticent because I believe that Americans must stand united before the world, particularly in the face of our foremost adversary, the Soviet Union. I also believe a President should be given fair time to pursue his goals and test his policies. In this sense, politics should stop at the water's edge. But this cannot mean that all criticism should be muted indefinitely, no matter how wrong a President may be or how critical the world situation may become.

President Reagan has had his fair chance, and he can no longer expect Americans to support policies that make our relationship with the Soviet Union more dangerous than at any time in the past generation.

This is the grim result of Reagan Administrative diplomacy: If present developments in nuclear arms and United States-Soviet relations are permitted to continue, we could face not the risk of nuclear war but its reality.

Note how the "translations" of the individual sentences are transformed. The first paragraph now reads something more like this:

For a long time now I have not criticized -- as would be inappropriate -- the Leader of Our Country. I have kept unusually quiet [linking backward], as I mentioned, for a good reason: I believe we've got to all hang together against our chief adversary, the Evil Empire. I also believe [linking backward] that a President should be allowed to do his thing. In this sense [linking backward], we should keep all political criticism an internal matter. But this kind of silence [linking backward] cannot be allowed to continue if things are going to get more terrible than they have ever been before.

Note also how the final sentence of the third paragraph no longer ends lamely on the inconclusive "to continue" but now shines and reverberates with the alliterative *r*, helping turn a "risk" into a "reality":

If present developments in nuclear arms and United States-Soviet relations are permitted to continue, we could face not the risk of nuclear war but its reality.

The style of this revised speech presents us with a man who is a tower of strength, a man of clear vision, a man who can lead us all *forward*. The *forward* lean is created primarily by each sentence's leaning forward, as the structural expectations would have us do, toward the Stress position.

I am not saying he would have won; but he would not have lost by such a huge margin. In looking at several others of his speeches from that campaign, I have not found a single sentence with a strongly filled Stress position. The weak Stress position was a major component of his style -- or rather of the style he was given.

This candidate is not alone. From a quarter-century of experience as a professional writing consultant, it is clear to me that the single most prevalent writing problem in professional America today is the inability to get the important material to the Stress position. It afflicts more than three-quarters of all the lawyers, scientists, business persons, and governmental workers with whom I have worked.

Here is a commonly encountered weak sentence structure in our contemporary professional world:

Topic position	Verb	Stress position
New, most important information	Necessary verb structure (no action)	Old, backward-linking information

The pervasiveness of this structure is not hard to explain. When a writer is struggling to create a sentence, trying hard to articulate an important thought, two anxieties tend to dominate:

1) I've got to find the right words for the crucial concept; and
2) I've got to get those words down on paper quickly before I forget them.

Having accomplished those tasks, the writer can relax a bit and complete the sentence with all the necessary grammatical and backward-linking material. This procedure may be the most convenient for the writer; but it creates great problems for the reader. The reader needs to encounter the material in exactly the opposite order.

Topic position	Verb	Stress position
Old, backward-linking information	Verb that communicates the action	New, most important information

In the world beyond the classroom, it is more important that the reader get delivery of the message than that the writer be able to record it in the easiest manner possible.

I have also observed a pattern in some writers who vary in the way they fill the Stress position. They will naturally place their new information in the Stress position when they are in relative control of the concept being expressed; but the moment they begin to struggle with a concept, their new information appears much earlier. Such a dichotomy makes sense: The absence of struggle allows them to tend to the shape of the thought; the presence of struggle makes them anxious about recording the new information before they lose control of it.

The best way to judge this Reader Expectation approach effectively is to experiment with it. During that experiment, make a temporary alteration in your normal reading procedure. Instead of trying to determine the substance of a given unit of discourse, investigate the organization of its structure. Instead of asking *"What* is here?" ask *"Where* are certain kinds of things located?" You should find that investigating the structure will lead you and your students deeper into the complexities of the substance. The following section exemplifies this by exploring a selection of typical undergraduate writing problems.

U sing Topic/Stress to Solve Typical Student Writing Problems

The *Ab Ovo* Beginning

Most teachers of composition are familiar with the student paper that begins not from *a* beginning but from *the* beginning -- *ab ovo*, "from the egg." We can try to talk to students about grabbing their audience or getting right to the heart of the matter or beginning swiftly or jumping right in. Sometimes that advice works; more often, it does not. In its place, I suggest we direct their attention to the probable effects the information in their Topic and Stress positions will have on their readers. That new perspective may lead them to discover the airiness of what they might have previously considered dense matter -- or the obvious emptiness of what they might have intended as effective bull.

Here is an opening paragraph from a freshman paper.

3a. The intricacy of human beings must confound even the most cynical of men. Personality serves as one of the many complex components that comprise the intricacy of man. To fully understand personality requires a great deal of thought and knowledge.

Aside from noting the misuse of "comprise" and the split infinitive ("to fully understand"), what might we say to this young man? To condescend to him for his intellectual shallowness might do serious harm. He might have struggled nobly to produce something of worth in this paragraph. Alternatively, he might have intentionally padded the whole paragraph just to fill the space; but to accuse him of such a tactic might do irreparable harm, if our guess is wrong. The safest and most productive tactic, I suggest, is to forego making assumptions about his motivations and instead to investigate the structure of his prose.

One of the great advantages of this approach: Even though you are the teacher, you do not have to know beforehand what the investigation will turn up. Since the student failed to communicate much, there is no reason to pretend you can perceive what that communication might have been intended to be. Without any idea of what might happen, I directed this student's attention, sentence by sentence, to his filling of structural locations -- especially to his Topic and Stress positions.

First sentence: The intricacy of human beings must confound even the most cynical of men.

I asked him what in his opinion deserved the Stress position. He chose "the intricacy of human beings." He also decided that the "even" phrase was the context out of which that emphasis on "intricacy" should come. Easy enough:

Revision: Even the most cynical of men must be confounded by the intricacy of human beings.

So far, this is likely to be a paper about "the intricacy of human beings."

Second sentence: Personality serves as one of the many complex components that comprise the intricacy of man.

I asked him to find the old information. He found it occupying the Stress position. I asked him what he wanted his readers to emphasize. He chose "personality." We transported it to the Stress position.

Revision: The intricacy of man comprises many complex components, an important one being personality.

Better. Now the paper's thesis seems to have something to do with that subcomponent of intricacy, "personality."[3]

Third sentence: To fully understand personality requires a great deal of thought and knowledge.

He identified the old information as "personality," located conveniently in the Topic position. But then he actually blushed to see that his whole paragraph now formed a crescendo to the climactic insight that all this required "a great deal of thought and knowledge." Some thesis for a paper. I did not have to tell him anything more about the paragraph. He grasped it for himself.

Note: Had I used his time and my energy at this point to complain about his splitting an infinitive ("to fully understand"), far more important matters might well have gone unexplored. Split infinitives are bad when they distract an audience by their supposed sinfulness or disrupt the smooth flow of reader energy in the reading process. Certain audiences and certain splittings cause no problem.[4] We do our students a kindness by discussing this at a moment when it can be the primary topic of interest. I think we do them a disservice when we allow the presence of such grammatical miscues to overwhelm all other matters of rhetorical importance.

The Nondeveloping Paragraph

The Topic/Stress approach also works well to bring students to the realization that although they have filled their paragraphs with information, they have failed to develop their thought. The more information they think they have included in the paragraph, the harder it is to get this across to them using conventional means only. Here is an example from a freshman essay on one of today's most popular freshman topics, "Violence on Television."

4. Violence on television may offend people of highly moral beliefs. These people live cleanly and despise any corrupt acts. For example, if people worship the devil then this could greatly disturb their life. These scenes presented on television demoralize people of definite tenets. Besides providing a bad influence, this type of violence may affront people considerably.

The student who wrote this was convinced she had packed the paragraph as full as a paragraph ought to be packed. She had followed all the advice she knew about topic sentences and exemplified her points with the support of three specific examples. She had taken great pains in the crafting of each individual sentence. What then could be problematic about this paragraph?

We used the same kind of sentence-by-sentence Topic/Stress analysis as above.

First sentence: Violence on television may offend people of highly moral beliefs.

She had wanted to stress "violence on television"; that needed to be switched to the Stress position. She had also wanted this to be the story of the "people of highly moral beliefs"; they needed to be switched to the Topic position.

Revision: People of highly moral beliefs may be offended by violence on television.

When we accomplished this revision, I could see her mind in her eyes. "This guy's weird, but harmless enough. If he thinks the revision sounds better than the original, why not just humor him?" Of course the revision does not *sound* any better; but it may *function* better.

Second sentence: These people live cleanly and despise any corrupt acts.

We looked for new information. According to her, "these people" referred to the "people of highly moral beliefs" and therefore were old information. "Live cleanly" referred back to "highly moral" and therefore was essentially old information. "Despise" overlapped a good deal with "offended" and therefore was also essentially old information. "Corrupt acts" sounded new to me but turned out not to be. She had been watching a television program the night before that was violent because of corrupt acts. "Corrupt acts" was therefore intended by her to be old, backward-referring information. We had run out of words: Everything was old information. She perceived that instead of *developing* thought in her second sentence, she had mostly been *repeating* that thought in slightly different terms.[5]

She was now somewhat puzzled. This Topic/Stress stuff had unearthed something mildly embarrassing. In terms of new thought in this second sentence, there was no there there.

We continued:

Third sentence: For example, if people worship the devil then this could greatly disturb their life.

Since we had found so much old information in the second sentence, we went through the third sentence asking whether each item was old or new. "For example" was old information, linking backward nicely, just as she wanted the beginning of this sentence to do. "People" also appeared to be old information, since we had heard about "people" before; but those highly moral people were hardly likely to be the ones to "worship the devil." These "people" were not those "people." "They" turned out to be the devil worshipers; and, since I had heard nothing of devils nor of worship to this point, they struck me as new information. But again I was wrong. That violent television show with all the corrupt acts turned out to have been about devil worshipers. They too were old information.

On we went. "Greatly disturb" was more old information -- the latest variation on "offend" and "despise." "Their life" referred to our old friends, the highly moral people. So in this sentence, once again there was no new information. Once again she had written a sentence that restated her first sentence instead of further developing its thought.

"Well, that was very interesting," she said, nervously. "We don't have to go any further." "Oh, let's," I responded.

We persevered and found the following.

Fourth sentence: These scenes presented on television demoralize people of definite tenets.

"These scenes presented on television"	(Old information -- the devil-worship show)
"demoralize"	(Old information -- related to "offend," "despise," and "disturb")
"people of definite tenets"	(Old information -- our old friends the highly moral beliefs people).

Again, nothing but old information.

Now kicking and screaming -- (not really) -- I dragged her into the fifth sentence.

Fifth sentence: Besides providing a bad influence, this type of violence
                    may affront people considerably.

"Besides providing a bad influence" Wait a minute!

This is *not* old information. This is *new* information. So lulled was I into
the complacent expectation that no new information would arrive until the
next paragraph that I almost missed it. Not only is this new information,
but it is the single most important piece of information in the whole essay.
It is essentially the conclusion of the argument she was wanting to make.
Bad stuff on TV, she wanted to say, can be a bad influence on kids and affect their future actions. But note where has she hidden this most important piece of information: (1) It is not in the Stress position; (2) it does not
even warrant a full clause, but is relegated to a mere phrase; and (3) it begins with "besides," which suggests that we have *already* heard about it,
which we have not.

The rest of the sentence held truer to form:

"this type of violence" (Old information -- the devil worshiping
                         TV show)
"may affront . . .   (Old information -- the last in the continuing
   considerably"   series of "offend," "despise," "disturb," and
                         "demoralize")
"people"   (Old information -- once again, our old high-
                         ly moral friends)

As a result of this investigation of structural expectations, this student
was able to defend against building this kind of paragraph in all future papers. She started to understand the difference between generating prose
and constructing an argument. This had been accomplished in a relatively
clinical manner that eventually succeeded in putting the power of analysis into her own hands.

Where had she learned to create such paragraphs? -- in high school
English classes, in which she had always received straight A's. Check it
out: (1) A "topic sentence"; (2–4) Three sentences of "support"; and (5) a
"conclusion," which repeats the topic sentence. All too familiar.

The Writer as Hunter and Gatherer

Many of our students reach college having discovered that a demonstration of assiduous work in the library often persuades teachers to grant high
grades. Such hunting and gathering can come to be synonymous for them
with thinking and writing. This unfortunate equation may be based on the
theory that high grades reflect either innate intelligence or sustained industry: Either one will do. In some cases, especially given time restrictions,
the more the industry in the library, the less intellect need be expended.
Topic/Stress analysis works well to set such a committed but misguided
student on a more productive path. Here is an example of a student who

has a particular structural habit that, unknown to her, presents constant problems for her readers. Solving that structural problem will contribute mightily in changing this hunter-gatherer into a thinker.

5a. The Breton lai became one of the most popular poetic forms in England in the twelfth and thirteenth centuries. The adventures of a single main character formed the content of this relatively short type of poem. The long continental romance, such as that written by Chretien de Troyes in France during the late twelfth century, preceded the lai as a popular form of literature among the Norman nobility. The concept of "amour courtois," or courtly love, was at the heart of most romances, and the development of the Breton lai was strongly influenced by the exaggerated attitude toward love and chivalry that was expressed in the courtly love tradition. A lower and illiterate audience was apparently the major consumer of this form, however; a form peculiar to England, therefore, evolved out of these concepts.

Long though it may be, this paragraph is worth analyzing through a combination of Topic/Stress analysis and the slow-motion approach used earlier. Together they reveal a great deal about the nature of the writer's paragraph and her habitual structural devices.

It is not important to me to help her make this particular paper better; it is *very* important to me to help her change this debilitating structural habit for good. That will help her improve all her other papers, in this course and all others, and beyond her coursework into her professional life.

THE BRETON LAI . . .

These are the first words of this essay; and for us (unless we happen already to be well read in medieval literature), they are distinctly new information. They turn out to be the *only* piece of information in the sentence that is not a familiar concept; therefore, they are the least likely to act as context for the reader. They also turn out to be what the writer actually wanted us to emphasize. According to her, they belong in the Stress position.

. . . BECAME ONE OF THE MOST POPULAR POETIC FORMS IN ENGLAND IN THE TWELFTH AND THIRTEENTH CENTURIES . . .

She could not choose among these various pieces of information to determine the best candidate for the Topic position. This inability indicated that she had no clear idea from what perspective she wished the reader to view this material. Was this to be an essay on "popular forms"? Or was it to focus on "England"? Or was it an essay about literature of "the twelfth and thirteenth centuries"? This indecision turned out to be significant. Whatever might be put up front, we were confident that the "Breton lai" ought to occupy the Stress position.

5b. One of the most popular poetic forms in England in the twelfth and thirteenth centuries was the Breton lai.

The paper promises to be all about the Breton lai.

THE ADVENTURES OF A SINGLE MAIN CHARACTER . . .

> What connection does this have to the previous sentence? None that I could see. This sentence might have continued, "The adventures of a single main character have nothing to do with the Breton lai." For a second time we have been presented with the new information at the beginning of the sentence, where (1) we do not yet know what to do with it, and (2) it makes no logical backward link.

. . . FORMED THE CONTENT OF THIS RELATIVELY SHORT TYPE OF POEM.

> The Stress position of this sentence is filled with the old information -- "this [. . .] type of poem" -- that we would have appreciated having at the beginning. "Short," to be sure, is new; but the author said she wished us to emphasize the "adventures of a single main character," which should therefore be switched to the Stress position.

5c. One of the most popular poetic forms in England in the twelfth and thirteenth centuries was the Breton lai. This relatively short type of poem concentrated on the adventures of a single main character.

The paper will be about the Breton lai, paying special attention to the adventures of a single main character.

THE LONG CONTINENTAL ROMANCE, . . .

> If this is old information, then the "long continental romance" must be another way of referring to the "Breton lai." However, an attentive reader will note that this cannot be the case: The Breton lai was short and English, not long and continental. (But a great deal of reader energy must be expended to ascertain those distinctions quickly and clearly.) For a third time in a row, then, we have been burdened with new information in the Topic position. For the second time in a row, the information located in the Topic position does not help us step with confidence and understanding from the previous sentence to the present one.

. . . SUCH AS THAT WRITTEN BY CHRETIEN DE TROYES IN FRANCE DURING THE LATE TWELFTH CENTURY, . . .

> The new information has now attracted to it a lengthy exemplification. We carry all this information with us, an increasingly difficult burden to bear, as we await not only the connective old information but also the verb. (We may, however, be impressed that she has done enough library work to have hunted down and gathered in "Chretien de Troyes.")

... PRECEDED THE LAI ...

> Finally we understand the relationship between this sentence and the previous two. Had she only begun with "The lai was preceded by ...," we would have had far less difficulty in assimilating all this information about the "long continental romance."

... AS A POPULAR FORM OF LITERATURE AMONG THE NOR-MAN NOBILITY.

> We note that the Stress position is occupied (for the first time) by *new* information -- the "Norman nobility." Surely we should expect soon to hear more about these high-ranking people from south of the Channel. (But don't hold your breath: How much more have we heard recently about "the adventures of a single main character"?)

5d. The lai was preceded by the long continental romance, such as that written by Chretien de Troyes in France during the late twelfth century, as a popular form of literature among the Norman nobility.

THE CONCEPT OF "AMOUR COURTOIS," ...

> By this point it comes as no surprise, to her or to us, that her sentence begins with new information; but even if we adjust to make this a temporary reader expectation, we still are without the connective and contextualizing material we need and expect from the Topic position. Whether or not we recognize "amour courtois," we do not know what connections it has to the short Breton lai and/or the long continental romance.

... OR COURTLY LOVE, ...

> Though this is shorter than the "Chretien de Troyes" material was in the previous sentence, we again have the same pattern: The sentence begins with new information and then is interrupted by a phrase of explanation before the verb arrives.

... WAS AT THE HEART OF MOST ROMANCES, ...

> At this point, we can see that the material on the Breton lai was but a prelude to the actual main concern of the paper, the long continental romance. Now that we are into the meat of it, we shall not encounter the Breton lai again.

... AND THE DEVELOPMENT OF THE BRETON LAI ...

> Wrong again. The Breton lai is back. We await further "developments."

... WAS STRONGLY INFLUENCED BY THE EXAGGERATED AT-TITUDE TOWARD LOVE AND CHIVALRY THAT WAS EXPRESSED IN ...

> Now that we have struggled through this long, unwieldy sentence, we are finally arriving at the Stress position.

... THE COURTLY LOVE TRADITION.

How annoying. "Courtly love" appeared first in the Topic position, where it was new information and did us no good. Now it appears again in the Stress position, where it is old information and therefore redundant. This sentence is a serpent that chases its own tail and catches it.

A LOWER AND ILLITERATE AUDIENCE ...

Old information or new? New, we say with confidence. She has always given us new information in the Topic position. But we are wrong once again. "A low*er*" audience -- lower than whom? Than "Norman nobility," of course. You remember them from two sentences back? She told us they would be important by placing them in the Stress position there. So what if we now have to jump high buildings in a single bound to be able to catch sight of them once more?

... WAS APPARENTLY THE MAJOR CONSUMER OF THIS FORM, HOWEVER;

The placement of "however" in the Stress position suggests that the author recognized the however-ness of the statement only as she was finishing the typing of it. "However" is, by definition, old information. It points backward to a recent statement and announces the advent of some sort of qualifying counterstatement. It therefore functions well when it is placed between the statement to be qualified and its qualification. Then "however" tells the reader, "The statement you have just read will now be qualified." Placing "however" after the qualification sends a much more complicated message: "You have just finished reading a qualification you did not know at the time was a qualification; it qualified something you had read even earlier."[6]

A FORM PECULIAR TO ENGLAND, THEREFORE, ...

Even if we had ascertained that "this form" before the semi-colon was the Breton lai, we would not be immediately convinced that "a form" here referred to the same form. Had this author consistently linked old information at the beginning of sentences to recognizable information in previous sentences, we might not have a problem at this juncture. The "therefore" fails to perform its proper logical function. It is actually only a bit of metadiscourse, informing us that the paragraph is coming to an end. Rarely has a "therefore" been less justly deserved.

... EVOLVED OUT OF THESE CONCEPTS.

The word "concepts" is no better warranted here than was the "therefore" which preceded it; but the author may well believe she has been dealing with concepts instead of gathering together the bits of information she hunted down in the library.

It will do little good and perhaps a great deal of harm to give this student a low grade or berate her for not thinking hard enough. She may well not yet be able to distinguish between "thinking hard" and "working hard"; she has clearly done a certain amount of "work." The "paper" seems to me not yet ready for a grade -- not ready to be called a "paper." She has not yet decided what to do with all her gatherings.

It will definitely do some harm to grade this paper "A for thought, C for writing." Those two activities cannot be separated. How do we *know* there is any "A" thinking here if the writing is "C"?[7]

On the other hand, it may do a great deal of good to help her discover her structural habits. If we ask her to restructure each sentence by announcing whose story it is up front and saving the new, important material for the end, she will most likely produce a series of sentences in which the Topic positions are occupied either by the Breton lai or by the long continental romance. If we ask of her "whose story" the paragraph as a whole was meant to tell, she will be hard pressed to decide -- because she never got around to making that decision in the first place. She hunted; she gathered; but she never synthesized.

She might decide the paper is to be both their stories -- or one story comparing the two. That might lead to investigating the revised Stress positions to see which facts she deemed most significant. From those she could then make comparative lists for the two substories and begin to *analyze* the material she had discovered in the library. In some respects, the two poetic forms are distinctly opposed (long versus short, elite versus popular); in other ways they overlap (twelfth/thirteenth centuries and late twelfth century, one influencing the other); in other ways they coincide (both concerned with "amour courtois"). From considering these oppositions and coincidences, she can generate a great many new possibilities for discovery. She can begin to see how the process of writing is inextricably linked to the process of thinking.

Once it becomes clear to her that information must be molded into concepts, subdivided into demonstrations, connected to present insights, and disengaged to indicate distinctions, then she can start to understand how discourse can be perceived to flow from sentence to sentence and from paragraph to paragraph. She would be aided at this point by understanding how readers perceive the distinction between a writer's stringing along of one continuing topic and a writer's changing cleanly from one topic to another.

The Multiple Uses of the Stress Position

Along the way in this chapter and the last, the Stress position has been used to achieve a number of differing effects. It may be helpful to bring them together.

That's All, Folks

The Stress position of a sentence that ends a document should usually afford the reader a full sense of closure. It does not have to be a great climax, or a dramatic moment, or a witty insight; it just has to allow the whole thing to come to rest.

The Stress position that ends a segment or section of a document either should produce a document-ending kind of closure or should perform a more subtle two-stranded task -- bringing closure to the present section while leaning forward to introduce or link to the approaching section.

Heeeeere's Johnny!

The Stress position is an excellent place to announce that a change of Topic is about to occur. If new, important-sounding information is (1) made yet more prominent by being placed in the Stress position, and (2) is not fully self-explanatory, then it creates an expectation that the reader is about to hear a good deal more about that subject. It is no surprise to the reader (when reading well-wrought prose) to find the occupant of that Stress position sometimes reappearing as "whose story" it is in the Topic Position of the next sentence.

I call this (with trepidation, because our communal memory of this is fading fast) the "Heeeeere's Johnny!" use of the Stress position. For many years on television's late-night talkfest called *The Tonight Show*, announcer Ed McMahon introduced the host, Johnny Carson, with a drum-rolling, crescendoing, scale-ascending, climax-producing "Heeeeeeeeeeeeeere's *Johnny!*" And then Johnny would step into the spotlight (a Topic position) and give his monologue ("*his* story"). The Stress position of the monologue was always obvious: As he said, "We'll be right back," he mimed a little golf swing. When the ad was over, we always found Johnny in his accustomed structural location, the interviewer's chair, from which he controlled the viewer expectations for the rest of the show. He would announce his first guest -- in a Stress position: "And now here is that wonderful . . . and terrific . . . Bette Midler." And on she would come, assume the spotlight, and sing. After the next ad, we found her in the "Whose Story" location -- the end of the interviewee's sofa. (Ed McMahon had to scoot down a bit to make room for her.) For a few minutes, almost everything was "her story" -- where she was singing, what she thought about recent developments in Hollywood gossip, etc., etc. Whenever Johnny broke in to tell some non-Midler story, it was a refreshing violation of expectation -- much needed to keep the audience off-balance and awake. Eventually, he would introduce his next guest, again in a Stress position. That guest would come on, do his solo thing, and then take his place in the "whose story" position on the Topic position sofa, forcing Bette Midler out of that spot and into relative obscurity for the rest of the show. (By the end of the show, poor Ed McMahon had almost no sofa left on which to sit.) It was a rhetorically structured show.

One of the common paragraph structures in English is the "Heeeeeere's Johnny" paragraph, in which a piece of new information in the Stress position of the first sentence takes over the "whose story" part of the Topic positions of all the other sentences in the paragraph:

First sentence: A B C D E F G H XX!

Second sentence: XX J K L M N. . . .

Third sentence: XX P Q R S T U. . . .

Fourth sentence: XX V W Y Z.

To see this in action, revisit the revision of the "insidious disease" paragraph, example (1k) of this chapter.

Multiple Strands

If the "Heeeeeeere's Johnny" Stress position were the only use of the Stress position, then no writer could discuss a particular topic or story for more than one sentence. He would be forced to change stories when he created the following Topic position. But often the stressworthy material in a sentence is only one strand in the fabric of a more complex thought. Sometimes a number of these threads must be produced before anything can be tied together. When that is the case, the occupant of the Stress position usually does *not* occupy the following Topic position; instead, the "whose story" of the one sentence repeats in that position for all the rest of the sentences that continue to tell that story.

First sentence: X. . . . . A

Second sentence: X. . . . . B

Third sentence: X. C

Fourth sentence: X. . . . . D

The sum of all these Stress positions is the developed story of X.

Epistrophic Emphasis

Epistrophe is the ending of several consecutive units of discourse with the same word or phrase. It has always been effective in Western literature and communication; but it always has a heavy dramatic ring to it and can therefore be used only occasionally. Part of its power comes from being a violation of the default value expectation that something new and different will appear in the Stress position. For a good look at this figure of speech, revisit example (16) in Chapter 2, which echoed "New Hampshire" throughout the courtroom.

The Intentional Anticlimax

The epistrophic Stress position is still a strong Stress position; but there are times when a weakly filled Stress position is the right rhetorical choice.

Sometimes the news you have to relate is so bad that to put it in a Stress position is just to rub salt in the wound. Consider the following piece of badly written bad news.

7a. We fire you.

Too abrupt, too harsh, too inhuman. This writer's immediate superior might first want to get rid of agency here, so "we" are not doing anything. That produces the first revision:

7b. You are fired.

Better for us; but worse for the employee. "Fired" is strong enough a word without its occupying the Stress position. And wouldn't it be kinder if the employee were not the target of this arrow? Why not make it the story of the employment contract and get all the people removed from the mess?

7c. Your contract must be discontinued because of your noncompliance with clause 3(d)i.

Better; but the Stress position still has something important in it, giving the sentence a forward movement toward a negative resolution. Why not weaken the Stress position to make a more cushioned, marshmallowed ending?

7d. Our employment relationship must be discontinued because of noncompliance with clause 3(d)i of the employment contract.

It is still not good news; but at least it does not add to the harshness of reality the coarseness of rhetoric. There are times when no emphasis is the best emphasis.

This kind of manipulation raises ethical questions. Teaching people how to submerge important information so it cannot be "heard" or "seen" as important can easily lead to abuse. Under what circumstances would (7d) be a better communication than the terse (7b), "You are fired"? (7d) will be a kindness to the employee if she already knows she is losing her job. She opens the letter, knowing beforehand its contents, and is relieved that the prose is fussy and marshmallowy, not nasty.

Under what circumstances would (7d) be a disservice to the employee? (7d) will be almost cruel to an employee who does not yet know what is coming and is cowed by the fussiness of the legalese. Once again, it all depends on context.

T opic Changing and Topic Stringing

If a writer consistently follows the advice offered here concerning the Topic and Stress positions, then two patterns of progression will naturally begin to appear. Often, either (1) the Topic position of a new sentence will be filled by the new information in the previous sentence, thus "changing" the topic of the prose, or (2) it will be filled by the occupant of the previous sentence's Topic position, thus "stringing" along a continuing topic to the new sentence. As a result, these two progressions can be called Topic Changing and Topic Stringing.[8]

Topic Changing

In this pattern, the key word in the Topic position repeats or refers back to a word at the end of the previous sentence. The cohesion that results can be charted as follows:

Topic	Stress
Old^1	New_1
Old^2 (=New^1)	New_2
Old^3 (=New^2)	New_3
Old^4 (=New^3)	New_4

In this progression, the writer never settles on a particular topic for more than a sentence. Instead, the writer focuses our attention on the way in which each new arrival connects backward and moves on into new territory in the next sentence. It produces a kind of domino effect. Therefore, each statement must be comprehensible in and of itself; the intent of the whole passage is to focus on the *connections* between these various statements and the forward-moving quality of the progression as a whole. Topic Changing, therefore, is a technique that highlights connectedness -- that highlights cohesion. As a result, it is the most effective technique to use in writing certain kinds of narrative or descriptive paragraphs or segments of paragraphs -- stories that concentrate on "what happens next."

An example, taken from Url Lanham's *Origins of Modern Biology*:

8a. Up to the time of Darwin, Lamarck was the only biologist to develop a theory of organic evolution in extensive fashion. Its failure as a scientific theory was discussed in the last chapter. The writings that will be taken up here as a background to the development of Darwin's theory will be those of such popularizers as Erasmus Darwin and Robert Chambers, whose work was read by Darwin. He apparently knew nothing of the development of evolutionary theory by the philosophers.

The Topic Changing proceeds with such subtlety that one would have to search for the connections to be aware that they exist.

8b. Up to the time of Darwin, Lamarck was the only biologist to develop a theory of organic evolution in extensive fashion. Its failure as a scientific theory was discussed in the last chapter. The writings that will be taken up <u>here</u> as a background to the development of Darwin's theory will be those of such popularizers as Erasmus Darwin and Robert Chambers, whose work was read by <u>Darwin</u>. <u>He</u> apparently knew nothing of <u>the development of evolutionary theory by the philosophers</u>.

Topic	Stress
Old^1 (Lamarck) . . . . .New^1	(a theory of organic evolution)
Old^2 (=New^1) (Its failure) . .New^2	(in the last chapter)
Old^3 (=New^2) (here) . . . . . . .New^3	(Darwin)
Old^4 (=New^3) (He) . . . . .New^4	(the development of evolutionary theory by the philosophers)

The prose moves with relative ease from sentence to sentence, establishing the connections by lighthanded lexical references and leaving us at the end with an introduction to "the development of evolutionary theory by the philosophers," which becomes the focus of the succeeding paragraph.

Topic Changing is neither a good thing nor a bad thing by itself. It certainly does not produce a template or paradigm one might use for the construction of paragraphs. It is highly effective when the business at hand moves from one statement to another without need of further development. It can be a disaster, sometimes even comically so, when the intellectual need is just the opposite -- that is, when the writer/reader needs to concentrate on one topic for a number of sentences before it is fully developed.

As an example of this sad comedy, here is the first page of a freshman paper written by a student who has just learned about Topic Changing but has no use for its necessary counterpart, Topic Stringing. I have underscored the connections.

9. Over the last several years, much doubt has been raised as to the future of <u>the US space program</u>. <u>The space program</u> received a major setback on January 28, 1986, when the space shuttle <u>Challenger exploded</u>. <u>The explosion of the Challenger</u> was more than simply the tragic death of seven brave Americans, it represented the death of <u>a dream</u>. <u>This dream</u> of the conquering of space is crucial to our continued growth as <u>a nation</u>. <u>Our nation</u> needs space exploration and development in order to maintain the worldwide balance of power, to provide new sources of raw materials, and also to establish a new frontier, against which another generation of Americans may be able to grow and rediscover the values that made our country <u>great</u>. <u>This greatness</u> has been diminishing of late, and today's space program is now a prime target of both governmental and nongovernmental critics. These critics argue that we must radically cut back on, if not eliminate entirely, our space program because it has allowed itself to be

dominated by the Defense Department (DOD) and has been unable to define a specific set of goals necessary for future <u>progress</u>. <u>Progress</u> must be made by designing new projects like the space plane and re-organizing NASA into <u>a joint, Cabinet-level agency</u>. <u>This agency</u> would be the sole directional institution for space-related activities within <u>the country</u>. <u>Our country</u>'s future is, despite the complaints of critics, inexorably linked to the future of <u>the space program; our space program</u> must go forward.

Eventually, one stops reading for content and concentrates instead only on "whether he will do it again." This is the first page of a 12-page paper, every sentence of which is Topic Changed from the sentence before it. It was, in its own technical way, a tour de force; but it never allowed the author to discuss anything for longer than one sentence. After a while, it became unreadable.

Notice how long two of his sentences had to become in order to allow the Topic-changing transition to the next sentence to be accomplished. The poor fellow just could not allow himself to end the sentence until he had reached a topic to which he was willing to change at the beginning of the next.

Topic Changing, like all the other structural advice offered in this volume, cannot be reduced to a rule-oriented technique. It will function well only when the writer wishes to move the reader from fact to linking fact. When that is the progression needed, it works wonderfully to keep the multiplicity of facts in the order in which the writer wishes the reader to encounter them. And like Topic Stringing, it often appears for just a short while within a paragraph instead of dominating the entire paragraph. Neither one is a "technique" to use while writing; rather, both are natural results of taking care of the reader's expectations on a sentence-by-sentence basis. As terms, therefore, they are therefore more descriptive than proscriptive or prescriptive.

Topic Stringing

Topic Stringing develops when (1) you consistently and accurately articulate "whose story" your sentences are, and (2) your text stays the story of the same person, thing, or idea for two or more sentences. Consider the following paragraph, which deals with the American wilderness of the eighteenth century and the European colonists who came to settle in it:[9]

10a. The wilderness masters the colonist. It finds him a European in dress, industries, tools, modes of travel and thought. It takes him from the railroad car and puts him in the birch canoe. It strips off the garments of civilization and arrays him in the hunting shirt and the moccasin. It puts him in the log cabin of the Cherokee and the Iroquois and runs an Indian palisade around him. In short, the frontier is at first too strong for the man. It imposes on him conditions which it furnishes or it destroys him, and so the Indian clearings come to fit him and the Indian trails lead him. Little by little, the wilderness changes because of him, but the outcome is not the old Europe. . . . The fact is, that here is a new product that is American.

In this paragraph, every sentence begins with "the wilderness" or one of its lexical references ("the frontier" or "it"). We call such a string of similar referential words a *lexical string*. Because of the Topic position placement of this lexical string, the paragraph is read by most readers as a *continuing story* of the wilderness. That story is a dramatic one: For the first half of the paragraph, the American wilderness is dominating the early colonists from Europe, forcing them to adapt to new circumstances. About halfway through, the domination stops as the colonist begins to adapt. By the end, the wilderness is the one doing the changing. The story is recognizably American, the subject of any number of films from the mid-twentieth century: The powerful figure holds sway until at first chastened and then eventually humbled and humanized by forces less powerful than it. But at the end of this paragraph/story, the result is not the defeat of the wilderness but its amalgamation, with the colonist, into a new hybrid called "America."

Now let us change the structure of the paragraph, thereby changing its continuing story:

10b. The colonist must submit to the wilderness. He comes to it a European in dress, industries, tools, modes of travel and thought. Because of it, he leaves the railroad car for the birch canoe. He must strip off the garments of civilization and array himself in the hunting shirt and the moccasin. He must adopt the log cabin of the Cherokee and the Iroquois and run an Indian palisade around himself. In short, the colonist is at first too weak for the wilderness. He must accept the conditions which it furnishes or perish, and so he fits himself to the Indian clearings and follows the Indian trails. Little by little, he transforms the wilderness, but the outcome is not the old Europe. . . . The fact is, that here is a new product that is American.

In this revision, the concept of Topic Stringing has been retained, but the occupant of the Topic position has changed. Now we have the story focusing on the colonist. The colonist is dominated by the wilderness for the first half, after which he adapts and eventually takes over. It is once again a recognizably American story, this time from the old Andy Hardy–type films: The weakling has sand kicked in his face by the bully but then builds himself up and perseveres until he overcomes his adversary, after which they become great friends and make each other better people as a result. Both (10a) and (10b) end with the insistence that neither party has been vanquished. The great strength of this "new product that is American" lies in the hybrid nature of this new country. It is neither a former wilderness made European nor a society of Europeans transformed into frontiersmen.

Try now yet another permutation:

10c. The wilderness masters the colonist. It finds him a European in dress, industries, tools, modes of travel and thought. It takes him from the railroad car and puts him in the birch canoe. It strips off the garments of civilization and arrays him in the hunting shirt and the moccasin. It puts him in the log cabin of the Cherokee and the Iroquois and runs an Indian palisade around him. In short, the frontier is at first too strong for the man. He must accept the conditions which it furnishes or perish, and so he fits himself to the Indian clearings and follows the Indian trails. Little by little, he transforms the wilderness, but the outcome is not the old Europe. . . . The fact is, that here is a new product that is American.

In this revision, the wilderness is the Topic String that dominates the first half of the paragraph, ceding the Topic position to the colonist for the second half. The transition is neatly accomplished by a Topic Change in the middle: "In short, <u>the frontier</u> is at first too strong for <u>the man</u>. <u>He</u> must accept the conditions. . . ."

This is the original paragraph by Frederick Jackson Turner, the central point of his influential work articulating the frontier thesis of American history. Version (10c) serves Professor Turner's needs far better than either of the preceding versions. Whose story is (10a) all the way through? -- that of the wilderness. Whose story is (10b) all the way through? -- that of the colonist. Whose story is (10c) all the way through? -- that of *America*. How is that the case when there are two different topic strings? Because in Professor Turner's paragraph (10c), the "whose story" occupant of the Topic position is always the one who is stronger -- the one who is "winning." As long as the wilderness is winning, it gets to keep control of the Topic position; but as soon as the colonist turns the tide, the colonist takes over the Topic position. As a result, when the paragraph ends, it has throughout been the story of *winners*. America is the hybrid amalgamation of winners. That, says Professor Turner, is what gives America its special character.

With apologies for disturbing Professor Turner in his grave, here is the paragraph revised again, with the opposite arrangement of Topic Strings: It is the story of the colonist in the first half and then switches to the story of the wilderness for the second.

10d. The colonist must submit to the wilderness. He comes to it a European in dress, industries, tools, modes of travel and thought. Because of it, he leaves the railroad car for the birch canoe. He must strip off the garments of civilization and array himself in the hunting shirt and the moccasin. He must adopt the log cabin of the Cherokee and the Iroquois and run an Indian palisade around himself. In short, the frontier is at first too strong for the man. It imposes on him conditions which it furnishes or it destroys him, and so the Indian clearings come to fit him and the Indian trails lead him. Little by little, the wilderness changes because of him, but the outcome is not the old Europe. . . . The fact is, here is a new product that is American.

In this strange version, America turns out to be an amalgamation of losers. It is what is left over after the stuffing has been kicked out of both combatants. The facts have not changed; but their varied locations change the way in which the facts will most probably be perceived.

Turner's thesis is not an accumulation of facts; it is the particular intellectual combination he makes of facts, thereby transforming information into ideas.

Transport yourself for a moment into the following fantasy: Professor Turner goes off to the library one morning to collect data for his famous theory, accompanied by a young friend of his, the author of the "Breton lai" paragraph. (See above, example (5), page 155). At the end of the afternoon, they agree to share with each other all the information they have unearthed. They return to their homes, each to write his own presentation of the day's combined findings. Professor Turner turns out "The Frontier Thesis of American History," including the above paragraph (10c). What kind of paragraph does the author of the Breton lai produce when she deals with the same material? Following true to her structural habit of beginning every sentence with new information, she makes one sentence the story of "moccasins"; in another she tells the story of "canoes"; and later we hear the story of "strength" and "acceptance." The whole paragraph might look something like this:

10e. Mastery was achieved by the wilderness over the colonist. European industries and tools mark his appearance, along with European dress, modes of travel, and thought. The birch canoe replaces the railroad car. The moccasin and the hunting shirt are worn by the colonist when he strips off the garments of civilization. The log cabin of the Cherokee and the Iroquois house him; he is surrounded by the Indian palisade. The strength of the frontier exceeds that of the man, in short. Acceptance must be afforded the conditions it furnishes, or he must die, and so the Indian clearings are accommodated, and he follows the Indian trails. Little by little a new product called America -- not the old Europe -- emerges from this transformed wilderness.

It *sounds*, for all the world, like there is a lot of "thinking" going on in this paragraph; but it would take someone like Professor Turner to perceive from it the thought presented in Professor Turner's article. We have to stop assuming that whenever prose *sounds* like it ought to be meaningful, it must be our fault as readers for not making the "proper" sense of it.

I have often argued that there is no such thing as good writing that is bad thinking or bad writing that is good thinking. If the thinking is bad, there is nothing there to write well. (It might be elegant, powerful in sound, impressively written; but it is not well written.) And if the writing is bad, how can anyone tell that there is good thinking underneath?

This concept was challenged one day by a senior colleague of mine, a highly respected scientist named Irving. According to him, a senior colleague of his had brought him an article in 1962, told him to read it, insisted that it was the most brilliant essay on the subject ever written, and predicted that it would change everything Irving would do for the rest of his career. Irving read the article and found it almost incomprehensible -- one of the worst pieces of writing he had ever encountered. But because Irving had such deep respect for his senior colleague, he persevered, making his way through the opaque article 11 times. On the eleventh reading, Irving finally discovered the brilliance of the article, and it did indeed influence the rest of his career. Was this not, Irving challenged me, the perfect example of the combination of bad writing and good, even brilliant thinking? I remember my reply: "Irving, by the time you had read that article for the eleventh time, you had become its coauthor." (Irving was pleased -- and rightly so -- to discover that he had coauthored one of the most brilliant articles he had ever read.) And so it would be for a budding history professor from our fantasy who might come across the Breton lai author's paragraph about moccasins and canoes and be able to extract from it, on the eleventh reading, Professor Turner's frontier thesis of American history.

Readers need more than just the building blocks of information; they need instructions for assembly.

Topic Strings and Lexical Strings

The more sophisticated prose becomes, the more important becomes the principle of Topic Stringing. Here for an example is the opening paragraph of an undergraduate essay:

11a.   The issue of terrorism is exemplary of the media's role in international affairs. It is the media which is largely responsible for the success of terrorism. Terrorism would have little impact if it were not for the extensive coverage that it receives from the world's newspapers, magazines, and news broadcasts. By threatening human life the terrorists acquire the world attention that they need. The public displays an emotional reaction to graphic pictures of the horrific aftermaths of terrorism. The reports not only stir up passionate responses from the public, but this type of reaction intensifies the issue because the public becomes involved. The media is aiding the terrorists by giving world coverage to their cause. On the other hand, the public definitely has a right to know, so coverage should be less intense. Sometimes the citizens sympathize with the terrorists' cause, if not their methods of resolving it. This was the case with the recent Shi'ite hijacking of a TWA airliner, which received extensive coverage.

I have presented this example to literally thousands of readers. When asked to suggest a grade for its effectiveness, they differ widely, suggesting everything from A– to C–, with a majority choosing something in the B range. Rarely does anyone suggest that the prose is entirely ineffective. I would rate the paragraph as not yet being ready for a grade.

If you wish to play the home version of this game, please re-read paragraph (11a) and circle all the words that create the lexical string having to do with "terrorists" and "terrorism" (i.e., circle any word, like "them," that seems to refer to "terrorists" and any word, like "hijacking," that seems to refer to acts of terrorism).

When I do this exercise with even as few as 20 people, the number of words circled normally varies from about 8 to 18; some find as many as 23, with the record being 27. That happens not because some readers are more perceptive than others but because different people interpret differently. This paragraph, like any other unit of discourse, is infinitely interpretable. A word that seems to one person directly relevant to "terrorism" will, to another, seem distinctly irrelevant.

Here is one possible list, the underlined words in the reprint below of (11a). Good arguments can be summoned for why some choices should be deleted and others added; but that is beside the point being made here. The more important concern is *where* in the sentence structure the underlined words appear -- in the Topic position, the Stress position, or the middle.

11a.   The issue of terrorism[1] is exemplary of the media's role in international affairs. It is the media which is largely responsible for the success of terrorism[2]. Terrorism[3] would have little impact if it were not for the extensive coverage that it[4] receives from the world's newspapers, magazines, and news broadcasts. By threatening human life[5] the terrorists[6] acquire the world attention that they[7] need. The public displays an emotional reaction to graphic pictures of the horrific aftermaths of terrorism[8]. The reports not only stir up passionate responses from the public, but this type of reaction intensifies the issue[9] because the public becomes involved. The media is aiding the terrorists[10] by giving world coverage to their[11] cause.[12] On the other hand, the public definitely has a right to know, so coverage should be less intense. Sometimes the citizens sympathize with the terrorists'[13] cause[14], if not their[15] methods[16] of resolving it. This was the case with the recent Shi'ite hijacking[17] of a TWA airliner, which received extensive coverage.

Terrorism/Terrorists

Word	Structural Location
1	Topic
2	Stress
3	Topic
4	middle
5	Topic
6	Topic
7	Stress
8	Stress
9	middle
10	middle
11	Stress
12	Stress
13	middle
14	middle
15	Stress
16	Stress
17	middle

Note that despite a large number of appearances in the paragraph, terrorists and terrorism do not dominate the Topic position. The paragraph therefore is not primarily "their story."

Here is a fresh copy of the same paragraph, offering you an opportunity to circle a second lexical string, this time the one for everything having to do with "the media" and "coverage."

11b. The issue of terrorism is exemplary of the media's role in international affairs. It is the media which is largely responsible for the success of terrorism. Terrorism would have little impact if it were not for the extensive coverage that it receives from the world's newspapers, magazines, and news broadcasts. By threatening human life the terrorists acquire the world attention that they need. The public displays an emotional reaction to graphic pictures of the horrific aftermaths of terrorism. The reports not only stir up passionate responses from the public, but this type of reaction intensifies the issue because the public becomes involved. The media is aiding the terrorists by giving world coverage to their cause. On the other hand, the public definitely has a right to know, so coverage should be less intense. Sometimes the citizens sympathize with the terrorists' cause, if not their methods of resolving it. This was the case with the recent Shi'ite hijacking of a TWA airliner, which received extensive coverage.

An interesting question: Did the paragraph seem to you a different paragraph this time through? Many people feel that way. (More on this later.)

Once again, people's lexical strings tend to vary in length widely, from 8 to 20+ members. Here is one possibility:

11b. The issue of terrorism is exemplary of the media's[1] role in international affairs. It is the media[2] which is largely responsible for the success of terrorism. Terrorism would have little impact if it were not for the extensive coverage[3] that it receives from the world's newspapers[4], magazines[5], and news broadcasts[6]. By threatening human life the terrorists acquire the world attention[7] that they need. The public displays an emotional reaction to graphic pictures[8] of the horrific aftermaths of terrorism. The reports[9] not only stir up passionate responses from the public, but this type of reaction[10] intensifies the issue[11] because the public becomes involved. The media[12] is aiding the terrorists by giving world coverage[13] to their cause. On the other hand, the public definitely has a right to know, so coverage[14] should be less intense. Sometimes the citizens sympathize with the terrorists' cause, if not their methods of resolving it. This was the case with the recent Shi'ite hijacking of a TWA airliner, which received extensive coverage[15].

Media/Coverage

Word	Structural Location
1	middle
2	Topic
3	middle
4	Stress
5	Stress
6	Stress
7	middle
8	middle
9	Topic
10	middle
11	middle
12	Topic
13	middle
14	middle
15	Stress

Like the terrorists/terrorism string above, the media/coverage lexical string, despite its numerous appearances, does not dominate the Topic position. The paragraph seems not to be primarily "their story."

One last time: You are invited to circle the lexical string having to do with "the public."

11c. The issue of terrorism is exemplary of the media's role in international affairs. It is the media which is largely responsible for the success of terrorism. Terrorism would have little impact if it were not for the extensive coverage that it receives from the world's newspapers, magazines, and news broadcasts. By threatening human life the terrorists acquire the world attention that they need. The public displays an emotional reaction to graphic pictures of the horrific aftermaths of terrorism. The reports not only stir up passionate responses from the public, but this type of reaction intensifies the issue because the public becomes involved. The media is aiding the terrorists by giving world coverage to their cause. On the other hand, the public definitely has a right to know, so coverage should be less intense. Sometimes the citizens sympathize with the terrorists' cause, if not their methods of resolving it. This was the case with the recent Shi'ite hijacking of a TWA airliner, which received extensive coverage.

"The public" produces a shorter lexical string for most people, ranging from 4 to 12 members. Again, here is one possibility.

11c. The issue of terrorism is exemplary of the media's role in international affairs. It is the media which is largely responsible for the success of terrorism. Terrorism would have little impact if it were not for the extensive coverage that it receives from the world's[1] newspapers, magazines, and news broadcasts. By threatening human life the terrorists acquire the world[2] attention that they need. The public[3] displays an emotional reaction to graphic pictures of the horrific aftermaths of terrorism. The reports not only stir up passionate responses from the public[4], but this type of reaction intensifies the issue[5] because the public[6] becomes involved. The media is aiding the terrorists by giving world[7] coverage to their cause. On the other hand, the public[8] definitely has a right to know, so coverage should be less intense. Sometimes the citizens[9] sympathize with the terrorists' cause, if not their methods of resolving it. This was the case with the recent Shi'ite hijacking of a TWA airliner, which received extensive[10] coverage.

Public

Word	Structural Location
1	middle
2	middle

<u>Public</u>

<u>Word</u>	<u>Structural Location</u>
3	Topic
4	middle
5	middle
6	Stress
7	middle
8	Topic
9	Topic
10	Stress

Note that like the members of the previous two lexical strings, the public does not dominate the Topic position. The paragraph seems not to be primarily "their story."

Here is the list of the Topic positions for each of the paragraph's ten sentences.

The issue of <u>terrorism</u> is . . .

It is the <u>media</u> which is . . .

<u>Terrorism</u> would have . . .

By threatening human life, the <u>terrorists</u> acquire . . .

The <u>public</u> displays . . .

The <u>reports</u> not only stir up . . .

The <u>media</u> is . . .

On the other hand, the <u>public</u> definitely has . . .

Sometimes the <u>citizens</u> sympathize . . .

<u>This</u> was . . .

In this ten-sentence paragraph, terrorists and terrorism occupy three Topic positions; the media and coverage occupy three Topic positions; the public occupies three Topic positions; and the tenth Topic position is filled with a nonreferential "This." As a result, this paragraph is the consistent story of no one. That is unfortunate, since it seems intended to explore a continuing, developing argument that needs to be anchored in one particular perspective, at least for a while.

Note that each of the three lexical strings dominates the Topic positions for two sentences in a row. The author constantly begins to form a Topic String but leaves off just when the going gets good. This author reminds me of the child entering a candy store with a five-dollar bill in his fist. He is determined to shoot the whole wad on one particular delight. Immediately his eye is caught by the peppermint sticks; but just as he begins to commit to the purchase, he notices the licorice whips.

Converted from sticks to whips, he begins once more to make his purchase -- only to notice the caramels. Clearly they should be the final choice . . . except, on second thought, those peppermint sticks really do look good. And so forth.

The author of this paragraph was probably not aware that she was being tempted from topic to topic, creating for the reader a kind of intellectual pinball machine experience. She could have discovered that hidden fact had she investigated the significant structural locations of his paragraph. Just a quick glance at the first few words of each sentence would have made the underlying problem apparent.

Note that the words "the issue" appear on all three of my lexical strings. There lies the problem of the paragraph in a nutshell: The author never quite made it clear to us -- or, I would wager, to herself -- what "the issue" of this paragraph really was.

To revise this paragraph, the author might well consider what the terrorists' (or the media's or the public's) "story" might be. Any kind of heuristic process, formal or informal, will be of help. What does each need or want from the others? How do they go about getting it? What is their relationship with each of the others? What might that relationship be? What ought that relationship be?

Whatever heuristic is used, the organizational principle of the topic string will help the writer stay on one topic until enough has been said for that topic to change. We start to see that this structural stylistics (reader expectation) approach creates simultaneously a method of revision and a method of invention. It not only indicates what has gone awry with the thought process to this point but also facilitates a reentry into that process to produce both clarification and amplification of thought.

I asked above what I called an "interesting question": Did the paragraph read differently during the circling of the media/coverage lexical string than it had during the circling of the terrorist/terrorism lexical string? For many readers, it does. The difference may well be caused by the nature of the exercise itself. In each case, readers are asked to pay special attention to a particular lexical string -- that is, they are requested to valorize it above all other lexical strings. On one reading, therefore, the paragraph is processed as the continuing story of terrorist/terrorism, all other information being subjected to that story's focus. On the other reading, the paragraph is transformed to investigate the continuing story of media/coverage, which therefore provides a different context for all the other information. The same paragraph "reads" differently given different reading instructions.

As thought becomes more and more complex, the number of lexical strings in a given paragraph tends to increase. The larger the number of lexical strings, the more complicated it becomes for the reader to perceive which story in the paragraph is the central story. Writers cannot stand over the shoulder of every reader, pointing out which lexical string should be particularly valorized at any given moment; nor can they print the dominant lexical string in a contrasting color -- nor underline it -- nor capitalize it -- nor add a rubric in the margin "effects of terrorism on media." The clearest instruction a writer can manage to send the reader is a structural one: The reader will know to value one lexical string over all the others *if that lexical string is also a topic string*. The topic string becomes a continuing contextualizer: The whole string of sentences becomes the story of the constant Topic position occupant.

If the terrorism paragraph were recomposed and amplified into several paragraphs, each of which offered as a topic string the party whose continuing story the paragraph was, then the reader would know to tie all other lexical strings in that paragraph back into the central, unifying lexical string -- the topic string. Picture the terrorism paragraph with its three main lexical strings graphically portrayed:

11d. The issue of terrorism is exemplary of the media's role in international affairs. It is the media which is largely responsible for the success of terrorism. Terrorism would have little impact if it were not for the extensive coverage that it receives from the world's newspapers, magazines, and news broadcasts. By threatening human life the terrorists acquire the world attention that they need. The public displays an emotional reaction to graphic pictures of the horrific aftermaths of terrorism. The reports not only stir up passionate responses from the public but this type of reaction intensifies the issue because the public becomes involved. The media is aiding the terrorists by giving world coverage to their cause. On the other hand, the public definitely has a right to know, so coverage should be less intense. Sometimes the citizens sympathize with the terrorists cause, if not their methods of resolving it. This was the case with the recent Shi'ite hijacking of a TWA airliner, which received extensive coverage.

One the one hand, this visual image of the interstitial network of lexical strings fairly represents the confusion a reader has in making sense of the prose. On the other hand, this representation is quite unfair: Even if the paragraph were clear as could be, with a topic string firmly dominating the flow of the thought, the visual presentation of the lexical strings would still look as confused as it does above because in all sophisticated prose, a number of lexical strings function simultaneously.

But picture both the terrorist paragraph and the Professor Turner paragraph printed on paper so wide that (a) no sentence need extend to a second line and (b) each sentence begins at the left margin. The terrorists paragraph will still look just as muddled:

11d.

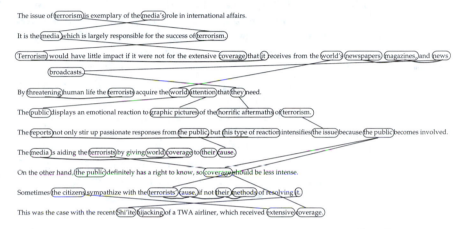

The issue of terrorism is exemplary of the media's role in international affairs.

It is the media which is largely responsible for the success of terrorism.

Terrorism would have little impact if it were not for the extensive coverage that it receives from the world's newspapers, magazines, and news broadcasts.

By threatening human life the terrorists acquire the world attention that they need.

The public displays an emotional reaction to graphic pictures of the horrific aftermaths of terrorism.

The reports not only stir up passionate responses from the public but this type of reaction intensifies the issue because the public becomes involved.

The media is aiding the terrorists by giving world coverage to their cause.

On the other hand, the public definitely has a right to know, so coverage should be less intense.

Sometimes the citizens sympathize with the terrorists' cause, if not their methods of resolving it.

This was the case with the recent Shi'ite hijacking of a TWA airliner, which received extensive coverage.

In contrast, Professor Turner's organization, given the same treatment, would manifest itself visually, the two topic strings forming a backbone of perspective:

10c.

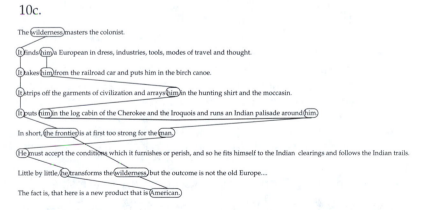

The wilderness masters the colonist.

It finds him a European in dress, industries, tools, modes of travel and thought.

It takes him from the railroad car and puts him in the birch canoe.

It strips off the garments of civilization and arrays him in the hunting shirt and the moccasin.

It puts him in the log cabin of the Cherokee and the Iroquois and runs an Indian palisade around him.

In short, the frontier is at first too strong for the man.

He must accept the conditions which it furnishes or perish, and so he fits himself to the Indian clearings and follows the Indian trails.

Little by little, he transforms the wilderness but the outcome is not the old Europe....

The fact is, that here is a new product that is American.

As children grow into young adults, we should abandon the counsel "Vary the way you begin your sentences to keep your reader interested" and replace it with "Construct topic strings when you wish to develop a point of view or an argument continuously, from its basis to its conclusion." When sentences become complex and sophisticated, a reader's desire for variety is naturally fulfilled by the nature of the content. That desire for variety is replaced by a need for coherence and control.

E *xerting Control over Revision Through Topic Stringing*

Again, Topic Stringing must not be taught as a new "rule" of how to *write* paragraphs; rather, it should be presented as a quick and convenient way for a writer to *perceive* how a paragraph is progressing and how it is leading the reader through the interpretive process. To make the point, I turn to a passage most generously offered to us all by Erika Lindemann, from her *Rhetoric for Writing Teachers*, in which she demonstrates in great detail the three drafts of her own rewriting process that produced the opening paragraph of her chapter on rewriting.

Three pages into the chapter, she shares with us her original version of the chapter's first paragraph, handwritten, with all the crossouts and scratched changes. The format itself is instructive and comforting: Students can see that even successful writers like Professor Lindemann scritch and scratch just like they do in trying to transform awkward beginnings into elegant finished products. Here is the last phase of her much revised first draft:

12a.   Rewriting -- a swear word in most English classes. Most students consider it a punishment, a penalty for writing poorly in the first place. Many teachers, bent on beating comma faults out of their students, require them to submit pages of corrections or to complete appropriate exercises in the composition handbook. If writing seems painful, as it does for most students, surely rewriting prolongs and intensifies the agony. They remain convinced that, having given the paper their best effort, there is no way to improve it by revision. For almost all writers, rewriting is a frustrating chore. When we contemplate an almost alien draft, we must admit that some of our ideas refuse to be governed by words, that in many ways the writing has flaws. To protect ourselves from viewing our mistakes as a personal failure, we construct defenses which permit us to ignore the draft altogether. Listen to these students as they rationalize their reluctance to rewrite their papers: [12 student comments omitted].

She was displeased with this draft, as she most candidly informs us:

> Almost a week later, after I'd drafted the entire chapter, I reread it. What especially displeased me about the first paragraph was its lack of focus. Although I had intended to present the students' perspective on rewriting, I shifted the focus several times from "rewriting" to "students" to "teachers" to "all writers/we" back to "students."

I wasn't secure about my audience either. Although I wanted to communicate how students feel about rewriting papers, their teachers would be reading the book. Some readers surely would resent phrases like "swear word" and "teachers bent on beating comma faults out of their students' papers." Some would resent my aversion to handbook exercises. . . . The last sentence didn't please me either; I needed a lead into the students' comments, but the alliterating *r*'s seemed too fancy.

While I agree wholeheartedly with these revisionary perceptions, I fear they must seem like sheer magic to a struggling student. How does one go about perceiving that revision is necessary? How does one revise successfully? First, be as intelligent and experienced as a professional English teacher; then struggle to spot where your intelligent perceptions failed to make it to the surface of your prose; then fix that.

The Reader Expectation approach will not by itself solve revision problems; it will, however, lead a writer to perceive where many problems exist and then suggest options for change. Professor Lindemann complains about the lack of "focus" on the student perspective. A less skillful writer of the same paragraph might not be able to detect that lack of focus merely by reading hard. However, that lesser writer could, with relative ease, check back through the sentences' topic positions and announced agents to find out exactly whose story most readers would perceive the paragraph to be. Here are the results of such a search:

Topic Position	Other Agents
Rewriting	
Most students	
Many teachers	
writing	rewriting
They	
For almost all writers	rewriting
we	we
	our ideas
	the writing
To protect ourselves	we
[You] Listen	

Whose story is this draft? Looking in the Topic positions, where we expect to find that answered, we discover it is the story of virtually everyone and everything that appears in the paragraph. Whose story *should* it be? That is entirely up to the writer. Professor Lindemann thought it should be the students' story. Someone else might have opted for it to be the story of "writing" or of "rewriting" or of "we" or of "our ideas" instead. No one of these choices is the correct one. There is no correct one. There is only the question of what a particular writer, in this case Professor Lindemann, is trying to communicate.

If we go along with Professor Lindemann's choice of focus, one possible path to revision is clear: We should try to get "students" into the Topic position as often as is reasonable. Note that she tells us about the problem -- how and to whom she shifted the focus several times -- but does not tell us why it is so or how to go about changing it. Note also that she tells us that she eventually shifts the focus back to "students" at the end; my lists of Topic position occupants and agents do not include students toward the end, suggesting that she had *not* succeeded in that refocusing attempt for a majority of her readers. It makes sense, therefore, that she should be puzzled at that point as to why "the last sentence didn't . . . lead into the students' comments." The students had not been in evidence for several lines; no wonder they seem out of place in the final sentence.

Here is the product of her much revised second draft:

12b.   Rewriting has become a dirty word in most English classes. Most students see it as a punishment, a penalty for writing poorly in the first place. Many teachers reinforce this notion by asking students to "correct the mistakes" in journals or on separate sheets of paper the teacher will collect for review. Some students are sentenced to complete exercises that mend their ways of misusing commas. Others remain convinced that, having done the best they could on the paper, there is no way to improve it by revision. It's too much of a chore. Listen to their own typically frustrated, honest reasons for not rewriting papers:

If we scan the second draft for Topic position occupants and other agents, we come up with the following:

Topic Position	Other Agents
Rewriting	
Most students	
Many teachers	the teacher
Some students	
Others [students]	
It [revision]	
[You] Listen	

Improvement: "Students" have found their way to the Topic positions of three out of the seven sentences. But a "focus" problem remains: Two sentences are still the story of "rewriting"; one features "teachers"; and the still problematic final sentence is still the story of the inferred "you" (that is, those of us reading).

Here are some of her comments on this draft:[10]

> The second version is considerably shorter than the first, probably because I kept asking myself as I wrote, "What do *students* think about rewriting?" The last sentence gave me fits; for all my tinkering with it, I just couldn't get from my own paragraph to the quoted materials. . . . Changing "Sometimes teachers" to "Some students" kept the focus of the paragraph on students (a deliberate passive construction helped).

Once again, her comments focus on what I would consider the most pressing concerns; but also again, they do not help the student understand how she revised -- or how they should go about revising -- effectively. *Why* does changing "teachers" to "students" keep the focus on the students? Because the change deposited the students in the Topic position, keeping the story *their* story. *Why* did the "deliberate passive construction" prove helpful? Because (1) the passive was the best way to get the students into the Topic position, and (2) their story is a passive one and therefore is best expressed by a passive verb.

Here is the third draft, the one she settled on for the published chapter:

12c. For most students, <u>rewriting</u> is a dirty word. They see it as a punishment, a penalty for writing poorly in the first place. Many teachers reinforce this notion by insisting that students correct mistakes in papers already graded or complete workbook exercises on writing problems in someone else's prose. Rewriting the <u>whole</u> paper, students believe, means they've failed the assignment. For almost all writers, rewriting remains an unpleasant chore, a process which confronts them with countless inadequacies in the draft and convinces them that words manipulate writers, not the other way around. Students rewrite their papers reluctantly for many reasons, as the following comments attest:

If we compare this time some of the *Stress* position occupants with those of the first draft, we can spot some of the reasons for the superiority of this revision.[11]

Stress position (1st draft)	Stress position (3rd draft)
most English classes	a dirty word
in the composition handbook	in someone else's prose
⎯⎯⎯⎯→	they've failed the assignment
the writing has flaws	[words manipulate writers,] not the other way around

A quick glance at the Stress positions of a paragraph can often tell writers whether the parts of the sentences expected to be interesting to readers actually are so. Through several revisions, Professor Lindemann's good ear led her to fill the Stress positions with the new, intriguing information. Understanding the reader expectations involved allow all of us -- those with good ears and bad -- to increase the chances that the "good stuff" will be read as "good stuff."

The last draft is also an improvement concerning the "student" topic string. Here are the structural locations of "students" in the paragraph's six sentences:

1) Topic position

2) Topic position

3) Agent of the subordinate clause. (Topic position ceded to "teachers.")

4) Parenthetical agent only. (Topic position ceded to "rewriting.")

5) Nonexistent. (Replaced by "almost all writers.")

6) Topic position

If we wanted to make yet a fourth draft of this paragraph, increasing still more the intensity of the focus on "students," all we need do is ensure that once the "students" take over the Topic position, they never let it go. That is, we would be establishing a writing perspective from their point of view by making them into a topic string. In doing that, we would be making decisions that Professor Lindemann perhaps would not make:

a) We would be undercutting the control, power, and presence of "teachers." That involves both gains and losses.

b) We would be choosing to talk only about "students," leaving the generalizations about "almost all writers" for some other paragraph. That seems to me an outright gain in intensity and cohesion, especially since the sixth (and still troublesome) sentence switches back to the agency of "students." That agency has to carry all the way through the 12 comments that follow the colon.

Here is one possible version of such a topic-strung revision:

12d. For most students, <u>rewriting</u> is a dirty word. They see it as a punishment, a penalty for writing poorly in the first place. They are forced by their teachers to correct mistakes in papers already graded or to complete workbook exercises on writing problems in someone else's prose. If they are requested to rewrite an <u>entire</u> paper, they immediately assume that their first draft was a complete failure. For so many students, rewriting remains an unpleasant chore, a process which confronts them with countless inadequacies in their draft and convinces them that words manipulate writers, not the other way around. If they do rewrite, they do so reluctantly, as their pained reasons attest:

   1) I wait until the last minute, so there's no time to rewrite. [and 11 more examples follow]

By itself, this rewrite is neither better nor worse; it just does a particular job more effectively. If the intent of the paragraph is to focus exclusively on students (as a preparation for the long list of student comments that follows), then one could well argue in its favor.[12]

Note also that with "students" reappearing consistently in the Topic position, the problem of redundancy surfaces. In the first sentence we are told that students do not like rewriting; the second, third, and fourth sentences develop and exemplify that statement; but then the fifth and sixth sentences do only a little more than restate the initial assertion. The paragraph now appears a good candidate for just a bit of pruning, especially in the penultimate sentence:

12e. For most students, <u>rewriting</u> is a dirty word. They see it as a punishment, a penalty for having written poorly. They are forced by their teachers to correct mistakes in papers already graded or to complete workbook exercises on writing problems in someone else's prose. If they are requested to rewrite an <u>entire</u> paper, they immediately assume that their first draft was a complete failure. Worst of all, they become convinced by the countless inadequacies in their draft that words manipulate writers, not the other way around. If they do rewrite, they do so reluctantly, as their pained reasons attest:

> 1) I wait until the last minute, so there's no time to rewrite. [and 11 more examples follow]

Compare this final revision to version (12a) with which we started:

12a. Rewriting -- a swear word in most English classes. Most students consider it a punishment, a penalty for writing poorly in the first place. Many teachers, bent on beating comma faults out of their students, require them to submit pages of corrections or to complete appropriate exercises in the composition handbook. If writing seems painful, as it does for most students, surely rewriting prolongs and intensifies the agony. They remain convinced that, having given the paper their best effort, there is no way to improve it by revision. For almost all writers, rewriting is a frustrating chore. When we contemplate an almost alien draft, we must admit that some of our ideas refuse to be governed by words, that in many ways the writing has flaws. To protect ourselves from viewing our mistakes as a personal failure, we construct defenses which permit us to ignore the draft altogether. Listen to these students as they rationalize their reluctance to rewrite their papers: [12 student comments omitted].

The final revision no longer suffers from the problems Professor Lindemann enumerated. It now has the focus she sought.[13]

S *eeking Control over Reader Response*

Some students have felt uneasy about this Reader Expectation approach because, they argue, it seems so manipulative. It *is* manipulative. It helps writers manipulate probable reader response. There is nothing unethical or even unsocial about manipulation per se; it becomes a negative quality only when it is abused. We are manipulating people every time we try to convince them to see something the way we see it. That rhetorical task is the stock in trade of almost every profession. It functions in literary criticism essays, in grant applications, in civil rights legislation, in political candidacies, in business agreements, in charitable solicitations, and in legal briefs. A major part of growing up is the transformation from being someone who merely responds and obeys to being someone who chooses and controls. We should not shrink from the task of helping our students grow up. The critical word is *choice*. Choice enables.

I have been claiming throughout that this approach is no mere cosmetic process and that it helps bridge the perceived gap between thought and expression of thought. The following extended example synthesizes the Reader Expectation principles developed in this chapter and demonstrates how disastrous badly written prose can be -- even when it does not *sound* so bad.

Here is the opening paragraph from the statement of facts of an actual legal brief.

13a. J sold all its assets and liabilities in 1956 to BCC. As part of this transaction a single share of J common stock was retained by BCC to continue the J trade name and corporate form, although J no longer conducted business as an independent manufacturing entity. Thereafter BCC manufactured the J power press line until the defendant, A, purchased BCC's entire manufacturing operation in 1962.

This again is "splat prose" -- dull, pedestrian, even unto being footsore. On first reading, few would call this disastrous or incompetent prose; but that is what it is. This paragraph loses the case. And the Judge may never consciously know what happened.

The background: J is a corporation, founded in 1926 to produce power presses -- large machines that are fashioned to shape hunks of metal into molded forms by mechanically or electronically lowering a heavy upper steel block onto a stationary metal base with molding capabilities. J owned and operated the company for 30 years, selling everything in 1956 to another corporation, BCC. BCC operated the company for six years and then sold to yet another corporation, A.

In 1986, one of these machines malfunctioned, the upper part descending when it should not have, thereby severing three fingers from the hand of the operator. The operator naturally wished to be compensated; in our legal system, which is accomplished through money damages. He wishes to sue for $2,000,000. Company A seems clearly in the direct line of liability; but Company A has little money. Any judgment rendered only against Company A would produce the company's bankruptcy and therefore little or no cash for the plaintiff. Company BCC no longer exists in any form and therefore cannot be sued. Company J, though no longer in the power press business, still exists and is flourishing. If the plaintiff wants $2,000,000, clearly Company J is his best source for it -- *if* J can be directly tied to the accident. The plaintiff sues J.

The case can be considered a moral tossup. On the one hand, the plaintiff has been seriously damaged and deserves whatever kind of restitution can be made him. J manufactured the original press and is responsible for its design and function. On the other hand, Company J has been out of the power press business for 30 years; it has had no opportunity to inspect the presses and no authorization to make repairs. Nor has it profited in any continuing way from those presses since the 1956 sale was concluded.

Question: Which lawyer wrote paragraph (13a) above: the one for the plaintiff? or the one for J? The fact that the paragraph by itself does not scream against injustice, one way or the other, is an indication of how poorly written and ineffective it is. Clarence Darrow, the great trial lawyer of the first third of the twentieth century, used to boast to his opponents, "If you let me write the facts, I'll let you argue the law -- and I'll win." By that he did not mean he would suppress all those facts that were harmful to his case; he meant he could tell the story so convincingly from his client's perspective that it would compel a judge to come up with a legal conclusion favoring his side.

Especially since the case is a moral tossup, we should be able to revise these facts to support either side. Let us therefore assume the role of J's lawyers and put the Reader Expectation approach to use in making the best possible case for him. That done, we will cross the street and join the plaintiff's law firm to see how we would recast the same facts in order to make the best possible case for him.

Before 1970, the outcome of this case would have been simple and straightforward. J, having abandoned the power press business in 1956, would have been considered too far back in the chain of events to incur any liability for an accident that happened in 1986. However, in the 1970s and 1980s, product liability law went through such a series of radical transformations that to collect for your leaky rowboat you could take a shot at suing Noah. J might be found liable under the present facts if the linkages between people and events can be kept intact throughout that 30-year period. As J's lawyers, we need to worry mainly about one legal principle: Can a direct line be firmly forged from J to the plaintiff's accident? If so, J might be in trouble.

As J's lawyers, we must try to get J out of the picture as soon as possible so we may later demonstrate just how far removed J was from the 1986 accident. We start with the first sentence:

J sold all its assets and liabilities in 1956 to BCC.

Since this is the first sentence of this narrative, we cannot use the Topic position to link backwards. We can use it instead to contextualize the reader for the rest of the sentence and perhaps even the rest of the paragraph. Since our need is to set our only action as far back in time as possible, we would do well to begin the sentence with "in 1956." Located there, that date promises most readers that some kind of chronology will follow.

We are not allowed to bolster that effect by adding "In 1956, thirty long years ago, . . . " because that would be an argument, not a statement of fact. No year, despite one's private perception, is longer than another. The conventions of legal briefs require that only facts be stated in the statement of facts and that all argument be reserved for the argument section. We know, however, that well-stated facts will argue for themselves, almost to the point of reducing the later argument section to the status of a conventional necessity.

At the moment, this sentence is the story of J. It might be nice if we could disappear from the storyline altogether, but we cannot; our name is on the title page of this brief, and the opponents' brief will concentrate on their version of our story at great length. We must take the opportunity here to tell our version of our story. Once we have done that, we then should disappear.

Our story is clear in this sentence. What action did we do? Look to the verb: We "sold." Fine.

Our revision so far has produced the following:

13b. In 1956, J sold all its assets and liabilities to BCC.[14]

BCC now occupies the Stress position. Good. We would like to put BCC in the spotlight. "We sold to THEM." They will then be available in the next sentence to take over the Topic position; the story will become *their* story. That is good for us.

The second sentence has two clauses, which we will consider separately.

As part of this transaction a single share of J common stock was retained by BCC to continue the J trade name and corporate form, . . .

"As part of this transaction" is indeed backward-linking old information, but not immediately perceivable as such. "This" sounds old; but there was no verb "to transact" in the previous sentence. Since "transaction" refers to J's having *sold* everything to BCC, the backward link can be better established by using the nominalization of the previous verb:

As part of this sale, . . .

Better. But then we run into serious trouble. This sentence is once again the story of J, in the form of "a single share of J common stock." J was supposed to have disappeared from sight by now. This sentence was supposed to have transferred the storyline to BCC. The problem lies in the disastrous passive construction, which puts J up front and buries BCC in the middle. By switching BCC to the Topic position, the sentence become BCC's active story:

13c. As part of this sale, BCC retained a single share of J common stock to continue the J trade name and corporate form, . . .

Even though we now have BCC up front, we should still be troubled by the continuing presence of J in the sentence. It will be *their* argument, not ours, that the single share of stock retains the presence of J; it will be ours that the share of stock is just a piece of paper. We therefore should remove J from the labeling of this stock, trade name, and corporate form:

13d. As part of this sale, BCC retained a single share of the common stock to continue the trade name and corporate form, . . .

Much better. The rest of the second sentence:

. . . although J no longer conducted business as an independent manufacturing entity.

Disaster: J is back. J has once again recaptured the "whose story" position from BCC and has become once again an active agent. To solve the problem, we might just do away with this clause altogether; but we thereby would be foregoing a dramatic statement that could be quite valuable to us. Not only did we *sell*; we also *died*. Where should such information appear? Since it is an important part of our story, it should appear when we are in the process of telling our story. We should therefore transport this item to the first sentence, where we were content to have J occupy the Topic position. That revised first sentence will now tell our story with a far greater sense of force and closure:

13e. In 1956, J sold all its assets and liabilities to BCC and thereupon discontinued doing business as an independent manufacturing entity.

Much better: In 1956 we sold and died. We have sacrificed something for this transformation: The spotlight of the Stress position no longer features BCC. We could recreate an internal Stress position for BCC by following it with a semi-colon; or we could allow the lack of internal Stress position to cause an even greater build to the moment of our death. Both work. In either case, BCC will be available as old information for the Topic position in the second sentence.

On to the third sentence:

Thereafter BCC manufactured the J power press line until the defendant, A, purchased BCC's entire manufacturing operation in 1962.

BCC appropriately appears in the Topic position; it is still BCC's story. In the Stress position, however, we might prefer the spotlight to shift not to the date but to the new future agent, A. We also should again eradicate the presence of J: It is no longer the "J Power Press line," but only "the power press line."

13f. Thereafter BCC manufactured the power press line until its entire manufacturing operation was purchased in 1962 by A.

So far, so good, it seems:

13g. In 1956, J sold all its assets and liabilities to BCC and thereupon discontinued doing business as an independent manufacturing entity. As part of this sale, BCC retained a single share of the common stock to continue the trade name and corporate form. Thereafter BCC manufactured the power press line until its entire manufacturing operation was purchased in 1962 by A.

The prose is distinctly stronger, more direct, and more clear in presenting the procession of agency. But trouble awaits us just around the corner. It will only be a sentence or two before the plaintiff appears and the accident happens. We discover to our horror that our statement of facts has neatly, even forcefully, done the plaintiff's job for him. In one paragraph, we have forged a strong and direct linkage from J to BCC to A to the Plaintiff and his injury. We have accomplished this anti-feat by relying on the tactic of topic changing. The 30 years have flown by in just a few sentences, making us the plaintiff's near neighbor in time, and therefore potentially liable for two million dollars' worth of damages.

What to do? We should tell the story so the Judge will experience the facts as we do. We can separate J from the plaintiff by separating our demise from his accident, not only in historical time but also in reading time.

To accomplish this, we can leave the solid first sentence as it is: "In 1956 we sold to BCC and died." We then use Topic Changing to transfer the story to BCC, as we have already done. But then we change our tactics: We Topic String. In the next sentence, we keep BCC up front, so the sentence tells BCC's story. Then the next sentence again tells BCC's story. And the next. And the next.

New paragraph. It too tells BCC's story throughout.

Another new paragraph. It too tells BCC's story throughout.

And perhaps another. We will tell all the ways in which BCC made this company and this product its own: They discontinued four models and created three new ones; they expanded into 14 new states; they discontinued the old advertising program and started anew; etc., etc., etc.

Somewhere on the bottom of the second page of the statement of facts, a paragraph ends by noting that in 1962, BCC sold the company to A. Now it is A's story, and A will take over the Topic position.

BCC had the company for 6 years; A had it for 24. Therefore, the next Paragraph is all A's story -- and the next -- and the next -- until, somewhere on the top of page 4, the plaintiff appears and the terrible accident occurs. At that point, the Judge should say, "Oh, the poor plaintiff. But he wants WHO to pay for this? J? All the way back there?" By spelling out the facts this way, we have given the Judge the <u>experience</u> of "30 long years ago." We stand a chance now of winning.

Now we cross the street and become the lawyers for the plaintiff. Without revisiting the individual sentences of the original paragraph, we can state the one Reader Expectation concept we will feature throughout our statement of facts: We will put J as often as possible into the *Topic* position, making almost everything J's story. It might seem at first that we would want J always in the Stress position; but that would produce prose with only one whiningly repetitive thing to focus on -- J. We want instead to tell a continuing story about a great many things, all done by the J company and its products. But we will not begin "In 1956"; we will begin "In 1926" -- and we too will demonstrate "30 long years," albeit a different 30.

After the J power press company has been sold by J, the J power press company will continue to sell its wares. The J corporate form, the J stock, the J trade name all will occupy Topic positions to demonstrate the continuity of the presence of J throughout this history. We may often find ourselves opting for passive constructions in order to keep the different manifestations of J in the Topic position. In 1956, when J sells to BCC, we will press the fast forward button, always indicating the continuing presence of the J corporation in the Topic position.

Both of these stories -- J's and the plaintiff's -- deserve to be told, each from the perspective of the party involved. Both deserve to be told with force and with intended influencing of reader expectations and responses. That response can be best gauged by recourse to our knowledge about Topic and Stress positions, old and new information, Topic stringing and changing, agency, action, and contextualization.

T he Tollbooth Syndrome

Why do people produce writing like the J power press facts, or the Breton lai paragraph, or the terrorism paragraph, or any of the many examples of uncontrolled and uncontrolling writing we have been investigating? At least in part, it stems from a misconception of the nature of the writing task.

We learn to write in schoolrooms. For a great majority of people, writing remains an academic kind of task -- a burden to be dispensed with at the earliest moment possible. They receive an "assignment"; they talk with the appropriate people; they search through the library; they read whatever they need to read; they "organize their thoughts," perhaps into some sort of outline form; and then, when the thinking has mercifully come to an end, they "write it up." They "reduce it to words." They "clothe the thought with expression." Wrong from the start. Writing is not something that happens after the thinking process has ceased. It *is* a thinking process. The English teacher's one-liner makes good sense: "How do I know what I mean till I see what I say?"

Naturally, if thinking has ceased before writing begins, then writing will probably remain sheer drudgery. But this misconception of the *process* of writing is based on a deeper misconception of the *purpose* of writing. This latter misconception can be described in a metaphor I call the Tollbooth Syndrome.

Picture the following: You are a well-known professional in your field. You have been summoned for three weeks to New York (a city that makes you uncomfortable) to consult on an important issue. You are staying with friends in southwestern Connecticut and commuting by car into Manhattan at 5:30 A.M. to avoid the rush hour. (You soon discover that in Manhattan, 5:30 A.M. *is* the rush hour.) On one particular day you have spent from 6:00 A.M. to 9:30 P.M. in the office with nothing to show for it. Everything that could go wrong did go wrong. At 9:30 you make your way down to the parking lot, through wind and rain. You fight your way through 90 minutes of crosstown traffic and finally find yourself battling the dark and the elements on Route 95 as you head toward Connecticut.

Just before you leave the State of New York, you see a sign: "Tollbooth, one mile, 40¢, exact change, left lane." You search in your pocket for change and find you have precisely three coins -- a dime, a nickel, and a quarter -- just the right amount. You enter the exact change lane. In front of you is a shining red light but no barrier; to the left of you, the hopper. You are tired and irritable as you roll down the window, the wind and rain greeting you inhospitably. You heave the change at the hopper. The quarter drops in; the dime drops in; but the nickel hits the rim and bounces out. What do you do? Do you put the car in Park, get out, and grovel in the gravel for your nickel? No. Do you put the car in reverse and change to another lane where a human being can make change for your dollar bill, after which you will return to your original lane? No. You go through the red light. It is raining; it is nearing midnight; there are no police in sight; and if you did get caught, you would be able to show the proof of your good intentions in the gravel. The alternatives are just too burdensome. You go through the red light.

If you do this, I would argue, you do it because you choose to ignore the fundamental purpose of paying tolls. Tired and irritated as you are, you do not wish to recognize that in order for you to continue on that road you must transfer 40 cents of your accumulated wealth to the Connecticut state government, with which it will keep the roads in good repair and pay tollbooth operators. Instead you rationalize that in order for you to continue on the road *you must be dispossessed of 40 cents* -- and you have been. It is therefore moral, if perhaps a bit risky, for you to plunge further on into the Connecticut darkness.

The same holds true for "the writing task." Most writers do not care whether the intended audience actually receives their 40 cents' worth of communication; they care only that once they have digested all that work of thinking they now dispossess themselves of it onto the paper. That done, all is done. If a reader complains of the lack of X later on, the writer can lead the reader to the hidden spot in the gravel where some traces of X exist, faintly gleaming through the grime in which it has become embedded.

That works in school. There, the student is usually rewarded for demonstrating that she has done a great deal of work and has found many of the right signal words or facts. In the professional world, it matters not how much work the writer has done; it matters only that the reader actually gets delivery of precisely that which the writer intended to send. Students tend to assume that the professor *already knows* what thoughts to make of all the information they have been able to gather on the subject. The mere presence of the information implies the presence of the thought. More often than not, they are right to assume as much. Given the semantic clues that accompany the "right" information, teachers perform the task of interpretation for the writer. Without an actual act of communication taking place, it naturally must be hard to teach students much about the act of communication. Down deep, they are convinced it is all a performance, a private charade between student and teacher, with both in on the game.

We cannot entirely avoid afflicting our students with the tollbooth syndrome. There is indeed a limitation of what we can create to be at stake or at risk in collegiate production of essays. But we can better prepare them for the day when things are quite literally at stake when they produce prose. We can do it better by concentrating on those who should be receiving the 40 cents.

Endnotes

1. See the discussion of the second sentence of the "turn-key" example (Example #16) in Chapter 4, page 115.
2. I borrow this example and its revision from Joseph Williams.
3. The revisionary process demonstrated here was not likely to produce a better paragraph. There was too little substance on the page that could be the object of revision. Instead, the process was used to demonstrate to the student just how little he had produced in the first place. When nothing can be made of nothing, it is time to start over. Because of this revision process, the student became capable of spotting such vacuity for himself in the future.
4. The rule against the split infinitive is a curious one. I suspect it is a holdover from Latin grammar, because in Latin the infinitive is a single-word verb form. The prohibition can be explained in expectation terms: Whenever a reader encounters the word *to* in an infinitive, the reader *expects* the verb to follow immediately. I would argue, therefore, that an adverb be allowed to split an infinitive when it so changes the nature of the verb that it becomes part of the verbal concept. I think "fully understand" is an action, different from "fully to understand" and "to understand fully." "Fully understand" is something I try to do every day. Therefore, it seems to me reasonable to allow writers to use

"to fully understand," since the word "to" is indeed followed immediately by "the verb."

5. In my description of this sentence, you might note that I have repeatedly filled my Stress positions with the same material, the words "old information." One might argue that I have broken the "rule" of always putting new information in the Stress position. I point this out to underscore again the importance of not letting these statements of reader expectations dwindle or rigidify into rules. My violation of reader expectation here is intended to convey that no matter where you look in her sentence, you always wind up with "old information." The ancients had a name for this figure of speech: *epistrophe*.

6. Many of us were taught that "however" cannot be the first word in a sentence. That prejudice comes from the Latin language, where the word usually appeared as the second word in a sentence. The argument might be made that "however" qualifies that which is to its left by that which will appear to its right; if it comes first in a sentence, there is nothing to its left. "This, however, . . . " would be the appropriate beginning. However, any reader of an English sentence beginning with "however" knows immediately that the new sentence will qualify the entire sentence to the left of "however." I see no reason not to use it as a first word. I see many reasons not to use it as a last word, except for comic or anticlimax effects.

7. Sadly, this paper -- if it continues in the same manner for a number of pages -- often receives a grade of A or A–. The grade is a reward for her diligence in finding "amour courtois" and "Chretien de Troyes" and the "Norman nobility." Some might give it a B+, with a comment suggesting that "the ideas are fine but need further development." *What* ideas?

8. I retain Joe Williams's use of the term *Topic Stringing* but use *Topic Changing* where he uses *Topic Chaining*. The "change" concept seems more immediately relevant to this shift in Topic position perspective. None of this is very new: See the "Theme/Rheme" work over a half-century ago by the members of the Prague School of Linguistics. (For more on them, see Chapter 6, below.) Our main contribution here is the adaptation of linguistic perception to the practical usages of rhetorical pedagogy.

9. I borrow this example, and the first three alternate revisions, from Joseph Williams.

10. I have omitted Professor Lindemann's comments when they applied primarily to diction. The Reader Expectation approach cannot by itself refine a writer's sensibilities where vocabulary is concerned. It can, however, make writers aware of which words have particular force in a sentence due to their structural location; that, in turn, might lead the writer to reconsider the effects of particular combinations of emphasized words.

11. I have switched here from concentrating on the Topic position to investigating the Stress position. Using a Reader Expectation approach, it does not matter which structural elements you consider or in which

order you consider them. Each connects to the others. Altering one will usually alter the others. There need be no hierarchy.

12. Professor Lindemann has explicitly articulated an intention to keep the focus on "students." Had someone else written the paragraph, that writer might have intended to locate students in a small world of teachers and in a larger world of "almost all writers." In such a case, my rewrite would be a step in the wrong direction. Again, the paragraph is neither good nor bad by itself but only in terms of the communicative task it is trying to perform.

13. The generosity Erika Lindemann demonstrates by sharing this revisionary process with us is typical of her character altogether. It has always been a pleasure to work with her and learn from her.

14. It is actually not possible to sell all of one's liabilities. But that legal consideration is extraneous to the concerns of the present discussion.

6

Paragraphs: Issues, Points, and Purposes

Procrustean Problems in Teaching the Paragraph

When we write, we expend most of our effort ands attention creating sentences. If you are writing a paragraph in a chapter of a book, your main focus at any given moment is usually on the creation of the presently unfolding sentence. For readers, however, the unit of thought -- and therefore the primary unit of experience -- tends to be the paragraph. Writing consistently handsome sentences will not suffice, therefore, if together they do not form coherent and persuasive paragraphs.

From the beginning of this country's educational history until the last two decades of the twentieth century, composition textbooks concentrated first on the grammar and correctness of the sentence and then on the structure and development of the paragraph. While Barrett Wendell, in the 1890s, was insisting that the sentence is more properly the subject of revision than prevision,[1] Fred Newton Scott was creating a composition course entirely based on paragraph construction.[2] Scott cites Alexander Bain as his authority for considering the paragraph a pragmatic microcosm of the essay:

> Adapting an old homely maxim, we may say, Look to the Paragraphs, and the Discourse will look to itself, for although a discourse as a whole has a method or plan suited to its nature, yet the confining of each paragraph to a distinct topic avoids some of the worst faults of Composition; besides which, he that fully comprehends the method of a paragraph will also comprehend the method of an entire work.[3]

But what have we been teaching as "the method of the paragraph"? For most of our history, textbooks have suggested that if the student can be taught to produce *correct* sentences, then the combining of several of these into a properly formulated *structure* will produce good paragraphs.

That structure has most commonly required that the opening sentence should be a "topic sentence," which, by definition, states the issue and point of the paragraph. The topic sentence is to be followed by "support" (examples, proofs, or reasons) -- usually three of them -- each encapsulated in its own sentence. Some particularly rigid formulations dictate that the final sentence of the paragraph must restate the issue/point articulated by the topic sentence. This produces a form we could call the Wizard of Oz paragraph -- with its innards singing "because, because, because. . . ." While this is no longer visible as a college level technique, it remains remarkably dominant in some states at the high school level.

Such a structure could not have remained this long in our institutional pedagogy had it not some underlying efficacy. For students in grammar school and middle school, it actually accomplishes a great deal of good:

-- It provides something most illusive but most necessary in the writing process -- a place to start. Once you have figured out the topic sentence, paragraph construction seems all downhill from there.

-- It makes students feel secure, grounded, founded, found. They like it because it provides a sense of orderliness and induces a sense of comprehensiveness.

-- It teaches that good writing demands good *structure*.

-- It allows teachers to evaluate students' efforts relatively objectively. Once the important point has been articulated in the opening sentence, it is only a momentary task to note whether the three support statements are there and the concluding repetition in place. Moreover, that one-sentence wonder also functions as a skim-master: The whole essay can be evaluated by quickly reviewing the topic sentences alone, which produce the Reader's Digest version of the text. This is especially important when you have 45 students in every class.

But there is a serious problem with this pedagogy: Although the Topic Sentence approach to teaching paragraphs works admirably well as a sixth-grade calisthenic, it does not accurately describe how professional adults structure their prose. Take any published book down from the shelf, open it, and select a paragraph at random. Beginning with that paragraph, examine 100 consecutive paragraphs. How many will contain precisely five sentences, the first of which is recognizable as a "topic sentence," the next three as "support," and the fifth as the "conclusion" that restates the topic sentence? Perhaps zero. Perhaps one. The odds are low that you will find two. This ironclad structure so many of us were taught as children simply does not describe the reality of adult prose.

It is not a problem that we teach this to sixth graders or eighth graders; it is an admirable way to start. It is a problem, however, that this early training is so clear-cut and so forcefully pounded into so many of us that the latter-day adult training we get in paragraph structure -- if any -- has difficulty dislodging that which was so fundamentally established. That five-sentence, topic-sentence-dominated construct lives on inside many of us. (This may not be the case for those of us who work in the Academy; it is clearly the case for a large percentage of the lawyers, scientists, and businesspersons I have dealt with over the years.)

Greek mythology tells us that in the days of Theseus there was a villain known as Procrustes who ran a macabre bed-and-breakfast just off the road somewhere between Corinth and Thebes. Knowing that travelers from one of those cities to the other would be unable to make the journey in a single day, he would wait on the road at sunset, ready to persuade a weary pedestrian to spend the night at his place. "You'll need a good meal and a good night's rest to finish the journey. Why not stay with me for the night?" It sounded like the kindest of invitations. But although the unsuspecting house guest might well have enjoyed the fine dinner, he could take little pleasure in retiring thereafter; for Procrustes suffered from a murderous compulsion that all visitors should fit the length of his guestroom bed -- precisely. Those who were too tall had their feet amputated or their legs shortened by their host and died from loss of blood. Those who were too short were stretched by their host on the rack and died from internal hemorrhaging. There were but few fortunate souls whose bodies were just the right shape to fit the structure that had been prepared for them. Those lucky few escaped unharmed and thought all was right with the world.

The five-sentence Topic Sentence paragraph structure so many of our students were taught is just such a Procrustean bed. One size fits all. It matters not what size the bulk of your thought might be: To fit this prescribed resting place, it must be foreshortened or (more often, in the sixth grade) unnaturally extended to satisfy the requirements of your pedagogical host.

We *know*, when we become adults, that we cannot function with such restraint; but few of us have received any guidance in understanding *the structure that readers expect to experience* when making their way through a paragraph. It should come as no surprise, when we stop to think about it, that there is no *single* structure that accomplishes this important task.

The five-sentence "Topic Sentence" paragraph model fails for many reasons, three of which are paramount:

(1) It assumes that the issue of the paragraph can always be stated in a single sentence.

(2) It assumes that the issue of a paragraph is always the same as its point.

(3) It limits our perspective on the paragraph; it looks inward, treating the paragraph as a self-sufficient unit, a piece of discourse unaffected by a context larger than itself. That belies the reader's normal experience. Readers rarely read paragraphs in isolation from each other. Most paragraphs proceed from a previous one and lead to a following one. Nor do readers stop at the end of each paragraph to analyze its contents in retrospect.

To put students more in touch with actual reader experience, a pedagogy of the paragraph should accomplish the following:

1) It should look both inward at the paragraph and outward toward the paragraph's larger context.

2) It should recognize that readers do not wait for the end of a paragraph to begin their interpretation of it. Instead, they experience a paragraph as discourse that is constantly *unfolding*. Their interpretation of a paragraph therefore shifts and changes with the appearance of each additional word.

3) It should take into account the distinctions between a paragraph's *issue* (the ground it might cover), its *point* (the intellectual claim it makes), and its *purpose* (the function it performs in the discourse as a whole).

I *ssue*

The Topic Sentence approach was right about one important reality of reading: It is generally the case that readers expect that a paragraph will be "about" whatever shows up first. Whatever comes first provides a *context* for all that follows: Everything that follows is read with that beginning unit already in mind. Try the following brief demonstration. Contemplate each of the following three words in isolation for about three seconds, visualizing as vividly as you can the color each suggests.

RED

YELLOW

BLUE

Now try to clear your mind of that experience, in order to contemplate afresh, in the same intense way, the following list of three words:

BLUE

YELLOW

RED

For most readers of these two lists, the word "yellow" summons up two slightly different colors. The first "yellow" may be tinged with orange, since it comes out of a context of "red"; the second "yellow" may be tinged with green, since it comes out of a context of "blue."

Context controls meaning. Whenever you encounter the word "yellow," it makes available to your brain *all* the "yellows" you have encountered in life to date. It has the potential to designate a large number of potential meanings: an area on the spectrum stretching from orange to green; or the qualities associated with brightness or sunshine or moonshine or gold or rottenness or cowardliness or decay or a large number of other possibilities. The particular *choice* of "yellowness" your mind will make will depend to a great extent on the other words in the sentence that surround it; but at the moment of encountering the word, its context is provided specifically by the words that have just preceded it.

> Every word a writer uses depends for its "meaning" on the reader's previous experience with the object or situation which this word suggests.
>
> (Kenneth Burke, *Counter-Statement*)

Context controls meaning. That is so not only for a mere list of words but also for a carefully ordered list of words encountered as a paragraph.

Our sixth-grade teachers were right that readers assume paragraphs will be about the issue announced at their beginning; and they were right to presume that sixth-graders never need more than one sentence to articulate the issue of a given paragraph. But for a large percentage of paragraphs in sophisticated, professional prose, a single sentence cannot suffice to define the issue, to articulate the matter at hand. Some paragraphs require two sentences to get the issue going; some even require three. Readers know this intuitively. Rather than looking exclusively at the first sentence, they will proceed up to three full sentences into the paragraph before deciding that they have fully experienced the paragraph's issue. But their tolerance for expansion is matched by their need for context: Once readers have wandered three sentences into the paragraph, they will seize upon the material in those first one, two, or three sentences and make it *their* issue regardless of whether the rest of the paragraph discusses it or not. If the issue was not clearly delineated, readers have to figure it out for themselves. Experience has demonstrated that when this is the case, ten readers are likely to make anywhere from five to ten different decisions as to what the issue of the paragraph was supposed to have been.

Given the old topic sentence model, issues should always be easy to spot. The first sentence should always translate, "This paragraph will be about X."

1. I like the Spring because of the pretty flowers. I like the Spring because of the tulips. I like the Spring because of the roses. I like the Spring because of the daffodils. I like the Spring because of the pretty flowers.

In sophisticated prose, however, the two-sentence issue is not only quite common but also quite necessary. Here are a few of the many, recognizable two-steps:

2a. "So you see where we've come to. Well, here's where we're going. . . ."

2b. "Here is a general statement. From that generalization, I'm going to focus on this more specific development. . . ."

2c. "You may think that things are X. Well, they're really Y. . . ."

Even three-sentence issues are possible, and not unfamiliar:

3a. "So you see where we've come to. It's not been much help. Let's take a look at X instead. . . ."

3b. "Here is X. Here is Y. The important thing to consider here is the relationship between X and Y. . . ."

3c. "X is intriguing. Just look at how intriguing X can be. But that is the case only when you ignore Y. . . ."

3d. "X looks convincing. Y looks convincing. But neither does the job very well when you consider Z. . . ."

Many issues, however, are not as clear-cut as some of these models -- no matter how unambiguous they might seem to any given reader. When I first started turning students' attention to spotting issues of different shape and size, I was constantly surprised at how much class time was consumed by disagreements concerning what the issue "actually" was. The disagreements often became unpleasant, resulting in the students' becoming convinced that the exercise (along with the insights it was intended to serve) was a great waste of time.

It took me a long while to understand those students were right to disagree. There was no actual or objectively verifiable issue. Each of them was interpreting the paragraph the best he or she could; the less simplistic the paragraph, the more likely that the individual perceptions and interpretations of it would differ. The intentions of the writer do not fully control the prose once it is in the hands of readers. If the interpretation of every paragraph is necessarily infinite (in the sense that there is always yet one more interpretation possible), then how can we teach the "correct" way to form paragraphs? Answer: There is no "correct" way. The best we can hope to do is to teach the writer to send readers enough instructions for interpretation that a substantial percentage of the audience will interpret the paragraph more or less as the writer intended. Those instructions, on the paragraph level as on the sentence level, are communicated mainly through structural location of information and ideas.

We therefore should be teaching our students not how paragraphs must be but rather how readers normally go about experiencing paragraphs. The reader's perception of a paragraph is not a static one -- a retrospective look at a finished unit; instead, it is a dynamic, constantly unfolding one, as each new sentence creates a new selection of interpretive choices, discarding some possibilities while opening up others. I suggest, therefore, that we teach paragraphs one sentence at a time and through time. I offer here a few examples of this relatively slow-motion technique. Please be patient with them: They "read" slower than they sound in class.

4a. Much has happened since the Apollo program and the Mercury and Gemini missions that paved the way for it in the early 1960s.

This sentence is the first in its paragraph. When I present it to a class, I ask a question based on the concept of reader expectation: "If the rest of the paragraph is about this sentence, what is the rest of the paragraph likely to be about?" Most (but not all) expect we will hear more about what has happened in the development of the space program. We proceed to the second sentence:

4b. Numerous scientific and communications satellites have been launched into Earth orbit.

Does this begin to fulfill the promise of (4a)? It could: It might be the first of several examples of the "much that has happened" in the space program. On the other hand, perhaps it does not: The paragraph may "settle down" to talk exclusively about "Earth orbit" experiments -- in which case it would have taken two sentences, not one, to state the issue. Here is the next sentence:

4c. Unmanned deep-space probes have been sent to the sun, the moon, and the planets, where they gathered a wealth of information about our solar system.

Apparently, since we are off to the sun and the planets, we are not going to linger over the "Earth orbit" experiments. Because we are hearing about yet more of the "much that has happened" in the space program, it now looks like the whole paragraph will be devoted to this continuing effort. In other words, we are now somewhat convinced that this paragraph has a one-sentence issue.

The next two sentences confirm this suspicion:

4d. Skylab demonstrated that American astronauts could live and work in space for months at a time.

4e. And a dramatically different launch vehicle entered service: the space shuttle.

The final sentence of the paragraph is not immediately as clear in its function:

4f. The winged reusable craft was supposed to make space flight routine and cheap.

Since "the winged reusable craft" refers to the space shuttle, this sentence speaks more to its immediate predecessor than to the first sentence of its paragraph (4a); but for the paragraph as a whole, it took only one sentence to get on the table the issue that would be discussed.

I am going to look at two more (somewhat contrasting) paragraphs in this manner, slow-paced though that might seem, to demonstrate how this approach uncovers complexities in the reading process that help students far more than sets of rules tend to do. Here is the first sentence of the next example:

5a. This book is the beginning of an attempt to move the study of American literature away from the small group of master texts that have dominated critical discussion for the last thirty years and into a more varied and fruitful area of investigation.

(Jane Tompkins, Sensational Designs, opening sentence)

Again I ask, "If the rest of the paragraph is about this sentence, what is the rest of the paragraph likely to be about?" The answers here vary a good deal more than did those to paragraph (4). Some focus on the concept of "beginning," suggesting that the paragraph will go on to talk about what should come *after* the beginning. Others suggest the paragraph will concern the concept of "moving away," demonstrating how that will be accomplished. Others expect to encounter examples both from the canonical list of "master texts" and from the "more varied and fruitful" list. In my experience, readers have not agreed on what is likely to come next. That does not mean that Tompkins did a "bad job" in writing her "topic sentence"; rather, it suggests that it may well take more than one sentence here to narrow the focus of this paragraph enough to let the discussion begin.

The path of development becomes clearer as the next two sentences unfold. Here is the second sentence:

5b. It involves, in its most ambitious form, a redefinition of literature and literary study, for it sees literary texts not as works of art embodying enduring themes in complex forms, but as attempts to redefine the social order.

Most readers do not perceive this sentence as beginning the development of the one-sentence issue that preceded it. I ask a slightly different question: "If the rest of the paragraph is about *these two sentences put together*, what is the rest of the paragraph be likely to be about?" Many people concur in their response at this point. They see in this sentence the principle behind the move from master texts to noncanonical texts; they expect (but are not sure) the rest of the paragraph will explore not the move, nor the texts, but rather the reason behind the move from one set of texts to another. At the moment, this looks like a possible two-sentence issue.

How will we know? When will we know? If the third sentence begins the *discussion* of the previous two-sentence unit, then we probably have a paragraph defined by a two-sentence issue.

We move to the third sentence:

5c. In this view, novels and stories should be studied not because they manage to escape the limitations of their particular time and place, but because they offer powerful examples of the way a culture thinks about itself, articulating and proposing solutions for the problems that shape a particular historical moment.

Most see this third sentence as fulfilling the expectation raised by the first two sentences considered together and moving on to develop that two-sentence unit: It further addresses the principle (announced in the second sentence) behind the move (announced in the first). When they read the paragraph's next sentence, they tend to agree that it continues the development begun in the third sentence:

5d. I believe that the works of fiction that this book examines were written not so that they could be enshrined in any literary hall of fame, but in order to win the belief and influence the behavior of the widest possible audience.

The final sentence invokes the same general agreement:

5e. These novelists have designs upon their audiences, in the sense of wanting to make people think and act in a particular way.

So for paragraph (5), it took not one but two sentences to get on the table that which the rest of the paragraph would develop. Stated more concisely, paragraph (5) has a two-sentence issue.

The third example of this slow-motion technique is a paragraph from Robert Gutman's biography of Richard Wagner, the great opera composer, who also wrote an extraordinary amount of prose concerning aesthetic and political theories. Among that prose is an article on revolution, written one year after the revolutions of 1848 had swept across Europe.

6a. His [Wagner's] poetic article of 1849, "The Revolution," had promised a new Europe.

"If the rest of the paragraph is about this sentence, what is the rest of the paragraph likely to be about?" Based on this sentence alone, most readers expect to hear more about that poetic political article. Some expect more specifically to hear about the "new Europe." The second sentence:

6b. To the jubilant strains of shrill, warlike music, a paradise was to rise from the devastation of a volcanic upheaval.

Most agree that this sentence fulfills the expectations raised by the first sentence. It continues to talk about Wagner's 1849 article, suggesting something of the paradisal nature of the "new Europe" after the revolution has succeeded. So far this sounds like a one-sentence issue, with the discussion likely to begin with the next sentence.

The third sentence:

6c. But in the finale of the *Ring*, hostility gives way to a calm resignation, knowing neither defeat nor victory.

For many, the "but" dashes the expectations that had been raised by the first sentence and confirmed by the second. We are no longer reading about an 1849 article promising paradise after the revolution; now we are shifting to considering his four massive operas known as the *Ring* cycle, which suggest that after the revolution life may not be significantly improved. I ask, "If the rest of the paragraph is about these *three* sentences put together, what is the rest of the paragraph likely to be about?" Some expect to hear about the pessimistic operas. Others expect to find the writer contrasting the article with the operas. Here is the rest of paragraph (6), which I offer to the students a sentence at a time. (All the proper names refer to characters in the *Ring* cycle operas.)

6d. Brynhild bids her father, Wotan, rest to music of infinite sadness, and the old world sinks down because it can no longer bear its load of deceit and treachery. Hagen, preaching Bakunian-style violence to the end, is pulled into the depths of the cascading river by the Rhine Daughters. But, though they happily ride the crest of destruction with their restored treasure, no new Eden can follow. Alberich is still at large, and the new world may well be as troubled as the old.

The operas took over; the prose article faded away. That 1849 article had been used as a contrast just to launch us into a consideration of the *Ring* cycle's pessimism about the effects of revolution. In paragraph (6), it took three sentences to get on the table that which the paragraph would proceed to discuss. This paragraph has a three-sentence issue.

What then of the possibility of a *four*-sentence issue? Or a *five*-sentence issue? To my knowledge, this just does not happen in good English prose. I have never encountered a successful issue stated in more than three sentences. Once a fourth sentence arrives and fails to make clear whether the issue of the paragraph is one, two, or three sentences, we tend to give up hope for coherence. We perhaps continue to struggle through the paragraph; but we are attempting only to accumulate *information* in the hope that *thought* will eventually reveal itself. That "paragraph" is not really the unit of discourse we call a paragraph: It is instead a hunting and gathering expedition on the part of the writer -- and we are along for the ride.

While I cannot fully *explain* why issues are limited to three sentences in professional English, I can point to other equally powerful (and equally mysterious) limitations imposed by the number three. When we are informed that we are about to be presented with a number of reasons or examples of something, our expectation includes the possibilities that the list will include one, two, or three items. Three is perfection. Three is complete. The arrival of three suggest the end and the beginning of things -- "ready, set, GO!" . . . "and *so* we *come* to an *end*" -- or the perfection of things -- "the red, white, and blue." Three is mystical, magical, and melodic. If we are handed more than three -- even if the number is only four -- we tend to feel overburdened. Can you imagine Goldilocks and the *four* bears?

"Somebody's been sleeping in *my* bed," said the Papa Bear.

"Somebody's been sleeping in *my* bed," said the Mama Bear.

"Somebody's been sleeping in *my* bed," said the Baby Bear.

"Somebody's been sleeping in ―-" [Oh shut up already!]

Three is our limit. Four is a million.

This sentence-at-a-time technique helps students discover how readers read and, consequently, how easy it is for readers to be distracted from the writer's intentions. In concentrates on the *fluidity* of the interpretive process.

Our middle school and high school training tended to teach us to build a paragraph structure by piling sentence-brick on sentence-brick, until the thought-edifice was complete.

The process goes something like this: We create sentence #1. It is a visible entity, whole unto itself, a brick. Call it brick #1. Then we create the second sentence, brick #2. If we are "good" writers, we might provide the reader with some sort of mortarlike connecting material that cements the two together. Then we create brick #3, perhaps with more mortar -- and then brick #4 and #5 and so forth, until we have "finished" our paragraph. A six-brick paragraph might look like this:

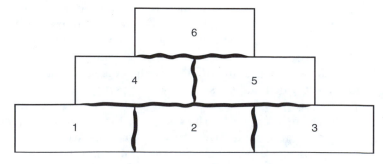

As we gaze at this paragraph-building, we can still see clearly the definition of each individual brick. The unit as a whole remains the sum of its individual, still perceivable parts.

This image provides a false representation of what actually happens to readers in their linear journey through a paragraph. It even more greatly falsifies the nonlinear experience the reader has of perceiving the paragraph holistically.

In the actual reading act, each sentence, as it arrives, may fulfill some previous expectations and simultaneously raise others. Let us not think of paragraphs as essentially linear:

nor as brick buildings,

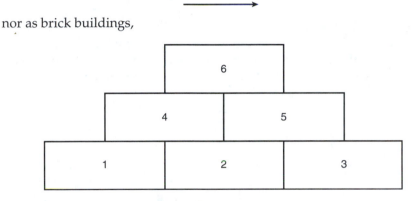

but rather as a liquid, fluid experience that produces a shape that continually changes as we progress further into it.

In the figure below, consider the dotted line a moment of time -- the moment when the reading eye encounters information. The wavy line represents sentence #1 of the paragraph, flowing toward the eye. As the eye encounters the words, the brain cumulatively forms a concept of the sentence's thought. Once the brain has taken in all the words of the sentence, the totality of that sentence thought is pictured at the right as a liquid pool.

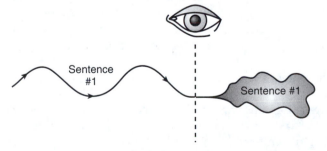

At that point, sentence #2 starts to flow past the eye. As the brain processes sentence #2, it *adds* that information/experience/thought to the pool generated by sentence #1. The result is not a bricklike juxtaposition of two distinct thoughts but rather a new, conglomerate pool that is shaped differently from the sentence #1 pool. The former pool is no longer perceivable as the unit it once was; it has been lost in the conglomeration.

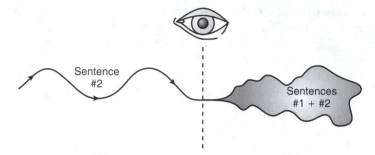

Then sentence #3 flows by the eye, is processed by the brain, and further changes the shape of the aggregate pool. Some parts of the pool may be enlarged; some may be constricted; some old shapes may have disappeared; and some new ones may have been generated.

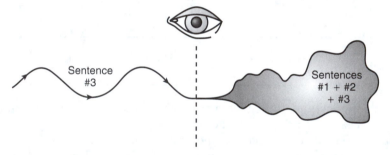

By the end of sentence #3, the pool often tends to have assumed what will more or less be its final shape. That is, by the end of the third sentence, we as readers should know what the *issue* is and be prepared for further strengthening and weakening of the shape that is now before us. Fourth, fifth, and other succeeding sentences may continue to fill up the pool. Whether that happens after sentence #3 or not, by the end of the paragraph, the pool will have attained a shape; but it will no longer be possible to "recognize" sentence #1 -- or any other of the individual sentences -- as a discrete unit. How different this is from the brick metaphor, where brick #1 -- and each of the others -- is *always* recognizable and rerecognizable in its original shape.

I would argue, that one can *never* see sentence #1 again in the way one experienced it the first time through. Even when we reread the paragraph, the experiencing of sentence #1 will be influenced and contextualized by our already having read the entire paragraph. One can never step one's toe into precisely the same textual pool twice.

The reading of a paragraph is indeed a liquid experience: Everything flows into everything that had preceded it; every moment is new and different in itself but is always part of a continuum; everything that newly arrives *changes* the "meaning" of what has already been experienced; everything that has already arrived contextualizes and controls that which will arrive thereafter. In order for a writer to control -- *insofar as possible* --

the continual and continuing interpretive process of the reader, the writer must understand what kinds of expectations a reader is likely to have concerning what will come next. *Placement* of information highly influences what kind of synthesis a reader will experience in trying to form information into idea. Rhetoric and real estate have much in common: For both, the three most important things are location, location, and location.

It seems Procrustes was the wrong myth model to follow in teaching our writing students; instead we should have used the mythical Proteus, the shape-changer. Whenever his freedom was threatened, he could turn into whatever shape he felt best suited the situation -- animal, vegetable, or mineral. Paragraphs should be Protean, not Procrustean. Their shape should not be preordained but rather suggested by the shape and complexity of the thought they struggle to present.

What happens in a paragraph that advances the progress of the discourse as a whole? I suggest each paragraph does some or all of the following:

It offers cohesion;

it presents unity;

it indicates purpose;

it raises an issue;

it makes a point;

it tells a story;

it generates development;

it provides coherence; and

it creates shape.

The last is of special importance. Paragraphs must not be crammed into a pre-existing shape but must help create structural shapes that in turn help to communicate their substance. A change of shape produces a change in meaning; a change of meaning requires a change of shape. And if we ask "Whose paragraph is it, anyway?" we must assuredly answer "It is the reader's." Since paragraphs should be judged by how well they show themselves to their readers and not by how well they conform to previously established "academic" regulations, we must avoid Procrustes and embrace Proteus.

Readers have expectations concerning the beginnings of paragraphs that parallel their expectations concerning the beginnings of sentences. Just as readers tend to read a sentence as the story of whoever or whatever shows up first, so they tend to assume that a paragraph will develop the issue stated at its beginning. The expectation is so strong that most readers consider the first sentence or two or three the issue whether it was intended as such or not. In other words, what may have begun as an expectation has become a habitual reading procedure. To demonstrate: If we delete the issue sentence of example (4) above (its first sentence) and put it back in at the paragraph's end, a reader of our new paragraph would remain confused from its beginning to its end. (I call this restructuring procedure *de-writing*. It has proved a highly effective teaching tool.)

Try to forget having encountered example (4) before, turning yourself into just such a new reader. Proceeding through the same slow-motion technique as we used before, notice how much less comprehensible the substance of this paragraph has become, demonstrating once more that it is the *structure* -- on the paragraph level, just as it was on the sentence level -- that sends 85% of the instructions for the interpretive process.

Here is the new first sentence of our paragraph:

4u. Numerous scientific and communications satellites have been launched into Earth orbit.

Could this first sentence be a one-sentence issue for this paragraph? The answer to that question is *always* "yes." Hand me *any* sentence you have ever encountered, and I can write another few sentences to follow it that will make it perform as the one-sentence issue of my new paragraph. Since we are usually hoping prose will speak to us as clearly as simply as possible, we always *presume* the first sentence of a paragraph will be its issue -- until we are otherwise informed. If this sentence (4u) is a one-sentence issue, then the rest of the paragraph will discuss earth orbit experiments. The paragraph's second sentence should help to clarify this matter for us.

4v. Unmanned deep-space probes have been sent to the sun, the moon, and the planets, where they gathered a wealth of information about our solar system.

Oops. Not only does this *not* launch us into an earth orbit discussion section, but there is no evident link -- that is, no explicitly articulated link -- between these two sentences. Since the promise of a one-sentence issue seems to have been undone, and we cannot see how the two go together to make up a two-sentence issue, our last hope for coherence is that the third sentence will show us clearly how this is the unfolding of a *three*-sentence issue. We would be pleased to find the third sentence beginning, "But whether in earth orbit or far beyond into outer space, our efforts. . . ." But here, alas, is what we actually get as a third sentence:

4w. Skylab demonstrated that American astronauts could live and work in space for months at a time.

Now we are in deep trouble. It is not impossible to figure out a way in which these three sentences could reasonable "talk" to each other; but we, as readers, would have to do that creative act for ourselves, which will cost us a substantial intellectual effort. That should have been the writer's job.

Three sentences is our normal limit for considering the possibilities of issue expansion. We now proceed with lessened hopes that some organization will become apparent. Here is the fourth sentence:

4x. And a dramatically different launch vehicle entered service: the space shuttle.

At this point we have four sentences that cover four different topics. (The "And" supports this conclusion.) All we are convinced of at the moment is that every new sentence will *not* be connected to its predecessor. Here, then, is the fifth sentence:

4y. The winged reusable craft was supposed to make space flight routine and cheap.

Oops, again. The one expectation in which we had generated some confidence is now violated. For some odd reason, the shuttle seems to have deserved two sentences to everyone else's one. Now, thoroughly baffled, we stumble on to the final sentence:

4z. Much has happened since the Apollo program and the Mercury and Gemini missions that paved the way for it in the early 1960s.

We hardly know what to make of this. Instead of seeming an umbrella statement that makes the whole paragraph cohere, it seems just one more dislocated fragment heaped on a pile of the same. The paragraph as a whole is a disaster. And yet not a sentence has been changed from the relatively clear and controlling prose of the original. Only a structural location -- a most significant one -- has been changed.

Structure is 85% of the ballgame.

Context controls meaning.

For easy comparison, here again is the paragraph in its original form. Note how the contextualizing first sentence helps us make sense of all the other sentences as we encounter them.

4a. Much has happened since the Apollo program and the Mercury and Gemini missions that paved the way for it in the early 1960s. Numerous scientific and communications satellites have been launched into Earth orbit. Unmanned deep-space probes have been sent to the sun, the moon, and the planets, where they gathered a wealth of information about our solar system. Skylab demonstrated that American astronauts could live and work in space for months at a time. And a dramatically different launch vehicle entered service: the space shuttle. The winged reusable craft was supposed to make space flight routine and cheap.

With paragraphs, as with sentences (and as with most experiences in life), people wish to be contextualized before they have to deal with new and challenging material.

Again I will borrow Joseph Williams's box paradigm, with slight changes. He pictures the top half of the paragraph as follows:

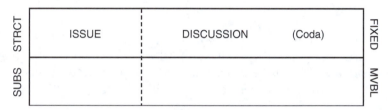

Readers expect the issue to begin each paragraph, with the discussion of that issue usually filling the remainder of that unit. (I discuss the concept of *coda* below.) Once again, we will consider the upper level of the boxes not as items of substance in a paragraph but rather as *places* in its *structure*. That structure is relatively fixed in terms of reader expectation and cannot be easily modified by any individual writer. As such, it parallels the sentence-level and Topic/Stress level boxes discussed in earlier chapters. The lower level of boxes, as before, will be occupied by substance, movable at the will of the writer. The advice will also remain the same: In general, place substance in the structural locations where readers tend to expect that substance to appear. And, once again, two major benefits will accrue as a result: (1) That substance will most likely be labeled and interpreted what you want it to be labeled and interpreted; and (2) the reader will spend a minimal amount of reader energy on unraveling the *structure* and have a great deal more energy left for contemplating the *substance*.

The Issue (with a capital *I*) then becomes a place, a structural location in the paragraph. That relatively fixed location brings with it relatively fixed expectations: It is the place in which readers expect the substantive issue (lowercase *i*) to appear. The same holds true for the structural location called the Discussion (capital *D*): That is where the reader expects to find the discussion (lowercase *d*).

The dotted line between Issue and Discussion sections is meant to indicate that the spatial ratio suggested by the Issue and Discussion sections does not remain constant. The Issue is not always approximately the first third of a paragraph.[4] Often it will consume only 10% of the space. On occasion it can extend to as much as two-thirds of a paragraph; that is commonly the case for three-sentence opening paragraphs, especially in professional research articles:

Sentence 1: Experts have long said. . . .

Sentence 2: Experts have failed to realize. . . .

Sentence 3: This article sheds clearer light on the subject by demonstrating that. . . .

Here is an example of such a paragraph, where the issue is our ignorance and the point (a different thing altogether) is the proffered illumination:

7. Like the immune system, the olfactory system discriminates numerous foreign molecules in the environment. Yet, surprisingly little is known about the manner in which the structures of odor molecules (odorants) are encoded in specific patterns of neuronal activity, which are then relayed to the brain and decoded as distinct odor qualities. This article discusses recent progress of biochemical studies on the molecular mechanisms that operate during the initial interactions between the odorant and the chemosensory membrane.

Although the subject matter of this paragraph may be foreign to most of us, the structure is remarkably familiar. Note how the "yet" that begins the second sentence informs us that this is not likely to be a one-sentence issue kind of paragraph: The "yet" denies the efficacy of the first sentence to stand alone as the paragraph's issue. The first sentence sounded for all the world like it was going to be a one-sentence issue; but that "yet" warns us that we may be dealing with a two-sentence unit. That turns out to be the case. And what is the point of raising this issue of our ignorance about how odorants function? That point is delivered in the third sentence, which invites us to stick around to hear all the interesting progress we have been making recently.

It is important to note that not all paragraphs present and discuss issues. Narrative paragraphs, for example, may simply tell a story in chronological (or otherwise logical) order. In such paragraphs, the Issue position should contain a clue for the reader *not* to expect issue and discussion but rather to expect a narrative.

8. The summer I was 16, I took a train from New York to Steamboat Springs, Colo., where I was going to be assistant horse wrangler at a camp. The trip took three days, and since I was much too shy to talk to strangers, I had quite a lot of time for reading. I read all of *Gone with the Wind*. I read all the interesting articles in a couple of magazines I had, and then I went back and read all the dull stuff. I also took all the quizzes, a thing of which magazines were even fuller than now.

Here the emphasis on setting a time frame ("The summer I was 16") and the presentation of simple fact ("I took a train") lead us to expect the ensuing travelogue. Whether or not you wish to think of this as an "issue," there is no "discussion." The Issue position is filled with the clue that raises the expectation of a narrative; the Discussion position is filled with the rest of that narration. Such paragraphs normally (but not always) present such a structural clue in the paragraph's first sentence.

Narrative paragraphs need not articulate a point because they are establishing knowledge that will be supportive of points made later in the text. They act as background or as a foundation.

The traditional topic sentence pedagogy oversimplifies paragraphs. It takes no account of different paragraph functions; nor does it recognize the frequent need of sophisticated writers to take more than a single sentence to state the paragraph's issue. If the latter were the only problem with the topic sentence approach, we could easily readjust that older pedagogy instead of discarding it. We would need note only that sophisticated writers often take two or three sentences to create what for younger writers would be a single topic sentence. Far more problematic, however, is this topic sentence pedagogy's insistence that the first sentence must always state the issue *and* the point. As example (7) above demonstrates, for sophisticated writers, issue and point are often not identical. That insight should lead us to discard the topic sentence approach altogether.

P *oint*

In the sixth grade, a paragraph's issue and the point the paragraph intended to make were almost always one and the same thing:

I like the Spring because of the pretty flowers.

The same continued to hold true throughout high school:

Capital punishment should be abolished because it is cruel and inhuman.

Violence on television should be eliminated because it influences people to go out and commit violent acts.

These statements were both the issue the paragraph would discuss and the point the paragraph was intended to make. Summoning three examples and restating the topic sentence created a complete, cohesive, and coherent paragraph, and the job was done. It was a doable task for the writer and a reviewable task for the teacher.

But in sophisticated, professional prose, the *issue* the paragraph will discuss and the *point* it will try to make are often not one and the same thing. The *issue* refers to the intellectual geographic boundaries within which the discussion will wander; the *Point* is the place within those boundaries at which we wish the reader to arrive. It should come as no surprise that readers expect the *point* of a paragraph (with a lowercase *p*) to arrive in a particular structural location, which we will refer to as the *Point* (with an uppercase *P*).

Readers delight in being told what the point of a paragraph is -- clearly and explicitly. They are grateful when that clear point is presented in a *single* sentence. They also want to *know* that sentence when they see it. The extensive investigation of thousands of professional paragraphs has made it evident that readers expect that point to appear at particular structural locations. They expect the point to be in a Point sentence; and they know where to look for it.

Unlike any of the other reader expectations we have explored, however, there are *two* possible Point locations in paragraphs. One is a fallback plan for the other: If the point did not arrive in the first expected location, then we look for it in the other.

In exploring with students where the point is likely to arrive, there are a number of different ways to put the pedagogical question:

i) I am a busy and intolerant reader. I haven't the time to read your whole paragraph. I'll read only one sentence. Which do you choose?

ii) Of all the sentences in this paragraph, which suffers least from the annoying question "*So what?*"

iii) Which of the sentences in this paragraph explicitly articulates the point the paragraph was trying to make?

Once having contemplated those three, it is simplest to do the job by asking a more compact fourth question:

iv) In this paragraph, which is the Point sentence?

Note: It is possible to leave the paragraph's Point unarticulated -- to allow it to hover over the surface of the prose, beckoning the reader and depending on the inexorable force of direction generated by the persuasiveness of the argument's development. That is possible to do, but risky. It can be advantageous in certain limited circumstances:

-- When the point is so clear and forceful that to state it would be to produce too much emphasis;

-- When the point is not yet ready to be articulated because more argument needs to be made; or

-- When you intend to present a question without indicating an answer.

Most students have had no experience in distinguishing between issues and points. To help them perceive that distinction, it makes sense to revisit whatever paragraphs you use to investigate the concept of Issue/issue. That is what we will do here. This time through, we will be trying to identify the point sentence. When I first experimented with this approach, I encountered the same kind of classroom disagreement and dissatisfaction I had when the class tried to identify issues. Once again, I eventually realized that the students were not being perverse or disruptive or dimwitted in refusing to recognize what I clearly saw as the point sentence of a given paragraph; they were simply interpreting the substance in ways I had not. Since all paragraphs are infinitely interpretable, that should have come as no surprise. It is possible to reap a number of benefits from such disagreements:

1) We can demonstrate to them how reasonable it is for intelligent readers to differ in interpreting what seems to them a paragraph with only a single meaning.

2) We can help them articulate the clues in the paragraph that led them to make their interpretive decisions.

3) We can help them investigate what we should do to revise the paragraph so it will lead a greater percentage of readers to formulate one particular interpretation.

As I did in the previous trip through these examples, I have the class consider the paragraph sentence by sentence. Approaching the paragraph as a whole raises too much chaotic interpretational dust before we are ready to deal with it. Also, such retrospective consideration belies the actual reading process. Readers encounter the paragraph a sentence at a time, fluidly formulating and reformulating its structure as the paragraph unfolds in a forward-moving (even if also a backward-reconsidering) motion. Readers do not make their way through a paragraph and only at its end begin to consider what it "meant."

Here again is the paragraph from Example (4).

4a.   Much has happened since the Apollo program and the Mercury and Gemini missions that paved the way for it in the early 1960s. Numerous scientific and communications satellites have been launched into Earth orbit. Unmanned deep-space probes have been sent to the sun, the moon, and the planets, where they gathered a wealth of information about our solar system. Skylab demonstrated that American astronauts could live and work in space for months at a time. And a dramatically different launch vehicle entered service: the space shuttle. The winged reusable craft was supposed to make space flight routine and cheap.

If we take the first sentence by itself, we cannot be sure that it will eventually be perceived as the point of the paragraph; all we can do is judge whether at this moment it is a likely candidate. It is reasonable to write a paragraph whose point is that much has happened to the space program since the 1960s. Unless a better candidate appears, this may well turn out to be the point -- for most readers.

It is important that our students understand that this is *always* the case. Every sentence ever written *could be* the point sentence of a paragraph. What a reader must discover, paragraph by paragraph, is whether a particular sentence is the point sentence of this particular paragraph. That cannot be completely ascertained when only the first sentence has been read.

Proceeding to the second sentence, we begin to see what role context plays in determining a paragraph's point.

4b.   Numerous scientific and communications satellites have been launched into Earth orbit.

Although that sentence *could* be the point of some other paragraph, given its position in *this* paragraph, it is unlikely to be the point here. Its immediate context, the first sentence, makes it sound more like an example than a point. It may still be transformed into the paragraph's point if (1) it turns out to be the only example offered, and (2) the rest of the paragraph busies itself with enumerating these "Numerous scientific and communications satellites."

The third sentence narrows the interpretive options:

4c. Unmanned deep-space probes have been sent to the sun, the moon, and the planets, where they gathered a wealth of information about our solar system.

Many readers interpret this sentence as performing a function parallel to its predecessor: Both exemplify things that happened since the 1960s as part of the space program. The readers who share this perception are becoming more convinced at this moment that the first sentence is indeed the issue of the paragraph; it could also be its point. Something may yet happen to reformulate that conviction; but at the moment the first sentence is the leading candidate.

The next sentence seems parallel in function to its predecessor:

4d. Skylab demonstrated that American astronauts could live and work in space for months at a time.

Like the two sentences before it this sentence could well be the point sentence -- of some other paragraph. Placed where it is here, it appears as the third of a progression of sentences that exemplify the point being offered by the first sentence.

The next sentence sends us a signal that the interpretation already suggested may be the most persuasive one:

4e. And a dramatically different launch vehicle entered service: the space shuttle.

The word "And" suggests that we have indeed been encountering a series, of which this sentence is the last. The first sentence now appears likely to have been the point; and the rest of the paragraph served to exemplify it.

I mentioned above that the last sentence of this paragraph caused some consternation concerning the placement of the issue:

4f. The winged reusable craft was supposed to make space flight routine and cheap.

This final sentence seems a subset of the one that precedes it. It hardly seems weighty enough as a possible target of the paragraph's motion to warrant considering it the point. It seems to be doing yet something else, to which we will return later.

By the end of paragraph (4), then, a majority of readers will have concluded that the first sentence did indeed establish the point that controlled the rest of the paragraph. This paragraph fits, in part, the predictions of the topic sentence paradigm, even without a final sentence recapitulation. The other two paragraphs will not.

Here again is Example (5):

5. This book is the beginning of an attempt to move the study of American literature away from the small group of master texts that have dominated critical discussion for the last thirty years and into a more varied and fruitful area of investigation. It involves, in its most ambitious form, a redefinition of literature and literary study, for it sees literary texts not as works of art embodying enduring themes in complex forms, but as attempts to redefine the social order. In this view, novels and stories should be studied not because they manage to escape the limitations of their particular time and place, but because they offer powerful examples of the way a culture thinks about itself, articulating and proposing solutions for the problems that shape a particular historical moment. I believe that the works of fiction that this book examines were written not so that they could be enshrined in any literary hall of fame, but in order to win the belief and influence the behavior of the widest possible audience. These novelists have designs upon their audiences, in the sense of wanting to make people think and act in a particular way.

Again in asking which is the point sentence, we investigate the paragraph sentence by sentence. Our previous consideration of the paragraph allows us to do this with greater speed than before. We remember the first sentence; it opened up a great many possible directions but chose none. That kind of opening gambit is hardly likely to be the point the paragraph has been formed to make.

The second sentence narrows those possibilities:

5b. It involves, in its most ambitious form, a redefinition of literature and literary study, for it sees literary texts not as works of art embodying enduring themes in complex forms, but as attempts to redefine the social order.

This sentence offers a reason why the move from canonical texts to non-canonical texts is being urged. That reason could well be the point of the paragraph -- if nothing else supersedes it later in centrality of importance.

The third sentence usually stirs some interesting discussion:

5c. In this view, novels and stories should be studied not because they manage to escape the limitations of their particular time and place, but because they offer powerful examples of the way a culture thinks about itself, articulating and proposing solutions for the problems that shape a particular historical moment.

Some argue that this is a specific example, a subset, of the second sentence. Others argue it goes beyond the second sentence to matters more specific, more tellingly important. But those who argue for the third sentence as the point sentence also find themselves dissatisfied with the previous decision that the paragraph has a two-sentence issue; they now vote for a three-sentence issue.

The fourth sentence continues the debate:

5d. I believe that the works of fiction that this book examines were written not so that they could be enshrined in any literary hall of fame, but in order to win the belief and influence the behavior of the widest possible audience.

If this sentence is yet another way of restating the second sentence, then the shape of the paragraph is becoming clearer:

> 2-sentence issue; second sentence = point
>
> 3rd sentence: restatement of point
>
> 4th sentence: restatement of point
>
> [final sentence, yet to be revisited]

If not, then we should expect some development of the thought offered by the third sentence -- a connection harder to predict. The final sentence convinces many readers that the paragraph reads best as a two-sentence issue with the point in the second sentence:

5e. These novelists have designs upon their audiences, in the sense of wanting to make people think and act in a particular way.

In some ways, this third restatement of the point is the simplest, the most direct of them all. Some readers argue that it, not the second sentence, is the point. Others argue that the point is stated twice, once in the second sentence and again in the last. Yet others argue that the point is made and remade in every sentence from the second on. All of this arguing becomes a helpful way for students to explain to each other how they go about interpreting this particular paragraph. It should be encouraged, not perceived as a hindrance to the establishing of rules about where readers expect points to appear.

The disagreement flows in part from the lack of a single clear signal indicating which of these sentences is the strongest, most spotlighted articulation of the central concept being reiterated. Many minds are changed about this matter when I inform them the paragraph is the very first in a book by Jane Tompkins entitled *Sensational Designs*. Suddenly the final sentence attracts a great many votes as being the point sentence:

5e. These novelists have DESIGNS upon their audiences, in the sense of wanting to make people think and act in a particular way.

The signal was there. The paragraph now appears to most to be a two-sentence issue with the point in the final sentence -- or in both the second and final sentences.

The concept of *point* functions well as a rhetorical perspective from which students can investigate the thought development of a paragraph. "Getting the right answer," therefore, is not "the point."

The other example above, paragraph (6), had a three-sentence issue:

6. His poetic article of 1849, "The Revolution," had promised a new Europe. To the jubilant strains of shrill, warlike music, a paradise was to rise from the devastation of a volcanic upheaval. But in the finale of the *Ring*, hostility gives way to a calm resignation, knowing neither defeat nor victory. Brynhild bids her father, Wotan, rest to music of infinite sadness, and the old world sinks down because it can no longer bear its load of deceit and treachery. Hagen, preaching Bakunian-style violence to the end, is pulled into the depths of the cascading river by the Rhine Daughters. But, though they happily ride the crest of destruction with their restored treasure, no new Eden can follow. Alberich is still at large, and the new world may well be as troubled as the old.

The first sentence, on first reading, could easily be the issue and possibly be the point. (We will be disappointed if it turns out to be the point; but we have often been disappointed in our reading experiences.) Perhaps this is a paragraph about Wagner's 1849 article.

The second sentence surely sounds like we have a one-sentence issue with a possible point in the first sentence.

But the "but" that begins the third sentence informed us that we probably have a three-sentence issue. Could the third sentence be the point? Could we be changing from Wagner's optimistic article of the first two sentences to his pessimistic operas of the third sentence? We could -- *if* the rest of the paragraph goes on to discuss and develop those pessimistic operas.

We have developed a confidence that the issue is a three-sentence unit; and the third sentence is now capable of being the point -- *unless something even more pointed appears later on.* Paragraph reading is a fluid experience. Every sentence thereafter exemplifies the third sentence -- not in isolation ("I like the Spring because of the pretty flowers -- (1) tulips; (2) roses; (3) daffodils"), but rather with a building sense of richness, depth, and expansion. There is a sense of crescendo throughout. To what is it all lead-ing? It leads to the last sentence:

Alberich is still at large, and *the new world may well be as troubled as the old*.

(emphasis supplied)

All those mentioned in those last four sentences -- dwarves, humans, demi-gods, and gods alike -- find the new world no more to their liking than the old one. Alberich, the sour and scheming dwarf who started all the trou-ble at the beginning of the first of the four operas, is *still* at large; and the sec-ond half of the last sentence reiterates or echoes the point made in the third sentence. After the revolution, it may not be any better than before.

The statistics for these three examples thus far:

Example	Issue	Point
4	1	1
5	2	last (and/or 2)
6	3	3 (echo in last)

Other paragraphs might offer different combinations. Here is a para-graph with a one-sentence issue that has its point not in the first sentence but in the last. (The issue is capitalized; the point is underscored.)[5]

9. THE OFFICE OF THE VICE PRESIDENT OF THE UNITED STATES IS OFTEN CONSIDERED ONE OF THE MOST POINTLESS POSI-TIONS IN POLITICS. John Adams, the first Vice President, referred to it as "the most insignificant office that ever the invention of man contrived or his imagination conceived." Daniel Webster refused to accept the job, saying, "I do not choose to be buried until I am really dead." Because the Vice President's only real duty is to preside over the Senate, the job is not very attractive, and Vice Presidents are not usually chosen because they are strong, experienced leaders. This is alarming because the Vice President sits just a heartbeat away from the presidency. Since he could become the President of the United States at any time, his job should be regarded more seriously, and he should be an independently elected official.

Sometimes a paragraph with a three-sentence issue can have its point not in the third sentence but in the last:

10. IN SCHOOL, CHILDREN WANT THE RIGHT TO DO THEIR OWN THINKING AND TO EXPRESS THEMSELVES FREELY. THEY DO NOT LIKE TO BE GOVERNED BY RULES AND REGULATIONS WHOSE PURPOSE THEY DO NOT UNDERSTAND. BUT FUNDA-MENTALLY NEITHER DO THEY LIKE A SCHOOL WHERE THERE

IS SO MUCH FREEDOM THAT THERE IS DISORDER. They find fault with a teacher in whose room the children are disorderly. They also find fault with teachers who are too rigid and unimaginative and who cannot enjoy a joke. <u>Apparently a schoolroom and a school where behavior is governed largely by understanding and good will afford the freedom that is most satisfying to both pupils and teachers.</u>

Now the statistics start to suggest a pattern:

Example	Issue	Point
4	1	1
5	2	last (or 2)
6	3	3
9	1	last
10	3	last

In general, it appears at the moment, readers expect the point sentence in a paragraph (if any) to arrive at one of two places: (1) as the last sentence of the Issue (e.g., the second sentence in a two-sentence Issue, or the third sentence in a three-sentence Issue); or (2) as the last sentence of the paragraph. However, that generalization also turns out not to control all cases. Consider the following paragraph by Steven Stark from his article in the *Harvard Law Review* explaining why lawyers write the way they do.

11. But anyone who writes about rules and not facts is going to have a difficult time composing an appealing piece. What intrigues most readers are stories about people; a story is usually the development of a character. For example, what would make the story in *Erie v. Tompkins* interesting to the typical reader is what happened to Tompkins, not what happened to the doctrine of *Swift v. Tyson*. But the legal writer must ignore the attractive part of a story and be content instead to discuss the application of rules in a way that tells lawyers what doctrines they should follow. Even Joan Didion would have trouble doing much within those constraints.

Let us explore this for Issue and Point simultaneously, using the slow-motion, sentence-by-sentence method as above.
The first sentence:

11a. But anyone who writes about rules and not facts is going to have a difficult time composing an appealing piece.

If the rest of the paragraph is about this sentence, then we might expect Stark to demonstrate further how writing about *rules* is hard and writing about *facts* is easier. If that turns out to be the reason the paragraph was written, then the first sentence will appear to be the point sentence.

The second sentence:

11b. What intrigues most readers are stories about people; a story is usually the development of a character.

This sentence fails to fulfill the expectations attached to making the first
sentence either the issue or the point of the paragraph. It takes one part of
the general statement of the first sentence and further refines it: By "facts,"
he really means "people"; by "people" he really means "character." If we
combine the first two sentences, the new two-sentence issue seems to be
that it is harder to write about *rules* than it is to write about *characters*. If the
rest of the paragraph develops that thought, then this is a two-sentence Issue. If so, it is likely that neither of the first two sentences can stand by itself convincingly to be the point sentence, because neither makes a
complete point in itself.
    The third sentence:

11c. For example, what would make the story in *Erie v. Tompkins* interesting to the typical reader is what happened to Tompkins, not what
happened to the doctrine of *Swift v. Tyson*.

Most readers of the *Harvard Law Review* would remember from their Civil
Procedure course (with a shudder) how impossible the opaquely written
Erie case had been to read. This sentence then becomes, as advertised, an
example of the two-sentence Issue raised before it. *Erie* was difficult to
write because it had to forget about the *character*, Tompkins, and concentrate instead on the *rule* announced in *Swift v. Tyson*. That is one of the possibilities the two-sentence Issue had promised.
    The fourth sentence:

11d. But the legal writer must ignore the attractive part of a story and be
content instead to discuss the application of rules in a way that tells
lawyers what doctrines they should follow.

Here is the recurring theme stated once again, but this time in the context
of legal writing: "The attractive part of a story" (*characters*) has to be ig-
nored in favor of "the application of *rules*" in legal writing in order to "tell
lawyers what doctrines they should follow." The issue was raised as to all
discourse; the point comes home by applying that general perception to the
lawyer's predicament. Surely this must be the point sentence of the paragraph; but it is neither the last of the Issue nor the last of the paragraph.
    There is still a fifth sentence:

11e. Even Joan Didion would have trouble doing much within those
constraints.

Chuckle. This is what Joe Williams refers to as a "Coda." I will use the term with a capital *C* to indicate a place in the structure; I use it with a small *c* to indicate the kind of material best reserved for that place in the structure.

The Coda, when there is one, is the last sentence in a paragraph. It functions as a wild-card spot. We can do all sorts of things there that we could not get away with elsewhere. As a result, it is used by good writers sparingly, but to good effect. It is the safest place, for example, to insert a wisecrack, a witticism, or even a slight pun. Professor Stark can get away with the light and pleasant sarcasm about the well-known essayist Joan Didion because he had already finished his serious, hard work in the sentence before. Had he begun this paragraph with "Even Joan Didion would have a difficult time with legal writing," the editors of the *Harvard Law Review* would probably have excised the sentence in an indignant huff: The *HLR* is no place for such levity. But coming where it does, it is welcomed by the most serious of the serious in the spirit of "All work and no play. . . ." To signal to a reader the existence of a coda, best place it in the Coda position.

Stark's Point, therefore, is not located as the last sentence of the *paragraph*; but it is the last sentence of the *Discussion*. That turns out to be the second location readers tend to expect to find a paragraph's point.

The Coda position is used a number of other possible functions, aside from being a place for wit, sarcasm, humor, or exaggeration:

1) It is a place you can repeat the point, just for emphasis.

2) It is a place you can overturn everything you have just constructed. (Example: "But all of this fails if we do not consider X.")

3) It is a place you can include that second example that is really unnecessary to your point but with which you have become so ego-involved you cannot bear to let it go.

We can now articulate a general statement about reader expectations of the placement of the point sentence in a paragraph.

> **Readers expect the point sentence in a paragraph (if any) to arrive at one of two places: either (1) as the last sentence of the issue; or (2) as the last sentence of the discussion.**

Visually, that can be expressed with the box paradigm as follows:

STRCT	ISSUE	DISCUSSION	(Coda)	FIXED
SUBS	POINT		Point	MVBL

This reader expectation differs from all others because it includes a second fallback possibility; but it also sounds to many people the most non-intuitive (not counter-intuitive) of a group of otherwise highly intuitive observations. It sounds like it must be memorized by rote. Here is a restatement of the same expectation that may sound much more recognizable from your own reading experience:

> **Readers expect the point of a paragraph to be made explicit either just before the discussion of it begins or just as the discussion of it ends.**

Either, (1) "Here's the *issue*, which culminates in this *point*, which I will now *discuss*"; or, (2) "Here's the *issue*, which I continue to *discuss* until I am ready to make this comprehensive *point*."

The Issue can last for one, two, or three sentences. The Discussion can be short or long. There may or may not be a Coda. Surely there is more than one Procrustean structure for professional English paragraphs.

Point Placement and Paragraph Types

It may come as no surprise that readers have discernible expectations concerning whether the point should arrive at the end of the Issue or at the end of the Discussion. (For ease of reference, I shall be referring to the end of the Issue as "the beginning" of the paragraph and the end of the Discussion as "the end" of the paragraph.) The five paragraph types listed here do not by any means cover all the possible shapes of paragraphs nor all the expectations concerning the arrival of the point. They do, however, cover a great percentage of the paragraphs normally encountered.

First Paragraphs

Readers have a remarkably fixed expectation that the point of an opening paragraph will arrive at the end. As readers, we greatly desire to be led gradually into a new piece of prose, to be made as comfortable as possible with the new surroundings before we have to go to work. We do not appreciate the following progression:

THIS IS THE POINT OF IT ALL.

And we'll be spending some time together.

This is what I sound like.

Did you know there was a problem?

Hello.

We much prefer the reverse order:

Hello.

Did you know there was a problem?

This is what I sound like.

And we'll be spending some time together.

So now that you have a sense of me and this document,

THIS IS THE POINT OF IT ALL.

There is the added expectation that in most pieces of expository or persuasive discourse the last sentence of the first paragraph will also state the thesis or contract for the discourse as a whole. Joseph Williams and Gregory Colomb completed but never published a convincing piece of research on this. They collected a number of essays by English graduate student, 20–25 pages each, all of which had received an A or A– at the University of Chicago. They made a second version of each essay by changing only one sentence -- the last sentence of the first paragraph -- so it no longer promised what the essay would consider. They then made packets containing some original essays and some revised ones and sent them to several professors across the country, requesting them to grade the essays and to append a brief comment in support of the grade. The original essays came back with grades of A, A–, or B+, with complimentary comments; but many of the revised essays returned with substantially lower grades, some at the C and D level, with comments about poor development of thought, lack of focus, and fuzzy writing.

I had an occasion to relate this experiment to a dean at Duke University. It especially piqued his interest because on the day of that luncheon, he had received a refusal notice for a manuscript he had submitted to a moderately ranked journal -- the first such refusal he had suffered in some 20 years. They had apparently not understood the whole purpose of his article. The next time I dined with him was some three months later. He sat down at the table with a broad grin and announced that (1) he had indeed found that his "contract statement" in that article had been totally misleading, that (2) he had changed *only* that sentence and resubmitted the article to a much more discriminating journal, and (3) on this very day he had received an acceptance from them, with glowing comments about the brilliance of his work.

This expectation -- that the last sentence of the opening paragraph will articulate the nature of the focus of the whole article -- may well be the single strongest of all the reader expectations in English. But even such a strong expectation as this cannot be rigidified into a rule for writers: "Always place your thesis statement at the end of your first paragraph" will not do. Just as some paragraphs take more than one sentence to state the issue of that unit of discourse, so some essays take more than one paragraph to get around to articulating their grand issue or thesis. If it does take (for example) three paragraphs to introduce the thesis, readers will expect to discover the thesis statement in the last sentence of the third paragraph. In other words, readers would like to know the issue of the discourse as a whole *just before it begins to be discussed.* Note that good writers and journals will let readers in on the unfolding of such an extended event. After that third paragraph, the reader will see some kind of visual signal that separates those three paragraphs from the rest of the prose: There might be a quadruple space instead of a double space, or a horizontal line, or a Roman numeral, or any other visual marker.

Counterexamples for this expectation abound; but they all seem to have good explanations for why they function the way they do. Business memos, for instance, almost always begin with the "thesis statement," if any, in the very first sentence. The explanations: (1) In business, time is money; there is no money available to buy time to make readers comfortable; (2) comfort belies the impression of hard work; (3) and, most importantly, there is usually a line preceding the first line of prose, headed by "Re:." That line will contextualize the reader far more quickly and directly than two or three sentences could manage. Like any other reader expectation, this one should be violated when there is a distinct purpose for doing so.

Last Paragraphs

Readers have an equally fixed expectation that the point of a final paragraph will arrive at the end.[6] We like our endings to bring with them a satisfying sense of closure. That closure can act as symphonic cymbals clashing or as a modest good-bye; it can produce a final thought not previously articulated or recapitulate material that has been thoroughly developed earlier; it can shock, or it can relax.

If the point were to appear at the beginning of a final paragraph, the progress of the sentences would produce a faltering sense of anticlimax rather than a fulfilling sense of closure:

SO YOU SEE I WIN,

since I produced certain general theories,

based on a number of individual details, I summoned.

But when the point of a final paragraph appears at its end, climax and closure combine to create a far more satisfactory effect:

So, having summoned a number of individual details,

I created from them certain general theories,

AS A RESULT OF WHICH,

I WIN.

Whatever form that closure takes, its nature, length, or impact should vary in proportion to the shape, size, and weight of the unit of discourse as a whole. Long or complex documents may take several paragraphs to achieve a sense of final resolution. Again, no rule is sufficient to handle all cases. The final paragraph(s) should reach out to the needs of the reader rather than merely express the relief of the writer.

A great majority of high school students have been taught that the final paragraph of an essay should summarize everything the essay has presented. By continuing to obey that command in college essays, students demonstrate to what extent they conceive of writing as a task to fulfill the requirements of others rather than as an opportunity to communicate with an audience. Once their reader recognizes that nothing new will appear in such a final paragraph, the reader loses interest. The document must not simply *end*; it must be brought to a state of *resolution*.

One major exception: Just as a paragraph may end in a coda that undoes what has just been done, so a final paragraph in a document can act in that coda-like way and "end" by generating new questions for a future, ongoing discourse in which a response would be expected.

Most Medial Paragraphs

In most paragraphs between the first and the last, readers tend to appreciate being given the point up front. Many a reader will dip into a paragraph just long enough to decide whether it holds anything of promise for them. If it seems unlikely to satisfy their present need, they skip to the next paragraph. The writer who does not put the point up front in these paragraphs runs the risk of having the audience disappear before the point actually arrives.

One might wonder why readers expect the point to be at the end of first and last paragraphs but at the beginning of most others. In the initial discussion of the Stress position in Chapter 4, we noted the difference between the Stress positions of the sentence and the location of the most important information in newspaper articles. Most readers finish reading any sentence they have begun; that allows the writer to take advantage of the reader's need for closure and the sense of reward-at-journey's-end. Readers of newspaper articles, on the other hand, more often than not, do not reach the article's end, making it foolhardy for journalists to place the most important information there. A paragraph is usually longer than a sentence but shorter than a newspaper article. Paragraphs that will probably be read in their entirety tend to resemble sentences; paragraphs that may not be read in their entirety tend to resemble newspaper articles.

For paragraphs, length by itself is an untrustworthy indicator of a reader's staying power. A much better indicator is location. Most readers will finish all of any paragraph that begins or ends a whole document. Most readers will finish all of any paragraph that begins a subsection of a document; a somewhat smaller percentage of readers will read all of a paragraph that ends such a subsection.[7] Readers seem to be willing to give writers a full paragraph's worth of attention at the beginning of prose; for the most part, they are unwilling to miss a potentially significant or dramatic point of closure at its end. Readers have become accustomed to finding the point sentence of an opening or closing paragraph at the end, which in turn will reenforce their willingness to stay around.

Those same readers may well stop short of finishing any other paragraph, making it a far greater risk for the writer to delay articulating the point. There are, however, some circumstances when the point of a medial paragraph will function better at the Discussion's end.

Medial Paragraphs: Clear, with Dramatic Point

A writer can effectively delay the point of a medial paragraph until the end if the paragraph is important enough to benefit from the dramatic emphasis brought about by a crescendo to closure. In order to maintain interest until that important moment, it is best to send the following signals to the reader:

1) Insofar as possible, the last sentence of the Issue should *not* give the impression that it might be the point;

2) There should be a sense of urgency about the development of the discussion that hints that the paragraph has a goal not yet disclosed;

3) The reader should be able to understand everything during the paragraph's development without having had the point articulated up front.

Such paragraphs, then, must exhibit a need for the dramatic build to closure. Each step of that progression must be clear enough to be understood without the point having been previously announced.

Medial Paragraphs: Complex, with Dramatic Point

What might the writer do if a point requires the dramatic emphasis of placement at closure but the development of the discussion is too complex to be understood without the point having been previously stated? In such cases, the writer would do well to state the point *both* at the beginning and at the end. When the point is first announced, the reader may be unconvinced or uncomprehending; but after the discussion has developed the supporting reasoning, the second coming of the point can be greeted with a sense of new recognition -- "Ah, so *that's* what was meant before." The point may be the same old point, but it will be comprehended in a new way.

Ironically, this somewhat scarce type of paragraph comes the closest to the old topic sentence model for writing paragraphs: State the issue and point; give your reasons; then state the point again.[8] This second serving of the point works poorly in easily comprehended paragraphs, where the reader is annoyed to be burdened a second time with material already understood. It works well in paragraphs where the reader could not comprehend the point fully in advance of its being discussed.

A Note on One-sentence Paragraphs

Can there be such a thing as a legitimate one-sentence paragraph? (Many of us were taught in high school that one-sentence paragraphs were strictly forbidden.) Certainly such rhetorical unicycles abound in journalism; but they also show up in the scientific literature, often enough not to be considered scarce. One-sentence paragraphs are appropriate, as long as they fulfill all the rhetorical "requirements" for definition as a paragraph. For paragraphs that intend to make a Point, these "requirements" are three:

1. There must be a clearly stated Issue.
2. There must be a clearly ascertainable Point.
3. There must be sufficient Discussion to establish that Point.

To accomplish all of this in one sentence, all of the following must happen:

1. The Issue must be able to be articulated in a single sentence.
2. The Issue and the Point must be the same.
3. All the Discussion that supports the Point must have already happened recently, in previous paragraphs, or will happen immediately thereafter.

The best uses for a one-sentence paragraph, therefore, are either as a kind of punch line that brings an elongated previous development to closure or as a challenging statement of claim that will require an elongated ensuing development to produce its justification.

In short -- and as an example -- a one-sentence paragraph, under the right conditions, can do just fine.

A *Typology of Paragraphs?*

Having described five generic types of paragraphs, I may seem to be suggesting that we should construct a typology of paragraphs. I have no such goal in mind. The number of possible paragraph shapes is infinite because the number of different jobs paragraphs try to do is also infinite. We can note recurring patterns; but we cannot with any hope of success establish unvarying rules concerning their construction.

Given just the issue and point placement information discussed above, we can generate a large number of paradigms for a single paragraph. Given subject matter to "insert" into those paradigms, we can generate as large a number of "best" arrangements for it as we can find readers to interpret it. Given its situation between two other paragraphs equally variable in interpretive possibilities, the mind begins to boggle at the thought of simplistic, rule-like restrictions.

An abstract example: For a paragraph that contains six sentences, how many variations of structure can we generate, using only the issue and point placement principles developed above?

Variation #	Issue length	Point placement	Coda
1	1	1	None
2	1	1	6
3	1	6	None
4	1	5	6
5	2	2	None
6	2	2	6
7	2	6	None
8	2	5	6
9	3	3	None
10	3	3	6
11	3	6	None
12	3	5	6

These are only the main permutations that might prove helpful to most readers most of the time. Any other permutation is of course possible; some of those might even prove effective, as long as the reader is presented with nonstructural (e.g., semantic or typographic) clues concerning the paragraph's shape. Add to that (a) paragraphs that are not intended to make points, (b) paragraphs that explicitly announce the presence of multiple points, and (c) the variability of reader perceptions of what the issue or point might be; the number of possible paragraph shapes increases geometrically. The paragraph is a long enough unit of discourse to include explicit indications of unusual structures. (For example, "Given this state of affairs, two plans of action become possible: (1) . . . (including as many sentences as are needed) . . . ; and (2) . . . (as many sentences as are needed).") Still, if writers know the general expectations readers harbor concerning issue and point placement, they will be better able both to send helpful interpretive clues and to predict what sense most readers will make of the paragraph.

In an earlier chapter, I disparaged the grammar school advice to "vary the way you begin your sentences." In this chapter I have disparaged the opposite kind of advice concerning paragraphs -- "Always begin your paragraphs with a topic sentence." I would replace those overly comfortable maxims with a single, less comfortable one: Vary the structure of your sentences or paragraphs in direct relation to the jobs those units of discourse are meant to perform. Form follows function; shape should reflect function. This is by no means news. It has long been the credo of architects, automotive designers, neurobiologists, art critics, and engineers of all types. It also works for constructing prose.

Good writers tend to vary their paragraph shapes to suit the function of the paragraph's substance. When I began looking for an example of this to share with you here, the first book I picked up was Lewis Thomas's *The Lives of a Cell: Notes of a Biology Watcher*. I investigated the first seven paragraphs and found six distinct paragraph structures. Here are those seven paragraphs. For each, I have capitalized what I consider to be the issue, underlined my choice for point sentence, and enclosed any codas within square brackets. Note: Do not be surprised if you disagree with some of my decisions concerning issues, points, and codas. Interpretation varies. On another reading, I might disagree with some of them myself.

A. WE ARE TOLD THAT THE TROUBLE WITH MODERN MAN IS THAT HE HAS BEEN TRYING TO DETACH HIMSELF FROM NATURE. He sits in the topmost tiers of polymer, glass, and steel, dangling his pulsing legs, surveying at a distance the writhing life of the planet. In this scenario, Man comes on as a stupendous lethal force, and the earth is pictured as something delicate, like rising bubbles at the surface of a country pond, or flights of fragile birds.*

B. BUT IT IS ILLUSION TO THINK THAT THERE IS ANYTHING FRAGILE ABOUT THE LIFE OF THE EARTH; SURELY THIS IS THE TOUGHEST MEMBRANE IMAGINABLE IN THE UNIVERSE, OPAQUE TO PROBABILITY, IMPERMEABLE TO DEATH. We are the delicate part, transient and vulnerable as cilia. Nor is it a new thing for man to invent an existence that he imagines to be above the rest of life; this has been his most consistent intellectual exertion down the millennia. As illusion, it has never worked out to his satisfaction in the past, any more than it does today. Man is embedded in nature.

C. THE BIOLOGIC SCIENCE OF RECENT YEARS HAS BEEN MAKING THIS A MORE URGENT FACT OF LIFE. THE NEW, HARD PROBLEM WILL BE TO COPE WITH THE DAWNING, INTENSIFYING REALIZATION OF JUST HOW INTERLOCKED WE ARE. The old, clung-to notions most of us have held about our special lordship are being deeply undermined.

D. Item. A GOOD CASE CAN BE MADE FOR OUR NONEXISTENCE AS ENTITIES. WE ARE NOT MADE UP, AS WE HAD ALWAYS SUPPOSED, OF SUCCESSIVELY ENRICHED PACKETS OF OUR OWN PARTS. WE ARE SHARED, RENTED, OCCUPIED. At the interior of our cells, driving them, providing the oxidative energy that sends us out for the improvement of each shining day, are the mitochondria, and in a strict sense they are not ours. They turn out to be little separate creatures, the colonial posterity of migrant prokaryocytes, probably primitive bacteria that swam into ancestral precursors of our eukaryotic cells and stayed there. Ever since, they have maintained themselves and their ways, replicating in their own fashion, privately, with their own DNA and RNA quite different from ours. They are as much symbionts as the rhizobial bacteria in the roots of beans. [Without them, we would not move a muscle, drum a finger, think a thought.]

E. MITOCHONDRIA ARE STABLE AND RESPONSIBLE LODGERS, AND I CHOOSE TO TRUST THEM. BUT WHAT OF THE OTHER LITTLE ANIMALS, SIMILARLY ESTABLISHED IN MY CELLS, SORTING AND BALANCING ME, CLUSTERING ME TOGETHER? My centrioles, basal bodies, and probably a good many other more obscure tiny beings at work inside my cells, each with its own special genome, are as foreign, and as essential, as aphids in anthills. My cells are no longer the pure line entities I was raised with; [they are ecosystems more complex than Jamaica Bay.]

F. I LIKE TO THINK THAT THEY WORK IN MY INTEREST, THAT EACH BREATH THEY DRAW FOR ME; BUT PERHAPS IT IS THEY WHO WALK THROUGH THE LOCAL PARK IN THE EARLY MORNING, SENSING MY SENSES, LISTENING TO MY MUSIC, THINKING MY THOUGHTS.

G. I AM CONSOLED, SOMEWHAT, BY THE THOUGHT THAT THE GREEN PLANTS ARE IN THE SAME FIX. They could not be plants, or green, without their chloroplasts, which run the photosynthetic enterprise and generate oxygen for the rest of us. As it turns out, chloroplasts are also separate creatures with their own genomes, speaking their own language.

Here is my scorecard:

Pgph	Pgph length	Issue length	Point placement	Coda
A	3	1	3	None
B	5	1	1	None
C	3	2	3	None
D	8	3	3	8
E	4	2	4	4
F	1	1	1	None
G	3	1	3	None

Note how only the first and the last paragraphs employ the same construction pattern. The variety of this prose does not stem from its sentences varying in the way they begin: Note the numerous topic strings. Its force does not derive from the use of dazzling vocabulary choices as verbs: Note the six uses of the verb *to be* in the four sentences of Paragraph B. Of the seven paragraphs, only the second might pass muster under the Topic Sentence theory of construction, using a one-sentence issue that simultaneously states the point. (But note that it does not have a "conclusion" sentence that restates its first sentence.) Paragraph F violates the old rule against one-sentence paragraphs. According to our school standards, this man does not know much about writing. My 13-year-old's English teacher this year would have given Lewis Thomas a failing grade.

If we wish to defend or attack the quality of this prose, we would do better to abandon those old school standards and ask instead whether his structures perform meaningful tasks for his readers. Do his points arrive at a time when we expect them and can handle them? Do we agree on what his points are? Are we aware of an issue stretching to more than one sentence on occasion? Do the sentences connect to each other in easily perceptible ways? Is each sentence actually the story of whoever shows up first? Are his most important moments located at Stress positions? Do the occupants of his Topic positions link backward with significant old information? Do his verbs articulate his actions? Structural rules and typologies will not do the job nearly as well -- or perhaps not at all.

A *Reprise of Fluidity*

Putting all of this material on paragraphs together, here is a paradigm of the experience a professional reader reading any six-sentence professional paragraph. None of us do this consciously; most of us do this most of the time without even knowing it.

First sentence: This could be the issue. This could also be the point.

Second sentence: Either this is the beginning of the discussion, or it transforms the issue into a two-sentence issue. If it seems that this is a two-sentence issue, then this could be the point.

Third sentence: This could be the second sentence of the discussion; if so, it confirms our suspicions that we had a one-sentence issue. Or it could be the beginning of the discussion, in which case we had a two-sentence issue. Or it could round out the issue into a three-sentence issue. If it seems that this is a three-sentence issue, then this could be the point.

Fourth sentence: If we had a one-sentence or two-sentence issue, this continues the discussion. If we had a three-sentence issue, this begins the discussion. If we are not clear about how long the issue was, then we are now confused and will probably remain so.

Fifth sentence: No matter how long the issue was, this could be the point. If so, the sixth sentence will be a coda. Otherwise, this continues the discussion.

Sixth sentence: No matter how long the issue was, this could be the point. Otherwise, it is either the last sentence of the discussion or a coda.

You should be able to tell by the complexities of the possibilities how multishaped professional paragraphs tend to be. Different readers may disagree on how to perceive the shape of the same paragraph.

Can a student ever have a "wrong" interpretation? They can certainly "seem" wrong at times; but to dismiss their conclusion will probably be seen only as an act of power, an asserting of superior knowledge on your part -- which is of questionable pedagogical value. It is usually more productive by far to explore not its "rightness" or "wrongness" but rather to challenge the student's support for it. Inadequate or faulty support for the claim will help make clear how the student was thinking; substantial or perceptive support may help you and the class see the paragraph in a light you yourself could not have produced. It is the *process* of interpretation on which we should focus rather than the efficacy of any particular interpretive decision.

To explore this with students, give them a few sophisticated paragraphs and ask them to identify the issue and the point. Instead of deciding for yourself what the shape "is" and reprimanding those who do not agree, have the students who see a different shape from yours defend why the paragraph is shaped the way they suggest. Everyone -- perhaps including you -- will learn something about the infinity of interpretation -- and something more about the paragraph in question.

P *urpose*

So far, all of this discussion of paragraphs has looked inward, treating the paragraph as a self-sufficient unit existing in a rhetorical vacuum. Once we begin to consider paragraphs in the context of the paragraphs that precede and follow them, then the infinitude of reader expectation becomes even yet more of a challenge to be dealt with by the writer. To *issue* and *point* I add a third term: *purpose*. The first two look inward at the paragraph; the last looks outward, both before and after. Often -- but by no means always -- a paragraph serves a purpose in the ongoing flow of the discourse that is distinct from the issue it explores within itself or the point it tries to make. Often -- but by no means always -- that purpose has something to do with getting from where the previous paragraph left off to where the next paragraph starts. To make this distinction, we return to the three paragraphs -- Examples (4), (5), and (6) -- with which we developed the concepts of issue and point.

4. Much has happened since the Apollo program and the Mercury and Gemini missions that paved the way for it in the early 1960s.

Numerous scientific and communications satellites have been launched into Earth orbit. Unmanned deep-space probes have been sent to the sun, the moon, and the planets, where they gathered a wealth of information about our solar system. Skylab demonstrated that American astronauts could live and work in space for months at a time. And a dramatically different launch vehicle entered service: the space shuttle. The winged reusable craft was supposed to make space flight routine and cheap.

In my interpretation of this paragraph, the first sentence stated both the issue and the point. The issue is that "*Much* has happened. . . . ," which leads us to expect we will hear more about some of those happenings. By the time we arrive at the end of those several examples, we are convinced of the point of the paragraph: "Much *has* happened. . . ." But the *purpose* of the paragraph seems to me something quite different; to me, the paragraph exists to introduce us to the space shuttle, which becomes the issue of the following paragraph. That paragraph begins, "Then came the fiery explosion that not only destroyed the shuttle *Challenger* and her crew, but brought the space program to a grinding halt." The purpose of paragraph (4) looks outward and onward. Its grace is evident in the way it manages to do all it does -- state the issue, emphasize the point through exemplification, and fulfill the purpose of making the transition to the discussion of the *Challenger* -- while maintaining a simple sense of linearity. It continually moves forward. In a more gracious age, this quality was referred to as *sprezzatura* -- the graceful accomplishment of a complex or difficult task without a surface sense of effort.

Here again is Example 5:

5. This book is the beginning of an attempt to move the study of American literature away from the small group of master texts that have dominated critical discussion for the last thirty years and into a more varied and fruitful area of investigation. It involves, in its most ambitious form, a redefinition of literature and literary study, for it sees literary texts not as works of art embodying enduring themes in complex forms, but as attempts to redefine the social order. In this view, novels and stories should be studied not because they manage to escape the limitations of their particular time and place, but because they offer powerful examples of the way a culture thinks about itself, articulating and proposing solutions for the problems that shape a particular historical moment. I believe that the works of fiction that this book examines were written not so that they could be enshrined in any literary hall of fame, but in order to win the belief and influence the behavior of the widest possible audience. These novelists have designs upon their audiences, in the sense of wanting to make people think and act in a particular way.

In my discussion of this example, I argued for a two-sentence issue. The first sentence announces the "move"; the second sentence explains the principle on which this move is to be made. In part, the purpose of this paragraph is indistinguishable from its issue and point; but a separate purpose is accomplished by the last sentence, where the use of the word "designs" makes sense for us of the as yet impenetrable title of the book, *Sensational Designs*. This purpose reaches backward, to the title, and propels us forward into the next paragraph, which begins as follows:

> Consequently this book focuses primarily, though not exclusively, on works whose obvious impact on their readers has made them suspect from a modernist point of view, which tends to classify work that affects people's lives, or tries to, as merely sensational or propagandistic.

Note that the Stress position of this sentence (though not heavy-handedly the very last word) presents us with the other term from her title: "sensational." The second shoe has dropped. Paragraph typologies cannot account for such subtleties.

Here again is Example 6, dealing with Wagner's concept of revolution:

6. His poetic article of 1849, "The Revolution," had promised a new Europe. To the jubilant strains of shrill, warlike music, a paradise was to rise from the devastation of a volcanic upheaval. But in the finale of the *Ring*, hostility gives way to a calm resignation, knowing neither defeat nor victory. Brynhild bids her father, Wotan, rest to music of infinite sadness, and the old world sinks down because it can no longer bear its load of deceit and treachery. Hagen, preaching Bakunian-style violence to the end, is pulled into the depths of the cascading river by the Rhine Daughters. But, though they happily ride the crest of destruction with their restored treasure, no new Eden can follow. Alberich is still at large, and the new world may well be as troubled as the old.

The issue here, articulated by a combination of the first three sentences, suggests we might explore Wagner's change from optimism to pessimism concerning life after the revolution. But Wagner's optimistic 1849 prose article never reappears; the paragraph abandons optimism and sinks into the pessimism of the operas. What, then, is the *purpose* of this paragraph?

Different readers will perceive different purposes; but when I consider the multiple examples offered in sentences four through seven, together with their inflated style, I sense the author wants me not only to notice a change in Wagner's attitude but also to be weighed down by the extremity of that change. By the end of the paragraph, that weight has become so extreme that the author can use (or needs to use) a coda to repeat the point made in the third sentence. Those two articulations of the point are not quite identical: The third sentence tells us that the world *might be* no better after the revolution; but by the last sentence, it has been demonstrated (in Wagnerian terms) that the world *really is* no better after the revolution. In summary, then:

issue	--	Wagner changed his mind
point	--	Wagner opted for pessimism
purpose	--	Wagner's opting for pessimism was extreme and thorough

The interpretation just offered is not the right one or the only one; it is, however, one that actually occurs. The same terms (issue, point, and purpose) will turn up different interpretations in the employ of different sensibilities. The terminology is important because it gives readers ways of identifying and consciously probing their responses. Those ways in turn help readers maintain an awareness of the reading process when they change hats and become writers.

In using these terms -- issue, point, and purpose -- it is difficult to keep students from wanting to create exactly the kind of typographies I have been trying to avoid. They may well want to ascertain the "true" structure or meaning of a given paragraph; they will argue whether it *is* a one-sentence or two-sentence issue and disagree as to which sentence is "actually" the point. If you avoid being dragged into such arguments (that is, avoid the temptation to superimpose your own interpretation of the paragraph on them), then the procedure will not only be productive of intellectual energy but also relatively failure-proof as a pedagogical tactic. You can "allow" whatever interpretive decisions a student wishes to offer; but at the same time you can use the opportunity to push that student to defend and explain his decision. Anyone who wishes to offer a contrary interpretation should be equally encouraged and equally pressed to come up with a similar defense or explanation. The course in writing becomes a course in reading. Both are acts of interpretation. Your students will begin to discover that the process of writing forces them through an act of interpretation. Writing and thinking cannot be clearly separated from each other; nor should writing and reading.

The Writer's Power to Shape and Change Reader Expectations Concerning Paragraph Structure

Reader expectations concerning paragraphs are far more various and varying than those that concerning sentences or even the connections between sentences. On the sentence level, places in the structure do a great deal to suggest interpretive values by themselves; there is not enough time or space at that level for words alone to make all those directions to the reader semantically explicit. But in paragraphs, the subsets of discourse are clauses and sentences; there may therefore be time and space to articulate connections. Whatever the reader expectations may be concerning paragraphs, the writer has significant opportunities to override them. Any reader expectation can be violated to good effect; but any reader expectation can also be overridden by an expressly articulated counter-intention.

One method of overriding expectations is to achieve recognizable consistency for whatever stylistic abnormality you wish to maintain. Such a tactic can breed power and elegance; it also will probably incur a significant risk that the text will be misinterpreted. I knew one writer, for example, who insisted on placing the point of almost every paragraph at its midpoint -- exactly the place readers in general are least likely to expect it. That writer valued and enjoyed the sense of crescendo toward the point and decrescendo away from it, paragraph after paragraph. He was by my standards a wonderful writer; but he always had difficulty getting his books accepted for publication. Read his work with the issue/point expectations described in this chapter and you will find yourself mystified over and over again. Read the same prose with an expectation of

[build ⟷ POINT ⟷ resolve]

and you will read with pace, with immediate comprehension, and with great enjoyment.

Such individualism always puts comprehension at risk. His last book, a large one, was refused by over 100 publishers. Then one of his smallest books was accepted and looked like it would sell well. As a result of that success, a major publisher decided to opt for the large, unwanted book. It received a rave review on the front page of the *New York Times Book Review* and went through three printings in forty days. Once people were *told* he was a good writer, they adjusted to that "fact" and figured out how to read him.

It would be somewhat safer, but still highly expressive of individualism, to find ways to announce to readers that they should alter their expectations at given moments. The first and worst way that comes to mind is the potentially bludgeoning use of metadiscourse. Metadiscourse is, quite simply, discourse about discourse. Instead of talking about *what* you are talking about, you talk about talking about it.

Examples:

-- "I will divide this discussion into three parts. . . ."

-- "Without pausing to consider X, let us. . . ."

-- "Changing perspectives altogether, the impossibility of X being permanent would. . . ."

Metadiscourse is neither good nor bad in and of itself; its quality depends on its usage. If readers will be lost without being told that the discussion will be divided into three parts, then writers would do well to tell them -- explicitly and up front. If the three-part division will appear in due time and be easy to perceive and digest, then explicit metadiscourse might act only as an insult.

The decision to use or avoid metadiscourse must be based on the individual writer's sensitivity to reader response. For example, we have seen that in non-narrative paragraphs, readers expect the point to be made explicit in a single sentence located either at the Issue's end or the Discussion's end. This suggests to rule-ridden and rule-desiring students that a writer must never include *two* points in one paragraph. Of course, there are any number of reasons why a writer might want or need to construct a two-points-in-one package. At those times, metadiscourse can be most effective. Toward the beginning of the paragraph, the writer uses the number "two," thereby planting an expectation in the reader that two of something -- in this case, points -- will appear. The first will appear immediately; the second will appear after the other shoe of metadiscourse drops (in the form of "Secondly," or "(2)," or "On the other hand").

Far more subtle, effective, and enjoyable are the structural clues that can be summoned to warn readers to expect the otherwise unexpected. For instance, a writer can, with care, declare time out from the expected forward plunge through a paragraph:

12. If we can believe Herodotus, Aesop was a storytelling slave who lived on Samos in the middle of the Sixth Century B.C. and was killed by the citizens of Delphos. Writers later than Herodotus identify Aesop as either Phrygian or Thracian by birth. Aristophanes and Plutarch both contend that he was hurled to his death from a cliff when the Delphians discovered in his baggage a golden cup stolen from the temple. (The story, however, is a common one; compare Joseph and Benjamin in Genesis, chapter 44.) By the Middle Ages these stories had gained acceptance as the truth and had bred a host of other episodes and details. Most accounts picture Aesop as a deformed hunchback, grotesquely ugly, partially crippled, and defective in his speech, whose lively wit and imagination in storytelling allowed him to escape disaster in the direst of circumstances. (This too, however, has been a commonplace in literature: compare the story of Scheherezade.) Some sources even resurrect him after death and send him off to fight in the battle of Thermopylae, handicap and all.

Watch the development of the narrative from sentence to sentence here, paying special attention to the Topic position's revelation of whose story each sentence is.

12a. If we can believe Herodotus, Aesop was a storytelling slave who lived on Samos in the middle of the Sixth Century B.C. and was killed by the citizens of Delphos.

Given the beginning of the first sentence, we are contextualized by Herodotus, that Greek historian, but find the main clause to be the story of

Aesop. Since we are presented here with biographical details of the fabulist, we may generate an expectation that this will be a narrative paragraph telling us either about the life of Aesop or about portrayals of the life of Aesop.

12b. Writers later than Herodotus identify Aesop as either Phrygian or Thracian by birth.

With the introduction of "writers later than Herodotus," the second sentence moves on from Herodotus (who appears as old, backward-linking information) to further channel our expectations that we will soon encounter a series of portrayals of Aesop's life. It is a subtle form of Topic Stringing: The repeated element is those who have written about Aesop. It now appears that Herodotus had just been our starting place.

12c. Aristophanes and Plutarch both contend that he was hurled to his death from a cliff when the Delphians discovered in his baggage a golden cup stolen from the temple.

The third sentence begins with "Aristophanes and Plutarch," both of whom are indeed "writers later than Herodotus." The linkage and the progression through history continue, as does the Topic String.
But suddenly there is a change.

12d. (The story, however, is a common one; compare Joseph and Benjamin in Genesis, ch. 44.)

We encounter a punctuation mark -- an opened parenthesis -- that signals to us a time-out. It says, in effect, "Reader, we will not be continuing the march through history in this sentence; I have a significant but tangential comment to interject." In that interjection we are told not to believe everything we read about Aesop; some of the stories about him are folkloric or mythical and, as a result, appear in other places as well. Then the parenthesis closes.

12e. By the Middle Ages these stories had gained acceptance as the truth and had bred a host of other episodes and details. Most accounts picture Aesop as a deformed hunchback, grotesquely ugly, partially crippled, and defective in his speech, whose lively wit and imagination in storytelling allowed him to escape disaster in the direst of circumstances.

These next two sentences resume the historical progression by jumping to writers of the Middle Ages. The Topic String continues, somewhat, substituting "account" for the writers of those accounts. That period of time is so long that it requires two sentences to generalize about it. Then we encounter yet another parenthesis.

12f. (This too, however, has been a commonplace in literature: compare the story of Scheherezade.)

This second time-out might be intrusive and obstructive in the extreme, were it not for its structurally parallel relationship to the previous parenthetical remark. Both of them tell us to take Aesopic biography with a grain of salt; both of them refer us to well-known analogues to the Aesopic details. In leading us aside for a moment, both lead us to the same waystation.

The last sentence of example (12) is a delightful example of the use of the Coda position.

12g. Some sources even resurrect him after death and send him off to fight in the battle of Thermopylae, handicap and all.

We wind up having a bit of a laugh, both at the writers who have set Aesop to such ridiculous tasks, and at the readers who fall for it.

The *Issue* position in this paragraph informed us (accurately) to expect a narrative paragraph. It being narrative, we had no expectation of the arrival of an explicit *point* sentence. The *purpose* of the paragraph, however, resides more in its parenthetical interruptions and its sarcastic coda than in the march of history through Aesop's biography; the purpose (I would argue) is to tell us not to believe all the biographical details we read about Aesop -- even as we are reading biographical details about Aesop. Our expectations were adjusted in each sentence by both structural and grammatical clues. No hidebound rules were obeyed; neither was there any need for explicit metadiscourse.

Another powerful tactic for establishing and violating expectations is parallel construction. Rhetoric textbooks since Cicero and Quintilian have been encouraging writers and speakers to structure in a parallel way any substance that is in its nature parallel. By doing so, we establish expectations that we then fulfill in short order. Even the rhythm of the unit will support the implicit and explicit relationships. But if invoking the expectations inherent in this structure can yield predictable results, violating those expectations -- carefully and skillfully -- can also produce unusually effective results.

13. The essential problem of humankind in a computerized age remains the same as it always has been. That problem is not solely how to become more productive, more comfortable, more content, but how to be more sensitive, more sensible, more proportionate, more alive. The computer makes possible a phenomenal leap in human proficiency; it demolishes the fences around the practical and even the theoretical intelligence. But the question persists and indeed grows whether the computer makes it easier or harder for human beings to know who they really are, to identify their real problems, to respond more fully to beauty, to place adequate value on life, and to make their world safer than it now is.

The author of this, Norman Cousins, writes with the reader vividly in mind. Note the care he takes of us and the control he exerts over us by his choice of structuring effects here.

He has constructed what seems to me a two-sentence issue. The first sentence posits the existence of a problem in general; the second sentence makes that problem specific. The second sentence could conceivably be the point of the paragraph. It is substantial enough, long enough, and definitive enough. Notice its parallel-but-unbalanced structure: We are set up with "The problem is *not* . . ." and given three anti-definitions, each preceded by the word "more." The "not" raises our expectation of the arrival of a "but," which we further expect will be followed by the same number of "more's" -- three. We get the "but," and we get the expected "more" labels; but instead of three, we get four. The structural message (I would argue) is that the material that follows the "but" is meant to outweigh the earlier series by a four-to-three ratio. At the end of the third member of the "but" series, we expect to be able to exhale the reader energy we had reserved for the parallel series of three. Having to go on to a fourth makes a significant difference in the way we lean forward into the sentence.

In the next two sentences we are presented with another parallel structure, by no means unexpected. This second parallelism we expect to be in some way repetitive of -- and therefore parallel to -- the first parallel construction. We get what we had been led to expect; but note that we are now expecting a parallel structure that *violates normal expectations*.

This second parallelism takes two sentences. In the first of those, we learn of *two* things that computers make possible. In the following sentence, we learn of *five* things that computers cannot do. The unbalanced four-to-three ratio earlier in the paragraph is responded to here by an even more unbalanced five-to-two ratio. In other words, as the paragraph progresses, the imbalance between what computers can and cannot do becomes more and more severe. That structural presentation of imbalance seems to me the *purpose* of this paragraph. It is distinct both from its issue and its point.

We have seen a variation of this misbalancing tactic before, in the space program paragraph of Example (4):

4. Much has happened since the Apollo program and the Mercury and Gemini missions that paved the way for it in the early 1960s. Numerous scientific and communications satellites have been launched into Earth orbit. Unmanned deep-space probes have been sent to the sun, the moon, and the planets, where they gathered a wealth of information about our solar system. Skylab demonstrated that American astronauts could live and work in space for months at a time. And a dramatically different launch vehicle entered service: the space shuttle. The winged reusable craft was supposed to make space flight routine and cheap.

Following the opening issue/point sentence, we are bombarded with a number of examples. Why is such a distinct expectation raised at the end of the paragraph that the next paragraph will proceed to discuss the space shuttle? It is raised in part because the space shuttle is deposited at the end of this paragraph, where it can more easily lean forward to the prose that follows. But perhaps even more significantly, the space shuttle is the only example in the paragraph to have two sentences devoted to it instead of one. That two-to-one ratio structurally prepares us for the possibility of the shuttle program taking over as the story of the next paragraph -- which it eventually does.

Most students can see these kinds of things for themselves, once the existence of these structures is brought up from the intuitive level to a conscious level. Teachers new to this approach may be uncomfortable with it at first; but that discomfort is usually short-lived. It is replaced by a confidence in the promised benefits of exploration.

P ointless Paragraphs

Not every paragraph must include an explicitly stated point. Some paragraphs have only a narrative or descriptive task to perform. Others may be fashioned to lead the reader to surmise or supply the point; the writer may have a purpose based on politics, politesse, or psychology for letting the reader play this greater analytical role. But more often than not, when a non-narrative paragraph omits its point, it is either because (1) the writer did not recognize that readers might miss the point, or (2) the writer did not develop the thought enough to produce a point. In either of those cases, the efforts to create and effectively locate a point will help all concerned. The eventual decision to include or exclude the point may not be as important to the writer as the process of making that decision. Such a re-entry into the thinking process can lead in many different directions. Two typical problems show up in Examples (14) and (15) that follow.

Example (14) is a paragraph from a published paper in a journal of medical research.

14. Several other authors have recently reported clinical studies evaluating the use of moxalactam for the treatment of bacterial infections. Livingston and coworkers treated 50 patients with a variety of infections, obtaining a cure in 45 of the 47 evaluable cases. Lentino et al successfully treated 40 patients who had lower respiratory tract bacterial infections with moxalactam. Tofte et al obtained cures in 42 of 45 bacterial infections treated with moxalactam. Side effects in all studies have generally included minor abnormalities in renal and liver functions, eosinophilia, mild anemia, anorexia, and drug fever. One patient in each of two studies had diarrhea requiring cessation of antibiotic therapy.

Many readers have found this paragraph informative but pedestrian, even unto footsore. (Tediousness, some have argued, is an occupational hazard for those who must read great amounts of medical research.) If we analyze the paragraph in terms of readers expectations, we discover that tedium is by no means the main problem here.

The first sentence:

14a. Several other authors have recently reported clinical studies evaluating the use of moxalactam for the treatment of bacterial infections.

If this sentence is the whole of the issue, then we will expect to hear more about "other authors" or "clinical studies" or "moxalactam" or "bacterial infections" or some combination of these. Though this sentence may well be the issue, we may hope that it will not be the point. Why should we be burdened with an entire paragraph to discover the point that, yes indeed, several other authors *have* done moxalactam studies?

The second, third, and fourth sentences seem to bear out our suspicion that the first sentence might be the issue:

14b. Livingston and coworkers treated 50 patients with a variety of infections, obtaining a cure in 45 of the 47 evaluable cases. Lentino et al successfully treated 40 patients who had lower respiratory tract bacterial infections with moxalactam. Tofte et al obtained cures in 42 of 45 bacterial infections treated with moxalactam.

Here are some of the "other authors," studying the use of "moxalactam" to treat "bacterial infections." However, no one of these sentences is likely to be the point of the paragraph; they exist in a series and function to exemplify, not prove, the issue previously stated.

With the fifth sentence, we have our hopes momentarily raised that we may reach the point of all this:

14c. Side effects in all studies have generally included minor abnormalities in renal and liver functions, eosinophilia, mild anemia, anorexia, and drug fever.

From the Topic position, we learn that this sentence is the story of "side effects in *all* studies." It gives us hope that a summative statement of some kind is about to arrive; surely this will be the point. What we find instead is an anticlimax -- a list of merely "*minor* abnormalities." Since nothing in the paragraph prepared us to expect that information concerning minor abnormal side effects will be the most important in the paragraph, we still await the arrival of the point.

The sixth and final sentence:

14d. One patient in each of two studies had diarrhea requiring cessation of antibiotic therapy.

This does not seem likely to be the point, either; it is only a footnote-like comment to inform us why two individuals failed to have their moxalactam experiments completed. Our sympathies might go out to those two patients for their distress, but we have reached the end of the paragraph without having been told *why* we have been given all these facts. We are left to ask what the point of all this has been.

The author knew right away; he was surprised that anyone could have had a problem. The point was that in all these many studies, moxalactam proved extremely effective in treating bacterial infections. (This was so despite a few abnormal side effects and the minor problem that two people had to drop out of the studies. It was not clear whether the diarrhea had been brought on by the taking of moxalactam.) The author thought that the several successes mentioned in the second through fourth sentences would have made his point clear enough to any attentive reader. In other words, he assumed that everyone would interpret the statistics as he did.

By publishing a pointless paragraph, he ran a serious risk of being misinterpreted. We could read this paragraph as a *negative* statement about moxalactam if we cared to do so. For Livingston, 45 of 47 out of 50 were cured? What happened to the other two patients? Did they die? Why were three cases "not evaluable"? Lentino treated 40 cases successfully -- but out of how many? Why is that number suppressed? Tofte failed about 7% of the time. How bad were the failures? Side effects occurred in *all* studies? Would *you* like a little problem with your liver? or a touch of anorexia? or how about a bout of drug fever? Yes? Well then, take moxalactam.

The author could have avoided this problem by including a new second sentence to inform us that the use of moxalactam had been a flaming success. That in turn would have led us to expect the series of "successful" statistics that occupy the next three sentences.

But that new sentence alone would not have solved all the problems of the paragraph. If we look back at the Stress positions of the individual sentences, we find a series of disappointments. In the (original) second sentence, we find "45 of the 47 evaluable cases." It sounds pretty good as a success rate, but we would have been more assured of that had we been told as much explicitly and emphatically, in the Stress position.[9]

The Stress positions of the third and fourth sentence are both filled with the old information "(treated) with moxalactam." If we search for stress-worthy information in those sentences, all we can find is the statistics. If the point had been made earlier that these studies all demonstrated success, then the specific statistics (45 of 47, 40, and 42 of 45) would have become stress-worthy in and of themselves. Had all those statistics appeared in Stress positions, they might cumulatively have suggested "success."

The other two Stress positions are also unconvincingly filled. In the fifth sentence, we find ourselves stressing a long list of things we previously have been told are "minor" and are only "side effects." In the sixth sentence, we are left with an inflated sense of importance that these two patients were required to cease their moxalactam therapy by their physical discomfort.

The structural problems of this paragraph turn out to be more far-reaching then we could have predicted from our first, brisk reading. Not only does the paragraph as a whole lack a specifically articulated point but also each sentence similarly lacks any directions from the author as to what we should value most highly in our interpretation. In short, the author has merely laid all his findings on the table before us, leaving it to us to do the intellectual work of evaluation. He has not helped us decide what to think. He could have solved the problem by inserting a timely sentence informing us that the moxalactam experiments produced consistently excellent results:

14e. SEVERAL OTHER AUTHORS HAVE RECENTLY REPORTED CLINICAL STUDIES EVALUATING THE USE OF MOXALACTAM FOR THE TREATMENT OF BACTERIAL INFECTIONS. THE STUDIES DEMONSTRATE A HIGH RATE OF SUCCESS. Livingston and coworkers treated 50 patients with a variety of infections, obtaining a cure in 45 of the 47 evaluable cases. Lentino et al successfully treated 40 patients. . . .

If he did indeed intend to emphasize the success rate of these studies above all else, he could make the following revisions as well: (1) He could place the important statistics in the appropriate Stress positions; (2) he could arrange the evidence in a climactic order; and (3) he could relegate the "side effects" and the two cessation of treatment cases to a single sentence in the position of a coda. The resulting paragraph might read as follows:

14f. Several other authors have recently reported clinical studies in which bacterial infections were treated with moxalactam. These studies demonstrate a high rate of success. Tofte et al obtained cures in 42 of 45 of their evaluable cases -- a success rate of over 93%. Livingston and coworkers treated 50 patients with a variety of infections, obtaining a cure in 45 of the 47 evaluable cases -- a success rate of over 95%. Lentino et al successfully treated the lower respiratory tract bacterial infections of all 40 of their patients -- a stunning success rate of 100%. The side effects, which occurred in all the studies, tended to include minor abnormalities in renal and liver functions, eosinophilia, mild anemia, anorexia, and drug fever; and one patient in each of two studies had diarrhea requiring cessation of antibiotic therapy.

Conversely, we could restructure all the information in this paragraph to make the moxalactam experimentation seem quite negative and threatening. To do so, we would need to highlight the negative news -- the bad side effects -- by depositing them in structural locations that announce their importance. Here is one possibility:

14g. Several other authors have recently reported clinical studies evaluating the use of moxalactam for the treatment of bacterial infections. In all studies, moxalactam had side effects. Livingston and coworkers treated 50 patients with a variety of infections, obtaining a cure in 45 of the 47 evaluable cases. Lentino et al successfully treated 40 patients who had lower respiratory tract bacterial infections with moxalactam. Tofte et al obtained cures in 42 of 45 bacterial infections treated with moxalactam. In each of two studies, one patient had diarrhea requiring cessation of antibiotic therapy. Side effects have generally included minor abnormalities in renal and liver functions, eosinophilia, mild anemia, anorexia, and drug fever.[10]

Example (15) is taken from an assignment I have often given Freshmen in order to provide them with a real audience. They must write a letter -- a real letter, to a real person -- of praise or complaint. (Almost everyone opts for complaint. As Milton discovered, it is easier to write about Satan than about God.) After drafts are circulated among writing groups and responded to, the final letter is submitted in two copies, with an addressed, stamped envelope. One copy is actually sent to the intended recipient.[11] Here is a letter written by a college freshman to President Ronald Reagan in 1987.

15. Dear Mr. President,

As a concerned citizen of the United States, I am writing to you to express my disapproval of the current state of affairs in South Africa. Certainly you are aware of the system of apartheid, which has been in effect for some three hundred years. Apartheid is a system of racial segregation in housing, education, and commerce throughout the various provinces of South Africa. It is propagated by the government of South Africa, which is composed entirely of whites, in a nation with a large black majority. The government keeps the black majority in a state of disenfranchisement and denies all means of self determination to the country's majority.

Mr. President, this flagrant disregard for human rights and democratic principles flies in the face of all accepted principles of democracy and morality. Seeds of rebellion are being sewn by black opposition leaders in South Africa. A liberated black majority in South Africa is a nation whose time has come. There will be no turning back. Considering the geopolitical position that South Africa maintains, I urge you not to alienate the emerging black revolutionary forces that will inevitably claim power in South Africa. Please pledge the complete support of the United States to ending apartheid in South Africa and ensuring a healthy relationship with the new government that is to come.

Yours truly,

When I use this example in faculty writing workshops, I ask everyone to suggest what grade they might give this letter as a writing assignment. Usually no one suggests a straight A; very few opt for an A–; there are many votes for everything from B+ to D. The average is usually a borderline B–/C+. Almost no one describes the author as particularly clever or insightful.

An issue/point analysis of the letter's two paragraphs is most revealing, both of the strategy of the letter and of the role of a sentence-by-sentence analysis technique.

The first sentence:

15a. As a concerned citizen of the United States, I am writing to you to express my disapproval of the current state of affairs in South Africa.

If this first sentence is the entirety of the issue, then we probably expect to hear more about the author's disapproval of the state of affairs in South Africa. This sentence is hardly likely to be the paragraph's point: "I am writing to you" is an unlikely focus for that kind of spotlight. Besides, we expect the point of an opening paragraph in such a letter to occupy the final sentence.

The second sentence:

15b. Certainly you are aware of the system of apartheid, which has been in effect for some three hundred years.

This conceivably might begin the discussion of the one-sentence issue of the first sentence. It is hardly likely, however, that the point of the paragraph would be the noting of President Reagan's certain awareness of apartheid. (If it were, the rest of the paragraph would have to concern itself with proving to Mr. Reagan that he indeed *was* aware of apartheid.)

The third sentence:

15c. Apartheid is a system of racial segregation in housing, education, and commerce throughout the various provinces of South Africa.

This sentence is also unlikely to be the point. It is, however, a bit of an insult. After assuring the President that he knows all about apartheid, this student somehow feels the need to offer a working definition of it.

The fourth sentence:

15d. It is propagated by the government of South Africa, which is composed entirely of whites, in a nation with a large black majority.

Like its predecessor, this sentence further (and merely) defines apartheid and is therefore unlikely to be the point of the paragraph. But all this time we have been expecting the point to appear in this opening paragraph's final sentence.

Here is the fifth and final sentence of the first paragraph:

15e. The government keeps the black majority in a state of disenfranchisement and denies all means of self determination to the country's majority.

This does not sound like the paragraph's point. Instead, it merely extends the ongoing definition of apartheid to a third sentence. Our expectation that this would be the point has been violated. We have here a pointless paragraph.

The first sentence of the second paragraph:

15f. Mr. President, this flagrant disregard for human rights and democratic principles flies in the face of all accepted principles of democracy and morality.

We assume this sentence will be the issue of the second paragraph; but that turns out not to be the case. The second paragraph concerns itself with predicting a black victory in the unavoidable revolution. What then is the function of sentence 15f? -- It is the point of the first paragraph.

All the flailing about we witnessed in the first paragraph makes far more sense if it builds to the climax of a charge of immorality. To improve the first paragraph immeasurably, all we need do is surgically remove sentence (15f) from the second paragraph and suture it onto the end of the first paragraph. Then the point appears exactly where we might expect it, and that paragraph becomes a structural whole that is also a substantive whole.

Second sentence, second paragraph:

15g. Seeds of rebellion are being sewn by black opposition leaders in South Africa.

What is the function of this sentence? It turns out to be the real issue of the second paragraph. With its predecessor transported backward into the first paragraph, this sentence now becomes the first in the second paragraph and can more clearly announce this paragraph's issue -- the eventually successful black rebellion.

Is this sentence also the paragraph's point? It certainly could be the point of *some* paragraph. It will not be the point of this one if the sentences that follow it grow even more interesting or intense.

Most composition teachers will call attention to this important sentence not for its structural significance but for its spelling mistake. Most people who read this paragraph for content only do not notice that "sewn" should be "sown." Yet many teachers will make that error the focal point of the student's attention. A small change of the *e* to an *o* here will do far more good than a large red circle and an angry-looking "SP."

Third sentence, second paragraph:

15h. A liberated black majority in South Africa is a nation whose time has come.

Could this be the point? It certainly could be the point of *some* paragraph; but it is neither the last sentence of the paragraph nor the last sentence of the Discussion here. We hope, therefore, that something yet more vital is yet to come. It even _sounds_ like an intensification.

Fourth sentence, second paragraph:

15i. There will be no turning back.

Continuing to develop the issue announced by the Issue sentence, this yet more dramatic sentence sounds like it could be the point of the paragraph; if so, then what does the writer expect to gain by making this point to the President? We are still in hope that a yet more compelling point will arrive before the paragraph ends. We can hear the crescendo building.

Fifth sentence, second paragraph:

15j. Considering the geopolitical position that South Africa maintains, I urge you not to alienate the emerging black revolutionary forces that will inevitably claim power in South Africa.

This sentence seems a reasonable candidate -- indeed, an admirable candidate -- to be the point of the second paragraph. The issue was that the black population would eventually rebel and win out over the whites of South Africa. The author is now urging the President to make use of this certain knowledge. We are Americans, it argues. We like to be on the side of the winners. The South African blacks will eventually win. If we befriend them now, we will be able to say we supported them all along. We should get in while the getting is good. Machiavelli himself would have been proud of this strategy.

There remains a problem here: Sentence (15j) does not seem to be located in one of the two places we expect the point to be announced -- unless, of course, the sentence that follows it acts as a coda.

We turn to that last sentence:

15k. Please pledge the complete support of the United States to ending apartheid in South Africa and ensuring a healthy relationship with the new government that is to come.

There is nothing about this sentence that suggests coda. Located as it is in this paragraph, it seems a lame way to end such a Machiavellian piece of political advice. If, however, this sentence were split off from this paragraph to form a paragraph of its own, it would function well in two ways: (1) It would allow the point of the second paragraph to be located in that unit's last sentence, where we expect to find it; and (2) It would transform what was originally a lame ending of the second paragraph into a perfectly acceptable (and perhaps somewhat clever) summative paragraph for the letter as a whole. Its first part ("Please pledge the complete support of the United States to ending apartheid") can be read as nodding backward to the moral statements of the first paragraph. Its second part ("ensuring a healthy relationship with the new government") is a clear reference to the pragmatic advice offered in the second paragraph. Note that this is a fine example of a legitimate one-sentence paragraph: It requires no discussion, since the discussion has already taken place.

This revised letter now becomes the product of a significantly clever and insightful young man, aware of political and rhetorical realities. After articulating the mandatory moral principle in the first paragraph, it offers a sly and pragmatic reason for following what will seem a moral course of action.

The structural locations of the individual sentences now offer the reader instructions for interpreting the whole:

15k. As a concerned citizen of the United States, I am writing to you to express my disapproval of the current state of affairs in South Africa. Certainly you are aware of the system of apartheid, which has been in effect for some three hundred years. Apartheid is a system of racial segregation in housing, education, and commerce throughout the various provinces of South Africa. It is propagated by the government of South Africa, which is composed entirely of whites, in a nation with a large black majority. The government keeps the black majority in a state of disenfranchisement and denies all means of self determination to the country's majority. Mr. President, this flagrant disregard for human rights and democratic principles flies in the face of all accepted principles of democracy and morality.

Seeds of rebellion are being sown by black opposition leaders in South Africa. A liberated black majority in South Africa is a nation whose time has come. There will be no turning back. Considering the geopolitical position that South Africa maintains, I urge you not to alienate the emerging black revolutionary forces that will inevitably claim power in South Africa.

Please pledge the complete support of the United States to ending apartheid in South Africa and ensuring a healthy relationship with the new government that is to come.

Yours truly,

Before the revision, the first paragraph was pointless; the second paragraph raised a misleading issue and ended lamely. After the revision, the points appear where expected, the development is surer, and the tone stronger. All this was accomplished by restructuring, without the alteration of a single word choice. The grade for the letter is now an A.

Did the author know or intend the contents of this letter as I have interpreted them? We will never know. I did not have the opportunity to ask him. Had I asked him, I would not have known how to judge whether his response was genuine or an attempt to save face after the fact. Could the author have discovered for himself the same things I discovered? Yes; he merely needed to ask himself *where he had located* the points he was trying to make in these paragraphs. He might well then have been led to exactly the revision employed here. In other words, the weakness of the *structure* could have led him to perceive the incompleteness of his *thought*.

Note the difference between his asking (1) *where* the points are and (2) *what* the points should be. The former is a relatively objective question with the relatively objective answers of "here," "there," and "nowhere." The latter is the more abstract inquiry into the thought process, all too easily answered by "I meant to say exactly what I said" -- an example of the coffee stain metaphor mentioned in Chapter 1 (page 16).

How can you go wrong in constructing a paragraph? It's easy. Make sure the issue is not clearly stated up front. Hide the point in an unexpected place; or leave it out altogether. No matter how "correct" all the data may be, no matter how insightful the observations might become, few readers will be able to put it all together in a meaningful and communally agreed upon fashion.

Connections Between Paragraphs

In some ways, connections between paragraphs resemble connections between sentences. In both cases, the reader is departing from a unit of discourse that has raised numerous possibilities for further development. In both cases the reader wishes to know as soon as possible exactly which strands of the former discourse will be the connecting links to the present and ongoing discourse. The writer can furnish that information (1) by signaling forward at the end of the previous unit, (2) by motioning backward at the beginning of the new unit, or (3) by doing both of these.

One might think that since sentences are usually much shorter than paragraphs, they might offer far fewer possibilities for linkage to future sentences than paragraphs do for future paragraphs. This turns out not necessarily to be the case. Any of the contents of a sentence are available for future development. On the sentence level, the occupant of the Stress position may often be the leading indicator of future linkage; it is never the only possible one. Any important word in a sentence can become old information in the next Topic position and take over the storyline. Paragraphs, on the other hand, usually work with much larger units of thought. Their structure and development often aim at limiting the likelihood of what can come next, far more than sentences tend to do.

Sentences offer a much larger number of future possible connections than one might think upon first reading them. I borrow an example from fiction -- the ironically argumentative opening sentence from Jane Austen's *Pride and Prejudice*:

16a. It is a truth universally acknowledged, that a single man in possession of a good fortune must be in want of a wife.

Consider the wealth of possibilities for development crammed into this one delightful sentence. Here is only a partial list:

truth	universally
acknowledged	universal truth
universally acknowledged	a single man
a man	possession
a good fortune	in possession of a good fortune
must be	must be in want
a wife	in want of a wife
must be in want of a wife	

Any or many of these stepping stones might be used to forge the connection to the next sentence. Ask 20 people who have not read *Pride and Prejudice* to create a logical second sentence to follow Austen's first; the chances are high that no two people will come up with precisely the same sentence.

Here is the one Jane Austen produced:

16b. However little known the feelings or views of such a man may be on his first entering a neighborhood, this truth is so well fixed in the minds of the surrounding families that he is considered as the rightful property of some one or other of their daughters.

Note how many of the candidates on my list she managed to cram into this single sentence. The rest of the book can be read as a virtuosic devel-

opment of precisely the information she has hurled at us, in ever so gen-
teel a manner, in the book's opening sentence.

One can argue that such interpretive richness is the greatest difference
between literature and non-literature; but any well-considered sentence
will have a surprisingly large number of connective possibilities. Literature
tends to make greater use of a larger number of those connections; it is the
job of non-literature, insofar as possible, to restrict that number to a size
that can be willfully controlled by the writer.

No text is either literary or non-literary in and of itself. That distinction
stems not so much from the way the text was written but rather from the
way it is read. "Literary reading" searches for and values multiplicity of
interpretation; "non-literary reading" searches for and values singleness of
interpretation. Some texts (e.g., James Joyce's *Ulysses*) make for excellent
literary reading and maddening non-literary reading. Directions how to
assemble a harpsichord from a ready-made kit, on the other hand, might
offer just the opposite experience: They might not uplift you, but they help
you get the job done. Either kind of reading can be done to any text.

This distinction between literary and non-literary reading is the basis for
a strong argument against using literature as the main text of a composition
course. Both are subject to the same general reader expectations; but literature, which invites numerous rereadings, can and often must involve a great
many more intentional violations of those expectations. People often point
out to me that Henry James and Faulkner create sentences that go on for more
than a page, cramming in far more viable candidates for Stress positions than
there are Stress positions. They ask if this means that James and Faulkner are
"bad" writers. No, they are not bad writers. They would tell you, I am sure,
that they are dealing with "life"; and "life" is too complex and multifaceted
to allow for clear indications of import at every moment. The overburdened
sentence, therefore, mirrors the overburdening quality of life.

The perfect piece of literature, when read by 1,000 readers, should result in at least 1,000 interpretations. The perfect piece of writing in the professional world, when read by 1,000 readers, should produce one and only
one interpretation.

But despite the intentions of non-literature writers constantly to narrow the focus of their prose, readers cannot often predict with confidence
and accuracy that which will come next. Consider for example these three
opening sentences from works on rhetoric:

17. One of the most distinguished privileges which Providence has con-
    ferred upon mankind, is the power of communicating their thoughts
    to one another.
    (Hugh Blair, *Lectures on Rhetoric and Belle Lettres*, 1783)

18. In his remarks on ancient rhetoric, Roland Barthes correctly observed
    that "rhetoric must always be read in its structural interplay with its
    neighbors -- grammar, logic, poetics, and philosophy."
    (Chaim Perelman, *The Realm of Rhetoric*)

19. There are as least as many conceptions of rhetoric as there are philosophical perspectives on human communication.

(Lawrence J. Prelli, A Rhetoric of Science)

To play with any of these would be to enter into a game of infinite possibilities. Try your hand at creating a second sentence for each. You will find the author's choices in the endnote that accompanies this sentence.[12] See how close you came. Note that there is no "fault" involved if you were way off.

Because the possibilities are so numerous, I will not even attempt to offer a detailed catalogue of the types of transitions that can be made from paragraph to paragraph. A brief discussion of just a few will have to suffice. I begin with the narrative paragraph.

Narratives take us from point A to point B in time and experience. As readers, we maintain a few dominating expectations for the beginning of the paragraph that follows:

1) It might continue the chronology of the previous paragraph, beginning from where the previous one left off.

2) It might continue to develop the issue of the previous paragraph, thereby stating again from where the previous had started.

3) It might choose a particular detail or moment from the previous paragraph upon which to dwell and expand.

4) It might shift dramatically to a topic that the reader has as yet been given no cause to expect.

Readers are pleased and relieved when they are told as early as possible -- preferably in the first sentence -- which of these options will be realized. For an example, reconsider example (8) of this chapter, briefly encountered on page 211 above:

8. The summer I was 16, I took a train from New York to Steamboat Springs, Colo., where I was going to be assistant horse wrangler at a camp. The trip took three days, and since I was much too shy to talk to strangers, I had quite a lot of time for reading. I read all of *Gone with the Wind*. I read all the interesting articles in a couple of magazines I had, and then I went back and read all the dull stuff. I also took all the quizzes, a thing of which magazines were even fuller than now.

The paragraph that follows this one could continue the discourse in any number of ways, including innumerable variations on the four general directions suggested above.

1a) [Continuing the chronology]: "After a nearly terminal case of boredom, I finally arrived in Steamboat Springs."

1b) [A different way of continuing the chronology]: "Having finished with the quizzes, three times each, I was heading toward reader's despair.

In a last gasp effort, I resorted to studying the prose on the back of my ticket. 'The Railroad is not responsible for personal items lost or damaged during passage.' I started to wonder: What if I lost the. . . ?"

2) [Continuing the earlier paragraph's issue]: "I took the train because of the extraordinary fear I have of flying.

3a) [Expanding on a particular detail]: "After all those quizzes, I started to appreciate the complexity of a sprawling novel like *Gone with the Wind.*"

3b) [Expanding on a different particular detail]: "The one that held my undivided attention was called 'How Masculine/Feminine Are You?'"

4) [An unexpected shift]: "Little did I know that the entire summer would pass by without my being allowed to read a single page."

There are no paradigms, no preset instructions that can help a writer decide where to take the reader next. That must come from the thought process of the individual writer. A writing course cannot produce thoughts for students; it can only help students formulate as clearly as possible the thoughts they are already capable of summoning. A writer can bend a narrative in any number of directions at any given moment. Readers may be willing to follow; they must be given adequate warning where to turn next. As with sentences, beginnings and ends are the main places readers look for such help.

Non-narrative paragraphs also resemble sentences in the way they connect to each other. As we explored in some detail in Chapter 5, in forming a new sentence in a continuing discourse, there are two favored candidates for that new Topic position: either (1) the occupant of the previous Topic position (thus continuing that occupant's story and forming a Topic String), or (2) the occupant of the previous Stress position (thus shifting stories and creating a Topic Change). Paragraphs are relatively similar in this respect: They often benefit from linking backward either (1) to the occupant of the previous paragraph's Issue position, or (2) to the last sentence of the previous paragraph. As a result, the linkage sends the reader either back to the beginning of the last similar-size unit of discourse (which could be either the issue or the point), or to its ending (which is often the point). Here are examples of both kinds of linkage, using once again the examples (5) and (6) we have seen before, this time augmented by parts of their next paragraph:

5. This book is the beginning of an attempt to move the study of American literature away from the small group of master texts that have dominated critical discussion for the last thirty years and into a more varied and fruitful area of investigation. It involves, in its most ambitious form, a redefinition of literature and literary study, for it sees literary texts not as works of art embodying enduring themes in complex forms, but as attempts to redefine the social order. In this view,

novels and stories should be studied not because they manage to escape the limitations of their particular time and place, but because they offer powerful examples of the way a culture thinks about itself, articulating and proposing solutions for the problems that shape a particular historical moment. I believe that the works of fiction that this book examines were written not so that they could be enshrined in any literary hall of fame, but in order to win the belief and influence the behavior of the widest possible audience. These novelists have designs upon their audiences, in the sense of wanting to make people think and act in a particular way.

Consequently this book focuses primarily, though not exclusively, on works whose obvious impacts on their readers has made them suspect from a modernist point of view, which tends to classify work that affects people's lives, or tries to, as merely sensational or propagandistic.

That second paragraph links to both the beginning and the end of its predecessor. It returns us to the issue raised at the beginning of that previous paragraph, where we learned that this book would shift the attention we pay to literature in certain ways. It also connects us to the end of that previous paragraph by dropping the second shoe of the book's title, *Sensational Designs*. This latter connection is elegant and fulfilling; but the former connection, back to the issue of the previous paragraph, establishes the main line of development for the next few paragraphs.

Back to Example (6) and Wagner:

6. His poetic article of 1849, "The Revolution," had promised a new Europe. To the jubilant strains of shrill, warlike music, a paradise was to rise from the devastation of a volcanic upheaval. But in the finale of the *Ring*, hostility gives way to a calm resignation, knowing neither defeat nor victory. Brynhild bids her father, Wotan, rest to music of infinite sadness, and the old world sinks down because it can no longer bear its load of deceit and treachery. Hagen, preaching Bakunian-style violence to the end, is pulled into the depths of the cascading river by the Rhine Daughters. But, though they happily ride the crest of destruction with their restored treasure, no new Eden can follow. Alberich is still at large, and the new world may well be as troubled as the old.

    At the end of both the first Nibelung scenario and "Siegfried's Death," Brynhild gives assurance that the dwarf [Alberich] would never again possess the Ring and, in fact, promised freedom to him and all the Nibelungs from their enslavement to gold's power. The final stage direction of "Siegfried's Death" describes the inconsolable and obdurate fellow [Alberich] as he "sinks down with a gesture of woe." It seems mute evidence of Wagner's growing pessimism that in [the last opera of the *Ring*] not only does Brynhild pass over the dwarf's fate in silence, but the action fails to dispose of him in any way.

This second paragraph, although somewhat complex, grabs on to both parts of the previous paragraph's final sentence: Alberich the dwarf becomes a main character of the new paragraph; he also acts as an example of the "growing pessimism" that "the new world may well be as troubled as the old."

How much explicit connection is needed at the beginning of a paragraph to link it to the previous paragraph? The answer is Talmudic in its combination of responsiveness and evasion: You need as much connection as is necessary to make it clear to your reader how to proceed, without insulting or delaying your reader by being unnecessarily explicit. It is always a judgment call; but the judgment should be made not in terms of what sounds good to the writer but rather in terms of what is needed by the reader.

The main principles to keep in mind are those inherent in all the reader expectations described in this volume: Readers need to be contextualized first, informed what action is taking place, and then presented with the stressworthy material. Readers expect stressworthy materials to arrive at the end of a sentence, at the beginning or end of a paragraph, and toward the beginning and/or end of a whole document.

A *Note on Whole Documents*

It may seem strange that in a work of this length I should spend only a few paragraphs on the question of reader expectations concerning whole documents. The reasons can be stated briefly.

(1) On the one hand, the possibilities for structuring and developing a whole document are geometrically more complicated than those for structuring paragraphs, which in turn encompass those of structuring many individual sentences. No two people would be at all likely to produce identical documents, even when they started with precisely the same materials.

(2) On the other hand, certain strong conventions for structuring and developing whole documents have been crisply communicated to writers by individual discourse communities. There may be great differences between the structures of a legal brief and an article on medical research and a federal grant proposal; but the courts, the medical academic community, and the federal government each have let it be known what expectations they have of the gross structure of those documents. Each discourse community forces its own neophytes to adapt to those expectations. Composition courses at the college level need not steal their thunder; they need rather to prepare students in

the awareness of structural expectations. Those generalized linguistic expectations can be adapted to the needs of any community the student will eventually join.

For example, medical journals in each separate subfield have well-articulated rules (and these *are* rules) for the submission of data and analysis. Those rules may differ from subspecialty to subspecialty; but an individual cannot be accepted in that community -- that is, be published -- without demonstrating an ability to conform to those standards. Certain kinds of information belong in the abstract; other kinds are relegated to the methods section; yet others appear in the sections on findings; yet others belong to the discussion sections. Tables and graphs have their places. The main point had better be announced up front and presented pictorially in a prominent location. Methods must not appear in places where argument should be taking place -- and vice versa. All this must be learned by the scientific novitiate.

All that knowledge might be of no avail to the writer of a legal brief, a business memo, or an article for a journal of literary criticism. Each of those documents is founded on a similarly indigenous set of community expectations. Some are parallel to medical expectations; some seem parallel but are not; others could hardly be more different.

In contrast to legal briefs and scientific publications, articles in journals of literary criticism will often leave their punch line for the last third of the document. That revelatory moment will be preceded by a number of familiar subunits, no explicit headings being necessary. The intended audience recognizes those subunits just as clearly as if they were marked by headings in bold type. Here is one common progression:

(1) "Critics have long said . . .";

(2) "Critics are wrong because . . .";

(3) "If we turn to the texts, we see . . .";

(4) "This is complicated by . . .";

(5) "However, we can understand the problem better if . . .";

(6) "Returning to the texts, . . .";

(7) "Now watch how imaginatively I can deal with this . . .";

(8) Now that you've experienced the excitement of my solution, I'll give you a few moments to calm down before we bring this

(9) to an end.

A single course in writing, even a two-semester course, does not provide enough time to investigate a great many of these discourse-specific documents. Any one of them can make an excellent vehicle for teaching large structures. Juxtaposing any two of them can help demonstrate the potential differences between large structures. The greatest danger lies in allowing students to believe there is only one large structure in existence -- the form of the academic essay.

For students who wish to get a head start on their chosen occupation, we can devise specific advanced composition courses. Investigating the prose of a discipline will lead them to understand better the intellectual problems and challenges of that discipline. In the more generalized freshman course, students will have more than enough to do being introduced to general reader expectations of discourse units smaller than whole documents.

Endnotes

1. Barrett Wendell, *English Composition*, New York: Charles Scribner's Sons, 1891, p. 117.
2. Fred N. Scott and Joseph V. Denney, *Paragraph-Writing*, Boston: Allyn & Bacon, 1896.
3. Alexander Bain, *Composition and Rhetoric*, vol. I., Section 178.
4. The vertical lines in all the other boxes could also, for the same reasons, be desolidified into dots. Subjects, verbs, and complements (for example) are *rarely* one-third of a sentence's length each. So why use dots here but not elsewhere? For two reasons: (1) The solid lines are easier to work with mentally. Since there is no cause to be worrying about what percentage of a sentence is occupied by the verb, why constantly raise the question by perforating the vertical line? (2) On the paragraph level, however, we would do well to unteach the lesson learned about the length of the issue and to emphasize that it may take much longer to get the job done in some paragraphs than in others.
5. Again I must add that my choice of issue and point in any paragraph is not absolute. Other readers might read the paragraph differently, perceiving a different issue or a different point. I am only reporting what most readers in my experience have determined to be the issue and the point of that particular paragraph.
6. Exception: Final paragraphs can effectively end with a point sentence followed by a coda.
7. I base these generalizations not on formal statistical research but on many years of experience teaching students, faculty, and members of professional communities.
8. In other respects, these paragraphs do not resemble the typical Topic Sentence–style paragraph: These often have a two-sentence or three-sentence issue; they do not necessarily have precisely three examples between the two statements of the point; and the sophistication of the argument often connects the medial sentences in one long development rather than staking three separate claims as support for the point.
9. It is entirely possible for the failure in the two cases would be serious enough to bar the official acceptance of some drug therapies.
10. This rewrite is the product of Judith A. Swan, my partner in the consulting firm we have called The Science of Style.

11. When I taught at a Midwestern Jesuit school, half of the letters would go to the President and the other half to the Pope. After I moved to Duke University, half of the letters went to the President and the other half to the head of Food Services. So much for cultural differences.

12. Blair: "Destitute of this power, Reason would be a solitary, and, in some measure, an unavailing principle."

    Perelman: "I would add that in order best to define and situate rhetoric, we must also clarify its relationship to dialectic."

    Prelli: "There are likely to be family resemblances among rhetorical theories sharing similar philosophical assumptions, but the content of rhetorical theories varies when we move among the philosophical perspectives of the sophists, Isocrates, Plato, Aristotle, Cicero, Quintilian, Augustine, Ramus, Vico, Campbell, Blair, Whately, Kenneth Burke, Perelman, and Weaver -- to name only some of the more prominent theorists."

Pedagogy

7

Learning and Teaching the Reader Expectation Approach

L *earning to Teach Writing from the Perspective of Reader Expectations*

Putting the Reader Expectation Approach to Work

As I suggested in Chapter 1, this Reader Expectation approach allows us to demonstrate to students the role habit plays in their individual style of writing. We no longer need be limited to demonstrating how a particular essay might be improved the next time they get a chance to write it, which in reality will be never. (Even a revision assignment does not often lead students to revise or rewrite but rather to respond to comments and do damage control.) We can show them much about their process of writing; we can show them much about their process of reading; and, combining those two demonstrations, we can show them much about how to improve their control over the results when readers read their writing.

A few generalizations can be made that apply to all the different units of discourse we have been investigating:

(1) Readers wish to be contextualized at the beginning of discourse units. They want to know how this new unit will connect backward and whose story (or what issue) is to be considered. (Cf. the materials on the Topic position of the sentence, the Issue position of the paragraph, and the positioning of the thesis of a whole document.)

(2) That need for context is sometimes so great that readers will interpret as context whatever happens to appear in the places context is expected to be found. (Cf. the materials on whose story a sentence is and what issue dominates a paragraph.)

(3) Readers of English have great needs for closure. As a result, when a unit of discourse is small enough (sentence) or compelling enough (first and last paragraphs) to be read as a whole, readers give natural emphasis to that which comes last.

(4) Putting all the above together, it appears that readers' greatest and most constant rhetorical need is to feel they are safely and sanely *leaning forward* into and through the discourse. They lean forward to Stress positions within sentences; they lean forward from one sentence to the next as they seek cohesion; they lean forward from one development of thought to the next (however long) as they seek coherence; they lean forward to the end of the discourse as they seek completion. Since all this leaning is precarious, they need to be able to rely on their guide, the writer, for safe conduct. Writers can be more sure they are providing that service if they are consciously aware of their readers' structural expectations.

At first, this reader-based approach provides students with a strategy for revision. We can teach them how to look at structure, what questions to ask concerning the location of substance, and how to go about revising the prose so the structure sends clearer instructions to readers concerning interpretation. Eventually, however, what began as a strategy for revision naturally becomes a procedure of invention. Investigating the structural locations of substance inevitably leads a writer to reconsider the nature of that substance. Brief examples: Recognizing that a link is missing helps the writer produce that link; asking "whose story" a sentence or paragraph currently is helps the writer decide whose story he intends that discourse unit to be; investigating a sentence to determine whether the stressworthy information is in the Stress position leads the writer to decide just what she intended to present as the information of highest value. Reconsidering reader expectations always sends a writer further into the thought process because it gives him specific ways of varying the question "What did I mean to say?"

Students can be overwhelmed by all this information if they are not given some kind of procedure for their first few attempts at using it. It is necessary to divide first and conquer thereafter. The procedure, writ large, is this:

I. Analyze the prose to determine which of the writer's structural habits (and we all are creatures of rhetorical habit) are already helpful to readers and which are not. This is done by looking at the same two or three paragraphs several times -- one investigation for each of the major reader expectations. Patterns of structural usage will be apparent. Make note of the bad habits, identifying the two or three most troublesome.

II. When the student writes the next new paper, all of this structural information should be set aside. The student should write as she has always written. To concentrate on all the new advice at this point could shut down the inventive process altogether. *Very* frustrating! But once that new text is created, it becomes a candidate for a sentence-by-sentence revision, focusing on the two or three most troublesome habits discovered in Step 1, above. By the end of that revision, it should start to become clear (a) what the old, reader-unfriendly habits look and feel like and (b) what the new, reader-friendly structures look and feel like.

III. In creating the next new text, whenever the old, unhelpful structure seems to be appearing, revise it immediately, before leaving that sentence to form the next one.

IV. By one or two more new documents, the writer should start to reach naturally for the new, helpful structure. Then the writer's writing procedure is changed for good.

Here is that procedure set out in greater detail, addressed to a student. Following it will slow the student down -- but only for a few documents. After that, the writing will not only be clearer and more forceful but also faster; and the changes will be permanent.

1. Choose for analysis three paragraphs from one of your documents. For best results, avoid opening or closing paragraphs, which function somewhat differently from the others. It is best to choose paragraphs that are at least several sentences long, since they should offer a large number of rhetorical choices and possibilities for problems.

2. For one of those paragraphs, analyze the prose structurally several times, one time for each of the expectational principles explored in this volume. This requires the turning off the substance-reading machine you usually use when reading and turning on this new structural awareness in its place. In other words, do not read a sentence to see if it makes sense or sounds good or seems to help develop your thought; the coffee stain problem may make your prose meaningful to you in ways unavailable to your readers.[1] The structural reading I outline below is intended to help you perceive patterns in your own writing, both helpful and unhelpful to your reader. To read structurally, do the following:

   a) The first time through, circle all the verbs in the paragraph. Judge whether you can sense what the developing action of the paragraph might be as a whole, just by reading the list of verbs.

   b) Then go back and determine whether the verbs in the paragraph are weak or strong. Do not judge them by their length or by their seeming strength when considered in isolation. Ask instead whether each verb actually articulates the action -- that is, what is going on --in that sentence. It is not enough that the verb express-es *an* action; it must express *the* action taking place in that very sentence. Short, puny-looking verbs often do that job well; long, impressive verbs often fail. The judgment is an intellectual one, not an aesthetic one.

c) Then go back and check each sentence for subject-verb or verb-complement separations.

d) Then go back and check the Topic position of each sentence to see if the occupant is indeed the person, thought, or thing whose story the sentence was intended to relate.

e) Then go back and check each sentence for the location (or existence) of the old information that makes the important link backward to the previous sentence. See if that information is located in the Topic position, where it will do the reader the most good.

f) Then go back and check each sentence for the location of the information you wished the reader to consider the most stressworthy. See if each piece of such information is located in a Stress position. (A Stress position is any moment of syntactic closure -- before a properly used period, colon, or semi-colon. It can never exist at a comma.)

g) Then go back and underline the first few words of each sentence or main clause, at least up to and including the grammatical subject. See if the progression of those sentence beginnings helpfully *changes* the story from sentence to sentence (Topic Changing) or helpfully keeps the story focused on one topic while a discussion of it develops (Topic Stringing). Whatever the case, determine whether the relationship between sentence beginnings directs the reader's attention exactly as you choose.

h) Then go back and determine what you meant the issue of the paragraph to be. See if it is announced by the paragraph's first one, two, or three sentences.

i) Then, if the paragraph was intended to make a point, go back and determine what that point was meant to be. See if it is articulated at either of the locations at which the reader expects it to arrive -- either just before the discussion of it begins or just as the discussion of it ends.

j) If the paragraph was not intended to make a point but rather to narrate a story, determine whether the reader is adequately signaled as much in the first sentence or two.

3. That may seem a great deal to do; but through all this you will be discovering the structural patterns that govern your individual writing

process. Some will prove helpful to the reader; some will not. Does the most important information consistently appear elsewhere than in the Stress position? If so, you now know you are creating a recurring problem for your readers. You also know what to do about it. Do the verbs almost always articulate the action of the sentence? If so, then you now can consciously control a strength in your writing that to this point you might have summoned only through intuition.

4. Keeping in mind all the patterns you have discovered, perform the whole analysis again on another of your paragraphs. If the patterns of the second resemble those of the first -- for better or worse -- that's probably you.

5. To make sure the repeating patterns are no mere coincidence, check a third paragraph just for the weak or problematic patterns to see if they surface again.

6. The next time you write something, do *not* keep all this structural information at the front of your consciousness -- or anywhere else handy. Put it all aside. Write as you usually write. Once you have produced a draft, go back through it, checking every single sentence for only the one or two or three worst structural habits you have discovered by the above analysis. Whenever you find an expectation unintentionally violated, change the structure of the sentence so the expectation is fulfilled. Do not allow yourself to pass one by in the false confidence that since the sentence seemed perfectly clear *to you*, it must not need revision. Of course it might mean something to you: You wrote it. Presume that if something is structurally out of place, the chances of it meaning that to a high percentage of your readers are not as great as you would like them to be.

    This procedure is time-consuming, tedious, and occasionally stomach-tightening. All this discomfort, however, should be temporary. By the time you are into the revision of your fourth or fifth paragraph, you should have become strikingly aware of your habits -- "Oh, I did it again!" -- and be able to make the structural revisions more quickly and more easily.

7. If you are meticulous about these changes, you will find behavior modification coming to your aid fairly rapidly: The next time you begin to produce your normal sentence with (for example) the stressworthy information unhelpfully up front, your stomach muscles will alert you to that fact, sensing as they do the future pain that would be involved in a revision process. That warning will allow you to weave the revision process into the present invention process. In the not-too-distant future, you will be choosing the reader-friendly structure naturally. Then you have it for life.

The ability to consider your own prose from the perspective of your readers will eventually allow you to be better and more quickly in touch with the ongoing development of your thought. It may slow you down for a bit at the start; but after a short while, it will speed you up for the rest of your career. What begins as a burden on your time quickly -- and permanently -- becomes a timesaving device. What starts out as a revision procedure soon becomes an important part of the invention process. You not only recognize the relationship between structure and substance; you put it to use.

When, then, should you think consciously about these structural guidelines?

1. At first, only as a revision tactic. Write like you write; then go back and revise with reader expectations in mind.

2. After a while, when you know your own habits and are trying to change the bad ones for good ones, switch into a structural way of thinking in the middle of any sentence that has already proclaimed to you, "Oops, this structure isn't going well."

3. Once you have changed your habits so you naturally contextualize first and lean toward the emphasis of closure at the end, you will need to think structurally only when a particular sentence is giving you significant trouble.

Advice Especially for Those Who Are Teaching for the First Time

Having spoken in a voice for students, I turn to speaking to new teachers. The first time through anything is likely to be rough. That realization can provide some comfort if you are teaching for the first time. I will be bold enough to offer some words of advice.

Most new teachers are not told that their task in the classroom will differ significantly from the one they have mastered in their many years as a student. Students are rewarded for demonstrating in class that they understand and control the material. They have no need to *transfer* the material to the teacher, since the teacher (presumably) already understands it.

Just the reverse applies to teachers. They are not doing their jobs if they strive only to demonstrate that they understand and control the material. They are being paid to transfer that knowledge and control to their students. New teachers, having been students for so long, are often slow to realize this difference and to make the necessary adjustments.

Such a transfer of knowledge cannot take place well enough, especially in writing classes, if you as teacher remain materials-centered rather than student-centered. Plowing through even the best of examples or exercises will not, by itself, produce education. It is necessary that most of your students be with you every step of the way. In order to ensure that, you have to be looking at them; their eyes, posture, and energy level will tell you whether they are getting delivery of what you are sending their way. If they are not with you, do not continue, no matter how flawless you believe your next logical connection to be. Go back and ask them questions, or attack the point from a different perspective or with a different example. It is not important that your students merely be exposed to the principles you teach; it is crucial that they learn how to employ them to good effect.

To be materials-centered in the classroom is to be self-centered. To "get it right" is to demonstrate that *you* have got it right. As a teacher, you need to ensure that *they* have got it right.

Even in your very first semester, it is possible to out-teach some of the most grizzled of veterans. The veteran who knows 100% of the substantive material but only communicates 10% will be out-taught by the rookie who has mastered only 25% of the material but successfully communicates everything she knows. The final score will be 25 to 10.

In teaching this reader expectation approach to writing for the first time, you need not have completely mastered it in order to make good use of it. Here are four important pieces of advice for anyone teaching this approach, but especially for those who are teaching it for the first time.

(1) Teach the material not deductively but inductively. The deductive method simply will not convince a large enough percentage of your students. Deductive teachers announce a principle first ("Articulate the action in the verb") and then demonstrate the efficacy of the principle by offering examples; but all students know that even the devil can cite scripture to suit his purposes. At best, they will write the adage down and reproduce it for you whenever you require it of them.

The inductive method not only works better but also is far more enjoyable to use. It requires that you slowly lead students through analytic experiences so when it comes time to articulate the principle that sums up that experience, they might well be able to do it for you. They find this much more convincing because the principle, when it arrives, confirms their own (quite recent) experience. It explains why they have just seen what they have seen or done what they have done.

For an example of the inductive method, we can return to the first example we examined at length in Chapter 2: "What would be the employee reception accorded the introduction of such a proposal?" This is the inductive procedure I followed there:

a) I presented a problem: (Why is "How would the employees receive such a proposal" easier to read?).

b) I demonstrated the inadequacy of the obvious answers: (It's shorter. It's active.).

c) Having asked a question without finding a reasonable answer, I then suggested a task that was doable, without yet articulating why I was doing so: (Please underline the words in both sentences that articulate actions taking place in that sentence.).

d) I noted the nature of the community experience. (As a community or class, people do not agree which words or even how many words represented actions in the original sentence; but I did note widespread agreement that only one word in the revised sentence represented that sentence's action.)

e) Now that we had shared an experience as a community, I was able to give that experience a local habitation and a name: (Readers expect the action of a sentence to be articulated by the verb. When the verb fails to do that, readers are left too much to their own devices to interpret what the action was intended to be.).

It may sometimes take you two or three times as long to reach a principle inductively as it would had you proceeded deductively; but if you can get there through induction, your students will be far more likely to retain what you have led them to discover. That is because they will have experienced the process of discovering the various reader expectations just before you articulate what they are. When you announce it, they realize they already "knew" it.

(2) The second piece of advice: Be wary of presuming to know what students (or any other writers) had intended to say in their prose. This is perhaps the single most widespread and most serious pedagogical error made by writing teachers in this country today. Never tell them they "have good thoughts but need help with the writing." First, you may well be wrong. Just because you were able to perform an interpretive act on their prose does not mean your interpretation was precisely the one they intended you to make. Second, they will have every right to call you a hypocrite. If you are there to teach them communication, and if their prose had successfully communicated to you their thinking, then the writing did its job.

When a student's prose consistently violates Reader Expectations, you will be able to demonstrate why it is you cannot be confident that you know what he intended to communicate. To some extent, that renders your teaching fail-proof. You are no longer in the position of having (1) to figure out what they meant to say, and then (2) to show them a better way of saying it. You need only show them the structural problems that indicate why it is you cannot be sure of what they intended to communicate. You need only ask them the appropriate functional/structural questions. "Here's what you placed in the Stress position. Is that what you intended me to stress?" "You have a different occupant of the Topic position in every sentence. Did you intend this paragraph to be the story of all those occupants?" "All your verbs here are either *to be* or *to have*. Did you intend the action of the entire paragraph to focus exclusively on existence and possession?" They are the only ones with the correct answers; you need only supply the questions. They are supposed to have furnished the answers for you, in their writing, with clues furnished by the structural location of information. In the future, if they want to attract your attention to a particular piece of information, they will know where to put it.

(3) Do not be threatened by your students' disagreeing about the interpretation of any sentence or paragraph you may use as a teaching example. Instead, utilize those disagreements to demonstrate interpretational problems created by the prose. Example: You have planned to help them analyze a paragraph that to your mind has a two-sentence issue with the point in the last sentence. Inductively, you lead them to discover the issue and the point; but then some hard-thinking, rebellious voice in the back row triumphantly announces that he thinks the paragraph has a three-point issue with the point in the third sentence. Rejoice at this offering. Instead of trying to beat him down, draw him out. Make him articulate precisely why he interprets the paragraph that way. Support that interpretation (unless it can be demonstrated to be merely and intentionally disruptive) -- not because you have been convinced but because the paragraph is infinitely interpretable. He is "right": He did indeed interpret the paragraph the way he said he interpreted it. Argue that since his dissenting interpretation is rational and defensible, it is all the more important to signal to readers as clearly as possible what the issue and the point are intended to be.

(4) Never give your students the sense that there are right and wrong answers to any questions you raise about structure, substance, or interpretation. Remember the argument that there is no such thing as a good or bad sentence -- taken by itself. Units of discourse, of any size, are "good' or "bad" only in context.

Each sentence can only be effectively judged in relationship to the sentences that surround it -- and perhaps some that surround those as well. Hand me the most stunning, elegant, powerful sentence you have ever encountered. I can make it a "bad" sentence simply by dropping it into the middle of a paragraph in which it does not belong. For example, insert a famous sentence by President Lincoln into a paragraph by the eloquent C.P. Snow:

> Scientists are the most important occupational group in the world today. At this moment, what they do is of passionate concern to the whole of human society. At this moment, the scientists have little influence on the world effect of what they do. Fourscore and seven years ago, our fathers brought forth upon this continent a new nation, conceived in Liberty, and dedicated to the proposition that all men are created equal. Yet potentially they can have great influence.[2]

President Lincoln's "fourscore and seven years ago" opening gambit of the Gettysburg address is a "bad" sentence in the C.P. Snow paragraph for a number of reasons, including its being on the "wrong" topic and its suffering from stylistic incongruencies. What is worst, perhaps, is that it almost seems to fit the flow of the thought. Look at the string of time references from each sentence:

....today

At this moment, . . .

At this moment, . . .

Fourscore and seven years ago, . . .

Yet potentially . . .

Readers unfamiliar with the famous sentence would give a good effort at "making it fit" the thought. They might even become convinced either that they had "understood" what was meant or, if not, that the "fault" lay in their inability to comprehend.

Conversely (and perhaps a bit perversely), I could transform the worst sentence you have ever seen into a stunningly fine one, if you gave me enough time and space to create for it a context within which it would function well. Hand me, for example, a sentence in which you have intentionally committed 11 grammatical errors. To make it a "good" sentence, I would write a 20-page essay in which I would analyze in detail "the 11 most common grammatical errors in English usage today" -- a page or two on each error. At the end of page 19, at the height of my summation, I would include your sentence. Far from being an example of incompetence, it would shine as a stunning triumph of wit -- that in a single sentence I could bring together all 11 errors, singing together a final chorus just before the curtain comes down. Anyone writing a critique of my essay would be sure to highlight that intensely imaginative, error-ridden sentence: "He was able to get *all 11* into one sentence!" What had been intended as a disaster would be transformed into a tour de force.

New teachers sometimes tremble throughout the whole course that their students will discover that teacher does not always know the right answer to everything. In teaching writing from the perspective of readers, we triumph in the belief and demonstration that *nobody* has or could have an exclusively right answer when interpretation is the name of the game. Context controls meaning; and an individual reader's mind provides a great part of that context. Any student can create a context different form the one you are assuming as you look at one of your sentence or paragraph examples; that, in turn, can transform your example completely. Praise such inventiveness, and work with it; but it need not force you to back off from what you were trying to make the example "mean," given the context you were assuming.

De-writing

By concentrating so much on reader expectations, we can transform our students from acting as critics -- a role few of them will play after graduation -- into acting as readers -- a role they will play frequently. Instead of urging them to demonstrate what is "wrong" with a piece of prose, we can show them ways of signaling readers how to go about valuing and synthesizing their information into ideas. If we do this enough, by the end of the term they may have become expert not in the quality of several individual pieces of writing but rather in the actual process of perception and interpretation. One of the most helpful techniques to accomplish this I call *de-writing*.

De-writing is distinct from revision. *Revision* refers to the rewriting of inadequate prose for the purpose of making it better; *de-writing* refers to the restructuring of adequate prose to demonstrate how structure affects signification. In de-writing textual examples, we change the way the prose goes about signaling readers by the structural location of its information. We therefore change the way the unit communicates; it winds up not necessarily being worse but always being different. We create, therefore, paired examples that are not necessarily "better" and "worse" but instructively "different."

On the sentence level, we can de-write by changing the structural locations of some or all of the substance; we could, for example, change the occupant of the Stress position, several times perhaps, to see how that affects our act of interpretation. (For an example of this, see the discussion of the third sentence of the "insidious diseases" example, Chapter 5, Example (1), page 138.)

De-writing is especially effective when applied to the teaching of paragraph structure. It helps move students away from their firmly held assumption that if they empty onto the paper their entire reserve of facts found and ideas spawned, they have done most of the work necessary to the writing process. All the rest, they tend to believe, is merely cosmetic, merely the good manners required of them if they are to ascend into polite, educated society. The de-writing procedure demonstrates to them how significant -- and how signifying -- is the structure of any unit of discourse.

On the paragraph level, de-writing can be used to two different but related ends. I offer an example of each: Example (1) demonstrates how by altering a reader-helpful structure, we might obfuscate the intended communication, even if we retain all the component parts of the substance; and Example (2) demonstrates how by altering the location of clauses or sentences we might change the way context is established, thereby changing the reader's perceptions of present connections and future directions for the prose.

Example 1:   A demonstration of how altering a reader-helpful structure can obfuscate the intended communication, even if all the component parts of the substance are retained.

(The "whose story?" occupants of the Topic positions are underlined.)

1a. In this paragraph, the topics (the occupants of Topic positions) are underlined. Topics are crucial because they focus a reader's attention on particular ideas toward the beginning of a clause. Cumulatively, these ideas provide thematic signposts that should focus your reader's attention on a well-defined set of connected ideas. If a sequence

of topics seems coherent, it will move the reader through the paragraph from a cumulatively coherent point of view. But if through that
paragraph the topics shift in what seems a random fashion, then your
reader has to begin each sentence out of context, from no coherent
point of view. Whatever you announce as a topic, then, will fix your
reader's point of view, not just toward the rest of the sentence, but toward sequences of sentences, toward whole chunks of discourse.[3]

It flows; it speaks; we can admire the topic string established throughout; we can benefit from the Stress positions being consistently filled with
material that sounds worthy of our primary attention. By the end of the
paragraph, we know something about its "topics."

Then we de-write it so that few of these helpful structural clues are allowed to remain. (Again the underlined words mark the "whose story?"
occupants of the new Topic positions.)

1b. Particular ideas toward the beginning of each clause focus the reader's attention, so topics are crucial. Cumulatively, thematic signposts
that are provided by these ideas should focus the reader's attention
toward a well-defined set of connected ideas. Moving through a paragraph from a cumulatively coherent point of view is made possible
by a sequence of topics that seems to constitute a coherent sequence
of connected ideas. A lack of context for each sentence is one consequence of making the reader begin sentences with seemingly random
shifts in topics. The rest of the sentence as well as whole chunks of
discourse will be the objects of a reader's point of view as a result of
topic announcement.

The de-written version contains all the substantive material of the original; but the connections have been clouded, the contextualizations undone
and redone, and the flow of discourse thereby obstructed. Most importantly, the topic string has been destroyed, forcing the reader to recontex-
tualize constantly. Since the new occupants of the Topic positions do not
prove helpful as contexts for the clauses they begin, the reader remains
mystified much of the time. Although there are no grammatical errors and
no demonstrable breaks in logic, most readers will arrive at the paragraph's
end without the firm conviction of understanding they might have experienced from reading the original version.

Example 2:   A demonstration of how altering the location of clauses
or sentences can change the way context is established,
thereby changing the reader's perceptions of present
connections and future directions for the prose.

In the following example, the structural reorganization does not ren-
der the prose obscure or uninterpretable. Instead, each version offers available interpretations, all of which differ from those of the original.[4]

In the above example, the structure of individual sentences was changed so words no longer appeared where they would be of most help to the reader. In the following example, the major changes involve instead the location of clauses or sentences within the paragraph, thereby altering the reader's possible expectations of where the prose is about to go. The example is repeated from Chapter 6 (see Example (8), pages 211 and 254). It is the opening paragraph of its essay.

8a. The summer I was 16, I took a train from New York to Steamboat Springs, Colo., where I was going to be assistant horse wrangler at a camp. The trip took three days, and since I was much too shy to talk to strangers, I had quite a lot of time for reading. I read all of *Gone with the Wind*. I read all the interesting articles in a couple of magazines I had, and then I went back and read all the dull stuff. I also took all the quizzes, a thing of which magazines were even fuller than now.

If we use a slow-motion reading technique, stopping at the end of each sentence, we can plot the expectations of most readers for future development and then note how those expectations are or are not fulfilled.

First sentence: The summer I was 16, I took a train from New York to Steamboat Springs, Colo., where I was going to be assistant horse wrangler at a camp.

Any of the information here -- summer, 16, train, took a train, New York, Steamboat Springs, Colorado, going to be, assistant, horse, horse wrangler, camp -- any of it would be available as old information in the second sentence. Any of it is a reasonable candidate for taking over the Topic position in that sentence, as long as it turns out to be "whose story" the second sentence is. The leading candidates are probably the occupants of the Topic position (the sentence's first eight words or so) and the occupants of the Stress position (the sentence's last five or six words). Therefore, we are most likely either to hear more about the train trip or more about horse wrangling camp.

Second sentence: The trip took three days, and since I was much too shy to talk to strangers, I had quite a lot of time for reading.

The Topic position here hearkens back to the Topic position of the first sentence, forming a short topic string. The Stress position is filled with "a lot of time for reading," new information that is presumably stressworthy. While the third sentence could take off from anywhere, we rather expect it will tell us more about the reading that receives special emphasis here. If it does not, then we will be somewhat perplexed as to why "reading" had deserved its privileged location.

Third sentence: I read all of *Gone with the Wind*.

"A lot of time for reading" should more than adequately be filled up with the lengthy, sprawling novel, *Gone with the Wind*. Where will we go next? We might expect a topic change, importing *GWTW* into the Topic position of the fourth sentence in preparation for pages of analysis of Margaret Mitchell and the burning of Atlanta. We could just as reasonably expect a continuation of an "I read" topic string. Either would seem smooth, logical, compelling; anything else would be jarring, disconnected, unsettling. (None of those adjectives need carry any negative value judgment. It might be effective to jar, disconcert, or unsettle a reader at times.)

Fourth sentence: I read all the interesting articles in a couple of magazines I had, and then I went back and read all the dull stuff.

The "I read" topic string wins. Instead of being the announced topic for the rest of the article, *Gone with the Wind* has now become just the first of a number of things our narrator got to read. We are even more impressed now, not only with how much time he had for reading but also with how voracious and capable a reader he must have been. After all, *GWTW* is a long novel, and the trip was by train to Colorado, not by goat-cart to Peru.

Where do we expect to go from here? We might well expect the topic string to continue, leading us on to even more of what he read; or we might be prepared for a topic change to the occupant of the current Stress position, the "dull stuff."

The fifth sentence: I also took all the quizzes, a thing of which magazines were even fuller than now.

Quite neatly, this Topic position reaches back to both the Topic and Stress positions of the former sentence: (a) It continues the Topic string, expanding the "I read" into describing all the things he did on this long trip; and (b) it changes the topic by categorizing the quizzes as part of the "dull stuff" -- perhaps, by declination, even the dullest of dull stuff.

The paragraph is over. Where do we expect the next paragraph to take us? We would not be at all surprised if the author launches into an analysis of magazine quizzes. He has taken us all the way across the country, read up a storm, and landed us at the end of the paragraph in a subject that is of no importance whatsoever unless it turns out to be the main concern of the approaching discourse. In other words, if this article is *not* about magazine quizzes, then the magazine quizzes are annoyingly and misleadingly located in this paragraph's structure.

The article indeed proceeds to investigate the nature of magazine quizzes and their reflection of American popular culture. The train trip, with its enforced boredom from not enough to read, explains why such an intellectual guy as this author ever even encountered such a low level form of entertainment as these quizzes.

Now to de-write this paragraph, several times, with interesting effects. Here is the first de-writing:

8b. The summer I was 16, I took a train from New York to Steamboat Springs, Colo., where I was going to be assistant horse wrangler at a camp. The trip took three days, and since I was much too shy to talk to strangers, I had quite a lot of time for reading. I read all the interesting articles in a couple of magazines I had, and then I went back and read all the dull stuff. I also took all the quizzes, a thing of which magazines were even fuller than now. I read all of *Gone with the Wind*.

The first two sentences remain the same as in the original. However, the next three arrive in a different order, which presents the author's reading with a different effect. He reads the interesting short stuff; he reads the dull stuff; he takes the quizzes; and then, finally prepared for the plunge, he takes on *Gone with the Wind*. The last sentence, being last, and being so much shorter and blunter than the others, persuades us, perhaps, that it is the true climax of this paragraph's development. We firmly expect the next paragraph to launch into either his experience of reading *GWTW* or something connected to the process he has mysteriously outlined. This might be, for instance, an article about his great struggle with procrastination -- always leaving the more daunting task for later. In any event, if this paragraph is "well written," the article is *not* going to be about quizzes.

Here is another de-writing of the original paragraph:

8c. The summer I was 16, I took a train from New York to Steamboat Springs, Colo. The trip took three days, and since I was much too shy to talk to strangers, I had quite a lot of time for reading. I read all of *Gone with the Wind*. I read all the interesting articles in a couple of magazines I had, and then I went back and read all the dull stuff. I also took all the quizzes, a thing of which magazines were even fuller than now. I was going to be assistant horse wrangler at a camp.

In this version, only the horse wrangling has been moved; but that small change has made a significant difference. The trip passes before us in the form of reading and quiz-taking activities, at the end of which is the arrival in Colorado for horse wrangling purposes. Why is horse wrangling the closure point for a paragraph that is otherwise about frantic reading? Could it be that this bookish sort is going to have a tough time in the wake-up-and-smell-the-coffee Wild West? Or will he discover "real" meanings of life once he gets his nose out of a book?

Here is yet a third de-writing of the same paragraph:

8d. The summer I was 16, I took a train from New York to Steamboat Springs, Colo., where I was going to be assistant horse wrangler at a camp. Since the trip took three days, I had quite a lot of time for reading. I read all of *Gone with the Wind*. I read all the interesting articles in a couple of magazines I had, and then I went back and read all the dull stuff. I also took all the quizzes, a thing of which magazines were even fuller than now. I was much too shy to talk to strangers.

The only change from the original is the location of the "too shy to talk to strangers." That piece of information had been buried in the middle of a sentence in all the other versions and therefore might have escaped our attention. It seemed to have functioned only as a supportive reason to justify all the reading and quiz-taking upon which we were invited to concentrate. In this version, however, all that has changed: The material may be the same, but the progression is different. The reading and quiz-taking takes on a kind of desperate quality as he goes to extreme lengths not only to entertain himself but to avoid interacting with other people. We may not have noticed in the earlier version that both of these activities are decidedly solitary occupations; that fact is revealed to us by his resolving the paragraph with the admission of his shyness. The very delay in its arrival seems itself a manifestation of the shyness itself. Given the placement of "strangers" at the end of all this, what are we to expect of the next paragraph? Perhaps we expect to meet "her" -- a local version of Scarlet O'Hara.

De-writing is not only remarkably revealing; it is fun to do. Once you have done it for your students, they can do it for themselves, either individually or (more revealing, more fun) in groups. Give them an interesting paragraph and have them de-write it, perhaps more than once; then have them explain *why* they think the new versions have the different effects they claim.[5]

This activity relieves both you and (more importantly) your students of playing the hypothetical and unrealistic role of critic; instead, you are all engaged in the role of being readers. You then can explore what it is you are doing as readers: What do you expect and why? From where do you get your interpretive clues? What happens when the expected moment arrives with (or without) an expectation being fulfilled?

De-writing can even be used adversarially. Take a well-written paragraph that tells a complicated story about two persons or things or ideas, with the "whose story" of one of them appearing as a Topic string throughout the paragraph. De-write a version that undoes that topic string and creates another one, equally strong, for the other side. Hand the original version to the right half of the classroom and the de-written version to the left half -- without telling them they are receiving different paragraphs. Have them discuss what the paragraph means to them. The chances are high that the two sides of the room will come to disagree with each other on salient points of interpretation. When the disagreement has reached the level of confounded mystification, let the cat out of the bag and distribute the other version to everyone. Then analyze why they had reacted the way they had. The procedure is not without risk; but the pedagogical payoffs are big.

De-writing undoes the corrective model of teaching writing. Instead of furnishing students with bad writing which they are to make better, we furnish them with good writing and allow them to transform it by de-writing it so they may understand better how structural location controls the issuing of interpretive clues. That having been learned, students are in a far better position to make their own prose mean to most readers what they intend it to mean. They learn they can influence reader responses by altering the structural location of their information.

Ten Practical Teaching Questions

One of the early reviewers of this book, when it was but a manuscript asking to become a book, raised the following ten questions. They were good ones. Here are my responses.

How soon in the course should students be writing?

In a writing course, students should be writing constantly. They need not, however, be graded constantly. Getting them to write without the burden of grades may well make them feel better about the act of writing. It may also help produce less stifled prose -- freer, easier, more flowing prose. However -- (and I am constantly surprised by this) -- it will not change their structural habits. Often, when a student and I have just finished exploring her style in a paper written for a course, she asks if we can look at this feel-good piece she wrote for the school newspaper. She is confident that her untrammeled writing will be "better" than her indentured writing. Each time, we find the same good and bad structural habits that displayed themselves in her more constrained writing. So let students start generating prose right away. It will all be grist for a later mill. And the more writing they do, the more comfortable they will grow with the act of writing. All of it will later present to them what their writing habits have long been. Then they will know better what it is they have to change.

How long should writing assignments be?

Two full pages. (Or 500 words.) (Or at least one line on page 3.) I have found that an assignment of less than two pages allows for a casualness that can belie their writing style "when trying hard." Perhaps this is because opening and closing paragraphs are different rhetorical animals than the others in between; and students do not have to generate much more than an opening and closing paragraph when allowed to write significantly less than two pages.

But why not *more* than two pages? Because it rarely takes more than two pages of sample prose to investigate stylistic habits. When I do individual tutorials with my consulting clients (see Question 5, below), it usually takes me only two (medial) paragraphs to establish and demonstrate for them their particular strengths and weaknesses. More than two or three pages, therefore, is unnecessary for the purpose of diagnosis.

That does not mean, however, that there is no efficacy in assigning longer papers. I typically end my Advanced Composition course with two seven-page assignments that often extend to ten. But by then, the stylistic investigation has already occurred; and the attempts at stylistic change have had several opportunities to play themselves out. By the end of the term, having learned how to drive the car, it is time to take it out for a spin.

It matters little how big or small the topic may be on which they write. Whatever they write will display their writing habits. It is especially helpful if they do not have to make a formal beginning and ending to their two pages. Let them start in the middle and end in the middle. There will be plenty of time along the way to discuss beginnings and endings.

What about the "Research Paper"? I apologize in advance to those I may offend, but I do not believe in the efficacy of research papers in writing courses. My reasons:

a) Research differs so widely from field to field that you cannot teach "research" in the abstract.

b) Having to write a research paper exclusively for the purpose of having to write a research paper is perhaps the most burdensome, unrealistic task we could impose on our students. They will never be asked to do this once they have left school. It is by its nature anti-rhetorical: There is no audience that "needs to know."

c) Since the main point of the exercise is to track down what other people have already said, students will not be writing a *larger* paper, just a longer one. Five additional required citations would elongate the paper; five fewer would shorten it.

d) It generates the worst possible ratio (in the confines of a single term's course) of work expended to profit gained.

e) With the presence of so many other voices, going on at such length in these essays, the student's voice tends to fade away. In a writing class, it is the student's voice that should be the primary focus.

f) There will be plenty of opportunities for them to do *real* research projects in the courses they will be taking in their major subjects.

If you think that teaching proper citation is essential to your course, there are any number of ways to teach it directly without forcing students to surround it with a substantive paper.

What should students be writing about anyway? Does the specific subject matter make any difference?

The specific subject matter makes no difference. Neither does the student's "enjoyment of the topic." The point is to get them to produce prose so you can see how they do it and then help them see how they do it.

That having been said, the general atmosphere of the classroom and the energy outside of it are probably better when students (and you) feel happily engaged. Since they have to write anyway, why not make it about something of interest?

The one subject matter I avoid altogether is literature. Good literature profits constantly from the violation of reader expectations. (See page 253 for "Why Faulkner and Henry James are not bad writers.") To achieve that skill, it is best to learn first how to fulfill reader expectations -- at least most of the time. Literature, then, is actually a bad model for our students' prose. With the precious few exceptions of those who will go on to become creative writers, practicing a "literary style" could actually hamper them, not serve them, in the world they will enter as professionals. William Faulkner wrote great novels. No one would wish him to use that style to write for them a legal brief or a grant application or a letter to a client.

Furthermore, there is a great risk that with literature in the course, the class discussion and primary energies can easily be shifted from writing to reading. That is especially true if the teacher is a new teacher -- steeped in literary study but unpracticed in teaching writing. Best to avoid it.

To what extent should the approach here be supplemented with lessons on audience, purpose, and context?

The RE approach I have explicated in such detail here need not be considered the exclusive content of a writing course. It can easily fill a 20-hour course all by itself with no problem. I can extend that to 30 hours if there is a need to do so. But when I teach my 42-hour Advanced Composition course, REA consumes only a bit more than half that time. (In case you are wondering, the other half is taken up with stylistic imitations of nonfiction writers from the sixteenth century through the present. By the end of the course, the two halves talk to each other nicely.)

Raising any other rhetorical questions or concerns can make a writing course richer and more effective. Questions of audience? Surely. We and our students are already more consciously in tune with our "audience expectations" than with our reader expectations. Here is an exercise I have used with good results over the years.[6]

> Hypothetical: You are a junior and a pre-med. You have been a biology major from the start, intent on getting into medical school because, well, because you have been intent on getting into medical school. Your freshman advisor is an interesting and interested man from the psychology department who, from the start, has been counseling you that your real interest and aptitude is in the social sciences, probably in psychology, and that you have been pursuing a pre-med course out of peer and parental pressure. As a junior, you now see the light and recognize he has been right all along. You decide to change your major to psychology and give up the pre-med courses.

> Write a note of about four sentences to your advisor informing him of your decision to switch fields.

> Then write a second note, same length, same information, to the chairperson of the biology department.

> Then write a third note, same length and information, to your favorite biology professor.

> Then write a paragraph of a letter to your parents, informing them of your decision.

Then write a paragraph of a letter to your best friends back home, telling them about it.

I then have them vote:

-- Which of the five was the hardest to write?

-- Which of the five was the easiest to write?

-- Which of the five do they consider the best written?

-- Which of the five do they consider the worst written?

Then I put them into small groups to read their versions to each other in an attempt to discover what rhetorical assumptions -- and therefore stylistic changes -- they all make when their audience changes. They consciously learn how much they already intuitively know about controlling audiences and being controlled by audiences.

Questions of purpose? Questions of context? Surely. Anything that helps our students understand that purpose must be perceived by readers (not just intended by the writer) is a rhetorical gain. Anything that helps our students understand that context of any proportion controls the meaning of that which exists in its shadow is a rhetorical gain.

How can individual conferences be used to support this approach?

The longer I use this approach, the more I believe that the individual conferences are the moments when it all comes together for the students.

My students and my clients -- everyone from age 18 to 65 -- listen to these theories and perceptions and nod their heads and say "I knew that, sort of" and "That's right -- that's what I do as a reader." But if they try to apply all this new information all at once to their own writing, they become overwhelmed. This is especially true of my consulting clients, who hear all this material in two eight-hour days of lecture. In order to apply this approach, it is best to use a divide-and-conquer approach.

I discovered what I consider the best one-on-one approach quite by accident. I used to prepare fastidiously for individual tutorials with my professional clients, combing through many pages of their writing to identify structural patterns and habits. Hard work. Often impossible work. How, for instance, could I be sure that X rarely put the important information in the Stress position if I was never quite sure what in X's sentence was the important information? Hard work. Impossible work. I arrived one morning at a client's office for what promised to be a strenuous day full of individual tutorials. I was informed that because of an emergency the scheduling had to be changed: As a result, I would be seeing three people for whom I had not prepared. What to do? Necessity? Invention.

The first of these uninvestigated persons arrived, with prose in hand. When I explained that I would be sight-reading his prose, it occurred to me that most of his prose would always be sight-read. Why not use that realistic experience as a teaching experience? What happened in that 30-minute session -- and in the two that followed it -- has become the process I have used ever since, even with students. Here it is:

Using a piece of prose I have never read before, I read the first few words of the first sentence of a paragraph -- up to but not including the verb -- and then tell the writer how I am going about the interpretive act, in accordance with the reader expectation principles I have previously explained. (I will reuse example (11) from Chapter 4 to demonstrate the process here, followed by my oral comments to the writer.)

11a. A gross violation of academic responsibility . . .

Whose story is this? The "gross violation's." What will that violation do? The verb is supposed to tell us.

Then I proceed, in slow motion, through the rest of the sentence, stopping whenever I have been able to put together the next interpretive subsection.

11b. ". . . is required . . ."

The violation "is required" for something. We should find out what that is right away.

11c. ". . . to dismiss a tenured faculty member for cause, . . ."

So if you want to get rid of a tenured faculty member, you've got to demonstrate a gross violation of academic responsibility. Problem: I've just heard something that sounds important enough to deserve a Stress position; but the comma after "for cause" does not allow for a Stress position. I am now perplexed: Should I be stressing something already, or not?

11d. ". . . and an elaborate hearing procedure . . ."

Is this the beginning of a new clause? If so, have we changed now to hearing the story of a "procedure"? And how does that connect backward to the first clause? I'm confused.

11e. ". . . with a prior statement of specific charges . . ."

More difficulty. So this second clause, if it is a second clause, is not solely the story of a procedure, but now appears to be the story of a "procedure with a prior statement of charges." I am still waiting for a verb to tell me what this "procedure + prior statement" is supposed to be doing. (And I still do not know how much to value the first clause, which is already fading a bit from my memory.)

11f. ". . . is provided for . . ."

This "procedure" is provided for something? By whom? By what? For what? I'm losing my grasp. But at least it sounds like we are descending now to the Stress position, where the most important thing will arrive and make all of my struggles to this point worthwhile.

11g. ". . . before a tenured faculty member may be dismissed for cause."

The Stress position is filled with stuff I've already heard before! My mind is a mess. I'll have to go back and figure out how to put all this together by myself.

Here is the sample sentence, uninterrupted:

11. A gross violation of academic responsibility is required to dismiss a tenured faculty member for cause, and an elaborate hearing procedure with a prior statement of specific charges is provided for before a tenured faculty member may be dismissed for cause.

The writer has now experienced the drama of his reader's journey through this sentence. He is surprised by how hard it was to synthesize all these words into thought, given the order in which they appeared. I point out to him that the major problem for me-as-reader here was a lack of awareness on his part of the importance of the Stress position in English prose. It caused two problems: (1) I had no Stress position for the "gross violation" in the first clause; and (2) The only Stress position in the sentence was filled with old information we had encountered earlier in the same sentence. I tell him that I will keep my antennae up for further Stress position problems.

I move to the second sentence, using the same start-and-stop, interpret-as-you-go slow motion technique. Guess what? He's got a Stress position problem in that sentence, too. He thinks to himself, "Gee, I did it again." When we move on to the third sentence, it happens again. This time he says out loud, "Gee, I did it again." There is a Stress position problem in all but one of his sentences in this paragraph.

We move on to the next paragraph, using the same approach. As I move slowly into the first sentence, he has impatiently -- (that's good) -- moved several words ahead of me to look for Stress problems. He finds one, which allows him to preempt me and say, "Look, I did it again!" He has now discovered and experienced his major structural problem. This is induction at its best.

Of all the reader expectations we have covered, four of them should be consciously sought during this process in the order in which they should appear in most sentences:

1) What is the backward link to the previous sentence? (This should be answered by the first appearance of old information in the new sentence.)

2) Whose story is this? (This usually should be answered by the grammatical subject of the main clause.)

3) What's going on here? (This should be answered by the main verb.)

4) What's the most important thing in this sentence? (This should be answered by the occupant of the Stress position.)

When any of these "should be's" result in disappointments, there is usually a structural problem with the sentence. When these structural problems occur on a regular basis, that indicates a bad writing habit. Changing that habit can improve this writer's prose permanently.

I was shocked, on that day that I was first constrained to try it, that this approach worked so well. I thought I had just gotten lucky. I happened to pick the perfect paragraph or two of a writer who just happened to have a marked and pervasive bad habit. What luck! But then it worked again the next half-hour with the second person. And then it worked again for the third. And it has been working ever since. It still astounds me with its consistency.

And think of the anti-burnout benefit: You never have to prepare for these conferences. As a matter of fact, if you prepare for them, you destroy their major efficacy -- that of demonstrating to your student how a person *who has never seen this text before* will most likely experience the reading of it.

Once I have discovered a possible set of patterns in the first paragraph and confirmed them in the second, I take just the one or two worst problems and do a spot-check for them on another page or two. Actually, the student does the spot-checking. She becomes convinced: Those are indeed her patterns. This entire procedure takes me an average of 22 minutes per person. It may take you longer while you are new to it; but you should get quicker in short order.

The best procedure at this point is to assign the student to do a revision of three or four paragraphs from this or some other document he already produced and bring you the before and the after. My experience of this second visit has been remarkably consistent: The student returns with a sense of having done a good job on the revision; but when we look closely at their work, he has failed about 50% of the time to repair the structural damage. He has replaced one word with another, but he has not transported it to another structural location. Or he had changed the location of something, but not to where the reader needed or expected it. He is surprised to find that despite his sense of having understood it, he did not understand. I send him away to do yet another revision. This time, he gets it. The light bulb has been illuminated.

Then I warn him: The next time you go to produce a new piece of prose, FORGET ABOUT ALL OF THIS as you write your first draft. If you do not, you become so hyperconcerned with structural matters that the substance freezes within you. You should write your first draft in the "old style." THEN you should do an arduous revision process, changing every sentence in that draft that shows signs of your one or two or three worst habits. I urge him to change EVERY sentence that displays a structural problem, even if the sentence seems to make sense *to him*. We want to make the sentence safe not for him but for his readers.

This revision process is unpleasant and time-consuming; but it should only need to happen once. The next time the student goes to write something and finds himself structuring a sentence in the old, reader-unfriendly way, behavior modification will set it: His stomach muscles will tighten, and he will think, "I will have to go through the PAIN of revision later on if sentence before proceeding to the next one." This should last for two or three documents. After that, he should be naturally reaching for the reader-friendly structures. The improvement will be obvious to everyone.

When teachers work with the approach here, should they show examples of prose from their students, from their own work, or from the work of professionals?

Answer: E. (All of the above.)

Professional prose is a good place to start. It is arms' length. It is non-threatening. It is you and them for or against the outsiders. Together you can laugh it to scorn, or admire its strength, and no one gets hurt. They will feel somehow matured when they can see what went wrong with the prose of professional adults.

Eventually, using a sentence or two (and even later a whole paragraph) from *each* of your students in the class can work well. Everyone has habits. If, by the midpoint in the term, you have fostered enough of a collaborative atmosphere (as opposed to a competitive one), they should be able to profit from each other's writing -- and perhaps enjoy it as well.

Using your own writing may or may not be effective, depending on your relationship with the class. If you are relatively comfortable with each other, using some of your own prose from a while ago -- (distance!) -- and then getting them to suggest helpful revisions could be highly effective. Effective use of your own prose can foster a highly positive sense of community in the classroom.

How should teachers spread these lessons out over the course of a semester?

That varies, especially depending on what else you wish to include in the course. But in general, teaching a lot of this at the beginning is a good idea. The faster students get some of these principles in their minds, the more you can do with them -- and the longer they have to absorb them.

Going slowly and steadily has its benefits. Teach a particular principle; then give them chances to look at that principle functioning (or malfunctioning) in each others' prose. Ideally, you should cover verbs, agency, backward links, "whose story?," and the Stress position by the middle of the term.

What lessons seem to need a particularly long time?

The Stress position is so variable in its applications that you would do well to spend a great deal of time making it available to them. If students come away from your course with only one principle firmly in mind, the Stress position is the one that will be of most help to them -- immediately and lastingly.

How long can students go without receiving a grade on any of their writing?

The response to this may seem counter-intuitive. Our students are so trained to base their performance on grades that it would seem they need to receive these early and constantly. I would argue to the contrary. Why give them grades based on what they brought to you instead of what they learned from you? In a course like this, it matters less how soon they are evaluated than how well they have it all in their systems by the time the course has ended. Ezra Pound put it nicely in his *ABC of Reading*, which I paraphrase here: It makes no difference which leg of a table you make first, as long as by the end it stands squarely upon the ground.

The student evaluation forms at my university ask specifically how they felt about the grading. Every term I have a great many students comment how they were made uncomfortable at first by this gradeless existence; but by the end they had realized how the lack of grades had freed them to concentrate on improvement. They tell me that they realized, somewhere along the way, that they "knew" how they were doing all along because they were so constantly seeing each others' writing. (I have them look at three other students' submissions almost every week.)

Anyone who listens hard and tries hard to put all this to work finds that he has improved greatly by the end of the term. As a result, all those people do "well." Most of my students receive grades of A, A–, or B+, unless they have refused to listen and work. This is not grade inflation. They deserved those grades.

How should one determine a final grade?

I grade students essentially on what they have been able to accomplish by the end of the term. They know that will be the case from the first day. I balance two factors: (1) The quality of their prose at the end of the term; and (2) how far have they come since the beginning of the term. Usually the straight A's go to people who wrote pretty well to start with and have learned much of what I have to teach them by the end. Many, however, are capable of getting an A– even if they started at quite a moderate level; they are the ones who were able to understand the habitual problems we identified and were able to do something about them.

I give a single grade for their journals taken as a whole throughout the term. I give another single grade for their job as responders to each other throughout the term. And I give a single grade for their performance on the longer final writing project. Because I have been reading their prose throughout, the first two of these grades can be assessed in just a few minutes' review per student. Looking closely at their early prose and their final prose does not take long; the comparison speaks for itself.

S *upplementary Techniques and Related Concerns*

Freshmen, Rules, and Power

Many students arrive at American colleges and universities with the impression that the main goal of their previous education was to introduce them to as much cultural literacy as possible. They have been taught things because in order to join the ranks of responsible adults in our society, they have to know certain facts. They feel they have been introduced to the mysteries of mathematics, foreign languages, history, literature, and the sciences not because all of these fields prepare them in practical ways for functioning in the world but rather as an elongated rite of passage. Learning it all was their job, their occupation. Some have become cynical about education; others trust that it all had a purpose that will become apparent at some future moment of clarification. Only a small percentage will have already begun to synthesize concepts from discipline to discipline and to seek ways of using their exposure to knowledge as a means to gain greater control over their own thinking processes.

I do not intend this description as a criticism of pre-college education. In many ways, that education accomplishes a great deal in priming the intellect with matter up to the age of 18, leaving the teaching of synthesis, expansion, research, and conceptualization for the most part to the college-level educational process. I wish only to emphasize that the fundamental task of college instructors -- especially those who teach freshmen -- is to help students make that significantly important transition from being information gatherers to being thought processors. In the present scheme of things, the freshman writing course can be the single best opportunity to help them discover not only that they have thoughts but that they have a right to have thoughts.

A writing course will fail in that objective if it seems to present to its students only another helping of the rules with which they have long been burdened. It will fail even more surely if it seems to present them with yet another, newer set of rules to replace the old ones. If the principles of this reader expectation approach are presented to them as just that -- a new set of rigid rules -- the whole course will be highly unsatisfactory for all concerned. The proscriptive warning "Always place your most important material in a Stress position" will sound to them not significantly distinguishable from "Never split an infinitive." Avoiding this pitfall takes constant diligence and a strong will; it is all too tempting to use your position in the classroom mainly to demonstrate your power over them. It is important to distinguish the difference between *rules* -- (polite people do not split their infinitives) -- and descriptions of generalized reader behavior -- (most readers most of the time give special emphasis to material located at a point of syntactic closure). But that distinction alone will seem to many students merely a smokescreen to disguise what they perceive really to be a new set of rules, promulgated by the newest authority figure in the classroom. To make the distinction meaningful, teachers must offer students constant opportunities of realizing their own power, constant opportunities for them to make choices; by making those choices skillfully, students can begin to manipulate the structure of their prose and thereby influence most readers' process of interpretation. The more our students do that, the more convinced they will become that this methodology actually frees them to take much more control over their readers and also over their thoughts.

Along the way, we must often remind students that discourse is always infinitely interpretable. They will never be able to control a reader completely; they will never be able to make their prose, of whatever length, "mean" only one thing. Eventually they might understand that it is the infinite nature of interpretation itself that frees them from the burden of obeying someone else's rules. Once they understand reader expectations, they can choose when they will play safe with their structure by satisfying those expectations and when they will take a chance at making a dramatic effect by violating them.

In my experience, the people most eager to learn this reader-based methodology and most appreciative of its power have been medical school faculty. That makes a great deal of sense. More than anyone else at this moment in American life, medical school faculty write for a living. In 1980, the vast majority of responsible applications for federal grants -- from 65% to 85% -- were funded; by 1990, that figure was hovering around 15%; and with only exceptional moments, nothing much had improved by the end of the millennium. Even long-established research professionals with good track records and voluminous publication lists run the risk of being turned down the next time around. As a result, these people have real and pressing needs to ensure their audience understands exactly what they are arguing or proposing. On that rhetorical task depends not only their continuing professional viability but their continuing professional existence. They are grateful for whatever help they can get.

What makes our freshmen different from these M.D./Ph.D. veteran professionals? For our freshmen, there is little at stake when they produce prose: No salary, no livelihood, no continuing professional status. They risk only a grade and, perhaps, some sense of personal satisfaction. Our freshmen at Duke used to complain to me (concerning the required nature of the writing course) that they would not have gotten into Duke had they not been able to write well. It took me some time to realize the way in which they were right. Up to that point in their lives, they had needed writing only to get good grades in high school and to write a good college application essay. For those tasks, their writing had been fully adequate. It is a challenge to demonstrate to them how they will need great rhetorical skills as they proceed further into college, and much greater skills after they graduate.

How, then, can we reach these freshmen? We cannot do it by making a neo-1960s attempt at "relevance" -- with long reading assignments on crucial and gripping contemporary issues. By itself, that would depend too much on their already possessing a kind of purified intellectual curiosity unlikely to have been developed by age 18. Nor do I think we can accomplish it with vague promises or threats about the importance of written skills to their future career hopes. The promises may well be true; but delayed gratification will not work when the delay seems to reach all the way into some later existence. Instead, I advocate giving students the immediate experience of that which they seem most interested in at this time in their development: power. This Reader Expectation approach, when well taught, actually empowers the writer to some degree over the construction of prose and over the reader's interpretive process.

I have found two particular teaching strategies to be especially helpful in this effort: (1) Peer evaluation; and (2) double submission of papers. While neither of these is a new idea in the teaching of writing, they work especially well with this reader-based pedagogy.

Peer Evaluation

The audiences for whom our students have always written were teachers who already knew what those students had to say. The rhetorical task was always once of *demonstration* -- showing teacher that they had been to the library and done their work. In later, professional life, the rhetorical task will become one of *communication* -- getting a variety of readers to understand something as yet undiscovered, undeveloped, and not yet "won." The question became, therefore, how to provide these students with *real* audiences -- not the always-and-already knowledgeable teachers but someone who was relatively unknowing and willing to learn.

That real audience is sitting right there -- their classmates. Writing for their peers presents them with a wholly different rhetorical task than writing for their teachers. How, then, could that audience be harnessed to best effect? One successful solution was the use of peer response evaluation.

A Procedure for Peer Evaluation

Any number of procedures can work well to allow students the opportunity of reading and responding to each other's prose. I offer one here that has a particularly good track record.

1. Each student prepares four copies of the assigned paper -- one for me and one for each of the other three members of the writing group. Each person therefore takes home three essays to evaluate. No part of the procedure is done anonymously; students are thereby encouraged to stand behind their opinions and to treat each other humanely.

2. Students are asked to make two separate sets of comments: (a) On the paper itself they make any mechanical comments or corrections they feel compelled to make (spelling, grammar, etc.); (b) On separate sheets of paper they make substantive and structural comments, coding them to numbers they insert into the original text. These latter

comments must take into consideration the rhetorical principles being taught in the course. It is inadequate for commentators merely to indicate judgment ("unclear," "awkward, "wordy," "needs more development," etc.); they must articulate *why* such judgments can be made, with special reference to the reader expectation principles of structural location.

This allows for a divide-and-conquer approach to their learning the Reader Expectation insights. As each locational expectation is taught, you can have students pay special attention to it in their next peer review. Looking just for (for example) Stress position occupancy in the work of three of their classmates will give students a well-defined experience with more enlightenment than they could imagine beforehand.

It is essential to have them separate the mechanical comments from the substantive/stylistic comments. If students are encouraged to put all their comments on the paper itself, the mechanical concerns tend to take over. The students cease being readers and instead become error-hunters. Having covered the page with responses to the paper's mechanics, they feel they have done a great deal, enough to satisfy the requirements of the assignment. Separating the mechanical from the more important comments helps them concentrate on what the essay is trying to accomplish. It also expands the space available for substantive and stylistic commentary.

They have a week to ten days for this task. Most find they put more hours into the peer evaluation process than they had into writing the original paper. Peer evaluation becomes a major part of the course.

3. If a revision process is structured into the assignment, the second submission can be distributed to three *different* peer responders. The audience for this text has now doubled.

4. To reward and control the commenting process, I have found it helpful to assign a grade at the end of the term to represent *all* of their commenting throughout. Grades for individual commenting efforts have proved stultifying; and no grades whatever fails to provide sufficient motivation.

Gains for the Student

It is hard to overestimate the potential gains from using peer evaluation in teaching this reader expectation approach. I list a few of them.

1. People tend to learn best by teaching others. In this kind of a writing course, students can all too passively accept the principles offered and be able to regurgitate them when called upon to do so. Through peer evaluation we turn our students into teachers, forcing them to apply these principles actively on real texts -- a number of their classmates' papers. They discover it is difficult to teach others this approach to writing without understanding a good deal about it themselves.

2. Peer evaluation provides students with multiple opportunities to investigate the methodology without having to write multiple papers themselves. They get the opportunity to contemplate reader expectations while acting as readers; they demonstrate to themselves that readers actually read the way REA predicts they will. That experience will bear fruit when they again assume the role of writers.

3. When most students produce a paper for a writing instructor, nothing more than a grade is at stake. If the grade is high, it elicits in some students a sense of pride and fulfillment but in others a sense of cynicism -- that such a paltry or slovenly effort should be so well rewarded. If the grade is low, many students will keep it a private matter between themselves and the instructor and manage to cope with whatever feelings are produced. But since students get a great many grades in college, this particular stake is not necessarily a high one for some; for others it is *too* high a stake, which in turn can destroy some of the learning process.

   If, on the other hand, students produce papers to be read and evaluated by their peers, a great deal more is suddenly at stake: They are risking their intellectual reputation in their peer community. The power of this incentive should not be undervalued. One teacher told me of a student who complained to her with some bitterness that he had been unaware a particular paper would be evaluated by his peers: "If I had known it was going to be peer responded, I would have written a *much* better paper."

4. Students will often believe the critical comments of their peers ("I couldn't follow the logic in paragraph five") when they will ignore or distrust the same comment coming from their instructor. To the student, the instructor seems merely to be simulating an audience; the student's classmates actually *are* an audience. The safety catches in the evaluation process described above help to keep the student's peers from turning into Little Red Pens in the Sky.

5. Peer evaluation gives students the opportunity -- even the necessity -- of entering into the kind of dialogue and dialectic that teachers are forever trying to create in classroom situations. We are so delighted when on a given day we have succeeded in getting a "really good discussion going"; how much better, then, this prolonged (not momentary), well-considered (not knee-jerk) written response from student to student. What a class it would be if each of 15 or 20 students responded at length (an hour or two's consideration) to three of the others in an orderly and contemplative fashion. (In order for a class period to embrace such activity, the course would have to last well over 100 hours.) In a certain sense, this happens every time an assignment is peer evaluated by the procedure suggested above.

6. If three or six peers replace the instructor as commentators, then students receive not one set of comments but three or six. Each student is

thereby forced to reengage with his or her essay not from one *ex cathedra* perspective (the teacher's), but from the multiple perspectives represented by their peers. Most students have found the volume and diversity of the peer commentary a more satisfactory counterbalance to the great effort they exerted in creating the paper than would be the sole (and often abbreviated) response of their teacher.

7. In writing the evaluative comments, even if revision is not involved, students find themselves engaging in the given assignment not one time but seven times: They write; they comment three times; and they read three commentaries on what they've written. The richness of this sevenfold immersion is evident to everyone involved -- especially when compared to the relative spareness of the traditional single-submission/single-response procedure. If revision is involved, the number of engagements is further increased.

8. Concerning the writer's handling of reader expectations, multiple responses from classmates are more persuasive than teacher's in two ways:

   a) If several students independently comment that (for example) the Stress position rarely seems to be occupied by something stressworthy, the writer begins to believe that this is a problem for her readers in general.

   b) If several students disagree on "what's important" in a given sentence or what the point is of a given paragraph, the writer can see firsthand how her text is not controlling enough readers' interpretation processes.

   So whether the multiple student commentators agree or disagree, there is something the writer can learn.

9. Students tend to write more in their commenting on the six other papers than they do in producing their own. It is therefore possible to limit a semester's writing assignments to only a half-dozen papers, totaling 25 to 30 pages, and still generate more than 75 pages of writing per student during the term. That is accomplished without changing topics, thinking up new assignments, or devising new ways for them to overcome the problem of inertia.

10. Moreover, the writing done for the commentary assignments differs in quality and nature from that done for the formal assignment that preceded it. The original paper was written, in all likelihood, as an academic exercise, a formal writing for a formal and highly synthetic purpose. In contrast, the commentary is written from real person to real person, without fear of recrimination for poor expression, and with a real need to communicate precisely what was on the mind of the writer.

    That "real need" has long proved one of the most perplexing problems facing composition teachers. The best-known example of the difference a real audience can make was given us by the revered rhetorician from the University of Chicago, Wayne C. Booth, in his 1969 article "The Rhetorical Stance":

> Last Fall I had an advanced graduate student, bright, energetic, well-in-formed, whose papers were almost unreadable. He managed to be pre-tentious, dull, and disorganized in his paper on *Emma*, and pretentious, dull, and disorganized on *Madame Bovary*. On *The Golden Bowl* he was all these and obscure as well. Then one day, toward the end of term, he cor-nered me after class and said, "You know, I think you were all wrong about Robbe-Grillet's *Jealousy* today." We didn't have time to discuss it, so I suggested that he write me a note about it. Five hours later I found in my faculty box a four-page polemic, unpretentious, stimulating, organized, convincing. Here was a man who had taught freshman composition for several years and who was incapable of committing any of the more ob-vious errors that we think of as characteristic of bad writing. Yet he could not write a decent sentence, paragraph, or paper until his rhetorical prob-lem was solved -- until, that is, he had found a definition of audience, his argument, and his own proper tone of voice.

It is these three crucial rhetorical components -- "a definition of audience, his argument, and his own proper tone of voice" -- that be-come far more available to a student when they have a real audience of fellow students replace the essentially artificial audience, the in-structor. Booth's student broke out of his rhetorical handcuffs not sim-ply because he finally "had something to say" but because he had both a *need* to say it and an audience that, he thought, *needed* to hear it. That made the communication "real."

It is important, then, never to comment on the commentary as if it were "a writing assignment." If you keep the students free from fear-ing a formal response to their writing, they will be far more likely to consider their comments "real" writing. Indeed, experience has demonstrated that this procedure works best if the instructor offers no written commentary whatever. Even a single word like "nice!" trans-forms the whole experience for the worse: It becomes an "exercise." The students will feel once again that they are writing essentially for the instructor, who has reclaimed through that one "nice!" the role of "real audience." That student will concentrate much of her effort for the rest of the term in trying to produce a second "nice!" After three or four weeks of silence from the instructor, the students begin to believe that they actually *are* each other's "real audience."

11. Even the strongest student opponents of peer evaluation acknowledge that they value the opportunity to read the work of others in their own class. It gives them a sense of community and of community standards. It lets them judge for themselves how their own imagination, skills, and efforts compare to those of their peers. For some, it bolsters confi-dence; for others, it inspires them to generate greater energy; for every-one, it seems to present a clearer and more complete picture of their educational process.

Gains for the Instructor

In addition to making the course far more meaningful for the students, the introduction of peer evaluation should make the course a great deal less burdensome and more engaging for the instructor.

If all goes well with this procedure, the instructor can cease writing comments altogether. I have taught an advanced writing course using the Reader Expectation Approach for several years now, with a dozen students each writing about 125 pages, and each improving markedly and permanently by the end of the term, without my having written a single comment on any of those papers. I comment generally in class; I meet with each student three or four times during the term; and I am available for anyone who feels he needs more individual attention. They are doing far better than they used to in the traditional courses; and I am saved from the traditional burnout. It has become for me, in part, a delightful spectator sport.

But even if you maintain your role as commentator, there are a number of significant advantages for you in this peer process. No longer must you shoulder the burden of being the *sole* responder to student writing -- a burden that causes a number of kinds of damage.

-- Being the sole responder tends to encourage instructors to overcomment. If there is an error or infelicity of some sort, then not responding might be taken by the student as the equivalent of approval. The sum total of such overresponding almost always has a more negative than positive effect on the student.

-- It also tends to make instructors look for things to which to respond. If one has the responsibility of being the sole responder, then one is failing to uphold one's duty unless one responds fully. If one has the power of being the sole responder, then one must use that power to demonstrate that it exists. In both cases, the instructor sacrifices responding as a typical reader in favor of responding as the power player in a metagame.

-- The instructor usually finds that the comments needed for one student's paper must be reiterated many times over on other students' papers. Soon the freshness of the commenting fades and a sense of drudgery sets in. Instructors can collect these repetitive concerns and issue one sheet of communal comments for the class as a whole.

-- The more diligent the instructor, the greater the sense of anxiety is generated, lest in responding to the paper something important might be omitted.

Not only can all these negative effects be avoided by the use of peer evaluation, but they are replaced by a number of positive effects.

-- It is actually interesting to watch one's students interacting intellectually with each other. As a spectator sport, it is a varied and often uplifting experience.

-- The instructor learns firsthand what students do *not* understand. This can prove extremely beneficial for everyone involved. It can also change the way the classroom time is used.

-- The adversarial quality of the student-teacher relationship can be greatly reduced. The student can start to view the instructor as the person who can offer help instead of the person who cracks the whip.

Student Complaints and Some Responses

The student complaints concerning peer evaluation come from many people but take only a few forms. I list the most recurrent of them below, together with my responses to them. I do not suggest that my responses should be or will be dispositive of all issues; but when supported by a lot of patience and some understanding, they have proved reasonably effective in allaying the majority of student fears.

1. "My parents didn't pay $X for me to come to this university and be taught by other students."

    I disagree. I think one does indeed come to college to "be taught by other students." One learns from them in every class where they offer opinions or solve problems or collaborate in laboratories or simply recite. One absorbs a great deal more from them between classes than from professors during classes. As noted above, students tend to believe each other's responses to their written work in different and often better ways than the responses of hired-gun writing teachers.

    In addition, under peer evaluation procedures each student receives from five to ten times the number of comments he or she would have received had the instructor been solely responsible for the essays. The money of the students' parents has been well spent.

2. Students are often frustrated by having their essay receive widely differing responses from a single group of evaluators. How, they wonder, can it be a meaningful process if the comments they receive vary all the way from admiring to befuddled?

    When they offer this criticism, I welcome them to the real world. The course material has been dealing with the concept of infinite interpretability all semester long; that must have some bearing on the contingencies of value judgments. It is perfectly normal for one piece of discourse to elicit widely varying responses from its readers. (For a probable example, look at any three published reviews of the same new book.) There simply is no "right" opinion. Any three professors might give the essay an equally wide range of response. It is not too early for students to be learning this.

    While it is possible that no one student response might be as helpfully perceptive as one from the instructor of the course, it is equally likely that a group of student graders collectively will notice much of what the instructor would point out and probably a good deal more.

3. Students complain that when they receive widely varying comments, they do not know which ones to believe. Which ones are the right ones?

   Two responses: First, it is a dangerous thing for a student to believe that all comments that come from an instructor would by definition be "right." (Actually, most of today's students seem to me quite ready to challenge comments even from the fullest of faculty.)

   Second, it becomes part of the learning experience of the course for students to be forced to winnow the intellectual wheat from the chaff. Thinking through these criticisms, accepting some, rejecting others, being challenged or even confused by others -- all these are educational, intellectual processes, much to be valued in a course that professes to teach clearer thinking.

   I have found it helpful to point out to students that this chaff/ wheat process is a lifelong activity. It pops up in reviewing responses to your grant proposal, in reading reader's comments to your manuscript, in considering alternate proposals from the company's think tank, or in deciding where to go on the summer vacation. Peer evaluation brings a touch of this reality into the classroom, where its appearance is somewhat unexpected but much to be valued.

4. Is there a problem with mean-spirited responses? That depends in part on how the instructor explains the whole process. If you do a good job of indicating how this is a collaborative effort, not a competitive one, mean-spiritedness should be rare. I have encountered what looked to be mean-spirited responses only a few times. Most of these turned out to be merely pretentious. The student had gotten carried away with sounding magisterial. When a real case presents itself, well -- you handle it. It may not be pleasant; but it is probably a necessary growing experience for the perpetrator and a helpful one for the victim in terms of dealing with real-life situations down the road.

5. What happens if a whole group of student commentators issues a judgment on a paper that differs significantly from what you as teacher would have said? You can always go out of your way to add your perspective; but since this interferes somewhat with the process you have established, the more casually you do it, the better. I would suggest you save such interference for the truly extreme cases.

6. Some students, but not many, articulate fears about lacking the protection of anonymity in this process. (Even if the instructor attempts to run a blind submission procedure, anonymity will not be well protected; enquiring minds will want to know and will succeed in determining who wrote what.) Once again, I welcome these students to the real world. For the most part in life, you have to stand up for your opinions. The same should apply to the classroom, especially one in which communication is the main subject under discussion. I require names on the papers and names on the comments.

Double Submission of Papers

If peer response does not appeal to you and you wish to retain the role of being the sole responder to student papers, you might well consider the following scheme for double submission. The two submissions of the student's paper actually demand less total time from the instructor than does the conventional single submission; at the same time, the procedure allows the student to receive helpful feedback before the final draft is written. In addition, that feedback is likely to have an effect that reaches beyond the submission of this particular paper.

When the paper is first submitted, the instructor spends only a few minutes with it, analyzing only two or three paragraphs, structurally. Focusing on the relationship between substance and structure, the instructor checks the significant structural locations that have been taught in the course to that point; for example, if only the verb/action expectation has been taught, the instructor looks closely at the verbs. It is important to make this structural analysis the primary reading goal; as readers and teachers, we should be caring not that we are able to make *an* interpretation of the paragraph but rather that we can judge how likely it is that our interpretation is the one the writer intended for us. If few or none of the verbs seem to announce the actions of their sentences, the chances are not as good as they should be that our interpretation will coincide with that intended by the student writer.

If the structural analysis of two paragraphs turns up consistent structural/expectational problems, then the paper is returned to the student with the single instruction to remedy that recurrent problem -- throughout the entire paper. Once an instructor begins to become adept at such analyses, this whole process should take about five minutes; after more experience, it should take only a minute or two.

In effect, the instructor tells students to identify their ideas more accurately. "Your important materials seem rarely to show up in Stress positions. Make a Stress position for everything you want me to emphasize." They will have to rethink the material with that in mind. On revision, the instructor will be able to see clearly what it was they wanted the reader to value. Then the instructor is in a far better position to offer an opinion of it. When that better, fuller paper is resubmitted, it usually requires far less time and effort for the instructor to read and comment upon it. The instructor is also in a far better position to judge what it is the students actually thought -- as opposed to what she thought they thought. Thus the two submissions simultaneously can reduce instructor reading time and increase the quality of the student's process and product.

On the other hand, should the investigation of two or three paragraphs show few signs of structural problems on first submission, then the instructor can read the entire paper, quickly, in order to make suggestions for other kinds of improvements. These may take the form of structural advice that would normally be offered later in the term; or they may be a direct response to the substantive matter -- a kind of dialectic that may deepen the student's involvement. That dialectic becomes possible because the instructor has greater confidence he or she has actually understood what the writer intended to be understood.

Students soon realize that they are ahead of the game if their first submission does not suffer from consistent structural problems. If they do that first revision themselves, then the instructor will help them more substantively to do the second revision. If they wait for the instructor to show them how to do the first revision, they forfeit the opportunity for that more explicit dialectical experience the first time around.

When the first submission is structurally weak, instructors new at this procedure are often amazed (upon reading the second submission) at how far removed their own sense of the prose had been from what the writer had intended. Again: Just because we can make *some* sense of a text does not mean that we have necessarily perceived *the* sense it was intended to make.

Here is a potential variation -- if class size is small enough to make it practicable: The first submission can be made in person, with the analysis and comment being made live and on the spot. The analysis becomes a dramatic and dialectic event in itself, as the instructor can ask the author straightforwardly whether she intended X to be the action of this sentence -- or the most stressworthy part of the sentence, or whatever the structural concerns of the moment might be. The interview can be very brief -- less than 15 minutes. Much can happen in that time beyond the specific exchange of information: Student and teacher will bond in certain ways; the student may well feel recognized, stretched, encouraged, inspired -- depending on the teacher's therapeutic skills; the teacher will seem to the student actively involved in the production of the paper; and the teacher will have a better sense of the students as individuals. Perhaps there is no need to add that when the teacher goes home at the end of the day, no pile of first drafts awaits the critical pen.

Teaching Grammar

I am often asked whether this reader-based approach should not be relegated to a second semester's course or an advanced course, since most students clearly need a great deal of rehearsal in the basics before they can handle this more sophisticated material. "The basics" often includes a great emphasis on matters of grammar and spelling. I answer straightforwardly: Teaching grammar as a separate, preliminary writing course at the college level is at best problematic. Few people -- and very few of those who need the training the most -- can absorb and retain dozens of grammatical details in preparation for using them at some later date. (By the term *grammar* here I am including the issues of punctuation and usage.) The time to teach grammar is when the individual grammatical needs actually arise in student papers.

The Germans seem to understand this much better than we do. When most American schools teach a foreign language, the preliminary course is often filled with chapters of grammar study, the actual readings being limited to the details of what Pierre and Hélène did at school today. In the second course, literature finally starts to take precedence over grammar. German schools throw you right into the literature, from the first day. You pick up the grammar and the vocabulary as you go, mostly because you need it in order to make sense of the literature.

This German approach works well for the teaching of grammar in English composition courses. If punctuation and other grammatical details are presented as part of the communicative effort from writer to reader, using actual contexts instead of prepared examples, students may begin to understand why our grammatical conventions exist. (By the way, the more informal type of writing required for the peer responses is often far less burdened by grammatical error.)

A great deal of grammar has some sort of rational basis for its existence. That rational basis usually has something to do with the writer trying to warn the reader about how to proceed or what to expect. I offer just a few examples:

1. The colon and semi-colon, properly used, create Stress positions in the middle of sentences through their notation of syntactic closure. Once that is understood, students realize that instead of being browbeaten by these arcane dots and squiggles, they can actually use them in an attempt to manipulate the reader's interpretation process. Conversely, the comma splice is inappropriate or "wrong" because in failing to effect syntactic closure, it also fails to signal the reader that the clause contains stressworthy material. (For examples connecting the colon, the semi-colon, and the problem of the comma splice, see Example (20) at page 124 of Chapter 4.)

2. A modifying phrase that begins a sentence raises an expectation that the person or thing modified will appear as the subject of the main clause. A dangling modifier dangles because the arrival of that subject violates that expectation.

   Floating in the gutter, I saw my Composition textbook.

   When we encounter the opening phrase "Floating in the gutter," we lean forward over the comma in the expectation that the subject of the main clause will disclose who is doing the flying. If there we find "I," the effect is either humorous or annoying, depending on the reading circumstances.

   If the author of this dangled sentence reviews it in the conventional manner for purposes of revision, the coffee stain problem arises, and he probably does not notice anything is amiss.[7] If, however, he investigates it in terms of a reader's structural expectations, he might well pause to consider "whose story" it is meant to be. At the moment, it is the book's story in the opening phrase and speaker's story in the main clause; yet no explicit transition has been made from one story to the next. Something has to give. To remain consistent, the phrase and the clause should present a single story. "After the collision, I was horrified to see my Composition textbook floating in the gutter."

3. Single subject, plural verb: This problem (or its reverse) usually results from one of two causes: Either common usage makes it seem correct, or the subject has been separated from the verb by so much material that the writer has forgotten the subject's number. The latter case can be remedied if a writer notices that such a long subject-verb separation is likely to be burdensome for the reader. When subject and verb reconvene, the mistake in number becomes apparent.

Many mistakes are the result of dialectal influence. Fortunately, we have had the insight and guidance of Mina Shaughnessy to teach us that dialectal mistakes are not perceived as errors by those within the dialect community. Indeed, if anyone within that community makes a mistake *within the dialect* (especially if the mistaken usage is considered correct by some other community), that person would invite quick and certain censure. Quite simply, grammatical expectations depend directly on the acceptance of the particular community in charge of the discourse. One person's expectation is another person's error.[8] Teaching writing from a reader's perspective enables us to present and work with the problem of dialect for what it is -- a case of the power to control discourse. (For a detailed look at English punctuation seen from the perspective of this reader expectation approach, see Chapter 6 of my textbook, *The Sense of Structure: Writing from the Reader's Perspective.*)

That said, we should still, I believe, teach our students to avoid error in the best ways we can contrive. We might do well to shift our emphasis: Instead of threatening that error will embarrass them in polite society, let us try arming them with the knowledge that error will interrupt the reading process and waste precious reader energy. Mina Shaughnessy:

> Errors, however, are unintentional and unprofitable intrusions upon the consciousness of the reader. They introduce in accidental ways alternative forms in spots where usage has stabilized a particular form (as is now true in spelling, for example, or in the familiar albeit "illogical" inflections). They demand energy without giving any return in meaning; they shift the reader's attention from where he is going (meaning) to how he is getting there (code). In a better world, it is true, readers might be more generous with their energies, pausing to divine the meaning of a writer or mentally to edit the errors out of his text without expecting to be rewarded for their efforts, but it would be foolhardy to bank on that kind of persistence except perhaps in English teachers or good friends. (That errors carry messages which writers can't afford to send is demonstrated by the amount of energy and money individuals, business firms, publishing houses, etc. spend on error removal, whether by correcting fluids, erasers, scrapped paper, or proofreaders.)[9]

Teaching Transitions

Two of the main products of mastering the Reader Expectation Approach are cohesion and coherence. Those qualities have also been the object of more conventional methods (often referred to as Current Traditional Rhetoric); but much of their effort has stressed the importance of individual words or phrases that mark transitions. We have unwittingly taught students that the mere presence of "however," "therefore," "in spite of which," and dozens of other expectation-raisers will ennoble their prose and make it more acceptable in the polite, professional, or learned worlds. Of course, we have always cautioned students to make sure the context actually justifies the presence of the transitional marker; but the caution often does not take.

Two interesting articles on transitional markers were produced by Gary Sloan.[10] In his 1978 article he reviews many studies that have expended their energies creating categories of referentiality. Ross Winterowd, for example, offers seven types of relationships that he calls "transitions": coordination, observativity, causativity, conclusivity, alternativity, inclusivity, and sequentiality. Jeanne Fahnestock suggests seven pairings of "continuative" with "discontinuative" relationships: sequence-anomalous sequence; restatement-replacement; exemplification-exception; premise-concession; conclusion-denied implication; similarity-contrast; addition-alternation.

Sloan gave his students paragraphs from published essays and asked them to categorize the semantic relationships between specified syntactic units, using three different systems of categorization. The results were predictable: The students disagreed with each other constantly on what labels to assign. The disagreements were born of two great perplexities: (1) The students could not agree on what a given sentence or sequence of sentences meant; and (2) they spent a great percentage of their total effort in trying to distinguish one category from another. These two perplexities seem to me unavoidable -- and fatal to the hope of any such effort at categorization proving helpful in the teaching of writing.

It is completely understandable that the students could not agree on what any given sentence meant: Any unit of discourse varies in its meaning with the sensibilities, experiences, and perceptions of the individual reader -- and the individual reading. The best a writer can do is to persuade most readers to value one set of semantic clues more than another; in that attempt, the context becomes a major control of the message. That context, however, is just as much in need of contextualization as that which it contextualizes. The problem is endless. In disagreeing on what labels to assign to the various transitional markers, the students were disagreeing both on the meaning the markers gave the surrounding prose and on the meaning the surrounding prose gave the markers. No set of categories, no matter how clever, no matter how seemingly all-inclusive, will solve this problem of interpretation.

The other problem: The students spent too much of their effort in trying to distinguish and demarcate one category from another. The categories presumably were intended to assist us in our understanding of the nature of referentiality. Soon, however, they take over as the prime object of our attempt at understanding. They replace the problem they were invented to solve.

In his 1984 article, Sloan produced interesting statistics on the frequency of transitional markers in discursive prose. He investigated 25 professional essays (from a traditional college readings anthology) to ascertain how many explicit and implicit transitional markers existed in T-Units, which he defined as "independent clauses along with any subordinate elements attached or embedded." His results: Out of the 3,754 T-units examined, only 7% required explicit markers to make it clear to the reader how to read cohesively. The percentage is much higher for student-generated prose.

With ambiguity such an imposing problem, why should only 7% of professionally wrought T-Units need to display words that tell readers how to connect one clause to its neighbor? According to Sloan's statistics, two thirds of the T-Units required some kind of connection to remain cohesive; apparently the linkage could be effected without an explicit marker most of the time by a combination of logic and structure.

Using one of Sloan's examples:

A. You do not need traffic police where there is no wheeled traffic. You do not need postal bylaws where no one knows how to write. (169)

The connection is made implicitly by the parallel construction. The addition of an explicit marker such as "and," "likewise," or "furthermore" would insult the intelligence of the reader while destroying the elegance of the repetitive syntax and rhythm. Conversely, such a marker would become essential if the parallel structure were not employed:

B. You do not need traffic police where there is no wheeled traffic. [Likewise,] in the absence of people who know how to write, postal bylaws would not be required.

Without the "likewise," the second sentence is a burden to the reader; with it, the sentence becomes a recognizable and somewhat effective chiasmus -- the figure of speech that combines repetition and reversal (XYYX).

$$\qquad\quad \text{X} \qquad\qquad\qquad\qquad\quad \text{Y}$$
-- no need for traffic police . . . . . no wheeled traffic

$$\qquad\quad \text{Y} \qquad\qquad\qquad\qquad\quad \text{X}$$
-- no people who can write . . . . no need for postal bylaws

The distinction between these two is accounted for by a consideration of the applicable reader expectations, which warn the writer of the need for the transitional marker -- in this case the "whose story?" principle. In (A) above, both sentences are the story of "you," whose action is one of "needing." The sentences both have the "You do not need X where there is

Y" format, inviting the reader to make obvious and immediate comparisons between the X's and the Y's. The structure, by itself, exudes the concept of "likewise."

In (B), however, the story of the second sentence seems to belong either to "people" or, more probably, to "postal bylaws." Neither of these are recognizable as old information; neither brings with it any clue as to how this new unit of discourse relates to the one just encountered. The added marker "likewise" would immediately raise an expectation in the reader that the present sentence repeats in some way the message of the preceding sentence. Positioned after the expectation-raising "likewise," the phrase "in the *absence* of people" would hearken back to "*no* wheeled traffic"; "postal bylaws" would then have the possibility of balancing "traffic police." That possibility would be confirmed by "would not be required," which echoes "you do not need." The chiastic cross-referentiality of (B) is more complex than the parallelism of (A); without the referential marker "likewise," the complexity becomes obscurity.

I am suggesting we can teach our students a great deal more about cohesion and coherence through making them conscious of reader needs and expectations than we can through constructing artificial categories for referential markers. Concepts like "causativity" or even lists of "helpful" words (like "moreover," "thus," "in addition to," and the like) do not help; they only further convince the student that pushing the right buttons or chanting the proper words will make their prose more acceptable to the world empowered to read and judge them.

Better writers use fewer explicit transitional markers because those writers make the structure do a great deal of the transition marking for them. Sloan reports that the usage of transitional markers increases in quantity as young writers mature; but that increase reaches a peak just before a competent writer develops into a highly skilled writer. The progression makes sense. In their early development, writers increasingly learn how important it is to make connections explicit; they forge those connections mostly through the use of explicit markers. As the same writer begins to develop elegance and power, the explicit markers give way to the more subtle and sophisticated transitions created by the structural placement of substance.

T*he Most Common Student Objections to the Reader Expectation Approach*

It may be helpful to be prepared for some of the objections most commonly raised by students against this Reader Expectation Approach.

Objection #1: "I've heard all this before." As of the publication of this book, that protestation is highly unlikely to be accurate. This approach has been developed mainly at the university and professional levels and has not been much experimented with at the high school level.[11]

Nonetheless, in order to respond to this objection, the instructor has to determine exactly what it is these students think they have previously heard. Many, for example, have been taught that "a verb is an action word." That sounds to them something like the principle that readers expect the action to be articulated by the verb. The two are by no means equivalent.

With more accuracy, others will say they have already been told that beginnings and endings are important *things*; but they usually do not understand as well that they are important *places*.

In both these examples, the students are referring to lore they have learned about the language -- not about the rhetorical discourse experience that unfolds between writers and readers. They think that language *is* a certain way and *has* certain requirements; they do not realize that success in writing depends on whether the reader actually got delivery of the message the writer intended to send. Teaching them how to manipulate readers' interpretive processes by relying on readers' expectations can free our students from perceiving language as imposing a constant burden of "requirements."

Objection #2: "When I write all my sentences following your advice about verbs and Topic/Stress, all my sentences sound the same. It's boring." Or, "When I revise my sentences the way you tell me, they all sound stupid and empty."

These students do not like the response I offer. The Reader Expectation Approach excavates and exposes thought. If all these students' sentences sound the same and sound unsophisticated, it is probably because the shape of all these students' thoughts is the same and is relatively unsophisticated. Often when sentences fail to vary in shape, the writer has failed to articulate (or even to consider) the *connections* between the various thoughts.

With such students, explore a paragraph they think suffers from this reader expectation malady. Check especially the relative values they intended to give to the materials in all the Stress positions. Was each Stress position occupant worthy of the kind of attention it was likely to receive? Was there *anything* in the sentence that deserved the prominence of a Stress position? See if there is any difference in kind between the materials in various Stress positions. Could they be combined into one Stress position without loss of emphasis and without creating confusion? For an extreme example, recall the grade school essay on "Spring" from the last Chapter:

1a. I like the Spring because of the pretty flowers. I like the Spring because of the tulips. I like the Spring because of the roses. I like the Spring because of the daffodils. I like the Spring because of the pretty flowers.

Was this information worth five Stress positions? Its author would probably list the occupants of the Stress positions as the items she wished to emphasize; but she has not performed any action of synthesis here. The

Stress positions are filled with "pretty flowers," "tulips," "roses," "daffodils," and "pretty flowers." Even in middle school, this student might be capable of noting the equation between these items:

$$\text{pretty flowers } = \left| \begin{array}{c} \text{tulips} \\ \text{roses} \\ \text{daffodils} \end{array} \right| = \text{ pretty flowers}$$

1b. I like the Spring because of the pretty flowers -- the tulips, the roses, and the daffodils.

The author of "Spring" might at this point complain that this editing effort has produced a rewrite that misrepresents her intentions. She had not wanted to present a cold list, a mere inventory of Spring likables. She had wanted us to savor each flower as it appeared, allowing us to luxuriate in its look, its smell, its touch. Fine. We need not demand that her prose take any particular form or shape. If she wanted her readers to look, smell, and touch, she must inform them of these things -- and in places where they are likely to consider themselves informed.

1c. I like the Spring because of the many pretty flowers. I like the roses, which look so beautiful with their many colors and their wonderful petals. I like the tulips, which smell like a perfume store, only outside. I like the daffodils, which feel furry and fuzzy and sometimes make me sneeze. The many pretty flowers make the Spring a special time for me.

Middle school children can *say* all these things. We could teach them to *write* them by explaining how they *think* about them and how readers will *perceive* what they think.

So, when a student complains to me that when he arranges the thought of every sentence by adhering to reader expectation principles, all his prose sounds "stupid and empty," I tell him that if when he makes explicit whose story it really is, and articulates up front the logical backward link to the previous sentence, and locates what is going on in the verb, and saves for the Stress position that which he wants his reader to emphasize, his prose then sounds "stupid and empty," it is because his thought was "stupid and empty." He can either continue to obfuscate that fact by writing the way he was writing, or he can begin to develop the sophistication of his thinking process by considering the rhetorical reality of a sophisticated audience.

Objection #3: "This system stifles my individuality and creativity."

This is perhaps the most serious and most often articulated objection; but it suggests that students view the material as a system of rules -- new rules that simply replace the old ones they learned in high school. Instead of the Big Red Pen in the Sky, they now are being controlled by the Big

Reader in the Sky. They envision an inflexible reader who demands that certain things appear in certain places. It also suggests they hear this material as suggesting there is a single, single-minded Reader out there. That is a serious misreading of this approach.

It is all too easy to promulgate this perception; all you have to do is translate the traditional noting of "error" into reader expectation terms. If you give them the sense that they are "wrong" if they do not conform to reader expectations, the attention they give to the student-teacher power struggle will displace the energy they could have devoted to understanding better the writer-reader relationship.

It is important to repeat (many times during a term) that these pronouncements about writing are not rules; they are only descriptions and *predictions* of reader behavior. They do not appertain to all readers or to any single reader all of the time. There is no way to pin down even as little as a sentence to mean only one thing to all people at all times. The best we can do is get the odds on our side.

When students complain about our forcing them to write their sentence someone else's way, they forget that the sentence is no longer theirs once they release the paper. They are allowing the concern for expression of individuality to obliterate the recognition of the presence and the needs of others. We must remind them that in the world they are preparing to join, *self-expression* (except in the case of artists and a few others) matters primarily to the self; only *communication* puts the self in touch with others. The Reader Expectation Approach teaches communication.

We can also remind them that every reader expectation can be violated to good effect. There may be times when the appearance of aggressive self-concern will be just what others want to see. When that is the case, the reader expectation principles will still indicate how to get the job done: Just do the opposite of the advice that puts you in better touch with others.

By making this complaint, students are expressing a legitimate fear of losing power or control over their self-expression. It is crucial to point out to them that what this approach does best is to put yet more control and power into their hands. With it, they have a better chance of influencing or even controlling reader response; and few things are more powerful than being able to influence someone else's acts of interpretation.

An Example

A Reader Expectation response to an essay will look different and function differently from any of the more traditional pedagogical responses. Here is an example, performed on an essay sent to me from a professor who was at a loss how to respond to it. (Note: The subject matter of this essay does not matter to us. This student's writing habits will surface in any essay on any subject, at least to some extent.)

Changing the World Single-handedly

[Asterisks appear where the writer used footnotes]

An odyssey is an intellectual or spiritual quest. In Miguel de Cervantes, *The Adventures of Don Quixote de la Mancha*, Don Quixote embarks on an odyssey to live the life of a knight-errant.

This writer believes that Don Quixote's quest is not only to live the chivalric life, but also to individuate. 'Individuation is the complex process in which an individual develops into a fully differentiated, balanced and unified personality . . . that differs from other people.'* Carl Jung, a famous psycho-analyst, studied this process in which a person tries to achieve psychic wholeness. Jung believed that all people were born whole, and through numerous experiences, the pieces of the psyche (personality) were broken up. Jung believed that this innate process of achieving wholeness is the ultimate goal of all individuals, although it is rarely achieved.

Jung explained that if individuation were to be achieved, it would occur during the stage of life called middle. He believed that the people in this stage of life are "likely to find that youthful objectives have been met or given up and that old sources of a sense of meaning in life no longer serve."* It is not only possible to say that

Don Quixote was mad, butthat he was also frustrated with his life, he believed:

'... that it was highly expedient and necessary, not only for his own honour, but also the good of the public, that he should profess knight errantry, and ride through the world in arms, to seek adventures, and conform in all points to the practice of those itinerant heroes, whose expliots he had read.'*

Jung also said that 'these problems of middle life can become impetus to further psychological development. Some people find that they need a change in job of life-style. We see Don Quixote abandon his previous lifestyle when he embarks on his odyssey.

Another frustration that inflicts Don Quixote is his idea to correct all the wrongs of the world. The objective of his odyssey was to go out:

'... in the world , where there was an abundance of griev-ances to be redressed, wrongs to be rectified, errors amend-ed, abuses to be reformed, and doubts removed.'*

He believed he could single-handedly change the world. We see this in his first attempt to 'redress a wrong.' Don Quixote found the countryman beating one of his servants because the servant was neglectful of his masters sheep. Don Quixote tries to save the boy from the torture by telling the master, ' . . . I am Don Quixote de la Mancha, the redresser of wrongs and the scourge of injustice.'* Doing his noble duties, Don Quixote tells the master to pay the boy and release him or else he will be penalized. As soon as Don Quixote believes that he has done justice and marches along, the master continues to beat the boy. Meanwhile, Don Quixote is content with his first "success" of solving the problems of the world.

Don Quixote's odyssey is an attempt to correct the wrongs of the world. We have learned that it cannot be done single-handedly. Yet, we don't know if Don Quixote learns it cannot be done. If he does learn so, he will be closer to the psychic wholeness that Jung described.

Here is the essay again, with the traditional kinds of responses that are geared to detect error and thereby prevent a recurrence of those errors in the future.

Never use a one-sentence ¶ in formal prose!

Changing the World Single-handed~~ly~~

[Asterisks appear where the writer used footnotes]

An odyssey is an intellectual or spiritual (quest.) ^ww^ In Miguel de Cervantes', *The Adventures of Don Quixote de la Mancha*, Don Quixote embarks on an odyssey to live the life of a knight-errant.

Avoid metadiscourse

(This writer believes) that Don Quixote's quest is not only to live
— *We use double quotation marks in this country*

the chivalric life, but also to individuate. "Individuation is the com-

plex process in which an individual develops into a fully differenti-

ated, balanced and unified personality . . . that differs from other

people."* Carl Jung, a famous psycho-analyst, studied this process

in which a person tries to achieve psychic wholeness. Jung believed

that all people were born whole, and through numerous experi-

are

ences, the <u>pieces</u> of the psyche (personality) (were) broken up. Jung
If they are "whole," then there are no "pieces" that in turn can be "broken up."

believed that this innate process of achieving wholeness is the ulti-

mate goal of all individuals, although it is rarely achieved.

Jung explained that if individuation were to be achieved, it

would occur during the stage of life called middle. He believed that

the people in this stage of life are 'likely to find that youthful objec-

tives have been met or given up and that old sources of a sense of

meaning in life no longer serve.'* It is not only possible to say that

proofread

Don Quixote was mad, (but that) he was also frustrated with his

comma splice!

life, he believed:

Do not use quotation marks (even double ones) with indented quotes

( ). . . that it was highly expedient and necessary, not only

for his own honour, but also the good of the public, that he

footnote?

should profess knight errantry, and ride through the world

in arms, to seek adventures, and conform in all points

to the practice of those itinerant heroes, whose (expliots)

he had read.'*   *proofread!!*

Jung also said (thta 'these problems of middle life can become
where does this quote end?
impetus to further psychological development. Some people find

that they need a change in job of life-style. We see Don Quixote
proofread!!!
abandon his previous lifestyle when he embarks on his odyssey.

Another (frustration) that inflicts Don Quixote (is) his (idea)

to correct all the wrongs of the world. The objective of his   AWK

odyssey was to go out (:) *improper colon use*

" . . . in the world , where there was an abundance of griev-

ances to be redressed, wrongs to be rectified, errors amend-

ed, abuses to be reformed, and doubts removed.'*

not the right quote
He believed he could (single-handedly) change the world. We

see this in his first attempt to 'redress a wrong) Don Quixote found

(the countryman beating one of his servants because the servant was
Do we know who you mean?   *reference?*
neglectful of his master's sheep. Don Quixote tries to save the boy
ww
from the (torture) by telling the master, ' . . . I am Don Quixote de la

Mancha, the redresser of wrongs and the scourge of injustice.'* Do-

ing his noble duties, Don Quixote tells the master to pay the boy
reference?   *ww*
and release him or else (he) will be (penalized) As soon as Don

Quixote believes that he has done justice and marches along, the

master ~~continues~~ to beat the boy. Meanwhile, Don Quixote is con-
      begins again

tent with his first "success" of solving the problems of the world.

    Don Quixote's odyssey is an attempt to correct the wrongs of the

world. We have learned that it cannot be done single-handedly. Yet, we

~~don't~~ know if Don Quixote learns it cannot be done. If he does learn
           Never use contractions in formal prose

so, <u>he will be closer</u> to the psychic wholeness that Jung described.
    tense?

Pat—

—Your paper is on a good topic but is marred by carelessness. You must choose your words with more care.

<u>PROOFREAD!</u>

– See the following sections of the Handbook:

42b – comma splice   71c – colon

119a – apostrophe   214 – metadiscourse

315 – 318 Paragraph construction

— The assignment was a "3-4 page paper." You have given us only 2 1/2 pages.

— Weak development of thought in places.

An ambitious paper, but much in need of revision.

D

The student who receives such comments is often led to believe that had she not made all the noted mistakes, she would have written a good paper. Writing well, this experience tells her, is mostly a question of not butchering the technicalities, once you have your thought well in hand. She was careless, and perhaps a little ignorant; but the teacher is finicky and probably more demanding where these things are concerned than would be most people in the real world. The exercise remains unpleasant for all concerned. The student may or may not have learned something about prose conventions; she has probably not learned anything about how to evaluate her own thought processes. All of this is heightened in effect by the grade, which tells her that she, through the metaphor of this paper, is unsatisfactory. There seems to be an implication that the quality of her mechanics reflects the present (or potential) quality of her mind.

Note that no single comment seems unreasonable; it is the cumulative effect that does the damage. Most "corrective" comments tend to be negative in effect. Teachers rarely circle a word and comment "well spelled" or "good proofreading" or "correct tense." The emphasis in this kind of commenting remains on wrongdoing, on sin; as a result, the corrective measure seems to have more to do with behavior than with thought.

The teacher has functioned here only as critic, not as reader. In most other circumstances in life, the student will be writing for readers.

This process is usually no fun for the teacher, either.

Here is a different response to the same paper. This one avoids the overconcentration on error and uses its energy instead to engage with the substance of the piece. It treats the author as more of an individual and more of an adult. It takes her intellectual effort seriously.

Changing the World Single-handedly

[Asterisks appear where the writer used footnotes]

An odyssey is an intellectual or spiritual (quest.) In Miguel de

Cervantes, *The Adventures of Don Quixote de la Mancha*, Don Quixote
  These were not "quest" knights,
  but public servants.
embarks on an odyssey to live the life of a (knight-errant.)

Good
topic   This writer believes that Don Quixote's quest is not only to
sentence   a conscious choice
               on his part?
   live the chivalric life, but also to (individuate) 'Individuation is

the complex process in which an individual develops into a

fully differentiated, balanced and unified personality . . . that

differs from other people.'* Carl Jung, a famous psycho-analyst,

studied this process in which a person tries to achieve psychic

wholeness. Jung believed that all people were born whole, and

through numerous experiences, the (pieces) of the psyche (personali-

ty) were broken up. Jung believed that this innate process of

achieving wholeness is the ultimate goal of all individuals, al-

though it is rarely achieved. *If they are "whole", then there are no "pieces" that in turn can be "broken up."*

Jung explained that if individuation were to be achieved,

it would occur during the stage of life called middle. He *Was Don Q. middle-aged at the time of his adventures?*

give examples

believed that the people in this stage of life are 'likely to

find that youthful objectives have been met or given up and that

old sources of a sense of meaning in life no longer serve.'* It

is not only possible to say that Don Quixote was (mad,) but

that he was also (frustrated) with his life, he believed: *would one necessarily lead to the other? Are they mutually exclusive?*

'. . . that it was highly expedient and necessary, not

only for his own honour, but also the good of the public,

that he should profess knight errantry, and ride through

the world in arms, to seek adventures, and conform in all

points to the practice of those itinerant heroes, whose

exploits he had read.'*

Jung also said that 'these problems of middle life can become impetus to further psychological development. Some people find that they need a change in job of life-style. We see Don Quixote abandon his previous lifestyle when he embarks on his odyssey.

Can we speak of "life-style changes" in D Q's time? Did the socio-ecomonic structure of society allow for upward or downward mobility? Isn't there something of the fracturing of the "Great Chain of being"?

Another frustration that inflicts Don Quixote is his idea to correct all the wrongs of the world. The objective of his odyssey was to go out:

Is he "frustrated" by it? Isn't he rather uplifted by it? Isn't it part of this power as a timeless character the very fact that he didn't suffer from "frustration"?

' . . . in the world , where there was an abundance of grievances to be redressed, wrongs to be rectified, errors amended, abuses to be reformed, and doubts removed.'*

I thought you said he was frustrated.

He believed he could single-handedly change the world. We see this in his first attempt to 'redress a wrong.' Don Quixote found the countryman beating one of his servants because the servant was neglectful of his masters sheep. Don Quixote tries to save the boy

Technically, the beating does'nt qualify as "torture."

from the torture by telling the master, ' . . . I am Don Quixote de la Mancha, the redresser of wrongs and the scourge of injustice.'* Doing his noble duties, Don Quixote tells the master to pay the boy

Try not to use words that you don't completely control.

Good example. We need more like this!

and release him or else he will be penalized. As soon as Don

Actually, he rode. (Don't forget poor Rosinante!)

Quixote believes that he has done justice and marches along

the master continues to beat the boy. Meanwhile, Don Quixote is content with his first "success" of solving the problems of

the world. *What do you think? This would be a good opportunity to look at the end of the book.*

Don Quixote's odyssey is an attempt to correct the wrongs of the

world. We have learned that it cannot be done single-handedly. Yet, we

don't know if Don Quixote learns it cannot be done. If he does learn

Do we want him to learn this? Which is more important— his "psychic wholness," or ours?

so, he will be closer to the psychic wholeness that Jung described.

Pat—

You have given us many good points in this paper. The connection of Jung and Cervantes is very promising. However, you need to take us further. More development of thought, please.

Your writing is not as good as your thinking. Lots of careless errors here. Work on your transitions. (And proofread, please!)

Isn't individuation a quest in itself? Are you suggesting we are all Don Quixote, in some sense? Would you wish us to end up like him? or are you suggesting that his family and friends were right? Could Jung have helped the Don? You never quite put the two parts of your paper (Jung and DQ) together.

C−

I would argue that this response also fails to be of as much help to the student as its good cheer, energetic involvement, and the substantive effort of the teacher was planned to generate. It again points out some errors, though it does not restrict itself to the notation of violations of prose conventions; but most of the comments suggest things she might do were she to have a future opportunity to write this paper again. The questions in the last paragraph of the final comment suggest she would have received a higher grade than C– had she perceived these important issues that (presumably) any reasonable person considering the topic would have discovered.

Many of the comments are accurate, informative, and indicative of a careful, probing reading. The student can benefit from a sense of someone's having paid attention to her efforts. That can be a great benefit indeed; but it will still leave her at a loss to discover how she might have done better by herself -- or how she can do better when she writes other essays in the future.

The grade is probably distressing to her -- unless it arrives in a context of many previous D's and F's. It colors all the comments; through it they become (however well intended) condemnatory and condescending. A grade of B+ in its place would make the same comments relatively superfluous; they would be reduced to specifying how the paper fell only a bit short of being a first-rate response to the assignment.

I would argue that this paper is not yet ready for a grade.

Here is the paper one more time, responded to from the perspective of Reader Expectations.

Changing the World Single-handedly

[Asterisks appear where the writer used footnotes]

contract?

An odyssey is an intellectual or spiritual quest. In Miguel de Cervantes, *The Adventures of Don Quixote de la Mancha*, Don Quixote embarks on an odyssey to live the life of a knight-errant.

This *writer* believes that Don Quixote's quest is not only to live

whose story?

the chivalric life, but also to individuate. Individuation is the complex process in which an individual develops into a fully differentiated, balanced and unified personality . . . that differs from other people.'* Carl Jung a famous psycho-analyst, studied this process in which a person tries to achieve psychic wholeness. Jung believed that all people were born whole, and through numerous experiences, the pieces of the psyche (personality) were broken up. Jung believed that this innate process of achieving wholeness is the ultimate goal of all individuals, although it is rarely achieved.

Jung explained that if individuation were to be achieved, it would occur during the stage of life called middle. He believed that the people in this stage of life are 'likely to find that youthful objectives have been met or given up and that old sources of a sense of meaning in life no longer serve.'* It is not only possible to say that Don Quixote was mad, but that he was also frustrated with his life, he believed:

Issue? Point?

Stress positions?

' . . . that it was highly expedient and necessary, not only for his own honour, but also the good of the public, that he should profess knight errantry, and ride through the world in arms, to seek adventures, and conform in all points to the practice of those itinerant heroes, whose exploits he had read.'*

Circle all your verbs to this point in the paper. What do you find?

Jung also said that 'these problems of middle life can become impetus to further psychological development. Some people find that they need a change in job of life-style. We see Don Quixote abandon his previous lifestyle when he embarks on his odyssey.

Another frustration that inflicts Don Quixote is his idea to correct all the wrongs of the world. The objective of his odyssey was to go out:

' . . . in the world , where there was an abundance of grievances to be redressed, wrongs to be rectified, errors amended, abuses to be reformed, and doubts removed.'*

He believed he could single-handedly change the world. We

Issue?
Point?

see this in his first attempt to 'redress a wrong.' Don Quixote found the countryman beating one of his servants because the servant was neglectful of his masters sheep. Don Quixote tries to save the boy from the torture by telling the master, ' . . . I am Don Quixote de la Mancha, the redresser of wrongs and the scourge of injustice.'* Doing his noble duties, Don Quixote tells the master to pay the boy and release him or else he will be penalized. As soon as Don Quixote believes that he has done justice and marches along, the

Point? What was —
your issue?

master continues to beat the boy. Meanwhile, Don Quixote is content with his first 'success' of solving the problems of the world.

Don Quixote's odyssey is an attempt to correct the wrongs of the world. We have learned that it cannot be done single-handedly. Yet, we don't know if Don Quixote learns it cannot be done. If he does learn so, he will be closer to the psychic wholeness

that Jung described.   *Note your stress position occupants throughout.*
You have a pretty good sense of what you want
your reader to emphasize. Keep it up!

Pat—

For each paragraph in this essay, do the following:

- Figure out the issue;

- Decide what your point was or should have been;

- Decide whose story it is for each sentence; and

- Make sure your verbs articulate your actions.

Having done that, produce a contract statement for the whole.

Whose story is the paper as a whole? Jung's? DQ's? A combination of both?

If the latter, articulate that combination in a sentence -- or a paragraph -- or several paragraphs -- whatever it takes.

I look forward to the revision, because by your making all these structural changes, I (and perhaps you) will understand far better what you are trying to say about Don Quixote.

Note how much less ink is expended on the text itself. None of the details of grammar, presentation, or mistaken fact are noted; there is time enough for that when the more important matters of thought and communication have been addressed.

Note also that the commentator makes no pretense of knowing what the perfect paper would have been like -- or even what this paper was trying to say.

The final comments offer the student ways of reentering her thought process and discovering why she recorded these connectable but unconnected sentences. They do not tell her what was on her mind; they ask her. They point out rhetorical habits she might do well to change (and, in some cases, to nurture) for every paper she writes in the future.

There is no grade; the paper has not reached a stage of completion where a grade would be meaningful. There are no substantive comments; the student has not yet furnished enough interpretive clues for the teacher to make confident substantive judgments.

How do you know when a paper "has not reached a stage of completion where a grade would be meaningful"? You know you do not know what a piece of writing is intended to convey when major reader expectations are consistently violated. If the verbs are always weak by REA definitions (see page 321 above), then you cannot be sure that what you think is going on was what the writer intended. If there are rarely strong backward links at the beginnings of sentences, then you cannot be sure that they way you are linking the sentences together is what the writer intended. If there rarely seem to be important things in Stress positions -- or if there are constantly important-seeming things elsewhere than in Stress positions -- then you cannot be sure what you considered stressworthy was what the writer intended. And so on -- for every reader expectation we have explored. I guarantee you will often be surprised to find out that the writer intended something quite different by a sentence or paragraph than you managed to discover for yourself as the reader.

I offer no rewrite of the paper because the student never got a chance to rewrite it. Were I to distribute this essay to 100 people and request revisions, I have no doubt but that 100 very different essays would result. The original comes with too few clues for interpretation for a majority of readers to concur in a single interpretation. Only the author could tell us what she meant by it; the revision -- written with the reader, and the reader's expectations, in mind -- will give her that opportunity.

Endnotes

1. For the coffee stain metaphor, see Chapter 1, page 16.
2. C.P. Snow. "The Moral Un-Neutrality of Science," from Lee A. Jacobus, ed., *A World of Idea*, 2nd edition. New York: Bedford Books, 1985, p. 416.
3. This example was the invention of a Duke University graduate student teaching in the University Writing Program. So many instructors have used the example that I have not been able to ascertain exactly who wrote it.
4. There is no "clear," single, agreed-upon meaning for any of the de-written versions; rather, each of them offers little problem of interpretation to readers and therefore appears clear. Readers still may vary in their interpretations. They are unlikely, however, to have to struggle much in performing the interpretive act on these de-written examples.
5. For those who have had bad experience with group activities, you should find that de-writing does not suffer from the usual calamities when more than one cook is contemplating a stew. This is due, perhaps, to the "substance" preexisting the group activity. When a group

is trying to generate new prose together, there conceivably might be one "best" product at which they could aim; but when the text to be worked on preexists the group, there are any number of ways they can change it -- especially when their goal is not to perfect it but rather to generate a number of different variations, each with a different interpretive effect.

6. For a more detailed explanation of this exercise, see my article, "Theme and Variations: The Concept of Audience," in *Collective Wisdom: A Sourcebook of Lessons for Writing Teachers*, eds. Sondra J. Stang and Robert Wiltenburg. New York: Random House, 1988, pp. 95–7.

7. See Note 1, above.

8. See Mina Shaughnessy, *Errors and Expectations: A Guide for the Teacher of Basic Writing*. New York: Oxford University Press, 1977.

9. Shaughnessy, p. 12.

10. Gary Sloan. (1) "Relational Ambiguity Between Sentences," *College English* 39 (1978): 154–65. (2) "The Frequency of Transitional Markers in Discursive Prose," *College Composition and Communication* 46 (1984): 158–175.

11. One notable exception has been the work done at the high school level in Dayton, Ohio, by Terry Bell and Joe Dixon, who report many kinds of successes.

8

"I Knew That"

T *wo Typical Responses*

When I have finished the 15 hours of lecture it takes to present this reader expectation approach to a group of scientists or lawyers or academicians, and some of the participants stop on their way out the door to offer a few comments, I almost always hear one or both of these two observations:

1. "I *knew* all that; but nobody before has ever put it into words for me what it was that I knew."

2. (with some degree of frustration) "Why has no one ever told me this before?"

This I-knew-it-but-I-never-knew-it response is so common that it is worth some attention. What is it we all already "know"? What sense of the language is it that we all have in common? And why hasn't it all been put like this before Joseph Williams began the procedure with his 1981 publication of *Style: Ten Lessons in Clarity and Grace*?

The answer to the former question is straightforward. We "know" all this material beforehand because it describes what most of us do intuitively in the act of reading. The entire effort of this book has been to raise what we know intuitively as readers to the level of the conscious when we become writers. We become far more in charge of our own writing process by becoming far more aware of our natural tendencies as readers.

The second question is more puzzling. So many people have commented that this change, like so many fundamental changes in perspective, seems obvious once it is seen for the first time. Why should it have taken so long to harness the insight?

Well, of course, the possible beginnings happened long before now. Look carefully through the works of the great classical rhetoricians and you will find individual pronouncements here and there that fit quite neatly into a Reader Expectation approach. In Appendix C you will find a host of such quotations from Aristotle, Cicero, Quintilian, and Longinus (or pseudo-Longinus). You will find similar quotes from Hugh Blair (the eighteenth-century progenitor of the traditional approaches to composition),

Richard Whately (the premier nineteenth-century voice on the subject), and I.A. Richards (a persevering language and literature reformer of the twentieth century); all of these make their authors sound like they could have been partners in Clearlines, the Williams-Colomb-Kinahan-Gopen consulting firm that developed reader expectation principles in the 1980s.

But all of these shards of quotation are just that -- shards. None of these renowned rhetoricians synthesized these individual insights into a working model that could change the way language could be approached and manipulated.

However, a small but striking attempt was made in 1852, when Herbert Spencer published his well-anthologized essay, "The Philosophy of Style."[1]

H *erbert Spencer's "Philosophy of Style"*

The focus of Spencer's essay was described by the turn-of-the-century Harvard rhetorician Adams Sherman Hill as follows:

> Herbert Spencer maintains that such a principle is to be found in what he calls "economy of attention." He thinks that the sufficient reason for choosing the best words for the purpose in hand and arranging them in the best order is, that the reader's attention, being thus subjected to the least possible strain from the machinery of language, can be more closely given to the thought; that, therefore, the best writer is he who, other things being equal, draws least upon a reader's mental powers and sensibilities.

When I first read Hill's description -- years after beginning to work with reader expectations -- Spencer's "reader attention" sounded to me a great deal like the concept I have been calling "reader energy." I eagerly found the Spencer essay, began to read, and was astonished. The first three pages, had they been written 140 years later, could have been plagiarized from the first 30 minutes of the introduction to my professional workshop. Step after step, his logic and mine followed the same path. But eventually, his structure imploded, collapsing in on itself -- and for the best of Victorian reasons.

Before attending to those reasons, let me tell you a bit about this remarkable man, sub-editor of the *Economist*, friend of Huxley, Tyndall, George Eliot, and John Stuart Mill. He was, to say the least, a renaissance man in the Victorian era. He took a sub-editor position in 1848 at the age of 28 and immediately started writing. He began with "Social Statics" (1850), "Theory of Population" (1852), and "The Development Hypothesis" (1852). He was a supporter of extreme individualism. He then turned to the development of the doctrine of evolution as applied in sociology, producing in 1855 a book called *Principles of Psychology* -- a remarkable anticipation of the theory Darwin put forth four years later. Darwin provided the evidence to support Spencer's speculations. In that work Spencer also discusses the possibility of infant sexuality -- a half-century before Freud shocked the world with the concept. The overwork on this volume, however, caused a nervous collapse and left him a semi-invalid for the rest of his life, unable to work more than three hours a day. Despite this limitation, he turned out a set of writings not only remarkable in their quantity (especially given his physical limitations) but stunning in the breadth of their intellectual comprehension. In addition to his work on social theory, psychology, and literary style, he published an astonishing range of articles that included the following: "The Genesis of Science"; "The Art of Education"; "Manners and Fashion"; "Progress, Its Law and Cause"; "Representative Government, What Is It Good For?"; "Transcendental Physiology"; "State Tamperings with Money and Banks"; "Moral Education"; "The Nebular Hypothesis"; "The Laws of Organic Form"; "Morals of Trade"; "Social Organism"; "The Emotion and the Will"; "The Physiology of Laughter"; and "Parliamentary Reforms, Their Dangers and Safeguards." Having then discovered how all of his interests and theories fit together, he produced a prospectus for a "System of Philosophy" that was to comprise books on biology, psychology, sociology, and ethics. He carried through on each of these promises, sometimes with multiple volumes divided into subcategories. These were followed by more books on "Principles of Morality." He added writings on religion. And by the way, he was a music critic. The breadth is, as you can see, breathtaking; but it immediately raises questions about depth. While he was extraordinarily energetic about finishing the projects he started, he tended to move as quickly as possible to the next subject rather than plummeting deeper into the still waters he had stirred into motion. His 1852 article "The Philosophy of Style" can therefore be seen as a microcosm of his work as a whole.

He begins the essay with the establishment of the concept he calls "the reader's attention." He quotes Blair: "Long sentences fatigue the reader's attention." He quotes Lord Kaimes: "To give the utmost force to a period, it ought, if possible, to be closed with that word which makes the greatest figure." He urges us to avoid parentheses and to prefer Saxon words to those of Latin origin. He then suggests that "the truths thus dogmatically embodied . . . would be much more influential if reduced to something like scientific ordination." Notice the word "reduced": Therein lies the beginning of his downfall.

Then comes the statement that seems to lean forward to a development of a kind of reader expectation system. This is from the section he labels #3:

> On seeking for some clue to the law underlying these current maxims, we may see shadowed forth in many of them, the importance of economizing the reader's or hearer's attention. To so present ideas that they may be apprehended with the least possible mental effort, is the desideratum toward which most of the rules above quoted point. When we condemn writing that is wordy, or confused, or intricate -- when we praise this style as easy and blame that as

fatiguing, we consciously or unconsciously assume this desideratum as our standard of judgment. Regarding language as an apparatus of symbols for the conveyance of thought, we may say that, as in a mechanical apparatus, the more simple and the better arranged its parts, the greater will be the effect produced. In either case, whatever force is absorbed by the machine is deducted from the result. A reader or listener has at each moment but a limited amount of mental power available. To recognize and interpret the symbols presented to him requires part of this power; to arrange and combine the images suggested by them requires a further part; and only that part which remains can be used for realizing the thought conveyed. Hence the more time and attention it takes to receive and understand each sentence, the less time and attention can be given to the contained idea; and the less vividly will that idea be conceived.

The basics concept of "reader attention" (my "reader energy") is thus established. In his section #4, he expands on this eloquently. Referring to language as "the vehicle of thought," he suggests that

> . . . there seems reason to think that in all cases the friction and inertia of the vehicle deduct from its efficiency; and that in composition, the chief, if not the sole thing to be done, is to reduce this friction and inertia to the smallest possible amount. Let us then enquire whether economy of the recipient's attention is not the secret of effect, alike in the right choice and collocation of words, in the best arrangement of clauses in a sentence, in the proper order of its principal and subordinate propositions, . . . and even in the rhythmical sequence of syllables.

I could hardly agree with him more. But in section #5, he assumes an all-too-easy correspondence between words and thoughts; and his "secret effect" begins to generate rulishness. He launches into a defense of English words that have their roots in Anglo-Saxon -- and an equally strong attack on those whose roots are in the Romance tradition he identifies with Latin. The Saxon English, as he calls it, is the language of our childhood; it therefore breeds in us, he says, "strong associations." In section #6 he adds that the Saxon-based English vocabulary tends to produce much shorter words (fewer syllables) than its Latin-based counterpart. Since he insists that words (here he wanders into dangerous territory) have distinct and definitive meanings, and multiple words in English often mean the same thing, the brevity of the Saxon vocabulary will demand less reader attention than the extended length of its more tiring Latin counterparts. Although there are occasions that call for the more elevated Latin-based term (he admits), he strongly urges that

> in the immense majority of cases, each word serving but as a step to the idea embodied by the whole sentence, should, if possible, be a one-syllable or Saxon one. (Section #7)

The concept of "reader attention" thus starts to fail because of his limited vision of cognition. It is actually rare to impossible for two words in English to summon precisely the same cognitive response. He pairs "have" and "possess"; but the two are not entirely equivalent. He pairs "wish" with "desire," "think" with "reflect," "play" with "amusement." These are not exact equivalents -- and in some cases nothing near exact equivalents. These words, supported by a syntactic structure, become synthesized into a "thought." And now we have what begins to sound like a rule for "the immense majority of cases" -- that we should constantly avoid a large percentage of the words available in the English language.

When he extends this semantic principle to sentences, the roof caves in. He begins from a reasonable assumption:

> As in a narrative, the events should be stated in such sequence that the mind may not have to go backward and forward in order to rightly connect them; as in a group of sentences, the arrangement should be such, that each of them may be understood as it comes, without waiting for subsequent ones; so in every sentence, the sequence of words should be that which suggests the constituents of the thought in the order most convenient for the building up of that thought. (Section #11)

Having established this as a principle, he applies it to a specific example; and from that example he generates a rule that is clearly inapplicable, clearly not in touch with how professionals use the language. The crucial example is that of the "black horse" -- an example lifted a few decades later by Alexander Bain almost word for word, without any attribution to Spencer. "Ought we to say," Spencer asks in Section #12, "with the French -- *un cheval noir* ["a horse black"]; or to say as we do -- a black horse?" His argument proceeds as follows:

1. If we were to say "a horse black," the word "horse" would summon to the mind a picture of a generic horse.
2. For most of us, that horse would be brown, since most horses are brown.
3. Therefore, when the word "black" appears, we would suffer an interruption of the thought process. We would have to go backward to re-color our mental horse, thus wasting time and effort. Our "reader's attention" would have been diverted from its forward movement.
4. But if we say "a black horse," the word "black" summons up not a definite object but rather an indefinite sense of color.
5. Therefore, when "horse" arrives, the blackness simply congeals around the horse, and no time, effort, or attention has been wasted.

(He does not take this opportunity to say, "And *that* is yet one more proof that the English are superior to the French" -- but we can sense he was tempted.)

Then comes the trouble. In Section #14, he argues that "What is here said respecting the succession of the adjective and substantive is obviously applicable, by change of terms, to the adverb and the verb." But the very sentence that pronounces this principle-congealing-into-rule demonstrates the fallacy of the rule. "What is here said" might be preferable to "what is said here" at times; but the mind balks at the notion of our *never* being able to say "what is said here" just because the adverb would (apparently inappropriately) follows the verb.

In Section #15, he extends this to the larger divisions of a sentence, increasing the vehemence of his pronouncement by claiming that "the same principle holds good, but that the advantage of respecting it becomes marked." "Marked" sounds ever closer to making the "principle" into a "rule." We hear an argument for why "Great is Diana of the Ephesians" is a superior in arrangement to "Diana of the Ephesians is great." (Since the greatness precedes Diana in the first arrangement, Diana is already great when she arrives.) But we hear no suggestion that the *context* of the sentence might at times make the latter arrangement the superior one.

This is expanded section by section. In Section #16 it is applied to verb/subject: "Then *burst* his mighty heart" is considered superior to "Then his mighty heart burst" -- in *all* cases. Once again, context is not to be considered. In Sections #17–19, it is applied to all predicates that have qualifications:

> Observe in the following example the effect of putting [the conditions under which any fact is predicated] last: -- "How immense would be the stimulus to progress, were the honour now given to wealth and title given exclusively to high achievements and intrinsic worth?" And then observe the superior effect of putting them first: -- "Were the honour now given to wealth and title given exclusively to high achievements and intrinsic worth, how immense would be the stimulus to progress."

Most caring and careful readers could easily summon a context in which the former "inferior" arrangement would work far better than its supposedly "superior" counterpart.

The "rule" finally arrives in Section #22:

> Regard for the economy of the reader's attention, which, as we find, determines the best order for the subject, copula, predicate and their compliments, *dictates* that the subordinate proposition shall precede the principal one when the sentence includes two. (emphasis supplied)

The dictator tells us, it now becomes clear, that whenever we have (for example) a "because" clause and a "main" clause, the "because" clause must *always* come first. This choice is not to be controlled by context but rather by "principle." But any of us could easily supply examples of well-written sentences that employ the opposite order. His building crumbles.

He does try to back away from the totalitarian stance -- but only in a classist or intellectually snobbish way today that would offend our sensibilities. If you are a skilled enough writer, he tells us toward the end, you can be trusted to use some Latin-based vocabulary. If you are writing for a highly educated audience, you can, on occasion, switch around the order of words or clauses for special effect, since that audience can be trusted to process the prose without incident. But throughout there is the assumption that any sentence, in isolation, can be "rightly" interpreted; it only stands for one thing. Nowhere does Spencer take into account the controlling and transforming force of context or the multiplicity of meanings possible of individual words. As a result, his rules are self-evidently not in touch with the realities of language.

Spencer was so clearly "wrong" that, despite the enduring presence of the article, no one was interested in picking up his theoretical ball and running with it. Rules simply have not and will not work as part of the pedagogical process that deals with the creation of sophisticated prose. "The Philosophy of Style" was a dead end; and with it died the concept of reader attention.

Where Are the Linguists When We Need Them?

Spencer, with all his intuition, failed to carry through on his good hunch -- that the reader's energy must be conserved and directed to best effect. Too many rules, too quickly summoned, tied him in knots; by the end of the article, they cut off his circulation. Of course, he was not intending to publish a linguistic thesis, nor even a rhetorical one. He meaningfully titled his article "The *Philosophy* of Style," suggesting (perhaps a touch grandiosely) an "approach" to style rather than an anatomy of it. These are things that can be seen from a distant prospect.

The people who get the closest to language tend to be the linguists. As a graduate student, faced with thinking about teaching the language for the first time, I asked one of my colleagues who was advanced in his linguistic studies what help linguistics might offer to the novitiate composition teacher. I remember his answer verbatim: "No help at all. We're not interested in *doing* anything about the language. We just describe it." It seemed an extreme answer at the time; but over the years I have found it more accurate than I expected or could have wished.

Back then I was expecting a great breakthrough to develop from the most exciting and well-publicized piece of linguistic theory of the recent past -- Noam Chomsky's early work on transformational grammar.[2] He led us, through his tree diagrams, to the "deep structure" of sentences. The sentences themselves were surface manifestations of language; but they were based on underlying concepts that could be discerned by finding the essence of the interactions between the major noun phrases and verb phrases. The whole procedure was a distillation of essence, not unlike the same efforts done a few decades earlier for music by Heinrich Schenker. Without offering an opinion on the quality of Chomsky's early work as linguistics, it is safe to say that his work was of no significant use to rhetoricians and teachers of composition. It suggested that any number of surface manifestations might have the same deep structure and therefore essentially "mean" the same thing on the surface level as well. Modern rhetoricians travel in exactly the opposite direction. We are intensely concerned with the ways in which *any* change in the surface of a sentence might change the ways in which that sentence is perceived by readers.

This was not always the case: The complex eighteenth-century Scottish philosopher George Campbell was one of the founders of the influential Philosophical Society of Aberdeen, which included Thomas Reid, John Stewart, and James Beattie, among others. Together they produced the "Common Sense Philosophy" -- the belief that we have a "sense" "in common" about the important things in life. These works were the major influence on Hugh Blair as he wrote his *Lectures on Rhetoric and Belle Lettres* (1873), which established the principles that dominated the teaching of English composition well into the 1970s. Here is a disastrous one-liner from Campbell:

> When two sentences differ only in arrangement, the sense, the words, and the construction are the same.
>
> (*The Philosophy of Rhetoric*, Bk. III, Ch. III, Sec. II, p. 354)

The words may remain the same; but how can the construction not demonstrate surface changes -- no matter what the deep structure similarities may be? "The sense" always changes, even if only slightly, with the removal or displacement of a single syllable.

It is not until the work of Ferdinand de Saussure (1857–1913) and Charles S. Peirce (1839–1914) that we can see the beginnings of a view of the language that will take into account the complexities of multiple interrelationships between words within a single sentence. Peirce argued that every sign (Saussure's "signifier") must be interpreted by another sign (Peirce's "interpretant"), thus making signification an endless network linking signs to each other.

> All dynamical action, or action of brute force, physical or psychical, either takes place between two subjects . . . or at any rate is a resultant of such actions between pairs. But by "semiosis" I mean, on the contrary, an action, or influence, which is, or involves, a co-operation of *three* subjects, such as sign, its object, and its interpretant, this tri-relative influence not being in any way resolvable into actions between pairs.[3]

This "three-ness" became the complexifying leitmotif of linguistic work throughout the first half of the twentieth century. For Peirce it was

sign // interpretant // object.

For I.A. Richards and C.K. Ogden it was

Symbol // thought // referent.

Roman Jakobson triangulated reader / writer / text, finding "thought" floating around somewhere in the innards of the triangle. The quality of "three" made sense. "Two-ness" is digital -- on/off, up/down, right/wrong. The dyad is ever so simplified, compared to the triad. In the first-year law school course in contracts, the cases that presented the greatest challenges were those involving third-party beneficiaries. (X and Y agree to something for the benefit of Z. Something goes wrong. What can Z do about it?) Compared to two, three turns out to be almost infinitely more complicated -- and therefore suitably subtle and rationally reflective of life. The best-detailed investigation I know of this phenomenon of the dyad/triad is that by the sociologist Georg Simmel. (See "The Isolated Individual and the Dyad" and "The Triad" in *The Sociology of Georg Simmel*, translated and edited by Kurt H. Wolff. New York: Free Press, 1950.)

None of this linguistic work -- however stunning it might have proven -- has been of much help to the composition teacher. We have tried; we have given conference sessions on the topics; we have written articles and even books; but we have not been able to harness linguistic energy for pedagogic production. Why not? Because linguists are indeed primarily interested in describing and explaining the phenomena of language; and that is a full-time job.

In the 1930s and 1940s, a whole school of linguists in Czechoslovakia produced a whirlwind of intellectual activity. "The Prague School," as they were known, were just as focused on linguistic description as any other linguists; but the nature of their interesting work made it more adaptable for practical application, should there come along a linguist/humanist/ rhetorician/pedagogue talented enough to perceive the potential and to actualize the transformation. That person was Joseph Williams.

The Prague School of Linguistics and Functional Sentence Perspective

The godfather or pioneer of this school of thought was Henri Weil, whose monograph *De l'ordre des mots dans les langues anciennes comparees aux langues modernes* was published as early as 1844 and reprinted in 1869 and 1879. It was translated into English in 1878 and inspired Vilem Mathesius (1882–1945), who was the prime mover of what became called Functional Sentence Perspective (FSP). Weil spoke of "the movement of the mind." He distinguished between the "movement of ideas" (in inflected languages) and "syntactical movement" (in modern languages that depend on word order). The "movement of the mind" itself is movement from the initial notion to the goal of discourse. In modern languages, he pointed out, we usually start the sentence with the grammatical subject and proceed toward the goal of the sentence; but sometimes we can invert the order, putting the goal first. He calls that the "pathetic order," because it so invokes your emotive notice.

-- I will not do that.

-- That I will not do.

The better part of a century later, with Weil's work in mind, Mathesius studied the Czech language and found a dominance of word order and linguistic progression from a "theme" through a "transition" to a "rheme." This "theme-transition-rheme" motion he characterized as "non-emotive" and "unmarked." The reverse order, which was not uncommon in Czech but not the dominant order, he called "emotive" and "marked." This concern with word order and its control over meaning is referred to as Functional Sentence Perspective.

To oversimplify a bit, the "theme" is where you are coming from in a sentence and the "rheme" is where you are going. The "transition" helps you get there; but it belongs more to the rheme than to the theme. This is an ordering to be distinguished from the grammatical ordering of a sentence, which has to do with the functions of subject, verb, and object. Both of these orderings are yet again distinct from a third consideration of order having to do with who is doing what to whom -- the agent, the action, and the goal.

Mathesius distinguished between "the sentence as a pattern belonging to the language system and the sentence as part of the context (a component of the discourse)." Eventually, three relatively distinct levels were identified:

Semantic Sentence Pattern (SSP)

Grammatical Sentence Pattern (GSP)

Utterance of FSP (or) Communicative Sentence Pattern (CSP)

Applying these three perspectives to the sentence "John wrote a poem," the following schema evolves:

	John	wrote	a poem.
SSP	agent	action	goal
GSP	subject	verb	object
CSP	theme	transition	rheme

Add to this the concept of communicative dynamism, (developed by Jan Firbas), abbreviated as CD, and defined as "the extent to which the element contributes toward the development of the communication." A word or phrase therefore has a certain "amount" of CD; and it is the relative levels of CD that control the growth, development, and motion of the idea the sentence is trying to communicate. The description of this dynamic is the essence of FSP.

Mathesius did not find nearly as much FSP control in English as he did in Czech. In English, he thought FSP of secondary importance compared to GSP. "English differs from Czech in being so little susceptible to the requirements of FSP as to frequently disregard them altogether."

Here is a good example of how this kind of description unfolds.

In Mathesius's terms the non-emotive structure "A girl came into the room" would have to be looked upon as insusceptible to FSP, because in its most natural use it does not display the theme-transition-rheme, but the rheme-transition-theme sequence. The semantic structure of the example is the following. The verb "came" expresses the notion of appearance on the scene, the adverbial "into the room" expresses the scene, and the subject "a girl" a newcomer appearing to it. Under the circumstances, i.e. in the case of the most natural use of the structure, the adverbial element carries known information (derivable, recoverable from the preceding context) and is in consequence contextually dependent. The offered semantic and contextual interpretation equally applies to the less frequent, but not impossible order "Into the room came a girl," which would most naturally be interpreted as theme-transition-rheme sequence. In either case, being contextually dependent, the adverbial element contributes least to the further development of the communication. Of the two remaining elements, the contextually independent subject announcing the person appearing on the scene is communicatively more important than the contextually independent verb merely expressing the notion of appearance. The contextual independence of the subject is sufficiently signaled by the non-generic indefinite article. In terms of communicative dynamism (=CD), the subject carries the highest, the adverbial element the lowest degree of CD, the verb ranking between them. By a degree of CD carried by a linguistic element, I mean the extent to which the element contributes towards the development of the communication.

I realize it may be difficult to slip comfortably into such language and such a perspective if you are not used to reading the work of linguists. Let me try to put it in slightly simpler terms.

These three orderings, SSP, GSP, and CSP (the latter being the heart and soul of FSP), are all functioning *simultaneously* in a sentence. The closest parallel I can imagine is the way music functions. As you listen to a few measures of a song, you are dealing with a number of kinds of ordering simultaneously: (1) You are noticing a *melody*, which is "going somewhere" or "reaching for" some kind of resolution; (2) you are being affected by the activity of *rhythm*, either by its regularity or its quirkiness, its sense of fulfillment or its shock of violation; (3) you are being directed by the progression of *harmony* (or the lack thereof), as the conventions of tonality direct your attention forward and backward, whether you are consciously aware of it or not. There are yet other influences on your experience -- timbre, coloration, volume, dynamics, accentuation; but the gang of three -- melody, rhythm, and harmony -- are suspiciously similar enough to SSP, GSP, and CSP to suffice for our present needs. If you are listening to a song you know well, you can deal with all three musical orderings with remarkably little effort. You do not feel that you are juggling three separate auditory balls in the air. They just somehow all go together.

The same is true when you undertake the task of reading the sentence "John wrote a poem," or "A girl came into the room." You follow the SSP without a problem:

J<u>ohn</u> (the agent)   w<u>rote</u> (his action)   <u>a poem</u> (the goal of the agent's action)

<u>A girl</u> (the agent)   <u>came</u> (her action)   <u>into the room</u> (the goal of the agent's action)

The GSP is a completely different kind of consideration -- even though it progresses in the same order. You can *contemplate* the difference between SSP and GSP; but you never have to *think* about that difference.

<u>John</u> (subject)   <u>wrote</u> (verb)   <u>a poem</u> (object/complement)

<u>A girl</u> (subject)   <u>came</u> (verb)   <u>into the room</u> (complement)

You also have no trouble being influenced by the CSP -- even though its ordering is different from one sentence to the other. This is based on the relative CD of each subunit -- the communicative dynamism, the relative importance that derives in great part from the oldness/newness of the information. "Theme" is what we already know; "rheme" is that which the sentence was created to deliver to us as a new arrival.

<u>John</u> (theme)   <u>wrote</u> (transition)   <u>a poem</u> (rheme)

<u>A girl</u> (rheme)   <u>came</u> (transition)   <u>into the room</u> (theme)

In CD terms:

<u>John</u> (least CD: We already know about him)

<u>wrote</u> (more CD: This explains what John, whom we already know, is doing)

<u>a poem</u> (most CD: This is the new arrival -- the result of John's activity)

<u>A girl</u> (most CD: She is the newcomer in this sentence)

<u>came</u> (less CD: This is how the newcomer got here)

<u>Into the room</u> (least CD: This pre-existed her arrival and her arriving)

All of this is happening all at once as we do the reading act. The interesting aspect of FSP (or CSP) is the way in which it may or may not coincide with either or both of the other two orderings. It can function like syncopation or fugal development or counterpoint in music. It produces the quality that is the label of its most significant component -- communicative dynamism. The basic distribution of CD is what Weil (back in 1844) was calling "the movement of the mind." It is the interplay between SSP and GSP on the one hand and CSP on the other that gives the *sentence* its *functional perspective*.

You can hear the beginning of Reader Expectation theory here, can you not? Even the terms are the same: Agent-Action-Goal has a relationship (not always a directly parallel relationship) to Subject-Verb-Complement.

And there is more. Mathesius tells us that there are two ways of talking about the term *theme*: (1) It expresses something that is spoken about; or (2) it expresses something that is already known or obvious, given the situation. The chief chronicler of the Prague School, Jan Firbas, (echoing František Daneš), redefines *theme* as "an element or elements carrying the lowest degree(s) of CD within a sentence."[4] Thus, in the sentence, "An unknown man has asked him the way to the railway station," both "man" and "him" would be "thematic"; but the latter would be yet more so, because (says Firbas), its CD is lower. Another member of the Prague School, E. Beneš, makes a distinction between *theme* and *basis*. *Theme* is the unit with the lowest CD; *Basis* is the phenomenon that "as the opening element of the sentence links up the utterance with the context and the situation, selecting from several possible connections one that becomes the starting point, from which the entire further utterance unfolds and in regard to which it is orientated."

All of this is reflected in the Reader Expectation Approach by the two sometimes-separate, sometimes-the-same functions located in the Topic position: (1) The prospective answer to the question "Whose story is this going to be?"; and (2) the perspective backward link to the previous sentence. Mathesius notes this duality: His "something that is spoken about" is the Reader Expectation's "whose story?" element; and his "something that is already known" is the expected "backward link." Benes decided to make two different terms to apply to the two different functions: *Theme*, for him, is our "whose story?" and his *Basis* is our "backward link." But why does Firbas not fit neatly into this distinction? And why do all these linguists not package their perceptions into a methodology for composition? Before trying to answer this, let me follow the CD trail a bit further.

According to Firbas, the linear arrangement of a sentence can effect the relative values of CD within it. Here are his examples. The first concerns a "contextually independent indirect object" ("a boy") and a "contextually independent direct object" ("an apple"). Firbas:

"He gave a boy an apple."

"He gave an apple to the boy."

> Of the two objects, the one occurring later evidently carries a higher degree of CD. Similarly, a contextually independent infinitive of purpose will carry a lower degree of CD when occurring initially than when occurring finally:

"In order to meet his friend, he went to Prague."

"He went to Prague in order to meet his friend."

> In all these cases it is the linear arrangement that decides the degree of CD.

Notice his word "evidently." The later-arriving piece of information "evidently" possesses a "higher degree of CD." Firbas is on the brink of discovering what we have been calling the "Stress position." Australian linguist M.A.K. Halliday stepped over that threshold; and yet the concept did not find its way into the composition world until 1980, when Joseph Williams first published <u>*Style: Ten Lessons in Clarity and Grace*</u>. Why the wait? I offer two answers, separate but intricately connected:

-- The linguists were dealing with language as a closed and perfectly balanced system, even though they knew it was not. They therefore

(a) dealt with sentences in isolation, and (b) assumed that such sentences had a solitary, specific, and knowable "meanings."

-- They were linguists, not rhetoricians. They acted like linguists, and not like rhetoricians.

Firbas, writing in 1963, expressed extreme frustration at the possibilities of a given sentence having more than one meaning.

> In my opinion, insusceptibility to FSP could be spoken of when in the very act of communication, written or spoken, a structure permits of more than one interpretation of its functional perspective. Such cases of malfunctionality or multivalence will certainly be far more frequent in written than in spoken language.

He did not realize that *every* sentence is "such a case." Interpretation depends on context; and the context of a single sentence extends infinitely -- out to the sentences that surround it, to the rest of the document, and to all other documents like it or related to it, and to each and every reader who reads it. Such "multivalence" is the nature and essence of a sentence's functionality; and as such, it becomes definitionally impossible to consider it "malfunctionality." Firbas concludes his paragraph with a heavy sigh of disappointment:

> On the other hand, as J. Vachek and other scholars of the Prague group have pointed out, language is not a closed and perfectly balanced system.

That is the point of view of a linguist, striving to get language to stay still -- to lie there on the page long enough and quietly enough to be inspected and examined and categorized and solved. Wonderful work has been done as part of that general linguistic endeavor. Fascinating work has been done by the specific endeavors of the Prague group. But as long as a single sentence lays on the page for isolated inspection, the results will be of little help to a teacher of composition or a struggling writer. Notice how their examples tend to feature highly simplistic sentences. John wrote his poem and the girl entered the room; but what happens to the SSP and the GSP and the CSP and the FSP and -- most especially -- the CD when two clauses have to function in the same sentence? What if the girl entered the room *as* John was writing his poem? Or *because* he was writing his poem? Or *despite the fact* that he was writing his poem? How much CD would everybody and everything get assigned to it in each of those cases?

And what happens when the contextualizing influence of an immediately preceding sentence is taken into account?

> Shattered by the news that both of his parents had been killed in the plane crash, John needed to focus his attention on something, on any activity, just to maintain his sanity. John wrote a poem.

versus

> Each of the students in the class had to choose whether to write a poem or a book report. John wrote a poem.

In one case, John is old information; in the other, he may be new. In one case, the poem is new information; in the other, it is old. We can even vary the CD of the verb:

> What a difference there was in the efforts Mary and John made to fulfill their English assignments last week. Mary read a poem. John wrote a poem.

Context controls meaning. A sentence devoid of its context is limited in its use as an example of what a writer should do or what a rhetorician could do. FSP is language-centered; Reader Expectation rhetoric is reader-centered. It is precisely the impossibility of assigning a given degree of CD in a sentence considered only by itself that makes language and the struggle with language so dynamic.

To make the jump from the linguistically descriptive to the rhetorically pedagogical, all that was needed was to ask (and try to answer) the question, *"How* does a given piece of information obtain its CD?" ("Evidently" will not suffice as an answer.) To a great extent, this book is an attempt formulate an answer to that question that is complex enough to reflect the realities of communication and simple enough to provide a set of tools that can help writers get better control of their prose, their thinking process, and their readers' interpretive process.

The complexity of the answer is reflected in the large number of questions that stemmed from the central assumption, presented all the way back in Chapter 1:

> Readers of contemporary American English prose have relatively fixed expectations of where in the structure of a unit of discourse they should look for the arrival of certain kinds of substance.

Here again are the major (reader's) questions for which the Clearlines group suggested locational or structural answers:

Whose story is this sentence?

What is going on in this sentence?

How does this sentence link backward to the one that preceded it?

What is the information in this sentence to which I should give the most emphasis?

What is the information in this sentence to which I should give little emphasis?

What is likely to come in the next sentence?

What is the issue of this paragraph?

How does this paragraph connect to the one that preceded it?

What is the point of this paragraph?

What is the next paragraph likely to do?

Add to those concerns the multiple ways of emphasizing information -- (location in the Stress position, underlining, italicizing, capitalizing, bolding, the use of semantic intensifiers like *especially*) -- and the ways of deemphasizing information -- (location in the middle of a sentence, location between a subject and its verb, the use of parentheses, the use of semantic undercutters) -- and the special effects of parallel structure for indicating parallel meaning, repetition for indicating emphasis, anaphora for creating auxesis, epistrophe for enhancing eventual closure -- and then throw in the weighing and balancing techniques -- (independent clauses weigh more than dependent clauses, which weigh more than phrases; final clauses weigh more than opening clauses; long units weigh more than short units, except when the pithiness of brevity provides energy) -- and, and, and. . . . (The discussions of all these are scattered throughout Chapters 1 through 6.)

There is *so much* to consider when we try to establish the rhetorical "meaning" for even a single sentence. Connect that sentence to the one in front of it, and the whole interpretive effort changes. Connect it to the one that follows it, and the effort becomes yet more complex, even though the context becomes more defined. And all of this completely disregards the enormous interpretive weight that must be assigned to semantics. Word choice, I have argued, is only 15% of the ball game; but it is a distinctly important 15%. Think just for a moment about the factors that influence the affect a given word might have: number of syllables; etymology and linguistic provenance; sound; connection to the sound, size, and other characteristics of the other words in the sentence and nearby; social status; evocative connections; and, and, and. . . . "Think," "ponder," and "cogitate" are *not* equivalent signifiers.

Although it has taken hundreds of pages to discuss all these influences and elements and structural phenomena, the wisdom offered by this Reader Expectation approach is relatively simple and straightforward:

1. Learn where readers tend to look to find certain kinds of things.

2. Most of the time, put those things in those places.

3. As a result of that, (a) readers will be more likely to label things the way you want them labeled; and (b) readers will use a minimal amount of energy to find things, leaving them more energy to contemplate them, once found.

4. Violate any reader expectation when the violation has a good purpose.

So if the hardworking, highly intelligent, and linguistically imaginative members of the Prague School never for a moment conceived of their efforts being translated into the beginning of a composition pedagogy, how did this translation happen? It happened because we were fortunate enough to have Joseph Williams perceive the possibilities for us. Joe is a first-rate linguist who happens to teach writing. His great contribution: He is the first person to be able to translate linguistic perception into pedagogical methodology for composition, in part because of his extraordinary knowledge and vision and in part because he was situated in and between both intellectual worlds. I was fortunate enough to be one of his partners in the first stages of that enterprise.

Firbas ended his article with a hopeful statement:

> I believe I am right in saying that the problems raised by H. Weil more than a hundred years ago have opened vistas of research that might bring us a little nearer to a better *understanding* of language as a tool of communication. (emphasis supplied)

He wanted to *understand* language; Joe Williams and Greg Colomb and I have tried to perfect a better way of *using* language as a tool of communication. Firbas was close to seeing the possibilities. Here is his penultimate paragraph:

> In the light of what has just been put forth, the basic distribution of CD seems to be a more suitable starting point for generating word orders than a primary grammatical sentence pattern.

Yes: And that is why "just" teaching grammar has never taught anyone how to write well.

Yes: And the key is *word orders* -- not *word order*. Structural location sends readers 85% of their clues for interpretation.

Yes: And "the basic distribution of CD" in English is directly dependent on *where* in the sentence a particular piece of information appears. That in turn is dependent on what has preceded that sentence and what follows it.

Linguist Michael Halliday, so much of whose far-reaching work is consonant with this Reader Expectations approach, has put it in yet a different way: "FSP can be defined . . . as the 'textual' component in the grammar of a sentence. . . . The grammatical system itself has a functional basis."[5] Halliday's work is always stimulating and provocative. It should be better known in the composition world.

For those interested in writing the language rather than in just viewing it, the primary concern is not what a sentence does, but rather what a writer can do with it.[6]

T hrusts and Parries

Over the years, a number of questions/complaints have been raised by a number of thoughtful people encountering this Reader Expectation approach for the first time. Since these concerns are so recurrent, it may be worthwhile to end this volume with some of the possible responses to those concerns. These are the four that seem to me the most significant:

A. Teaching everyone this approach to writing will rob students of their individuality and tend to make them all sound the same on paper.

B. This approach is essentially Formalist and presumes there is one model only of the Reader.

C. This approach, like all others, is doomed to failure because writing cannot be taught.

D. The successful teaching of this approach is (as Plato argued) immoral, because it would empower unprincipled writers to hide from responsibility, to obfuscate the truth, and to make the worse argument appear the better.

I will respond to them in that order.

A. <u>Teaching everyone this approach to writing will rob students of their individuality and tend to make them all sound the same on paper.</u>

This concern is discussed in Chapter 7. There are two main reasons we could not make self-imaged clones of our students, even if we wanted to do so:

(1) Any five people, each with his and her own individual sensibilities and intellectual predilections, will take the same material and make of it five significantly different pieces of prose. Instructing someone to put *what they think is important* in a Stress position is not at all the same thing as instructing them what they should consider as important. One could argue that a writer's individuality becomes all the more evident when his or her intentions are made as clear as possible.

(2) Every Reader Expectation can be violated to good effect. Our best stylists often turn out to be our most skillful violators. However, in order to violate effectively, one must fulfill expectations most of the time -- so the violation appears as an unusual occurrence. Constant violation produces mental turbulence. By making this complaint, students are expressing a legitimate fear of losing power or control over their self-expression. It is crucial to point out to them that what this approach does best is to put yet more control and power into their hands.

B. <u>This approach is essentially Formalist and presumes there is one model only of the Reader.</u>

This concern is easy to understand. All the statements concerning the expectations of readers can sound all-encompassing. In the hands of teachers new to the method, they can actually become so -- if the teacher disregards the ringing and repetitive caution against definitive pronouncements that has accompanied almost every pronouncement in this volume: No rules. No rules. Any Reader Expectation that rigidifies into a rule is sure to crumble soon thereafter. (Cf. Herbert Spencer.) It is important to be hypervigilant about this. The moment you say, "Readers naturally assign extra emphasis to anything that appears in a Stress position," you are in trouble. You would do far better to say, "Most readers tend to assign extra emphasis to anything that appears in a Stress position." "Most readers, most of the time . . .": That is the actuality.

To add to that, readers are distracted from their usual behavior at any given moment by whatever force is capable of distracting them. For example, if excessively burdened by having to deal with three badly constructed dependent clauses before the main clause arrives, the poor reader may well be so out of breath and weakened by the time the Stress position is reached that no reader energy remains with which to invest the final piece of information with stressworthy emphasis. Each Reader Expectation is clearly enough delineable when considered in isolation; but when a number of them collide in a single sentence, it can become difficult to predict what a reader -- never mind that nonexistent "Reader" -- would do with it all.

I have not presumed anywhere in this volume that the mind works in any particular way. I have presumed, however, that we can and have trained ourselves as a society to respond consistently to certain kinds of structural stimuli. Those responses vary from place to place, from dialect to dialect, and over time; but they change slowly and noticeably. It is worthwhile to note those Expectations under which we as a reading society tend to function here and now.

C.   <u>This approach, like all others, is doomed to failure because writing cannot be taught.</u>

This is a far more pervasive and serious problem than those above. Several years ago, in my capacity as director of writing programs at Duke, I served on a committee to hire an assistant director. We interviewed 13 semifinalist candidates, all of whom had or were just about to have a Ph.D. in Rhetoric and Composition Studies. We put the same question to each of them: "Assume that I am one of your students and that I have just produced a long paragraph in which I have displayed every major flaw that plagues my writing style. How could you use that paragraph to show me *not* how I could have written that paragraph better but rather how I could write better *the next time* I go to write something else?" Four of the candidates offered fuzzy, heuristic-based answers like "I would show you how to make an outline" or "I would show you how to use free-thinking techniques." The other nine said, "It can't be done." I found that stunning.

But they are in good company. Many thoughtful people who do not teach writing for a living think it cannot be done; but there are also a few who have been up close, who have made a wholehearted effort, and who have retreated from the task with the pronouncement that it must be an impossibility. Some have even written about it. To contest the matter, I have chosen an article by one of the best minds who has made this return-trip voyage -- the inimitable Stanley Fish. Since he was my chair for a number of years and my colleague for twice that long, I can think of him only as Stanley and not as Fish.

Stanley's mind is amazingly quick and agile; it is also active; and it is also restless. Before coming to Duke University (in 1985), he had been at Johns

Hopkins, where for two years he had undertaken the responsibility of heading their writing program. I was not there at the time; but I have not a shadow of a doubt that he invested the same time and energy and imagination in that effort that he always brings to a problem that needs solving. After two years, he abandoned the effort. In 1987 he published an article (republished in his 1989 book of essays, *Doing What Comes Naturally*) called "Anti-Foundationalism, Theory Hope, and the Teaching of Composition." His conclusion: Writing cannot be taught. Let us take a look at his argument.

For more than 20 years, beginning in the early 1970s, high-level literary criticism was dominated by a fascination with Theory. Stanley outlined the development of his own descent/ascent into his theoretical perspective in the long introduction to his most captivating of books, *Is There a Text in This Class?* Trained as he had been in New Criticism, he began by presuming that meaning was embedded in the text. He then discovered the possibility that meaning was really emanating from the reader. Eventually he came to believe meaning was a combined product of reader and text, producing infinite interpretations and the impossibility of precisely perceiving authorial intentions. Meaning always depended on context; context was supplied by the text, by the circumstances surrounding the text, by the writer, by the reader, and by the circumstances surrounding both the writer and the reader. "Meaning" was such a complicated matter that it would be better to abandon the word altogether. There is no "meaning" because there are too many "meanings."

As the theory wars grew warmer, two great armies seemed to form in the mist, descendants of the Rationalists and the Nominalists of the fifteenth century. In the late twentieth century, these foes were the Foundationalists and the Anti-Foundationalists. Here is Stanley's definitional effort to capture Foundationalism in his "writing can't be taught" article:

> By foundationalism I mean any attempt to ground inquiry and communication in something more firm and stable than mere belief or unexamined practice. The foundationalist strategy is first to identify that ground and then so to order our activities that they become anchored to it and are thereby rendered objective and principled. The ground so identified must have certain (related) characteristics: it must be invariant across contexts and even cultures; it must stand apart from political, partisan, and "subjective" concerns in relation to which it must act as a constraint; and it must provide a reference point or checkpoint against which claims to knowledge and success can be measured and adjudicated.

Such an approach, he continues, results in a method or recipe based on standard ingredients and complete with rigorous instructions that "will *produce*, all by itself, the correct result." This leads in turn to the production of fundamental and invariant *rules*; the rules lead the writer to all the products of good writing -- which Stanley lists as coherence, intelligibility, readability, persuasiveness, etc.

To see this composition foundationalism at work, all you need to do is to pick up almost any composition textbook written at any time in American history before 1975 (and many written thereafter). You can find bits and pieces of examples in my Appendices from Blair, Hill, and Wendell. The handbooks tell us the rules of grammar and the rules of usage. They show us paired examples from a digital world-- "acceptable/unacceptable"; "incorrect/correct"; "confusing/clear." Nineteenth-century rhetorics warned us against solecisms and barbarisms; twentieth-century texts warned us of most of these same problems but shied away from the old-style name-calling. But the rules persisted -- whatever they were called. If you ever have a question, you can "look it up." Or, if you are bold enough, you can call the director of writing programs at your local university. (I think the thing I miss most from my administrative days, besides working with new teachers, is the mischievous glee of settling bar bets on grammar for total strangers -- about four times a year -- phoned in to me by the more aggressive of the bettors.)

As a result, students wrote on eggshells, always fearful of "getting something wrong." The papers came out stiff and self-protective and just plain dull. I would agree with Stanley. These students were *not* being "taught how to write." They were, perhaps, being taught how not to embarrass themselves in print and in public; but, at best, that is being taught how *not* to write.

Then, in the last quarter of the twentieth century, Theory exploded onto the literary critical scene. It was just as natural for literature-based interests to leak over into the composition field as it had been unnatural for linguistic concerns even to flow in that direction. (Linguists were linguists and had always wanted to be linguists; composition teachers, at that time, were mostly literature students who had failed to find full-time employment in literature and had found a safe haven in the world of composition.) The brash, new voices in Theory -- Stanley's being one of the loudest and, I should emphasize, one of the clearest -- were those of the Anti-Foundationalists. Here is Stanley's definition:

> Anti-Foundationalism teaches that questions of fact, truth, correctness, validity, and clarity can neither be posed nor answered in reference to some extra-contextual, ahistorical, nonsituational reality, or rule, or law, or value; rather, anti-foundationalism asserts, all of these matters are intelligible and debatable only within the precincts of the contexts or situations or paradigms or communities that give them their local and changeable shape. It is not just that anti-foundationalism replaces the components of the foundationalist world-picture with other components; instead, it denies to those components the stability and independence and even the identity that is so necessary if they are to be thought of as grounds or anchors. Entities like the world, language, and the self can still be named; . . . [but] will be inextricable from the social and historical circumstances in which they do their work.

Most faculty, at any university, were shocked -- especially (but not always) the hard scientists. If everything is always and already dependent on multiple contexts to be ascertainable, they argued, then no certain or stable or "true" meaning can ever be found. Anything means everything and everything means no one thing (= nothing?). "Knowledge" disappears as a concept; chaos reigns. But, as Stanley and many others were quick to point out, that is a misreading of the whole project: Perception may not be unique-ly identifiable and communicable; but it is rooted -- in "situatedness."

> A situated self is a self whose every operation is a function of the convention-al possibilities built into this or that context. Rather than unmooring the sub-ject, . . ., anti-foundationalism reveals the subject to be always and already tethered by the local or community norms and standards that constitute it and enable its rational acts. Such a subject can be many things: certain, confused, in turmoil, at rest, perplexed, sure. But the one thing it cannot be is free to orig-inate its own set of isolated beliefs without systematic constraints.

Having said that, he sets out the bait for compositionists, which he seems to take himself as a natural result of his definitional process.

> . . . if the true picture of the human situation is as anti-foundationalism gives it . . . then surely we can extrapolate from this picture a better set of methods for operating in the world we are constantly making and remaking, a better set of rationales and procedures for making judgments, and a better set of so-lutions to the problems that face us as teachers of writing.

This is what he refers to in his title as "Theory Hope." It sounds hope-ful indeed.

But as we read further, we find that those hopes are to be dashed. His argument, bedrocked in Jacques Derrida's "The situation has always al-ready been announced," resolves in his conclusion that

> . . . any claim in which the notion of situatedness is said to be a lever that al-lows us to get a purchase on situations is finally a claim to have escaped situ-atedness, and is therefore nothing more or less than a reinvention of foundationalism by the very form of thought that has supposedly reduced it to ruins.

You cannot escape situatedness, he warns, by recognizing it; that act of recognition is itself situated, thus making the conscious gaze at it an im-possibility. Since you can never escape your situatedness, you can never get to a point or a place from which situatedness as a concept can teach you to write about your situation "better." Knowing you are controlled by context does not free you from that context.

But hope (Theory Hope) still seems to percolate just under the surface of the philosophical restrictions. If all knowledge depends on situations (situatedness, context), then why not teach situations? Stanley says it can-not be done -- or that it is always and already done anyway. We cannot get far enough away from the controlling situation to see it or say it. Indeed, the situation is not a thing unto itself, an "entity," but rather

> a bundle of tacit or unspoken assumptions that is simultaneously organizing the world and changing in response to its own organizing work. A situation is always on the wing, and any attempt to capture it will only succeed in fixing it in a shape it no longer has.

The teaching of situations turns out to be a contradiction in terms.

What is "wrong" here? Nothing, I believe. If you get used to thinking these kinds of theory thoughts, Stanley makes excellent sense. Foundationalism fails as an approach to composition. We have witnessed that for centuries now. And anti-foundationalism fails in that its own definitional nature makes it impossible that it should be used in a way that could succeed. The problem here is not in either of these two points, considered by themselves, but rather in the digital way in which the argument is set up. It presumes that foundationalism and anti-foundationalism between them cover the universe of thought and the possibilities of function. They are offered as the only two measuring tools available or possible. I suggest that the number of actual measuring tools is infinite. The task is not to find the "right" one; rather, it is to figure out *how* one should go about making choices at any given moment.

To explain what I am intending to say by that vague-sounding statement, I turn to a concept of Benoit Mandelbrot, one of the best known of the scientists who have done work on a new science called Chaos. Chaos science was developed to provide a description of turbulence. (Werner Heisenberg, on his deathbed, insisted he would pose two questions to God: Why relativity? and why turbulence? Heisenberg is quoted as saying, "I really think He may have an answer for the first question.")[7]

Chaos and pattern seemed to be opposite concepts. Set a system in motion and watch it over a long period of time; if you fail to see any pattern of regularity as it flows or progresses, then you are experiencing chaos. Start the same system a number of times, each from a different starting point; if the progressions or evolutions do not resemble each other, then you are experiencing chaos. It is an Anti-foundationalist's dream come true.

Before the mid-twentieth century, mathematicians struggled with such seemingly non-repeating systems. If they generated 500 or 1,000 solutions and plotted them on a Cartesian graph, no pattern appeared. Then, in the 1950s, everything changed with the arrival of computers. Suddenly it was possible to grind out a million, or five million, solutions. And lo and behold: In some cases, on the Cartesian graph, patterns began to appear. One famous example shows a fishlike form with smaller fishes in tow -- for a while. Then chaos sets in, and nothing looks patternable. But after a while, the fishes reappear, with their brood again in tow. But there was something much more remarkable than that: If you took any tiny little square of space on one of those fishes and blew it up 1,000 times, you would find the fishes reproduced in little. And then if you took a minuscule square from those microfishes and blew it up, you would find yet more finny prey. The images were "self-similar." Mandelbrot developed a system of coloring different kinds of solutions to a single irrational equation that demonstrated the patternings in exquisite and highly intricate ways. Fractals, he called them.

You look long enough and hard enough at the chaotic, and generate enough experience data, and patterned behavior can start to emerge. Writing is infinite? Writing is therefore essentially chaotic and cannot be taught? Perhaps with language too it is possible to perceive -- at long last -- patterns that emerge from large amounts of seemingly chaotic data. It all depends on how you go about the process of perceiving and measuring.

Mandelbrot, a Belgian, once had occasion to look up in a Belgian encyclopedia the length of the boundary line that separated Belgium from France. When he looked up that fact again in a French encyclopedia, he found a different figure. That stayed in his head for a while. Then one day he was flying in a plane at a low altitude over the English Channel. He looked down and came up with an answer, announcing it in his article "How Long Is the Coast of Britain?" His answer: The British coastline is infinitely long. Measure it from a plane flying 20,000 feet above: The curves and bumps of the coastline are clear and are calculable with your aerial surveyor's equipment. Descend to 500 feet: You can now see more intricate twists and turns, more bumpy bumps, and bumps on the bumps. The coast line now measures "longer." Descend, disembark, and walk out on the beach. Take along your landlubber's surveying equipment. The bumps on the bumps have a huge number of bumps on those bumps on bumps. The coastline now measures "longer." Take out your microscope and look at those grains of sand that are the outer edge of the naked-eye-available bumps. Each of those sand grains has a coastline of bumps. The coastline as a whole now measures longer. Take out your light microscope -- etc., etc. The coastline of Britain is infinite. It all depends on your measuring stick.

And therein lies the response to Stanley's pedagogical despair. The coastline is infinite; but it is not unmeasurable. It is infinitely measurable. If you are writing an encyclopedia, you've got to include certain kinds of unfactual facts, like coastlines and borderlines. And if you use a different measuring stick than the people across the border, you'll come up with a different answer. Problems will arise only when you have to put that fact to work. Then it becomes situated. Of course, it was situated before; but we didn't *care* about its situation then.

When we teach writing, we make a choice of measuring sticks. Since there are lots to choose from, no one stick will function perfectly or pervasively; if you are going to teach, you have to choose one, or two, or three. Nothing is digital here. Everything depends on context, on situation, on *location*. And that is precisely what this Reader Expectation approach comes back to, over and over again. By recognizing the *function* of certain *locations*, we do not escape from situatedness or locationness; we learn how to manipulate it to produce the greatest probability of response we can know. It will not produce a 100% agreement among all readers, because they will be bringing along their own measuring devices. In order to communicate with them at all, we have to guess just what kind of measuring equipment they are likely to bring. We cannot guess right all the time.

> Perfection could exist only if the entire range of the reader's and the writer's experience were identical down to the last detail. Universal and permanent perfection could exist only if this entire range of experiences were identical for all men forever. (Kenneth Burke, *Counter-Statement*)

That is why the foundationalist efforts of 200 years of writing instruction did not do the job well enough. Knowing what most readers are likely to do most of the time gets us closer to probable communicative success. And *that* you can teach.

Infinite interpretability? Right. The impossibility of perceiving authorial intention? Right. But those only state the problem. Readers interpret; but it is in our best interest to *limit* the probabilities of interpretation, even though we know we cannot control them completely. We cannot ensure that our intentions will be communicated; but it is in our best interest to *maximize* the possibilities that much of our intention will make it through to them. And of course we ourselves are never fully in touch with our own intentions. By knowing how we will most likely be interpreted, we can be led further into our own thinking processes.

Stanley admits at the end of his essay that writing cannot be taught. "This leaves me and you only a few worn and familiar bromides: practice makes perfect; you learn to write by writing; you must build on what you already know." He needn't have despaired. What we need is a supple pedagogy, a mobile, shifting pedagogy, based not on theory but on practicality. The questions should not be "Should it work?" or "Might it work?" but rather "Does it work?" We need a pedagogy not tied down to conventions and its concomitant rules but based on expectations and their multivalent possibilities. It requires one set of measuring devices to approximate the coastlines of sentences and of paragraphs and or essays as a whole. It needs yet others to recognize the differences in audiences -- styles that used to be called "high" or "low" and now are "formal" or "familiar." And it needs yet others to accommodate the different natures of different tasks -- grant applications, legal briefs, letters to parents asking for more money. Such a pedagogy needs to recognize its inherent self-similarities (for example, that which appears first contextualizes that which comes thereafter -- on any level) and guard against the easy parallelism of artificial self-similarities (for example, the five-sentence paragraph, with its Topic-Support-Support-Support-Conclusion shape, and the five-paragraph theme, with its Topic-Support-Support-Support-Conclusion shape). The writer who has conscious knowledge of Reader Expectations has no lock on truth or clarity or persuasiveness. That writer is, as suggested several chapters ago, more like a recording engineer in a sound mixing studio, with an array of buttons and levers and dials that can all be turned to various positions, making for an infinite variety of possibilities in the final sound emitted: Emphasis can be made more or less evident by the use of Stress positions or parallel structures or placement in anti-stress locations (like between subject and verb); expectations can be violated to good effect; expectations can be used in reverse (undercutting information by *not* putting it in a Stress position or softening action by *not* expressing it by the verb); combining controls over multiple expectations can increase, decrease, or ambiguate emphasis (see Fred and his dog in Chapter 4). It is overwhelming to realize, as noted in Chapter 1, that every time we read a single word, we read it as part of a number of units of discourse simultaneously -- phrase, clause, sentence, paragraph, subsection, section, whole document, etc. The only way to approach that whirlwind is to divide and conquer. Treat each unit by itself. And do not be surprised when a solution to the problem of one unit conflicts with the solution to another. Thought is complicated. There is no way around that.

To what is Stanley referring when he says "practice make perfect"? ("Perfect" would seem too high a standard for our merely human aspirations; but we know what he "means," yes?) I suggest it has to do with ear training. You try over and over again. You read good writers and then try to sound like them. You try some more. You sound a bit more like them. You try again. If you do eventually get good at it, what have you done? I would argue that you have, by ear, perceived the *shape* of good writing; and that shape, in turn, is entirely dependent on the *structural location* of information. Establish an expectation; move toward it; arrive at it. That is "shape." It can be learned by a really good ear with a lot of effort; but it can be learned better and far more easily by an eye trained to recognize structural locations.

Let us take an example from Stanley himself.

> To put the matter in a nutshell, the knowledge that one is in a situation has no particular payoff for any situation you happen to be in, because the constraints of that situation will not be relaxed by that knowledge.

What makes this sentence work? It deals with a complex thought that doubles back on itself: It is that very doubling back that is the crux of the thought. Such a thought is made more available to readers if the *structure* of the sentence also doubles back on itself -- which in this case it does. Stanley has used the old rhetorical figure of speech we have encountered before -- chiasmus, the stating of two or more element followed by the restating of them in reverse order. That XYYX form is familiar to us in President Kennedy's famous "Ask not what *your country* can do for *you*, but rather what *you* can do for *your country*." Stanley's sentence is yet more complex, requiring a *three*-element chiasmus -- XYZZYX. The X's are "knowledge"; the Y's are "situation" and the Z's are "payoff" and "constraint." Here it is again:

> To put the matter in a nutshell, the *knowledge* that one is in a *situation* has no particular *payoff* for any situation you happen to be in, because the *constraints* of that *situation* will not be relaxed by that *knowledge*.

It would have been a yet better chiasmus had he not thrown in the extra "situation," which does not form part of the XYZZYX pattern.[8] Maybe Stanley "perfected" the ability to do this by practice and more practice, having read rhetorically sophisticated writers for many years and having listened hard. If so, he could have been saved a lot of his struggle by a teacher who showed him chiasmus in action, named it, and thereby made it available to him on a conscious level. "Use it," the teacher could have said, "whenever you want to go into the forest and come back out again, changed by the experience." These things are teachable.

Stanley Fish is a good, clear writer. He once said to me, "I don't consider myself 'finished' writing a sentence until it is 'leaning forward.'" I think he is right; and this book tries to tell him why. He is always leaning forward to the Stress position; and the Stress position is often leaning forward to the next sentence. If it isn't, something else is -- usually found in the Topic position.

Knowing about Reader Expectations will neither help us understand nor predict the state of mind or cultural background or any particular controlling situation of the reader's mind; but it will help us make good guesses as to where in our sentences and paragraphs most readers will tend to look for certain kinds of informative clues in the interpretation process. These expectations are indeed social conventions; but until now they have remained available only on an intuitive basis to readers. This book tries to make them available now on a conscious level to writers. It goes against what Stanley refers to as "tacit knowledge" (a term of Polanyi's).

> Tacit knowledge is knowledge already known or dwelt in; it cannot be handed over in the form of rules or maxims and theories; there is, as James Reither observes, "no transition from 'knowing that' to 'knowing how.'

If it is tacit, it has to stay tacit to be tacit. It is therefore unarticulatable. Our tacit knowledge about how to write, then, Stanley might say, is unteachable, by definition. I would argue that our intuitive knowledge about our own interpretation processes is not tacit but simply unacknowledged. To acknowledge it is an act somewhere between the neuroscientist's explanation of how the brain tells us to scratch when we itch and the psychiatrist's explanation of why we break into a sweat whenever we see someone who reminds us of horrible old Uncle Irwin who tormented us when we were kids. We need not locate it on such a spectrum. We need only to discover for ourselves if it works. It does not have to rise to the level of an exact science or an infallible plan; it just has to work much better than anything else we have tried before.

It reminds me of a favorite story of my colleague, Judy Swan -- the conversation between the philosopher and the engineer, as they stood at the entryway to a banquet hall. They both looked longingly across the room to the banquet table, heaped high with the most inviting delicacies. The philosopher moaned, "Too bad we can never get there to eat all that marvelous food. Xeno's paradox tells us that before we can get all the way across the room, we have to go halfway first. And from that point, we must again first go halfway. And then again we must go half of the way. By logical extension of this argument, we can never get all the way across the room." The engineer replied with a smile, "It's all right. We can get close enough."

Had we as teachers of writing wanted to accept guidance from a famous and brilliant mind, we should have been embracing the suggestive work of

Kenneth Burke. His first book, *Counter-Statement*, offers a wealth of insight into the relationship between text and readers and forms and expectations:

> [F]orm, by our definition, resides in the fulfillment of an audience's expectations.
>
> [T]o guide the reader's expectations is already to have some conquest over him.
>
> *Form* in literature is an arousing and fulfillment of desires. A work has form in so far as one part of it leads a reader to anticipate another part, to be gratified by the sequence.
>
> Thus a pinioned bird, though it has learned that flight is impossible, must yet spread out its wings and go through the motions of flying; its muscles, being equipped for flight, require the process. Similarly, if a dog lacks a bone, he will gnaw at a block of wood; not that he is hungry -- for he may have his fill of meat -- but his teeth, in their fitness to endure the strain of gnawing, feel the need of enduring that strain. So the formal aspects of art appeal in that they exercise formal potentialities of the reader.

These forms and expectations and desires and fulfillments are teachable, but only if we can convert them into usable perceptions and procedures that keep real readers in mind.

D. The successful teaching of this approach is (as Plato would agree) immoral, because it would empower unprincipled writers to hide from responsibility, to obfuscate the truth, and to make the worse argument sound the better.

At the 1990 Conference on College Composition and Communication, the Clearlines group at that time -- Joseph Williams, Greg Colomb, Don Freeman, and I -- offered a panel on our method of teaching writing. The audience was large, stretching back to fill a large, shoebox-shaped room. During the question and answer period, a gentleman in the rear stood and spoke in earnest anger. Why, he asked, were we employed in teaching this material to lawyers, who would then use it to distort, falsify, and hide the truth? Were we not committing an immoral pedagogical act?

This point of view is an old one indeed, extending at least as far back as Plato's *Gorgias*. The appropriate rejoinder, I believe, insists on two points. First, almost everything good that is teachable can be turned around to be used for ill. Aristotle was arguing that 2,500 years ago:

> And if it is argued that great harm can be done by unjustly using such power of words, this objection applies to all good things except for virtue, and most of all to the most useful things, like strength, health, wealth, and military strategy.... (*On Rhetoric*, I.i.13)

What a painful scene it was to watch, in the movie *Marathon Man*, when Sir Lawrence Olivier's character (a sadistic former Nazi concentration camp officer turned dentist in New York) used his dental skills on the character played by Dustin Hoffman not to heal but to torture. Teachers cannot control the ethics of their students -- especially after the students have left the classroom; but that should not deter us from teaching that which can do good.

Second, I would offer as a response to the angry gentleman in the back of the room one of the primary arguments used by those in favor of developing nuclear weapons. (It works better for Rhetoric than it does for bombs. Rhetoric leaves behind no toxic fallout.) If we give *everyone* rhetorical understanding, then no one will be taken unaware, no one will be left defenseless in the face of the skillful rhetoric of those who do intend harm. Rhetorical understanding strengthens those who try to do good and levels the playing field when a struggle with the opposite kind of people arises. Again, this is an old argument, made at least as far back as St. Augustine, in his underread and still exhilarating pro-rhetoric work, *De Doctrina Christiana*. (Read Book IV. Great stuff.)

> Now, the art of rhetoric being available for the enforcing either of truth or falsehood, who will dare to say that truth in the person of its defenders is to take its stand unarmed against falsehood? For example, that those who are trying to persuade men of what is false are to know how to introduce their subject, so as to put the hearer into a friendly, or attentive, or teachable frame of mind, while the defenders of the truth shall be ignorant of that art? That the former are to tell their falsehoods briefly, clearly, and plausibly, while the latter shall tell the truth in such a way that it is tedious to listen to, hard to understand, and in fine, not easy to believe it? That the former are to oppose the truth and defend falsehood with sophistical arguments, while the latter shall be unable either to defend what is true, or to refute what is false? That the former, while imbuing the minds of their hearers with erroneous opinions, are by their power of speech to awe, to melt, to enliven, and to rouse them, while the latter shall in defense of the truth be sluggish, and frigid, and somnolent? Who is such a fool as to think this wisdom? Since, then, the faculty of eloquence is available for both sides, and is of very great service in the enforcing either or wrong or right, why do not good men study to engage it on the side of truth, when bad men use it to obtain the triumph of wicked and worthless causes, and to further injustice and error? (IV.ii.3)

Those were my answers to the man in the back. I regret that I neglected to add that I have interacted with thousands of lawyers in my career and have found them as a group predominantly ethical, hardworking, and remarkably devoted to doing things right.

E *pilogue*

I began this volume with a quote from Kenneth Burke's wonderful first book, *Counter-Statement*; I will end it with another.

> "What we find words for," says Nietzsche, "is that for which we no longer have use in our own heart. There is always a kind of contempt in the act of

speaking." Contempt, indeed, so far as the original emotion was concerned, but not contempt for the act of speaking.

This has something to do with the sense of burden one often has in the writing process -- of having to deal with thoughts and emotions that have already been felt, that no longer are new news. Writing tends to fail when the writer is consumed by a sense of loss in terms of the vitality or efficacy of the thinking process. It seems to so many students that by the time they begin writing, their thinking process has already been completed. Only "expression" remains. As long as the writing process is not considered a thinking process but merely a mechanical or cosmetic afterprocess, the writer will find writing a distasteful burden. Whenever the writer can consider the writing process not as afterthought but as a necessary component of the thought process itself, arrangement and style become as essential as invention. This Reader Expectation approach, if well used, creates for the writer a sense of dialect or dialogue with self. By investigating the relationship of substance to structure, the writer becomes both reader and writer, allowing a virtual dialogue to take place, artificially producing that perspective which heretofore has been obtainable (if at all) only by the passage of time. That is quite a bit to claim; but the proof of this pudding is in the reading.

Endnotes

1. Herbert Spencer, The Philosophy of Style, Boston: Allyn & Bacon, 1892. (First published in 1852). A senior colleague of mine recalls reading the Spencer article for his own freshman composition class in 1938.
2. See Noam Chomsky, *Aspects of the Theory of Syntax*. Cambridge: Harvard University Press, 1965.
3. Charles S. Peirce, *Collected Papers*, ed. Charles Hartshorne and Paul Weiss. Cambridge: Harvard University Press, 1974. 5:332, Pgph.5.484.
4. Jan Firbas, "Some Aspects of the Czechoslovak Approach to Problems of Functional Sentence Perspective." *Papers on Functional Sentence Perspective*, ed. Frantisek Danes. Prague: Academia, 1974.
5. Michael A.K. Halliday. "The Place of 'Functional Sentence Perspective' in the System of Linguistic Description." *Papers on Functional Sentence Perspective*, ed. František Daneš. Prague: Academia, 1974., pp. 43–53.
6. For another striking example of the Prague School perceiving linguistic function and Joe Williams turning that perception to pedagogical use and practical application, see František Daneš's article, "Functional Sentence Perspective and the Organization of the Text," in *Papers on Functional Sentence Perspective*. František Daneš, ed., Prague: Academia, 1974., pp. 118–119, where he sets out the patterns we have called Topic Changing and Topic Stringing. He sets them out, but he does not put them to use.

7. Chaos is a fascinating subject, made attractively available for nonscientists in James Gleick's excellent introduction to the subject, *Chaos: Making a New Science*. New York: Penguin Books, 1988.
8. Here is a version of Stanley's sentence, omitting the third use of "situation." Does the chiasmus now appear more clearly? "To put the matter in a nutshell, the *knowledge* that one is in a *situation* has no particular *payoff*, because the *constraints* of that *situation* will not be relaxed by that *knowledge*."

Appendixes

A

A Structural Definition of Rhetoric

To Aristotle, Cicero, and Quintilian, rhetoric was the art of persuasion, the art of speaking well. Their work has influenced all work on rhetoric since their time; it was expanded upon in the Middle Ages, rediscovered in the Renaissance, strained through the sieve of "common sense philosophy" in the eighteenth century, and once again rediscovered at the end of the twentieth century. However, in adopting and adapting classical rhetoric as a potential foundation of college writing instruction, we have been ignoring two substantial facts: (1) The classical rhetoricians were attending primarily to the needs of orators, not to the needs of writers; and there are great differences between oral and written communication. (2) They were concerned not with the English language but with Greek and Latin; and there are great differences in structure and function between those two ancient languages and our modern English. For the purposes of teaching English composition in our time, we need a revised definition of rhetoric.

The very word *rhetoric* has survived, until recently, with mostly negative associations and implications -- "mere rhetoric," "empty rhetoric," "only rhetoric." These associations carry with them Plato's warnings that rhetoric is nothing more than a "knack," like cooking (cf. his *Gorgias*); neither an art nor a science, he argued, it is a process of insidious ornamentation superimposed on thought by the speaker or writer. As such, according to Plato, it raises the possibility that a weak or evil thought can be made by its glossy rhetorical exterior to seem strong or good.

Aristotle attempted to counter the Platonic attack on rhetoric by insisting that the only way an argument could appear stronger than another was for it to have the stronger grounding in either truth or logic. He filled his *Rhetoric* with categorizations and subdivisions intended to help us construct and present the logic that will make the truth apparent. Rhetoric, for Aristotle, was the great facilitator in the production of truth and persuasion.

Quintilian tried to solve Plato's moral problem by insisting that one could not become a powerful rhetor without also being "a good man" (a *vir bonus*). This "goodness" turns out to be a more complicated matter than it first appears. On the one hand, when he first mentions the term, he argues for an inherent connection between the ability to perceive justice and an ability to make that justice seem reasonable to others. On the other hand, several books later, he advises us not to shrink from lying or distorting the facts in order to win a case, should our side be the one worthy of winning. By intertwining the seemingly naïve *vir bonus* concept with pragmatic, lawyerly advice, Quintilian fails to settle the dispute established by Plato and Aristotle.

St. Augustine, three hundred years later, finds a solution to the problem that made for him perfect sense. The study and use of rhetoric (art, science, knack, or whatever) is perfectly moral as long as it is in the service of God's truth. Since that truth, he argued, is revealed to us (or coded for us) in the Bible, any rhetorical device that makes that truth more apparent and more convincing must, by definition, be a moral endeavor. Rhetoric is a moral tool if it is used in the undertaking of the most moral of tasks -- spreading the good word.

In the seventeenth century, François Fénelon reverses Quintilian's approach, arguing that the good rhetor must take special care to become and remain the good man. Rhetoric being a powerful and potentially dangerous tool, those who learn to use it must develop their moral sense simultaneously to avoid abusing their power. He turns his attention from the law courts that so interested Cicero and Quintilian to the pulpit. In the service of preaching the holy word, the rhetor could maintain the necessary moral consciousness. Fénelon manages to neutralize the potential danger Plato feared from rhetoric by combining the techniques of Aristotle with the moral arguments of St. Augustine. He thus achieves a moment of synthesis in rhetorical history, but only at the expense of deemphasizing rhetoric's secular applications.

While some were engaged in debating the morality of rhetoric, others were developing its technical and procedural side. Many attempted to reduce the art or science of rhetoric to artistic or scientific rules of thumb. One result was a string of how-to books, from the anonymous Ciceronian *Ad Herennium* through the letter-writing and preaching manuals of the Middle Ages to the rhetorical handbooks of the Renaissance (of Sherry, Wilson, Puttenham, and others) and all the way to our present-day Fowler's *Usage*, *Harbrace Handbook*, and composition textbooks. In one way or another, almost all of these have employed a divide-and-conquer tactic, categorizing and subcategorizing information so each rhetorical weapon can be made conveniently available in the arsenal of argument, ready for the use of the writer knowledgeable enough to have learned of its existence and mastered its function.

Major controversies have arisen concerning such categorization. Peter Ramus, in the sixteenth century, insisted on a clear-cut distinction between dialectic (which included the discovery and arrangement of thought) and rhetoric (which concerned itself exclusively with the style and delivery of that discovered thought). Whatever belonged to one category could not possibly be included in the other. Despite energetic refutations of Ramus from his own day to our own, the influence of his conception of rhetoric is still felt throughout our institutions, as we distinguish problems in thinking from problems in writing. (It is curious that the ideas of Ramus have had such deep and lasting influence, since his own writings are not fully translated into English and difficult to find. Until recently, only specialized scholars in the English-speaking world knew much of anything about him.) How many times have we heard the criticism that a document is well conceived but badly written? I would argue that can never be the case. Thought does not exist until it is expressed (by writing, speaking, dancing, painting, etc.). Until then, it exists only as potential thought. If that seems too extreme a position, backing off a centimeter or two produces the argument that "thought might as well not exist before it is expressed." It all depends on whether *thought* by definition must *accomplish* something in the world or whether it is merely something for which the thinker obtains credit.

The alliance of Aristotelian (classical) thought with Ramistic thought has brought about major difficulties with which teachers of English have been struggling for the last 200 years. The classical rhetoricians were dealing almost exclusively with the oral presentation of material already conceived. Rhetoric, for them, was both a method of inventing what to say and a way of enhancing oral performance. For them the two combined nicely; from our perspective, they seem quite separable. As a result, we speak of "clothing our thoughts with words" and "reducing our thought to words." The Ramus dialectic/rhetoric separation has continually been misinterpreted to limit the classical definition of rhetoric to the written word. The oral tradition, so much a part of the development of rhetoric, plays a relatively small part in our contemporary needs; but we unknowingly maintain its principles in our conception of written rhetoric, whether appropriate or not. Therein lies the problem.

Longinus and Erasmus played their part as well, complicating matters. Longinus recognized sublimity in writing and tried to demonstrate what qualities of rhetoric transport discourse (and us with it) above mere communication to exaltation and persuasion. Erasmus demonstrated that thought and rhetoric lived a symbiotic relationship much like the one Mozart would create in developing a theme and variations movement. When Erasmus showed us how we could say "I was delighted to receive your letter" in a 150 ways, presumably with an equally diverse number of effects, he was suggesting that there are standard artistic/scientific methods we can practice and perfect to master writing. If it were so, it suggests any of us, with enough study and practice, could become a verbal Mozart.

In attempting to teach writing on the college level in America, we have expended most of our energy on three tasks: (1) helping our students find something to say (which we refer to as the *Invention* process); (2) helping our students develop elegance and power in presentation (which we refer to as *Style*); and (3) helping our students perfect a conventionally accepted manner of articulation (which we refer to as *Grammar and Usage*). We keep these attempts more or less separate, as Ramus would have us, the first belonging to dialectic and the other two belonging to rhetoric. Within the teaching of Invention, we create methods for finding something to say (some of which being formal patterns we call *heuristics*) and we counsel students in outlining and other helpful division procedures (which Aristotle called *Arrangement*). Until recently, all of this effort presumed or seemed to presume that thought could be separated from the expression of thought.

In all of this history, rhetoric has been conceived of as something that the writer/speaker can do *to* discourse in order to make it more effective. That suggests that the discourse itself, by itself, possesses a kind of estimable worth. We grade papers, expending great effort to arrive at the "right" grade, even though we recognize that different graders will often come to different conclusions concerning value. In this volume, I have been suggesting we reconstruct our perspective on the problem, deemphasizing both the writer and the discourse in favor of the traditionally less honored member of the communication triangle, the reader.

The eminent linguist Roman Jakobson -- and by now a host of others as well -- presented the act of communication as a triangulated set of relationships. The labels at the three points of the triangle vary, but without significant distinction for the present purpose. Here is a common set:

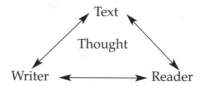

The triangulation attempts to dispel the logically flawed but more commonly accepted concept of linearity in communication:

Writer ⟶ Text/Thought ⟶ Reader

In the linear model, the writer encodes thought in a document and sends it on to the reader. The thought is presumed to exist in the document for everyone to see and decode. The writer, knowing how to write, makes the thought intelligible by choosing the "right" shape and content for the document; the reader, knowing how to read, perceives the writer's intentions because the shape and content of the document were "right."

Those who ascribe to the triangular concept of communication have demonstrated the inadequacy of the linear model. Both writer and reader have a relationship to the document, but it is not the same relationship. Simultaneously, the writer and reader have a direct relationship with each other, but not so much *through* the document as *because* of it. "Thought," the theory runs, is somehow surrounded by this triangle of relationships: The more clearly established the three separate relationships are, the more hermetically the thought becomes sealed within them. Any weakness in any of the three relationships creates a leak through which the thought can escape. We have come to discover that all three of these lines are irremedi-ably porous.

Traditionally, we have segregated the members of this triangle theory (writers, texts, and readers, with thought inhabiting the interior of the tri-angle) into corresponding academic houses. (1) *Writers* have traditionally been the exclusive prime targets of composition courses; as a result, our students often sense that the concerns of the writing course do not really carry over into other disciplines, where the substance matters more than the delivery. I recall overhearing one student assure another that she would well be able to produce in one night the ten-page paper due the next morn-ing because "after all, it's for a *history* class, not an *English* class." Profes-sors in other departments are often heard to complain that since student writing is so poor, English teachers must not be doing their job. Even the English teachers support the segregation of these tasks: Those who teach both composition and literature classes naturally tend to read essays for each of those classes with different eyes and different objectives -- and, most often, a different sense of enjoyment.

(2) *Texts* receive the bulk of attention in literature classes. That concen-tration was firmly established by the philological approach originally used in the study of literature; it was further solidified by the critical approach known as New Criticism, which dominated the middle fifty years of the twentieth century. Texts, by themselves and in isolation, "meant" something. Our efforts were directed toward unearthing that something. Reader-re-sponse theory, rising to prominence in the 1970s and 1980s, shifted the focus from the text to the reading experience. Under the auspices of the old New Criticism, we had naturally developed the concept of "different levels of meaning"; under the influence of Reader-Response theory, we have done away with the spatial metaphor of levels and have tried to deal with the more temporal metaphor of simultaneous, multifarious *interpretations* that are all part of a single response. But even now it is hard for any of us, teach-ers and students alike, to read a piece of discourse without trying to "make sense" of it; and no matter how enlightened we feel we are about these mat-ters, we tend to assume that the sense we manage to make makes eminent sense -- and perhaps is *the* sense the text was trying to make.

(3) *Thought* (the centrally located of the four players in the triangulat-ed scene) dominates almost all other academic courses, which advertise that they teach "substance." Mathematics offers the purest example, at least in its lower forms. Even in geometry, we quickly forget the presence of Eu-clid and concentrate on conceptual matters like the radius, the hypotenuse, or the parallelogram. In organic chemistry, we try to keep our carbons straight. In the introductory philosophy class, we do not ask, "In how many ways can Descartes be interpreted to mean something by this statement?" but rather "By this statement, what did Descartes mean?" In all these fields, however, the higher the level of the coursework, the more involved the stu-dent becomes in matters of interpretation and contextualization -- often in the process of attempting to discover authorial intention.

(4) Where in Academia, then, do we concentrate on the fourth member of the triangle, the *reader*? Until recently, we tended to value the reader's perspective primarily in creative writing classes, which traditionally have involved and valued peer response. Aside from that slight exception, the variation of reader response to a document has not been considered a particularly vital academic concern. That began to change with the onset of interest in literary theory in the early 1970s. Suddenly, the ways in which readers interpret (or are led to interpret) discourse became more important than the text itself. As a result, English courses expanded their jurisdiction to include almost all other previously foreign fields of investigation -- most notably philosophy, psychology, sociology, political science, history, and anthropology, but also including various fields of science, medicine, business, and law. They have done so not because all those other fields have been converted into literature but because they all deal with the reader's act of interpretation. Major controversies arose, attracting coverage in the nation's most important newspapers and journals, over what was called *canon revision*, the turning aside from the traditionally approved list of appropriate texts to less well-known or less well-valued texts, which have been popularly well received. Essentially, canon revision is the depowering of the text in favor of the empowering of the reader -- or at least of the critics calling for the canon revision.

Although the perspective I offer in this volume on teaching writing did not grow out of recent literary critical theory, it exists most comfortably in that climate. As many teachers of literature have turned from the poem, the play, and the novel to the reading experience of poem, play, and novel, so I would have teachers of writing turn from the writer's effort in producing a text to the probabilities of readers' responses to that text. It is a highly pragmatic step. In the world after college, graduate school, or professional school, it will not matter much how much effort the writer expenses in producing the text, nor how much better this one happens to be than previous ones had been; it also will not matter much whether the text is *capable* of performing its appointed task to communicate, request, persuade, or defend. Instead, it will matter a great deal how well the text actually *does* what it was supposed to do -- communicate certain thoughts to its readers. To determine if that has happened, we must look neither to the writer nor to objective conventional standards; we must look to the reader. I suggest, then, we cease concentrating on what strategies writers can use to fill empty pages and shift our attention to contemplating how readers go about reading. Knowledge of the reading process will naturally help empower writers over the writing process by helping empower them -- to the extent possible -- over the probable response of readers.

For the purposes of this volume, therefore, the ancient definitions of rhetoric must be laid aside. Here, rhetoric is neither the art of speaking well nor the art of persuasion. Instead, rhetoric is the combination of all the forces in and of a text that influence a reader's choices in the act of interpretation. Another way of putting it: Rhetoric is everything about a text that makes the reader interpret it in the way that reader interprets it.

This may appear at first to be a circular definition; it is not. The rhetoric of a text includes all its hows and wheres and whys -- not only for it's supposedly abstract thought but for all the elements of its construction. It concerns not only the nature and quality of the words selected but also their arrangement and sounds and relative weights and structural locations. It has to do with how sentences connect, linking backward and leaning forward. It has to do with what appears where -- within sentences, within paragraphs, and within whole documents. It has to do with the relative lengths and weights of the units of discourse (words, phrases, sentences, paragraphs, sections, etc.). It has to do with repetitions and variations and dynamics and tempi. Because these matters are all at least in part (and I would argue in great part) matters of *perception*, the emphasis of this new definition must be put not on the intentions of the writer but on the actual effects experienced by readers.

Structure and substance are inextricably intertwined: It is the structural location of information, and not the words chosen to represent it, that produces the major clues for the reader's interpretation process. *Where* a word (or phrase or sentence or paragraph) appears controls the most important part of what that fragment of text "means." Writing is 15% word choice and 85% structure.

An example. On a Saturday in November 1989, amid a series of stunning political events in Eastern Europe, the Berlin Wall suddenly no longer functioned as a barrier between East and West. Both the political and metaphorical significance of that occurrence were beyond the political expectations of most people on either side of the Wall. On that historic day, I heard five broadcasts (three on radio, two on television) of President John F. Kennedy's memorable 1963 speech in Berlin: " . . . I can say -- and I am proud of the word -- *ich bin ein Berliner*." ("I am a Berliner" ⟶ "We all are Berliners.") The summoning of these words of our martyred leader recaptured not a simple statement of policy but rather a moment of political prophecy. It was 26 years later, and that prophecy was being fulfilled.

It was no surprise that not one of the five announcers of those five rebroadcasts managed to point out that famous moment's extraordinary faux pas. President Kennedy's speechwriter had not been the German specialist the occasion had required. In order to say "I am a Berliner" in German, the appropriate phrasing would have been not "Ich bin ein Berliner" but rather "Ich bin Berliner." *Ein Berliner* does not mean "*a* Berliner"; it refers instead to a kind of pastry made popular by that city. President Kennedy had actually proclaimed, in all solemnity, " . . . I can say -- and I am proud of the word -- I am a jelly doughnut." Knowing that, one can discern in the recordings that half the roar from the crowd was appreciative applause and the other half was delighted and derisive laughter.

Why could that misspoken speech be played 26 years later to millions of Americans as a prophecy fulfilled -- a great moment in American political rhetoric? Because although Kennedy had gotten the semantics wrong, he had gotten the structure right. The carefully prepared structure told us most of what we needed to know; the inadequate semantic effort was adequately corrected (and for many entirely obliterated) by the forcefulness of the structural placement -- at the end of the sentence, at the end of a paragraph, at the high point of a crescendo, in the strife-torn city of Berlin, at a serious moment of international tension. Had he reversed it and gotten the semantics right but the structure wrong, I maintain that the moment would never have been preserved for our collective memory -- not then, and not 26 years later. Had he said "Ich bin Berliner" but buried it in the middle of a sentence in the middle of a passage and uttered it without a sense of dynamic arrival, it would have been at best a botched job; had he said it at some other place and at some other less appropriate time, it would have been entirely without historical significance.

English teachers have traditionally taught both literature and writing classes, often struggling to combine aspects of both into a more holistic approach to reading/writing. But struggle it has been, as articles continue to appear in our journals on how to succeed -- (or perhaps get away with?) -- using literature in the composition classroom, or how to inject -- (painful metaphor) -- more writing into substantive courses in all fields. The redefinition of rhetoric I suggest appears most timely because of recent developments in the history of English studies and English departments.

The English department as we know it was founded in the late nineteenth century, mostly for the purpose of organizing the activity of investigating literature from a philological and factual perspective. That activity had been underway for some time in individual courses, structured to replicate the kinds of activities undertaken by the investigation of Latin and Greek texts. Relatively few English texts were singled out for such prestigious attention; all of them were already considered classics.

In 1837, a group of Harvard undergraduates led a minor revolt in an English class, insisting on the opportunity to study something more modern than *Paradise Lost* -- and even daring to suggest the appropriation into the classroom of something absolutely contemporary. Their instructor assured them that even the day's current best-seller would seem unappetizing to them when subjected to his normal pedagogical techniques. They challenged him to make good on this boast. They chose for their experiment the number-one best-seller of that year -- a long work of fiction by a rising young British writer named Dickens -- something called *Pickwick Papers*. Courtesy of Professor Harry Levin, I have seen the eight-page, short-answer form examination on this work. Representative of the 70 or so questions on that exam is the one that sticks most in my memory: "State the three occasions on which we see 'the fat boy' during which he does *not* fall asleep." Such was the study of English literature at Harvard in 1837.[1]

In the early twentieth century, a division developed between attention paid to literature and attention paid to matters of communication, resulting in a split of both of identity and function: Literary concerns remained primarily the concern of English departments, while most communication skills were siphoned off for the newly created, less prestigious speech departments. English maintained jurisdiction over the composition course, presumably because it was both self-sustaining and income-producing; but within the department there was a clear caste system established to separate the doers of the two tasks. Literature was the concentration of choice; the composition course was considered by most to be no more than a necessary burden.

That dichotomous definition of English as an academic discipline was maintained steadily until the early 1970s, when economic hard times in the country combined with bad business planning on the part of academia to create an extraordinary shortage of positions for English Ph.D.s and even a threat to the tenure of established professors. It is possible, I believe, to trace the seismic moment of greatest change to the Arab oil embargo of 1973. America was shaken to its core by waiting in line for 45 minutes to purchase minimal amounts of gasoline -- that is, shaken by the realization that our control over the quality level of our daily life was seriously and realistically threatened. Businesses, governments, and whole professions reconsidered concepts of essential need and relevance, resulting in a flurry of reconstruction of the most basic assumptions about what was necessary to life. Suddenly, graduate programs in English were downsized at a stunning rate.[2] English departments had to be reconceptualized, as the number of English majors fell by as much as 80%.[3]

In order to survive, "English" had to rediscover itself -- producing both a higher intellectualization, as represented by the literary theory movement, and a higher pragmatism, as represented by the dramatic increase in the teaching of composition. The former afforded a way of retaining high-mindedness and standards of intellectual excellence; the latter afforded a way of retaining the services of a faculty that suddenly found itself offering a far greater supply than its new demand could justify.

I suspect that this economic turn of events also had something to do with creating the sudden, intense focus on literary critical theory that flourished at exactly the same time in the early 1970s. English professors had been sent the message by society that when the economy was in recession, one more book on flower imagery in Wordsworth's poems was expendable. Searching for a new self-definition within the late 1960s concept of relevance, English professors turned their attention to matters that appeared to be of more widespread import -- matters of social and political structures, human interactions, psychological and economic responses, racial concerns, gender concerns, sexuality concerns, and, above all, matters of interpretation. The latter seemed natural: Since English professors, consciously or not, had been teaching interpretations for years, why not refocus that concentration on the *act* of interpreting? The political realities of the late 1960s and early 1970s added their weight to this accommodation; and the texts generated by *any* other department became fair game for the act (and the game) of interpretation.

At the same time, in order to survive, more and more English professors found themselves teaching composition courses. These employment opportunities were generated by universities suddenly discovering that the low quality level of student writing mandated the requiring of a writing course -- and in many cases two courses. (This decrease in ability was probably a fiction; but no one could argue against the perception that students could not write as well as they needed to write.) More and more new Ph.D.s found themselves accepting jobs defined as rhetoric/composition posts; five years earlier they would have considered themselves exclusively literature professors. This was the case no matter what their teaching assignment might actually be: A position that in 1970 had involved two courses of composition and one of Milton would have advertised for a Miltonist; by 1980, the identical position would have advertised for a compositionist. At the same time, professors who had never taught anything but literature found themselves newly engaged in the teaching of composition. With a decline in the number of students interested in studying literature, it was an economic necessity.

Simultaneous with the economic necessities of teaching composition and the new interest in critical theory, a new field of composition studies appeared. Composition teachers discovered they had been looking too much at the products of writing and not enough at the process by which those products were produced.

The field adopted "process, not product" as its motto. That move was a necessary corrective; but it was unclear exactly how such a change should be effected. Attention was turned to what appeared to be the different moments in the writing process -- Pre-Writing, Invention, Revision, and Editing. "Process" seemed promising enough, until the processes started to seem like products themselves.

By the mid-1980s, we had spawned a counter-revolt against process: "Process" began to sound too mechanistic, too segregative, too reified. It was argued that every part of the writing process was involved at every moment in the process of writing. Our delight in the discovery of the linearity of process transformed into an awe (sometimes a helpless awe) at the realization of its non-linearity. The proscription of separable categories (Pre-Writing, etc.) failed because of its excessive clarity of division. One was always "pre"-writing; one's invention constantly incorporated simultaneous revision; and every moment of one's revision was in some sense a moment of new invention.

At this anxious moment, while large numbers of literature professors found themselves relegated to teaching writing, composition studies discovered rhetoric. The word had long been used positively by composition teachers (in opposition to its negative usage by the general public), though mostly either as a term of endearment or as an attempt at heightened respectability; but out of the mists of the past a sense of a rhetorical tradition started to emerge. Sessions at major conferences were devoted to Plato and Quintilian and Hugh Blair and Alexander Bain and Gertrude Buck. It became clear that if composition studies had a claim to academic respectability, it must be through the study of and alliance with our honorable ancestors who had populated the long and formerly distinguished history of rhetoric.

At that same moment, the literary critical theory people across the hall experienced a parallel epiphany. Terry Eagleton brought his *Literary Theory: An Introduction* (1983) toward closure with the following:

> [Rhetoric] saw speaking and writing not merely as textual objects, to be aesthetically contemplated or endlessly deconstructed, but as forms of *activity* inseparable from the wider social relations between writers and readers, orators and audiences, and as largely unintelligible outside the social purposes and conditions in which they were embedded.

Literary studies, it seems, just like composition studies, was turning out to be essentially an investigation of rhetoric.

Just as English departments in the early twentieth century had undergone a Ramistic split into departments of literature and speech, so the English department of the last quarter of the century found itself undergoing a self-similar split into the areas of literature and composition. In good Ramistic fashion, the members of the newly defined categories rarely encountered each other. Few professors before 1980 attended the annual meetings of *both* the Modern Language Association (MLA) and the Conference on College Composition and Communication (CCCC); fewer professors, even in the year 2000, attended the annual meetings of both the MLA and the Speech and Communication Association. But as the century came to a close, all parties found themselves meeting at a crossroads marked *rhetoric*: All parties had become interested in the Reader. Whether these fellow travelers will ever fully acknowledge having met each other at this crossroads remains to be seen.

To shed more light on the writing process, it makes sense that we turn the attention of composition studies to the reading process. Of course, there is no single reading process. Much depends on the nature of the material being read, the nature of the reader's purpose for reading, the nature of the reader's expectations of the kind of experience it will be, the depth of a particular reader's reading experience, the amount of time allotted, the needs and identities of individual readers, and several other equally viable and variable factors. With world enough and time, one might teach a course that investigates all these factors one by one; but the exigencies of the composition course will usually force us to choose. For this volume, I chose to concentrate on the kinds of texts students can expect to encounter after they leave the university -- texts in which the primary purpose is to communicate the author's specific intentions to the reading audience. Even with this limitation, the reading process remains infinitely variable, allowing no rule-like pronouncements to control it; but since we have always taught writing through rules and generalizations, those rules need to be considered and reconsidered if we are to find new and better ways to do the job.

Endnotes

1. I cite this example from the memory of Professor Levin, who discussed it in his graduate Dickens seminar at Harvard and showed us the examination (c. 1973).
2. This development was not entirely unanticipated. In 1967, Harvard University's English department accepted 120 new Ph.D. candidates -- the number they had been accepting yearly for decades. In 1968, they reduced that acceptance number to 90. In 1969, they dropped it further, to 47. Harvard was right to take these measures. Of the class that numbered 90, many did not finish the degree; but all who did managed to get some kind of academic job offer (the very last offer coming in August, two weeks before the start of that year's fall term at West Chester College.) But of the 47 graduate students in the next year's class -- my class -- to my knowledge only five of us ever got full-time academic positions; and of those five, only three of us remain employed in the field in the year 2002. My class's initial job hunt took place in 1974–1975, demonstrating the disastrous effects of the 1973 oil embargo. By 1975, Harvard was accepting only 16 graduate students in English. Two years later the number fell to seven. Even then it was difficult to find positions for everyone.
3. In the early 1970s, the English majors at Harvard University and at Loyola University of Chicago (similarly sized institutions) numbered about 800. By the late 1970s, the number at both schools had dropped to about 125.

B

A Backward Look at Error Avoidance

Throughout the nineteenth and most of the twentieth centuries, a great deal of the communication between writing instructors and their students concentrated on present error detection, presumably in the service of future error avoidance. Even though our pedagogy has calmed some of this fervor, the concern has not abated in the consciousness of the public. Whenever I am asked by a non-academic person at a social gathering what I do for a living, and I answer "I teach English," I usually hear one of the following three responses:

(1) "English was my [best/worst] subject in school";

(2) "Oh, then, I had better watch my grammar"; or

(3) "No one seems to be able to write anymore. Why just yesterday someone handed me a report with four spelling mistakes and two split infinitives. What are you people teaching your students nowadays?"

This interchange has been going on for some time now. Barrett Wendell wrote about it in 1891:

> During the past ten years I have been chiefly occupied in teaching, to undergraduates at Harvard College, the principles of English Composition. In the course of that time I have been asked a great many questions concerning the art, mostly by friends who found themselves writing for publication. Widely different as these inquiries have naturally been, they have possessed in common one trait sufficiently marked to place them, in my memory, in a single group: almost without exception, they have concerned themselves with matters of detail. Is this word or that admissible? . . . Are not words of Saxon origin invariably preferable to all others? Should sentences be long or short? These random memories are sufficient examples of many hundreds of inquiries.[1]

This emphasis on detail and error sent the message that good writing has less to do with good thought than with good literary manners. Concern for the latter has often obliterated or been confused for concern for the former.

Note how the pervasively influential Hugh Blair (in his *Lectures on Rhetoric and Belles Lettres*, 1783) takes his favorite prose stylist, Addison, to task:

The Addison passage:

> We cannot indeed have a single image in the fancy, that did not make its first entrance through the sight; but we have the power of retaining, altering, and compounding those images which we have once received, into all the varieties of picture and vision, that are most agreeable to the imagination; for, by this faculty, a man in a dungeon is capable of entertaining himself with scenes and landscapes more beautiful than any that can be found in the whole compass of nature.

Blair's comments:

> It may be of use to remark, that in one member of this sentence there is an inaccuracy in syntax. It is proper to say, *altering and compounding those images which we have once received, into all the varieties of picture and vision*. But we can with no propriety say, *retaining them into all the varieties*; and yet, according to the manner in which the words are ranged, this construction is unavoidable. For *retaining, altering,* and *compounding*, are participles, each of which equally refers to, and governs the subsequent noun, *those images*; and that noun again is necessarily connected with the following proposition, *into*. This instance shows the importance of carefully attending to the rules of Grammar and Syntax; when so pure a writer as Mr. Addison could, through inadvertence, be guilty of such an error. The construction might easily have been rectified, by disjoining the participle *retaining* from the other two participles in this way: "We have the power of retaining those images which we have once received; and of altering and compounding them into all the varieties of picture and vision." The latter part of the sentence is clear and elegant.[2]

He does just what many old-school composition teachers tended to do:

(1) He concentrates on one "error" above all things;

(2) In doing so, he ignores the substance of the sentence entirely;

(3) He rewrites it to teach by example;

(4) When he does praise something, he merely labels it positively.

He does no better for us when he chooses to praise Addison for what he considers good writing.

The Addison passage:

> Besides, the pleasures of the imagination have this advantage above those of the understanding, that they are more obvious, and more easy to be acquired.

Blair comments:

> This is also an unexceptional sentence.

Yet any number of things can be excepted in Addison's sentence. Are the two qualities really one advantage? How are the terms to be understood? What does "easy" mean? Does an understanding person necessarily have a more difficult time of it than an imaginative person when it comes to perceiving? Blair's lack of "exception" to the sentence seems to be based on his inability to find within it a perceivable stylistic or grammatical error.

If we examine the composition textbooks of the nineteenth century and earlier, we discover error spoken of most often in terms of manners and morality. The authorities seem to be implying a kind of grammatical Calvinism: If you do not appear to be one of the chosen -- (for that read "educated") -- then for certain you are not one of the chosen. This combines with an early form of behavior modification: If you present yourself grammatically, then you might eventually become the kind of approvable person that is marked by good grammar.

The Calvinistic parallel includes a depressing converse downside: Although a lack of grammar surely brands you as a lost soul, a firm control of grammar will not ensure your salvation.

> To be able to comply with the simplest matters of usage in composing sentences is something for which, on self-defensive grounds, every educated person strives. It gives him no credit if he can do it, but to be unable to meet the demands of correctness in ordinary oral discourse betrays a certain sort of unrespectability.[3]

Correct writing, then, was something one should practice so it would not get in the way of thought. From this perspective, rhetoric is tainted by a kind of original sin: Thought, Blair implies, is pure; but when it comes out of the mouths of mortals, it becomes tainted by the very language through which it seeks to be expressed. The best we can do is to expiate our sins by avoiding further error; perhaps then the external expression may correspond to the purity of the unexpressed thought.

An 1817 advertisement for Blair's book states it elegantly and respectably: "That the knowledge of Rhetoric forms a very material part of the education of a polite scholar must be universally allowed." Without such manners, a student will forever appear not merely unschooled but unworthy to join the ranks of educated, competent, adult society. I suggest that this, at its base, may be a matter of morality, power, and class.

It comes as no surprise that leadership in the development of composition pedagogy came for a long time from Harvard. Adams Sherman Hill taught composition there from 1872 to 1904, holding the Boylston Professorship of Rhetoric for all but four years of that time. In 1878 he published his influential textbook, *The Principles of Rhetoric*, revealing in the arrangement of that volume his priorities concerning the moral and societal underpinnings of writing instruction, many of which survive to the present.

His Introduction speaks most promisingly about rhetoric. He defines it as "the art of efficient communication by language." He praises it as an art, not a science, using "knowledge not as knowledge, but as power." He calls its rules "not absolute" and admits that "the ways of communicating truth are many."[4] From reading the Introduction, we have great hopes of his unveiling for us the mystery of the relationship between thought, language, and power. But we find something quite different as soon as we turn to the text proper. Morality rushes into the foreground as we read the title of his Book I: "Grammatical Purity." The titles of its subdivisions are similarly behavior-conscious:

Chapter I: Good Use. (12 pages)

Chapter II: Rules in Cases of Divided Usage (7 pages)

Chapter III: Barbarisms (12 pages)

Chapter IV: Solecisms (19 pages)

Chapter V: Improprieties (13 pages)

The message: If you do not learn to *conform* (a word he uses in the Introduction) to the rules of proper use, you will be considered in Chapter III "barbaric" (of another country), in Chapter IV "solecistic" (breaching etiquette), in Chapter V "improper," and in Chapter I downright bad. Of such are the impure made.

Chapter II's "Rules in Cases of Divided Usage" are delivered in "Canons," semantically recalling for us the canon law of the Catholic Church. Chapter III's "Barbarisms" worry about the threat of unwelcome incursions such as "barn-burner" and "soft-shell"; there he warns against the impropriety of using unapproved abbreviations such as "phiz" (for "physiognomy") and "poz" (for "positive") and "hyp" (for "hypochondria," not, as we use it, for "hyperbole"); and he rejoices that some previous offenders have now disappeared, such as "rep" (for "reputation") and "exam" (for "examination"). While these fears may entertain those of us who have seen the language either survive them or incorporate them, the sheer quantity and prominence of them should give us pause -- especially when they are the very first issue to which our attention is directed. By their prominence, they mark their author as linguistically ultraconservative, elitist, and classist. The final paragraph in the chapter on "Barbarisms" clarifies his position:

> How, then, is a language to grow? How is literature to avail itself of the new words it needs for complete expression? The answer suggests itself. In the art of writing, as in every other art, it is the masters, and they only, who give the law and determine the practice. The poets, the great prose writers, may be safely left to determine what words are needed by the language.[5]

Those who are in charge must stay in charge; all others must conform. This power of correction brings with it the powers of condescension and exclusion, especially when the rules concern formality and convention.

On his second page, Hill quotes DeQuincey on the pervasiveness of grammatical error: Says DeQuincey, "We have never seen the writer . . . who has not sometimes violated the accidence or the syntax of English grammar." In the footnote to this statement, Hill quips, "See p. 34 for an example taken from this very essay." In other words, Hill caught DeQuincey in a grammatical error in the very essay in which DeQuincey was fretting that everyone does it. Here we have a condescender condescending to another condescender. Deliciously, Hill himself makes it through only two more sentences before committing a grievous error of his own -- a faulty parallelism:

> With a few exceptions, to be hereafter noted, it should (1) contain none but English words, phrases, and idioms; (2) these words, phrases, and idioms should be combined according to the English fashion; and (3) they should be used in the English meaning.

Put down Professor Hill's book and pick up one of any of the other keepers of the flame before World War II; you will find the same sort of *ex cathedra* approach -- decrees, rules without explanations, social condescensions, moral approbations, and self-supporting prohibitions. Barrett Wendell (1891):

> I have dwelt this long on good use because, as I have said more than once already, good use is inevitably the basis of all good style. Whoever strays from it is first "original," then eccentric, then obscure, then unintelligible. Whoever writes a totally foreign language is of course unintelligible, but unintelligible only because in every word he formulates, and sometimes in every mark he puts down, he serenely violates every rule of the *reputable*, national, and present use that makes modern English the thing it is. . . . [T]here is no more absolute rule than the one which *prudent* people habitually exemplify; namely, that *a wise man should keep good company, and use good sense.*[6] (emphasis supplied)

Note that he equates "keeping good company" with "using good sense" by referring to them jointly as "one" rule. It is the sense of the dis-"reputable" that links the sin of "imprudent" error to the distinguishing factors between classes. The implicit (though shaky) syllogism settles the question: No one of a base nature is capable of producing a noble thought; base people do not sound grammatical; therefore poor grammar is a sure sign of ignoble thought. We find the essence of this syllogism in the opinions even of the enlightened David Hume (1747):

> Fine writing, according to Mr. Addison, consists of sentiments which are natural, without being obvious. There cannot be a juster and more concise definition of fine writing.
>
> Sentiments, which are merely natural, affect not the mind with any pleasure, and seem not worthy of our attention. The pleasantries of a waterman, the observations of a peasant, the ribaldry of a porter or hackney coachman, all of these are natural and disagreeable. What an insipid comedy should we make of the chit-chat of the tea-table, copied faithfully and at full length? Nothing can please persons of taste, but nature drawn with all her graces and ornaments, *la belle nature*; or if we copy low life, the strokes must convey a lively image to the mind.[7]

Once again we are told that education, especially when it concerns rhetoric, serves to separate the worthy from the unworthy; the worthy turn out to be representatives of the higher classes, the unworthy of the lower classes or the female sex. From this we derive the sense of sin that accompanies solecisms and barbarisms. They betray a fraudulence in one's pretensions to class and distinction. The metaphor extends all the way from the choice of topics to the choice of words.

> Nor can the "lower classes" of words, so to speak, perform the highest work. A complex feeling requires complex means of expression, and a writer who mounts into the region of ideas must use words adapted to the communication of ideas, -- words of which a larger proportion come, directly or indirectly, from the Latin or Greek.
>
> (A.S. Hill)[8]

The tell-tale signs of this unworthiness appear even more in the *presentation* of the prose (referred to then as *rhetoric*) than in the substance of the thought:

> The body and substance of any valuable composition must be formed of knowledge and science. Rhetoric completes the structure, and adds the polish; but firm and solid bodies only are able to receive it.
>
> (Blair)[9]

We might trace the source of these class distinctions to the historical formation of our hybrid language. When the Normans conquered the Anglo-Saxons in A.D. 1066, they brought to England their Norman French, a Romantic language with Greek and Latin roots, which both conflicted with and integrated with the resident Teutonic language, Anglo-Saxon. Neither the ruling aristocratic Normans nor the conquered Anglo-Saxon serfs were willing to allow their own language to disappear; and they each had to learn enough of the other's in order to communicate. The middle class had to look above and below, communicate in all directions, and synthesize wherever possible. Eventually the two languages intertwined to form an early version of our English, which necessarily retained a great number of class-marked synonyms.

The Teutonic words that survived tended to be those that described the basic functions of life. They were the sort of words, short and essential, that a ruling class would be willing to learn in order to make their orders known to a servant class: go, do, walk, talk, sleep, eat, live, die. Alongside them thrived longer, more complex, Romantic words with their Graeco-Roman ancestry and their somewhat more subtle applications: proceed, function, perambulate, communicate, repose, ingest, survive, expire. In retaining the synonyms, we have retained the class distinctions as well. You are what you speak.

Knowledge of language, then, seems always to have been a marker of class distinction for English-speaking peoples; but what began as mostly a semantic phenomenon in medieval England seems to have expanded into a grammatical phenomenon in nineteenth-century America. Perhaps our insistence on grammatical purity is rooted in an attempt to salvage vestiges of a caste society while otherwise engaging in a bold, democratic experiment. On the one hand, we insisted that "all men are created equal"; on the other hand, we had no glimmer of a thought of universal suffrage. The new upper class entrusted itself with making all the most important decisions. Democratic opportunities to make large amounts of money had allowed Americans a social mobility more volatile than that of the English; but that very mobility raised a serious new social problem for those people who rose to the top of American society. In fearing for the stability of their new power and recognizing that wealth was no longer an absolute indication of class, they might well have wondered how they could manage to go about telling "them" from "us." At the time, one could usually recognize one of "them" by their ignorance of the semantic and syntactic niceties of the quirky and often illogical language in common. If certain grammatical rules could be retained because of convention rather than logic, then only those educated in the conventions would be able constantly to avoid error. Thus, the man who ended his sentence with a preposition would be telling a tale thereby.

Originally, therefore, the knowledge of grammar might have been related directly to the possibilities of position and power. That scene was replayed over and over in classrooms whenever a teacher condescended to a student who was not yet in control of certain linguistic technicalities. Part of the sense of annoyance at students committing grammatical errors may have stemmed from a feeling that they were disgracing themselves by their sin-tinged and class-betraying ignorance. The outrage may also have functioned to protect the instructor's position in the power structure of the student-teacher relationship. No matter what the source of the rules -- truth, convention, faux necessities -- they produced a relationship founded on power.

If the teacher were presumed to be in touch with truth, then the resulting professional mission could be fulfilled by imparting that truth downward to the dependent and receptive students. The safety of catechism could overcome the dangers of dialogue. As a result, early textbooks tended consistently to state their principles as aphorisms or rules, without indulging in causal explanation.

> XII. An adverb should not be placed between "to," the sign of the infinitive mood, and its verb.
>
> (A.S. Hill)[10]

Professor Hill hands down the traditional rule against splitting infinitives (1) without explaining why splitting anything might cause difficulty, and (2) while splitting his own sentence. While his moment of inelegance admittedly does not involve an infinitive, it does create confusion for those young readers who do not already understand that his interruptive phrase is explanatory of *to*. He is safe, however, in that there was no rule that prevented this kind of interruption.

Such a proscriptive approach would lead naturally to a grammar and rhetoric of control: Categories were constructed, rules were multiplied, pieces of advice became canonized. Not until recently have teachers and scholars begun to search for underlying principles that might tie together and make sense of all this accumulated lore. The work of Martha Kolln is a delightful departure from the traditional. Rules are few and relatively neat and easy to apply. Principles require interpretation and application, which in some cases lead to the destruction of rules. Above all, grammar is seen as a way to gain control of readers, not as a way to prove yourself to society.

It is all too easy to distinguish semantically between principles and rules while neglecting to ensure the principles do not rigidify into larger versions of rules. If rules work badly in teaching writing, we will make no progress by replacing one set with another -- no matter what they are called. Rules legislate action. In order for principles not to dwindle into rules, they must tell us what not what we must do but rather what will happen if we choose to do certain things. That will leaves the choice more in our control.

For example, consider the following conventional rules.

1) Do not split the infinitive.
2) Do not overly qualify a subject before stating its verb.
3) Omit needless words.
4) Do not include in a paragraph any material that does not relate to the topic sentence of the paragraph.

When these rules are juxtaposed, their interdictions might combine to suggest the possibility of a single emerging principle by which they all are informed. That principle, in turn, could create the possibility of choice and the delineation of consequences. It would inform us why the rules were concocted in the first place; in turn, that would let us suit our rhetorical choices to the spirit rather than the letter of the grammatical law.

The emerging principle: All four of these rules involve interrupting and overburdening the reader. If we could develop a principle about making things easily available to the reader, then we could dispense with the miscellany of detailed rules -- which tend not to appear listed together in the first place. Once we understand something about not interrupting the reader, we might well find ourselves chipping away at rules like the prohibition against split infinitives. Those split infinitives that are likely to burden the reader might remain bad choices. Readers expect the verb stem will immediately follow the infinitive indicator *to*. Any delay causes problems: "To warmly and without hesitation recommend" makes us struggle through too much interruptive material before the second shoe of the verb drops. However, there are a great many splittings of infinitives that do not act as interruptives for the reader. If the interruptive word bonds with the verb stem to form what might be considered a two-word verb phrase, will any reader fail to fully understand its meaning? Such a principle of reader-interruption could create meaningful choices that would destroy inflexible rules.

As an example of just such an uninterruptive split infinitive, here again is a sentence from the previous paragraph: "If the interruptive word bonds with the verb stem to form what might be considered a two-word verb phrase, will any reader fail *to fully understand* its meaning?" If you missed this upon first reading, there were probably two causes: (1) The concept "fully understand" can be considered a verbal unity, an action that many of us try to do every day. To "fully understand" describes a different kind of effort than "fully to understand" or "to understand fully." (2) If you missed this uninterruptive error, you were probably reading for content. Most people, most of the time, read for content.

Even the most eloquent defenses of error avoidance fail to construct a link between lack of error and the production of thought. Hugh Blair's *Lectures on Rhetoric and Belles Lettres* offers once again a prime example:

> But though rules and instructions cannot affect every thing which is requisite, they may be of considerable use. If they cannot inspire genius, they can give it direction and assistance. If they cannot make barrenness fruitful, they can correct redundancy. They present proper models for imitation; they point out the principal beauties which ought to be studied, and the chief faults which ought to be avoided, and consequently, tend to enlighten taste, and to conduct genius from unnatural deviations into its proper channel. Though they are incapable of producing great excellencies, they may at least serve to prevent considerable mistakes.[11]

Some of us mark all the errors in student writing not as a power trip or in scandalized outrage but rather as an act of generosity and support. We suggest that while we personally are not offended by such peccadillos, we wish the student to know that many other readers do not share our enlightened attitude. To protect the student from suffering harm at the hands of those intolerant others, we note the errors in a spirit of edification. Good enough; but how is this effort interpreted by our students? Can they possibly avoid thinking that the same paper *without* the errors would not have been "better written"? As they scan our many markings, can they avoid being impressed by how much time and effort we have given to those corrections? If our error notations are definitive and our substantive comments are vague or merely suggestive, will they not conclude that cleaning up future errors is the only or at least the best way to improve?

If we could find a powerful way to deal with the substance of writing, then we could afford to treat error correction as part of the fine-tuning process -- something to be done after the writing was otherwise finished. If that new, powerful way dealt with substance through the perspective of structure, then many of the errors might have disappeared before the fine tuning was necessary. That is part of the mission of this book.

Endnotes

1. Wendell, p. 1.
2. Blair, p. 293–294.
3. Percy H. Boynton. *Principles of Composition*. Boston: Ginn & Company, 1915, p. 89.
4. Adams Sherman Hill. *The Principles of Rhetoric*. New York: Harper & Brothers, 1887, iii–iv.
5. Ibid., p. 30.
6. Barrett Wendell. *English Composition*. New York: Charles Scribner's Sons, 1891, 25–26.
7. David Hume. *Essays: Moral, Political, and Literary*. Oxford, U.K.: Oxford University Press, 1963, p. 196. From Essay XX: "Of Simplicity and Refinement in Writing" (1747).
8. A.S. Hill, p. 75.
9. Blair cite from Lecture 1, p. 5.
10. Hill (1878), p. 42.
11. Blair, Lecture I, p. 6.

C

Reader/Listener Expectations from the Past

Many of the concepts presented in this volume as Reader Expectations have been articulated many times over the course of the history of rhetoric; but they appear piecemeal and never as part of an organized vision of the communication experience of the reader. I bring together here a series of quotations from a number of famous rhetoricians: two ancient Greeks, Aristotle and Longinus; two ancient Romans, Cicero and Quintilian; the eighteenth-century Scottish founder of our traditional composition methodologies, Hugh Blair; one of the main British voices on the subject in the nineteenth century, Richard Whately; and the twentieth-century critic and innovator, I.A. Richards. (Please recall that the ancient rhetoricians were referring to Greek and Latin prose that was heard, not read.) Here we find opinions on a number of issues discussed at length in this book:

-- The importance of structure to communication;

-- The function of verbs;

-- The disabling effect of rhetorical rules;

-- The false relationship between length and wordiness;

-- The importance of closure to the effect of emphasis;

-- The control of context over meaning; and

-- The concept of reader energy.

L onginus on Structure

Longinus was a third-century A.D. Platonic philosopher and rhetorician, to whom the famous essay "On the Sublime" has been ascribed and then, by some, de-ascribed. Whoever wrote the essay, here he is on structure:

1. The beauty of the body depends on the way in which the limbs are joined together, each one when severed from the others having nothing remarkable about it, but the whole together forming a perfect unity.

379

Similarly great thoughts which lack connexion are themselves wasted and waste the total sublime effect, whereas if they co-operate to form a unity and are linked by the bonds of harmony, they come to life and speak just by virtue of the periodic structure. . . . I have shown elsewhere that many poets and other writers who are not naturally sublime, and may indeed be quite unqualified for grandeur, and who use in general common and everyday words which carry with them no special effect, nevertheless acquire magnificence and splendour, and avoid being thought low or mean, solely by the way in which they arrange and fit together their words. (40.1–2)

Quintilian on Structure

Quintilian (Marcus Fabius Quintilianus), Spanish-born, was a Roman rhetorician in the first century A.D. He was recognized as Rome's greatest teacher and elected to the Senate late in life on the basis of his rhetorical knowledge and skill. He was pressed by his admirers even later in life into recording what he knew of teaching and of rhetoric in a 12-volume opus, the *Institutio Oratoria*. This continually engaging work is one of the most fascinating and delightful ever written on either subject -- well worth a read, even in the twenty-first century.

Here is Quintilian on the structural location not of sentences but of arguments.

2. . . . for it is not only of consequence what we say, and how we say it, but also where we say it; there is need therefore also for *arrangement*." (Bk. III, Ch. III 2) (Watson)

Quintilian on Verbs

3. For the more ancient, among whom were Aristotle and Theodectes, said that there were only *verbs, nouns,* and *convinctions* [sic], because, that is to say, they judged that the force of language was in verbs, and the matter of it in nouns (since the one is what we speak, and the other that of which we speak), and that the union of words lay in convinctions, which, I know, are by most writers called *conjunctions*. . . . (Bk. I, Ch. IV 18) (Watson)

Quintilian on the Disabling Effects of Rules

4. . . . for rhetoric would be a very easy and small matter, if it could be included in one short body of rules, but rules must generally be altered to suit the nature of each individual case, the time, the occasion, and necessity itself. . . .   (Bk. II, Ch. XIII 1–17) (Butler)

5. Still such artifices, although they may be employed at times to good effect, are not to be indulged in indiscriminately, but only when there is strong reason for breaking the rule.   (Bk. IV Ch. I 70) (Butler)

6. Let [oratory] hold its course, therefore, not along foot-paths, but through open fields; let it not be like subterranean springs confined in narrow channels, but flow like broad rivers through whole valleys, forcing a way wherever it does not find one. For what is a greater misery to speakers than to be slaves to certain rules, like children imitating copies set them, and, as the Greeks proverbially express it, *taking constant care of the coat which their mother has given them?* (Bk. V, Ch. XIV 31) (Watson)

W *hately on Wordiness*

Richard Whately was an English logician and theologian, writing in the first half of the nineteenth century. He produced both a *Logic* and a *Rhetoric*, becoming perhaps the most influential voice on the subject of writing after Hugh Blair and before the turn of the twentieth century. Here he warns against making too facile a connection between the number of words in a sentence and the sense of "wordiness." Note that he demonstrated what he says by constructing a VERY long sentence in which to say it. (Note also that, in an age of increasing outrage at faulty grammar, he ends that long sentence with a preposition.)

7. In respect to the Construction of Sentences, it is an obvious caution to abstain from such as are too long; but it is a mistake to suppose that the obscurity of many long sentences depends on their length alone. A well-constructed sentence of very considerable length may be more readily understood than a shorter one which is more awkwardly framed. If a sentence be so constructed that the meaning of each part can be taken in as we proceed, (though it be evident that the sense is not brought to a close,) its length will be little or no impediment to perspicuity; but if the former part of the sentence convey no distinct meaning till we arrive nearly at the end, (however plain it may then appear,) it will be, on the whole, deficient in perspicuity; for it will need to be read over, or *thought* over, a second time, in order to be fully comprehended; which is what few readers or hearers are willing to be burthened with.   (Part III: Chap. I; section 3, p. 263)

Q *uintilian on the Stress Position, Reader Energy, and the Mental Breath*

8. For that which as a rule occurs to us first, is just that which ought to come last in our speech.   (Bk. VII, Ch.1 25) (Butler)

9. . . . sentences should rise and grow in force.   (Bk. IX, Ch. IV 23) (Butler)

10. It is, however, not infrequently possible to give special significance to a word by placing it at the close of a sentence and thereby stamping and impressing it on the mind of the hearer, whereas if it were placed in the middle . . . it would remain unnoticed. . . . (Bk. IX, Ch. IV 29) (Butler)

11. It is at the close of periods, however, that regard to numbers is more requisite, as well as more observable, than anywhere else; first, because every body of thought has its limit, and requires a natural interval to separate it from the commencement of that which follows; and, secondly, because the ear, having listened to a continuous flow of words, and having been led on, as it were, by the current of the speech, is better able to form a judgment when the stream comes to a stop, and gives time for consideration. There should be nothing, therefore, harsh or abrupt in that part where the *mind takes breath*, as it were, and is recruited. The close of the period is the natural resting-place of the speech; it is this that the auditor *expects*, and it is here that approbation bursts forth into applause. (emphasis supplied) (Bk. IX, Ch. IV 62) (Watson)

Cicero on Closure

Marcus Tullius Cicero is perhaps the most famous of all orators and rhetoricians. In and out of Roman government in the first century B.C., he was lionized and derogated, banished and recalled; and throughout it all, he never stopped writing. His *De Inventione*,[1] written at the age of 17 or so, is not greatly improved upon by his *De Oratore*, written when he was about 55, or by his *Orator*, written five years later. No one was an adversary more to be feared in argument. Here he is on the importance of closure.

12. My ear, at any rate, rejoices in a full and rounded period; it feels a deficiency, and does not like an excess. Why say *"my* ear?" I have often seen the whole assembly burst into a cheer, in response to a happy cadence. For the ear expects the words to bind the sentence together. (*Orator* 1.168)

Aristotle on Closure

One of the most compendious minds of all time, the Greek philosopher Aristotle (fourth century B.C.) studied under Plato and became the tutor of Alexander, later to be known as "the Great." He wrote on almost every subject of thought available to the world of his time, including an influential

Rhetoric, in which he attempted to answer the serious criticisms launched at the whole rhetorical endeavor by Plato. Here is Aristotle on closure.

13. The strung-on style is the ancient one; for in the past all used it, but now not many do. I call that strung-on which has no end in itself except in so far as the thought is completed. It is unpleasant because it is unlimited, for all wish to foresee the end. Thus, as they complete the course [runners] pant and are exhausted; for they do not tire while the goal is in sight ahead. This then, is the strung-on style of *lexis*; but the turned-down style is that in periods. I call a "period" an expression having a beginning and end in itself and a magnitude easily taken in at a glance. This is pleasant and easily understood -- pleasant because opposed to the unlimited and because the hearer always thinks he has hold of something, in that it is always limited by itself, whereas to have nothing to foresee or attain is unpleasant. And it is easily understood because easily retained in the mind. (*Rhetoric*: Book 3, 9:2–3, p. 240)

H ugh Blair and Richard Whately on the Use of (What We Have Called) the Stress Position

Hugh Blair was a Scottish clergyman who lived through most of the eighteenth century. As professor of rhetoric at the University of Edinburgh, he published the highly influential *Lectures on Rhetoric and Belle Lettres* (1783), in which he attempted to unite the teaching of writing and the investigation of literature. This work proved to be the fountainhead for all work done on the teaching of writing in Great Britain and America until the 1970s -- even though most writing teachers in the twentieth century had never heard his name. He established canons of good taste and standards of propriety as he attempted to demonstrate why "good literature" was *good* literature. He is much referred to and quoted in Appendix B of the present volume. Here he is recognizing some of the power of what we have been calling the Stress position.

14. In general, it is always agreeable to find a sentence rising upon us, and growing in its importance to the very last word, when this construction can be managed without affectation, or unseasonable pomp. (Vol. I, p. 239)

Here is Whately on the same subject.

15. It must be the aim then of an author, who would write with Energy, to avail himself of all the liberty which our language does allow, so to arrange his words that there shall be the least possible occasion for

underscoring and italics; and this, of course, must be more carefully attended to by the *writer* than by the *speaker*; who may, by his mode of utterance, conceal, in great measure, a defect in this point. . . . The proper remedy is, to endeavour so to construct the style, that the collocation of the words may, as far as is possible, direct the attention to those which are emphatic. (pp. 314–315)

Hugh Blair warns us not to extend beyond what seems to be a promised Stress position:

16. But very often we meet with Sentences that are, so to speak, more than finished. When we have arrived at what we expected was to be the conclusion, when we have come to the word on which the mind is naturally led, by what went before, to rest; unexpectedly, some circumstance pops out, which ought to have been omitted, or to have been disposed of elsewhere; but which is left lagging behind, like a tail adjected to the Sentence. . . . (Vol I, p. 223)

Here is Whately on the same subject.

17. An unexpected continuation of a sentence which the reader had supposed to be concluded, especially if in reading aloud, he had, under that supposition, dropped his voice, is apt to produce a sensation in the mind of being disagreeably balked; analogous to the unpleasant jar which is felt, when in ascending or descending stairs we meet with a step more than we expected: and if this be often repeated, as in a *very* loose sentence, a kind of weary impatience results from the uncertainty when the sentence is to close.   (pp. 317–318)

A ristotle and I.A. Richards on "Context Controls Meaning"

Whatever the language, it seems that what appears first controls some of the effect of what comes thereafter. Here is Aristotle on the subject.

18. The unlimited leads astray; he who gives, as it were, the beginning into the hand [of the hearer] allows him, by holding on, to follow the speech.   (3.14.6)

Ivor Armstrong Richards, known as I.A. Richards, was a twentieth-century English literary critic who wrote a number of books on the meaning of meaning. He was both devoted to the past and way ahead of his time, writing with a disarming clarity of thought and leanness of style.

Here is an excerpt from his *Philosophy of Rhetoric* on how meaning does not reside within words but rather within words within contexts.

19. A chief cause of misunderstanding, I shall argue later, is the Proper Meaning Superstition. That is, the common belief -- encouraged officially by what lingers on in the school manuals as Rhetoric -- that a word has a meaning of its own (ideally, only one) independent of and controlling its use and the purpose for which it should be uttered. This superstition is a recognition of a certain kind of stability in the meanings of certain words. It is only a superstition when it forgets (as it commonly does) that the stability of the meaning of a word comes from the constancy of the contexts that give it its meaning. Stability in a word's meaning is not something to be assumed, but always something to be explained. And as we try out our explanations, we discover, of course that -- as there are many sorts of constant contexts -- there are many sorts of stabilities.   (p. 11)

H *ugh Blair on Reader Energy*

Reader energy is my term; but the concept goes back a long way. Here is Hugh Blair on the subject.

20. If we are obliged to follow a writer with much care, to pause, and to read over his sentences a second time, in order to comprehend them fully, he will never please us long. Mankind are too indolent to relish so much labour. They may pretend to admire the author's depth, after they have discovered his meaning; but they will seldom be inclined to take up his work a second time.   (Vol. I, p. 185)

21. We are pleased with an author, we consider him as deserving praise, who frees us from all fatigue of searching for his meaning; who carries us through his subject without any embarrassment or confusion; whose style flows always like a limpid stream, where we see to the very bottom.   (Vol. I, p. 186)

S *ources for Appendix C*

Aristotle. *On Rhetoric*. George A. Kennedy, trans. New York: Oxford University Press, 1991.

Blair, Hugh. *Lectures on Rhetoric and Belles Lettres*. 2 vols. Harold F. Harding, ed. Carbondale, Ill.: Southern Illinois University Press, 1965.

Cicero. *Orator*. Translated by H.M. Hubbell. Cambridge: Harvard University Press; London: Heinemann, 1971.

Pseudo-Longinus. *On Sublimity*. D.A. Russell, trans. Oxford, U.K.: Clarendon, 1965.

Quintilian. *Institutes of Oratory*. 2 vols. Rev. John Selby Watson, trans. London: George Bell & Sons, 1892.

Quintilian. *The Institutio Oratoria of Quintilian*. 4 vols. H.E. Butler, trans. Cambridge: Harvard University Press; London: Heinemann, 1980.

Richards, I.A. *The Philosophy of Rhetoric*. New York: Oxford University Press, 1965.

Whately, Richard. *Elements of Rhetoric*. Douglas Ehninger, ed. Carbondale, Illinois: Southern Illinois University Press, 1963.

Endnotes

1. Although *De Inventione* has been ascribed to Cicero for centuries, there is now some doubt as to its authorship. Whoever wrote it, it is highly Ciceronian.

Works Cited

Aristotle. *On Rhetoric*. George A. Kennedy, trans. New York: Oxford University Press, 1991.

Aristotle. *Poetics*. Gerald F. Else, trans. Ann Arbor: University of Michigan Press, 1967.

Augustine, Bishop of Hippo. *On Christian Doctrine*. J.F. Shaw, trans. Edinburgh, U.K: T.T. Clark, 1892.

Bain, Alexander. *English Composition and Rhetoric*. Enlarged edition. New York: American Book Company, 1887.

Blair, Hugh. *Lectures on Rhetoric and Belles Lettres*. 2 vols. Harold F. Harding, ed. Carbondale, Ill.: Southern Illinois University Press, 1965.

Booth, Wayne. "The Rhetorical Stance." *College English* 20 (1969), pp. 139–145.

Boynton, Percy H. *Principles of Composition*. Boston: Ginn & Company, 1915.

Burke, Kenneth. *Counter-Statement*. Berkeley: University of California Press, 1931.

Campbell, George. *The Philosophy of Rhetoric*. Lloyd F. Bitzer, ed. Carbondale, Illinois: Southern Illinois University Press, 1963.

Chomsky, Noam. *Aspects of the Theory of Syntax*. Cambridge: Harvard University Press, 1965.

Cicero. *Brutus*. G.L. Hendrickson., trans. Cambridge: Harvard University Press; London: Heinemann, 1971.

———. *De Oratore*. 2 vols. E.W. Sutton and H. Rackam, trans. Cambridge: Harvard University Press; London: Heinemann, 1979.

———. *De Inventione*. H.M. Hubbel, trans. Cambridge: Harvard University Press; London: Heinemann, 1976.

———. *Orator*. H.M. Hubbell. trans. Cambridge: Harvard University Press; London: Heinemann, 1971.

Daneš, František. "Functional Sentence Perspective and the Organization of the Text," in *Papers on Functional Sentence Perspective*. Frantisek Danes, ed. Prague: Academia, 1974, pp. 106–128.

Erasmus, Desiderius. *On Copia of Words and Ideas*. Donald B. King and H. David Rix, trans. Milwaukee, Wis.: Marquette University Press, 1963.

Fénelon, François. *Dialogues on Eloquence*. Wilbur Samuel Howell, trans. Princeton: Princeton University Press, 1951.

Firbas, Jan. "Some Aspects of the Czechoslovak Approach to Problems of Functional Sentence Perspective," in *Papers on Functional Sentence Perspective*. František Daneš, ed. Prague: Academia, 1974, 11–37.

Fish, Stanley. *Is There a Text in This Class?* Cambridge: Harvard University Press, 1980.

———. "Anti-Foundationalism, Theory Hope, and the Teaching of Composition," in *Doing What Comes Naturally: Change, Rhetoric, and the Practice of Theory in Literary and Legal Studies*. Durham, N.C.: Duke University Press, 1989.

Flesch, Rudolph. *The Art of Clear Thinking*. New York: Harper's, 1951.

———. *The Art of Plain Talk*. New York: Macmillan, 1962.

———. *The Art of Readable Writing*. New York: Harper & Row, 1974.

Gleick, James. *Chaos: Making a New Science*. New York: Penguin Books, 1988.

Gopen, George D. *Writing from a Legal Perspective*. St. Paul: West Publishing, 1981.

Gopen, George D., and Judith A. Swan. "The Science of Scientific Writing." *American Scientist* 78 (1990): 550–558. Reprinted in *Exploring Animal Behavior*, eds. Paul W. Sherman and John Alcock (Sunderland, Mass.: Sinauer Associates, 1993). Japanese translation: Yosuke Kawachi, *A Collection of Geologic Sample Sentences: A Guide for Scientific Writing*, pp. 293–313 (1994). First Spanish translation: "La Ciencia de los Escritos Cientificos," Dr. Victor W. Gonzalez Lauck, trans.; Publicacion Especial Num. 3; Instituto Nacional de Investigaciones Forestales Y Agropecunarias; Campo Experimental Huimanguillo; Cardenas, Tabasco, Mexico (1995). Second Spanish translation: "La Ciencia de la Escritura Cientifica," Jorge R. Talbot, trans. for the June, 1996 Conference of the Fundacion de Investigaciones Metabolicas, Buenos Aires, Argentina.

Gopen, George D., and David A. Smith. "What's an Assignment Like You Doing in a Course Like This? Writing To Learn Mathematics." *College Math Journal* 21 (1990): 2–19.

Gutman, Robert W. *Richard Wagner: The Man, His Mind, and His Music*. New York: Time Incorporated, 1968.

Halliday, Michael A.K. "The Place of 'Functional Sentence Perspective in the System of Linguistic Description" in *Papers on Functional Sentence Perspective*. František Daneš, ed. Prague: Academia, 1974, pp. 43–53.

Hill, Adams Sherman. *The Principles of Rhetoric*. New York: Harper & Brothers, 1887.

Hume, David. "Of Simplicity and Refinement in Writing," in *Essays: Moral, Political, and Literary*. Oxford: Oxford University Press, 1963, p. 196.

Lanham, Url. *Origins of Modern Biology*. New York: Columbia University Press, 1968.

Lindemann, Erika. *A Rhetoric for Writing Teachers*. New York: Oxford University Press, 1982.

Mathesius, Vilem. *A Functional Analysis of Present Day English on a Special Linguistic Basis*. Josef Vachek, ed. Lisbuse Duskova, trans. Prague: Academia, 1975.

Peirce, Charles S. *Collected Papers*. Charles Hartshorne and Paul Weiss, eds. Cambridge: Harvard University Press, 1974.

Perelman, Chaim. *The Realm of Rhetoric*. William Kluback, trans. South Bend, Ind. Notre Dame University Press, 1982.

Plato. *Gorgias*. Walter Hamilton, trans. New York and London: Penguin, 1960.

——. *Phaedrus*. Walter Hamilton, trans. New York and London: Penguin, 1973.

Prelli, Lawrence J. *A Rhetoric of Science: Inventing Scientific Discourse*. Columbia: University of South Carolina Press, 1989.

pseudo-Cicero. *Rhetorica ad Herennium*. Harry Caplan, trans. Cambridge: Harvard University Press; London: Heinemann, 1981.

pseudo-Longinus. *On Sublimity*. D.A. Russell, trans.. Oxford, U.K.: Clarendon Press, 1965.

Puttenham, George. *The Arte of English Poesie*. Facsimilie Reproduction of 1906. Reprint published by A. Constable and Co., Ltd., and edited by Edward Arber. Kent, Ohio: Kent State University Press, 1970.

Quintilian. *Institutes of Oratory*. 2 vols. Rev. John Selby Watson, trans. London: George Bell and Sons, 1892.

——. *The Institutio Oratoria of Quintilian*. 4 vols. H.E. Butler, trans. Cambridge: Harvard University Press; London: Heinemann, 1980.

Ramus, Peter. *Arguments in Rhetoric Against Quintilian*. Carole Newlands, trans. Dekalb, Ill.: Northern Illinois University Press, 1986.

——. *Questions of Brutus (Brutinae Quaestiones)*. Carole Newlands, trans. Davis, Calif. Hermagoras Press, 1992.

Reid, Thomas. *An Inquiry into the Human Mind on the Principle of Common Sense*, 6th ed. Glasgow: Gray and Maver, 1804.

Richards, I.A. *The Philosophy of Rhetoric*. New York: Oxford University Press, 1965.

Richards, I.A., and C.K. Ogden. *The Meaning of Meaning: A Study of the Influence of Language upon Thought and of the Science of Symbolism*. New York: Harcourt, Brace, 1956.

De Saussure, Ferdinand. *Cours linguistique generale*. From the notebooks of Albert Riedlinger. George Wolf, trans. Oxford: Pergamon, 1996.

Scott, Fred N., and Joseph V. Denney. *Paragraph-Writing*. Boston: Allyn & Bacon, 1896.

Shaughnessy, Mina P. *Errors and Expectations: A Guide for the Teacher of Basic Writing*. New York: Oxford University Press, 1977.

Simmel, Georg. *The Sociology of Georg Simmel*. Kurt H. Wolff, trans. and ed. New York: Free Press, 1950.

Sloan, Gary. "Relational Ambiguity Between Sentences." *College English* 39 (1978): 154–65.

——. "The Frequency of Transitional Markers in Discursive Prose." *College Composition and Communication* 46 (1984): 158–175.

Spencer, Herbert. *Philosophy of Style.* Boston: Allyn & Bacon, 1892. First published in 1852.

Stark, Steven. "Why Lawyers Can't Write." *Harvard Law Review* 97 (1983–4) 1389–93.

Thomas, Lewis. *The Lives of a Cell: Notes of a Biology Watcher.* New York: Viking Press, 1974.

Tompkins, Jane. *Sensational Designs: The Cultural Work of American Fiction, 1790–1860.* New York: Oxford University Press, 1985.

Weaver, Richard M. *The Ethics of Rhetoric*, Chicago: Henry Regnery, 1953.

Weil, Henri. *The Order of Words in Ancient Languages Compared with that of the Modern Languages.* Charles W. Super, trans. Boston: Ginn & Company, 1887.

Wendell, Barrett. *English Composition.* New York: Charles Scribner's Sons, 1891.

Whately, Richard. *Elements of Rhetoric.* Douglas Ehninger, ed. Carbondale, Illinois: Southern Illinois University Press, 1963.

Williams, Joseph M. "The Phenomenology of Error." *College Composition and Communication.* 32 (1981): 152–168.

——. *Style: Ten Lessons in Clarity and Grace*, 7th edition. New York: Longman Publishers, 2002.

Index